T0348205

MINEFIELDS

MINEFIELDS

A life in the news game

HUGH RIMINTON

hachette
AUSTRALIA

hachette
AUSTRALIA

First published in Australia and New Zealand in 2017
by Hachette Australia
(an imprint of Hachette Australia Pty Limited)
Level 17, 207 Kent Street, Sydney NSW 2000
www.hachette.com.au

This edition published in 2018

10 9 8 7 6 5 4 3 2 1

A catalogue record for this
book is available from the
National Library of Australia

ISBN: 978 0 7336 4081 0 (paperback)

Cover design by Christabella Designs
Cover photographs with thanks to Richard Malone (above) and Richard Moran (below)
Text design and digital production by Bookhouse, Sydney
Typeset in Sabon LT Pro by Bookhouse, Sydney
Printed and bound in Australia by McPherson's Printing Group

To John and Jackie,
my parents.

CONTENTS

AUTHOR'S NOTE

OF ALL THE STORIES I HAVE WRITTEN, THIS IS THE ONE I HAVE BEEN most reluctant to write. Several publishers have been kind enough to ask me to tell my story over the years. I have tried to buy them off with my brilliant – but still unpublished – novels. I have made excuses.

The best reporters' memoirs are wonderful. Books by Ryszard Kapuscinski, Anthony Loyd, Fergal Keane, Edward Behr, Phillip Knightley are among my favourites. Mark Colvin's *Light and Shadow* is a gentle masterpiece. There are so many other books I would love to see published, by Michael Ware, Sally Sara, Peter Cave, Steve Levitt, Robert Penfold, Matt Brown, Sophie McNeill – and those are just some of the Australians.

My reluctance to go to print comes from a common folly. As journalists – hell, as shoe salesmen – we all believe our best work is still ahead of us. To write it down now would be to miss the best bits that are still to come. But I am not sure the best bits *are* still to come – for me or for journalism. The well-funded enterprise that sent bright young things across the suburbs and out into the world is now largely gone.

The very notion of 'the media' no longer holds. For two centuries – and only for two centuries – the press, and then radio and television, really were the conduit between power and the population.

Now, people, whether powerful or largely powerless, communicate directly. President Trump rarely bothers with press conferences. He tweets. Groups that share a common identity, whether they are Midwestern American farmers or Syrian rebels, communicate with each other and with the world through shared social platforms. Journalists are left taking notes and trying to catch up.

There are strengths in the new world. Many people feel empowered by hearing their perspectives amplified when previously they felt marginalised and ignored. This is the best of it. On balance, though, what tends to be communicated is not understanding but complaint. For all the new possibilities in communication, what emerges is often simply noise, mutually incomprehensible and mutually antagonistic.

In part, this book is motivated by a desire to explain a world that has all but passed. Much of what happened in these pages took place before the digital age, before social media or even cell phones. It was a time when a reporter might decide to disappear into the backblocks of Africa and turn up days or weeks later with stories to tell. If they were good enough, he or she would be encouraged to disappear again. The reporter worked with no desire beyond the telling of events they hoped would interest their home audience. There were some subtle pressures: don't report stuff that might put viewers off their evening meal, or prompt them to switch over to another channel. But generally, there was money and freedom to back yourself. No longer do reporters get sent off into war zones with US$250,000 in cash and an order to stay filing for as long as they can. The full story of why is in this book.

It is not just journalistic practice that has changed. The world has changed. A teenage cadet might imagine all the great human shifts are in the past and the world has settled into something reasonably permanent. Time proves that false. Change is constant and often momentous. Reporters witness history at its hinges – at the moment when what seemed to be solid breaks. The world goes through doors and emerges altered. The journalist takes a pledge to go through those same doors, wherever they may lead. And over time, the reporter is also changed.

These are my stories and my changes but they also capture a world that is rapidly passing, as worlds always do.

Hugh Riminton
Sydney, 2017

PROLOGUE

THE CITY OF DEATH

I ARRIVED IN THE CITY OF DEATH AROUND NOON, THE SUN HIGH, THE heat raising willy-willies in the colourless dust. The military Hercules lowered its ramp to reveal a *Mad Max* landscape of patchy desert scrub marked by an abandoned MiG fighter jet.

Baidoa in Central Somalia once had a population half the size of Adelaide but in the twelve months before we arrived 170,000 people had starved to death there. The Australian military had come to try to save some. And a collection of reporters, photographers, cameramen and techs – a crew for whom 'motley' would be too generous an adjective – were there to watch the diggers do it.

By 1992, two decades since its last major war, the Australian Army was effectively a peacetime force relearning its craft. And us hacks, with few exceptions, knew nothing of conflict at all.

The US marines bulldozed a patch on the edge of town. They stretched a perimeter fence around it, called it a military base and left the Australians to it. For infrastructure, they had dug two dunnies – actually, one dunny with two holes side by side – and left a water-purifying plant that was woefully inadequate for a battalion-strength force.

We journos numbered thirty-two in all. The big TV networks and newspaper groups were represented, plus others from the diggers' hometown newspapers. There was radio – ABC and commercial – and a couple of magazine writers who had talked their way on board. One of them was a lovely chap who normally wrote Sydney society gossip for Kerry Packer's *The Bulletin* magazine. After a few days in Somalia, he took to his bedroll and refused to shift.

There were some genuine legends in the mix – none more so than Bruce Wilson, veteran foreign correspondent for the Murdoch Press. He had life worked out. 'Happiness,' he declared, 'is directly proportional to the distance from head office.' Bruce was comfortable anywhere. In the deserts of central Somalia he extracted from his pack not only a nifty little folding chair but a full bottle of single malt whiskey and an actual glass.

Most of the journalists, though, were like me: new to military operations. But we were all keen to start filing stories.

Most of the TV newsmen – and TV sent only men; Jodie Brough from the *Canberra Times* was the only female reporter – raced off to explore the MiG. It was an incongruous sight, a legacy of Somalia's time as a client state of the Soviet Union. Moscow's contribution to the country were warplanes that could no longer fly, Kalashnikov rifles by the hundreds of thousands and not much else. The jet sat perched among the weeds, still mostly intact, in a place where the next most sophisticated form of transport for most people was a donkey cart.

But I had a better idea. At the back of our dusty camp I had spotted a grain crop. Sorghum, I later learned. This, I decided, symbolised the whole point of our being there. If the Australian troops, as part of this historic UN deployment, could bring security and stability to Baidoa, the people wouldn't need food aid. They could feed themselves.

Taking a long-suffering cameraman with me, I strolled down to the field. The crop was high, towering above my head, but sparse enough for me to walk among it. The cameraman stayed behind the low stone wall that formed the perimeter and framed up a shot that would compress the grain heads to increase the impression of abundance. The trick is called 'using the long end of the lens' and I walked twenty-five metres into the vegetation to make it work.

I was rehearsing my lines when I noticed a group of Somalis clustering along a track at the far side of the field. I waved at them. They waved back. Friendly enough. In fact, very cheerful. They seemed to be laughing.

'See,' I said to the cameraman, 'they don't have electricity but they're still fascinated with television.'

I knocked off a first take.

'Mate,' said the cameraman, 'they seem to be trying to tell you something.'

I glanced back at the tallest, most animated of the men. He was grinning wildly, then pointed to the ground and with a big uprush of both hands said:

'BOOM!'

In an instant, starting from the crown of my head, a frigid feeling rushed down to my feet. Blood really does run cold. At the same time the thought hit me – in a city where 170,000 people have just starved to death, why would a full crop of grain have gone untouched?

I was in a minefield.

I looked up at the cameraman. For once he wasn't taking the piss.

'Shit, mate, what are you gunna do?'

I had walked into the minefield. I could walk back out again. All I had to do was step where I had already stepped. I could see the slight scuff of a footprint. I forced myself to stand on top of it. But there the trail ended. The sorghum, rather like maize, dropped leaves. A lacing of desiccated brown tendrils covered the ground in front of me. I couldn't see anything that even remotely resembled a path.

Still, I had sauntered in. If I could match my gait going out, perhaps I would be lucky with my foot placement.

I looked at the distant wall, behind which the cameraman was starting to take cover, I focused on the middle distance and began strolling. Oddly, having decided to act, I felt free of fear. Call it fatalism, the acceptance that bad things might happen and there's nothing you can do about it. It is a feeling I have drawn on many times since.

With a couple of dozen steps, I reached the wall and climbed out.

The cameraman had kept rolling even as he took cover. If a reporter was going to get himself blown up, he wasn't going to miss the shot.

Afterwards, the army came down and swept the field and blew up a dozen mines. A major later treated us all to a lecture on the theme of stupidity.

To make things worse, the rest of the TV reporters had done macho, war-thumping pieces to camera, known as stand-ups, on the MiG, looking magnificent in the long shadows of the African sunset.

My boss hit the roof.

'Everyone else does a stand-up on a bloody warplane, and all we get from you is a fucking broccoli patch!'

I was too embarrassed to tell him about the minefield.

I was in Africa working as a foreign correspondent. It was the best job on earth, every reporter's dream. But it was already clear I wasn't the sharpest tool in the shed.

1

BEGINNINGS

THAT I WAS IN THE SHED AT ALL WAS THE PRODUCT OF A SERIES OF happy accidents.

I had the great good luck to be born to adventurous parents. Neither had university degrees, but they had energy, curiosity and integrity that carried them far.

I was born in Sri Lanka, or what was then Ceylon, the second of four sons to John and Jacqueline Riminton.

Mum was a fiercely tribal Irish Catholic. If Ireland was ever mentioned – and it frequently was – it was so Mum could reflect glowingly on its many advantages over any other society. Dublin was her Jerusalem. It was a love affair sharpened by exile. She spent very little of her life actually in Ireland.

Mum was born, in fact, in Malta. She was the daughter of a Royal Navy captain, hardly the career choice of a hardened Irish rebel. But he was born in 1900 when all of Ireland was part of Britain. Chronic asthma drove him to find employment that came with good health care and the navy fitted the bill. He was no Captain Hornblower. He was a dentist. The chief dentist in the Royal Navy.

His daughter, in time, would train as a nurse in England and follow him into uniform. It was as a flying officer with the Royal

Air Force that Jackie took off from grey post-war England to a posting in Sri Lanka just north of the capital, Colombo.

My father, John, was born in 1928 on the island of Jersey to a lawyer who had made a fortune with his own brand of cigarettes. My grandfather sold his company to British American Tobacco for a tidy sum. By the time of my father's unexpected arrival, his father was fifty-six years old and living a well-padded retirement in a grand house on the beachfront in the Jersey capital, St Helier. For young John, there was no family play. His one sibling, a sister called Nancy, was nineteen years old when Dad was born. He never saw his father do a stroke of work, or even move much. When Dad was nine, the old boy, long nourished on rich foods and fine cognac, carked it.

More disruptions would follow. In 1940, the Nazis were on the march. Dad was eleven years old when they trooped into Jersey, where they would remain until the fall of Berlin five years later. Others had tougher wars, but the years of German occupation in Jersey were trying just the same. After the D-Day landings, Allied troops pressed on towards victory but did not bother liberating Jersey because it had no bearing on the outcome. Cut off from France, food was tight. Dad remembers half-starved German soldiers crawling through the hedges looking for nettles to turn into soup.

His own protein chiefly came from periwinkles, limpets and other small shellfish harvested off the rocks and converted into a foul-smelling, gelatinous broth. By war's end, Dad was nearly seventeen. As his diet improved, he shot up fifteen centimetres, a sign of the importance of the nutrients he had been missing.

The war had a lasting effect on my father. It had levelled Jersey society. Dad saw the strength of community – people working for each other and for common benefit – as the real source of resilience in hardship. He dedicated his life to that impulse.

Peace brought new losses. His mother was dying of cancer. He went to the United Kingdom to begin medical school but he couldn't settle down. His father's fortune had been largely expended on black market treatments for Dad's mum and other necessities. The grand house was not worth much in a small post-war backwater. Jersey's tax-haven status and the vast fortunes that would come to reside there were in some unimagined future. In short, when his mum died, Jersey offered nothing, medical studies couldn't hold him, and adventure was what was required.

Dad had enough cash for a Piccadilly tailor, a sports car and impulsive journeys to exotic spots like Iceland, but nowhere near enough money to sustain him indefinitely. One day, strolling down London's Bond Street, he saw a sign outside the Ceylon Tea Plantation company. He went in.

'Any chance of a job in Ceylon planting tea?'

'We are not an employment agency,' he was archly told.

He left, but was then chased down the street. It turned out many of the younger men on the plantations had gone off to war and, for various reasons, had not returned. Perhaps he might be the right sort of chap after all.

A few weeks later he was sailing off to the tropics.

In Ceylon, he learnt to speak Tamil and encouraged and supported the building of Hindu temples on the plantations, recognising the strength the Tamil people drew from traditional rituals and beliefs. It was plain that the relationships he built were genuine and strong. As he was promoted to ever more important estates, he amassed boxes of letters from workers lamenting his departure and celebrating their time together.

One evening in the high country, he went to a village cinema and bumped into a feisty Irish nurse up from Colombo for the weekend. And, soon after, sixty years of marriage would begin.

—

So it was that I was born in one of the most beautiful places on earth. My early memories are of green. The green of the tea bushes, row on row. The darker, deeper green of the always pressing jungle.

By the time I came along, fifteen months after my older brother, Paul, my father was making rapid progress in the tea-planting business. I was brought home from the Hatton Dickoya base hospital to an estate called Forres in the shadow of Adam's Peak, or Sri Pada, the holiest mountain in a god-crowded island.

My memories of Ceylon were not of Forres though, but the next estate my father was given to manage. Tangakelle came with sweeping lawns, a swimming pool, and a bungalow built from rough-hewn stone with a deep verandah. My earliest coherent memory is of toddling down a long driveway to find my father fiddling with the engine of a motorbike. He looked up at me, smiled, straddled the bike and sped off up the shingle mountain road that was our one link with the rest of the world.

Not that I needed anywhere else. At Tangakelle, I had my brother to play with and soon a younger brother, Sean, as a distraction. There was a pre-school over the mountain pass where I would occasionally be taken to play with other kids. But I was happy in my world. A photograph from the time shows me playing with a bicycle with training wheels with a Sri Lankan boy, but I don't remember his name or anything about him. I do remember our nanny, Bridgit. She was a young Sinhala woman whom we adored. She would sing us songs and smuggle us sugar sandwiches. I have a clear memory of being astonished to discover that she was not my mother – and that my real mother was the goddess-like woman with yellow-white hair falling to her waist who lived in the big house. Sad as I was to feel a rift with Bridgit, I remember the thrill of feeling associated with such a potent and mysterious creature.

All things end.

The Sri Lankan government was determined to get the Brits out of the tea business. Fair enough. We had to go.

A photograph captures our family on the day of departure, my father with his planter's beard freshly removed to improve, he hoped, his employment prospects in far off Blighty.

2

SISTERS OF MERCY

ENGLAND WAS HELL. WORSE THAN HELL, BECAUSE HELL CARRIED THE promise of warmth. For children who knew only the tropics, the British winter was incomprehensible. It was physically painful.

We stayed with my mum's recently widowed mother in the West Midlands town of Droitwich, not far from the Welsh border. Dad was constantly away, driving through the sleet to London in search of work, shopping around a skill set ill-suited to industrial England.

Us kids, meanwhile, went down sick. I contracted pneumonia. My brothers fared no better. When we were upright, we were bundled in layers of clothing that made movement all but impossible and sent out on 'walks'. On one, Paul found what looked like a pane of glass lying flat on the ground. He stepped on it and went crashing down, bawling in pain, much to my amusement. I, naturally, stepped on the glass too, and suffered a similar fate: a bone-crushing impact that rocked me even through many layers of clothing. We had discovered ice.

It must have been near Christmas. One day we were encouraged to feel excited about the arrival of a flatbed truck with a brass band on the back. They were playing Christmas carols. Snow was heavy on the ground. The musicians, with their red Santa suits and gleaming golden instruments, at least brought colour into the relentlessly grey and white landscape. But I couldn't figure them out. Why were adults exposing themselves to the freezing wind just to tootle out tunes for a handful of distracted kids?

My parents briefly flirted with the idea of moving to Connemara, in the west of Ireland, to try their luck in the tourism business. That idea fizzled. Then came an announcement. Dad had gained employment with a London-based finance company called Lombard. There was one interesting detail. The job was in New Zealand.

All that mattered to me was that we were going on a ship again.

For me, Sri Lanka had been paradise and Britain was Siberia. A place never to be remembered without a shudder.

I don't remember leaving the UK. I do remember long days crossing a shining sea. Warm again.

The SS *Himalaya* was tiny compared with modern cruise ships but it felt like an entire world. There was a toy shop and a swimming pool. My parents were relaxed until I went down with pneumonia again – but even that episode ended with my relieved father buying me the toy car of my choice from the ship store.

We pulled into Sydney and spent a day exploring. Most of it was spent at Taronga Park Zoo. A photograph captures my brother Paul and me smartly dressed, with identical grey woollen shorts, long socks, polished sandals, white shirts and matching red ties. The highlight was seeing a shark and a stingray in the aquarium. I also remember being presented with a long metal cup containing something pink and frothy. I looked at it dubiously; my parents had a distressing willingness to be adventurous with food. In fact, it was delicious. My first milkshake.

My brothers and I have always bemoaned our parents' decision to get back on the ship and keep going. Our lives might have been simpler if we had just ended our journey in Sydney. For three of us four boys (Adrian would soon be born in Christchurch), Sydney would end up being our home. But it would take us decades to get back to that sparkling city by the sea.

First, we ploughed on across the Tasman. The southern winter had kicked in by the time we disembarked on a foggy morning at Lyttelton Harbour and found our way to Christchurch over the hill. My early childhood was over. The real business of growing up was about to begin.

—

We moved first to a rental house in Wiggins Street, Sumner, a pretty beachside suburb on the eastern outskirts of Christchurch. For some reason, 'wiggins' – or 'wigs' – was a family euphemism for male genitalia, so not the least of the many mysteries of our new home was why they named streets after penises.

We went on outings on the grey sands of Sumner Beach and explored Cave Rock, a gnarly castle of volcanic extrusion shot through with holes that the surf thundered into at high tide. At low tide, heart in mouth, we could clamber through the cave that ran the full distance of the rock as Mum waited anxiously nearby shouting at us to be careful. Dad was already at work.

Warm weather had finally arrived when we made a trip to the far western limits of the city where Dad revealed the house that he had bought. It was a white-painted besser-brick split-level piece of classic outer suburbia. The small yard was little more than a lumpy gravel pit. The address was 73 Grahams Road, as anonymous a location as it was possible to imagine. Past a little cul-de-sac of similar homes lay the entrance to a large park marked out with rugby fields, the New Zealand equivalent of a church. Beyond that lay a few fields dotted with cows, then the airport, then more fields stretching to the foot of the snow-bright Southern Alps.

A boy's head popped up over the fence, sized us up, and invited us to play. And that was how it was. For those early Christchurch years, Paul and I would get home from school, drop our bags and race through the streets or the park. At first it would be on foot. Very soon, we would shift to bikes. We began to accumulate the scrapes and scars that come with reckless riding through trails in the forested edges of the playing fields. Mum, with a toddler on hand (Sean) and a new baby born within a year (Adrian), cared only that we were home in time for dinner.

They were innocent times. But innocence had its limits.

Paul and I started at the local state school – Westburn primary – but, as migrants, my parents did not know whether to trust the public education system. They should have done. In New Zealand it was the best around.

Instead, my mother's Catholicism asserted itself and we were dispatched off to Loreto College, a primary school attached to a convent in far off Papanui. Paul and I rode the three kilometres there and the three kilometres home. I was six years old.

The cycling, except on the bleakest days of winter, was not a problem. The danger lay in the classrooms themselves.

Loreto was run by the Sisters of Mercy. It was a poor choice of name. They were in fact dedicated to never-ending violence. Those were still the days of 'spare the rod, spoil the child'. Every school, private or public, beat small children. To do otherwise was considered morally weak or even dangerous to a child's upbringing.

The nuns took to their disciplinary duties with enthusiasm. Perhaps it was Proverbs 23:13 that encouraged them: 'Withhold not correction from the child: for if thou beats him with the rod, he shall not die.'

Indeed, we did not die. But we were daily reminded of our sinfulness and taught to learn the error of our ways. The sternest rebuke from the sisters – or worse, from the mother superior – was to be called 'a bold fellow'. Well, I was a bold fellow, and I was frequently caned.

The teaching style, between rote learning of times tables, involved a nun standing in front of the class and calling out children for various offences. One that got them particularly riled was 'yawning'. But any sign of inattentiveness, sloppiness of dress, whispering, bad handwriting or quiet weeping would do. The offending child would then be ordered to stand in front of the class and left there until the next major break – lunch or the end of the school day. As the hours passed, more children would be required to join those awaiting their fate. Safe to say, their learning during that period of terror was limited.

At the major break, the nun would pull out a thin cane and with a flourish whack each of the kids over the palm of the hand. The worst would get 'six of the best'. The sting of it would leave that hand out of action for the rest of the day.

The following day, the ritual would be repeated.

Other than reciting arithmetical tables and doing handwriting exercises, I can't remember anything useful that we were taught. We did, however, get interminable lectures about God, Jesus, the perfect mother Mary, and the glorious example of the martyrs. We also learned a lot about our sin. Everything, it seemed, was a sin: speaking loudly, being boastful, running not walking – except when speed was required and it was sinful to walk and not run. Failure to finish my weekend homework was enough to see me up before the whole school to be told by the mother superior that I was 'a bold fellow'. She possessed a mighty thick cane which got a turn on my outstretched hand.

To a six-year-old, the levels of violence were bewildering. As an adult, I can reflect more kindly on the nuns. Who knows what made them take holy orders? Some, doubtless were pressed into it to save them from dangerous involvements with boys, others no doubt fled to the convent to avoid marriage, especially if their sexual impulses lay in other directions; others might well have been inspired by the genuine desire to dedicate their lives to God.

To many, consignment to a life of teaching small children must have been a hellish frustration. Now, with second-wave feminism, new recruits to convents have all but disappeared. Loreto College itself closed decades ago. I saw the last flicker of a dying world, one that had existed for over one thousand years.

The final straw for me came when my teacher screeched from the front of the class at an unusually meek and timid boy.

'You yawned!'

'No, sister, I didn't,' stammered the horrified lad.

'You did – you looked out of the window to disguise it but I saw it.' The nun, in full black habit and veil, strode down to the little boy's desk.

'No, sister, please!'

'See! You've got tears in your eyes! You get tears in your eyes when you YAWN!'

And with that the whimpering child was marched to the front to wait in misery for his belting. That was enough for me. I can't remember the boy's name. But I knew he was one of those – as most were – who were too cowed to argue back to a Sister of Mercy. I was certain his tears were tears of fear.

I was suddenly seized with a tumult of anger. It was hypocrisy. It was injustice. The endless lectures about God loving us, about forgiveness, the pious nonsense about confessions and our first Holy Communions, the cant about the sisters being mysteriously 'close to God'. It was all bullshit and I raged and raged.

The Sisters of Mercy left me with three legacies: an unshakeable grasp of my times tables, a cold disbelief in religion, and a lifelong distrust of self-appointed authority in any form and particularly when dressed in ecclesiastical garb.

Such was my fury at these bat-winged, boy-bashing charlatans that my parents, to my eternal gratitude, visited the school and it was agreed that my education would proceed more profitably elsewhere.

As a footnote, my departure from Loreto College did not disqualify me from – bizarrely – winning the end-of-year class prize. The reward was a book. An elderly nun who I quite liked, Sister Mary Sebastian, told me with a twinkle in her eye that she had chosen it for me. It was called *Exploration and Discovery* and was packed with pictures and stories of the great explorers. It was an excellent choice. These were my interests. It surprised and touched me that somewhere in all that institutionalised violence someone had actually noticed me as a person distinct from others. That was the deepest mystery of all from my brief life in the hands of the nuns.

3

WHO ARE THE GOOD ONES?

IT WAS WHILE AT LORETO COLLEGE THAT MY FIRST SENSE OF NEWS filtered through to me.

One autumn morning I rode to school through a particularly ferocious storm. The conditions were far worse just to the north. It became known as the Wahine Storm, a cyclonic belting that forced the inter-island ferry, the *Wahine*, to run onto a reef at the mouth of Wellington Harbour.

Fifty-one people died that day. New Zealanders, then even more than now, considered themselves to be one people. What wounded one, wounded all. I was aware of a deep sense of national mourning. As far as I knew, it was the first big thing to happen in my lifetime, the first sense I had that shifts could take place outside my immediate world of family, friends and classroom and still somehow reach out and shake me.

I have no recollection of the assassination of Martin Luther King the week before the Wahine Disaster. But when Robert Kennedy was assassinated that June as he was running for the US presidency, it was another event that stirred up our parents. Ours was a Catholic world and the Kennedys were martyred Catholics. I remember my mother lamenting 'Why do they keep killing all the good ones?'

This left its mark on me on two levels. One was a child's logical processing that I was always being told to be good, so perhaps the reward for being good was being killed? Oddly, it had the effect of making 'being good' something noble, rather than a tedious instruction to seek a standard that could never be met.

The other impact came from questioning who 'all the good ones were'. Here Mum explained not only Robert Kennedy but his brother JFK, whose assassination had escaped my notice as I was only two and still living in the tropical highlands. But she also explained Martin Luther King, murdered just nine weeks before. Give my parents credit, they were not racist. Far from it. Their Sri Lankan experience, combined with their upbringings and natural instincts, made them avowed proponents of equal human value.

It was from Mum that I first learned of King's 'I have a dream' speech. It was, of course, way before the internet. She could not have called up vision of the actual speech. She must have told me something about it – and about the civil rights movement in the United States. Whatever she said, Martin Luther King was lodged in my head as a Great Man, requiring further investigation if the chance arose.

In time, I did get to see vision of the speech Dr King delivered in Washington in 1963. It still shivers my skin. It contains within it the strongest and simplest argument for human dignity there is – that people should be judged not by the colour of their skin but by the content of their character. Fifty years on, this idea remains the central value of my life.

However we identify ourselves, or are identified by others, the content of our character alone is how we must be judged. There are rogues and despicable people of every colour, religion and social standing. There are people of honour – friends to be made – in every colour and religion. Stand beside the good – who are many – and fight against the bastards. Pretty simple really. And in that year of dark wonders, 1968, as a seven-year-old boy, I was starting to build up the ideas that would shape my whole life.

—

After the disappointments of my Catholic education, my father's influence came into play and I was sent to an Anglican private primary school transplanted intact – cricket pitch and vowels – from the Home Counties of England. Medbury was its name, nestled among quince trees and towering chestnuts in Fendalton, the most elite suburb egalitarian Christchurch had to offer.

It was an eccentric joint. The teachers – and especially the headmaster, Frank Chennells, who owned the school – still beat the children from time to time. But it was nothing personal. The beatings were background irritants, like riding bicycles in the rain, and no one took them too seriously.

In the 1960s, several of the school teachers were veterans from World War II. The little school library consisted almost entirely of books about heroic commandos or fighter pilots. Swimming lessons were conducted naked, in some bizarre nod to the traditions of *Tom Brown's School Days*. Latin and French were compulsory. Boys addressed their fellows by their surnames only, or by nicknames straight out of 'jolly, what-oh' English comic books. My best friends were Phillips and Tiddles.

It was in reading a war comic that I first saw a picture of a 'flying tackle' in rugby. I couldn't wait to try it. I was a tiny kid, always the smallest in the class, but I was a nifty enough runner. I quickly discovered that using the technique demonstrated by dashing Flight Lieutenant Wilcox, or whoever it was, I could launch myself above the ankles of much larger boys, grab them around the knees and bring them down.

It was a revelation. I could neutralise the advantage of size. My love affair with rugby had begun. I was never remotely a star, I was barely even competent, but I played in a couple of competition-winning club sides in my middle teens and my enthusiasm for the tackle never faded.

A distaste for authority, a delight in bringing the powerful to the ground . . . who says you learn nothing in primary school!

Another bonus from Medbury was the annual winter ski trip when the whole school shut down and took off to the snow. This sounds extremely luxurious. In fact, skiing in the 1960s was more like a colder version of bushwalking. The ski fields were invariably a blank mountain face at the back of some high country farm. Getting there usually involved a hike up steep snow-covered tussock. There were no chairlifts or snow-grooming (heaven forbid!). Once at the crude accommodation hut, the skier ascended using rope tows that were grabbed with a hinged metal 'nutcracker' hanging from the waist. On my first trip, my boots were leather lace-ups and my skis were made of wood. But the thrill of that first downhill rush was never to be forgotten. And the sight of dawn across high rugged mountains struck me then for the first time. Mountains have been a big part of my life and every dawn carries the echo of that first one, the awed discovery of a landscape wilder than imagination.

4

FEMINISM ARRIVES, JUST IN TIME

MOST OF MY MEDBURY COHORT WERE DESTINED FOR A HIGH SCHOOL education at Christ's College, the waiting room and training ground for what passed for a Christchurch establishment. I had no desire to go there. For one thing, I was conscious that I was getting an expensive private education while my brothers were in the Catholic system or public schools. My parents believed that I was an unusually bright child. It was true, I was a precociously early reader. I was granted special dispensation to take books out of the adult section of the Fendalton public library. A five-year-old who can read fluently and with authority is a bit of a freak. But by ten years old, the pack had caught up. Worse, my parents had realised that my younger brother Sean really was bright. My slack approach to schoolwork was also starting to be noticed. I could not justify, nor did I want, any special, expensive treatment.

Adding further to the mix, my father was unemployed.

Dad had moved to New Zealand as provincial manager of the London-based Lombard Banking Group. He built a network across the city, and one day a friend offered to train him up as a stockbroker with a view to a rapid rise to a partnership in his firm.

Dad took the job but quit after just a few weeks. The moment of crisis came when a wealthy woman of the town complained that her investments were not giving her sufficient return on her capital and suggested that her money was being managed by hopeless layabouts.

As Dad put it later, 'I decided I would not be spending the rest of my life working to make the rich richer.'

All well and good. But he had four kids, one at an expensive school, and whatever capital had followed him out of Jersey was long since spent.

It wasn't long before I was being called into the headmaster's wood-panelled study, which I had previously only visited for a belting.

'So tell me, young Riminton, what is your father doing for work these days?' rumbled old man Chennells.

'He's unemployed, sir,' I chirruped back.

'Is he now?' Chennells gazed at my guileless mug for a while. 'Oh, well. Carry on.'

Mum worried like hell but Dad was utterly serene through this time. He was going to find something worth doing. Some months later an announcement was made that a medical school was going to be established in Christchurch. Dad applied and was hired as the quaintly titled 'Academic Secretary' – effectively CEO. It was perfect for him, returning him to his early interest in medicine, while allowing him to use his administrative instincts in the name of a noble cause. He stayed with it until he retired.

The risks he took in turning his back on a potentially lucrative stockbroking career meant little to me at the time. In my own middle age, I feel inspired by his courage. He knew he could never be satisfied, no matter what the financial rewards, with something that did not fit his values of serving the community. He backed his values at the risk of real financial strain. Ultimately, his faith was rewarded and he lived a much happier life as a result. I hope, should I need to, that I can live up to his example.

My mum was also remaking her life. Both of my parents had been involved in grassroots charities. One in particular, called Birthright, supported families that had lost their breadwinner. We came to know a couple of those families quite well. On a few occasions, kids would come to live with us for a while to take pressure off a grieving and harried mum. One lad shared my room on several occasions. I would love to say I was saintly in my appreciation of the difficulties the boy was facing and that I offered counsel, friendship and support. In fact, we seemed to niggle and fight a fair bit. I recall it now with shame.

It was perhaps inevitable that Mum would go to university and retrain as a social worker. She could only commit the time to get a low-level certificate of social work, but her years of nursing and her volunteer work saw her quickly hired. She would finish up as provincial head of Catholic Social Services. In retirement, she would play a significant role in reforming New Zealand's adoption laws.

All of this suggests a life of unblemished worthiness.

In fact, life was especially tough for Mum. She was a ferociously bright woman who had enjoyed a life of independence and respect in the British Armed Forces, in hospitals and – later – as chatelaine to a fast-rising figure in the Ceylon tea industry.

In Christchurch, she found herself without family, friends or networks, reduced to household drudgery. Her Catholic doctrines and her robust affections for my dad meant she was destined to produce babies until menopause or death in childbirth.

Something had to give. She was miserable, ragged, unappreciated by her children and, most of the time, on her own. The parish priest, Father Curnow, was a regular visitor. For Mum it was a spiritual crisis as much as a domestic one.

She was caught in the cross-currents of her own Catholic tribalism and the Age of the Pill. Second-wave feminism was on the march. And Mum had a choice to make. Would she defy papal rules against contraception, or submit to the ancient Catholic role of domestic breeder?

Feminism won.

I am glad it did, because the alternative, I have no doubt, would have been a breakdown for my mother.

As kids, we were still required to attend church but Mum never again did. There were no more children. In time, she didn't even care that my brothers and I spent Sunday mornings riding our bikes around rather than attending church. The important thing was that she had a couple of hours to herself. She still worked for church agencies as a social worker but the faith and the dogma were gone.

The family marched on into modernity – or perhaps, post-modernity – and, so far, have counted ourselves the better for it.

Meanwhile, I was accepted into the high school of my dreams, launching a period that would bring great satisfactions but also the darkest phase of my life.

—

If Medbury was a little enclave of English privilege, Christchurch Boys' High School was an education factory. In my intake year, 1974, there were more than twelve hundred students, with three hundred in my year alone. At Medbury I had known the names – or at least the surnames and nicknames – of every child. At Boys' High I would never know all the names of even those in my year.

The place was an ornament to a Kiwi ideal – that the best schools should be free of charge and open to the public. I came from outside the school residential zone and owed my place to a former French teacher who had influence over the selection process and whom my parents had assiduously courted. His name was Gordon Troup, a Francophile who had played, it was said, a secret role in co-ordinating the French resistance against the Nazis. Whatever the truth, he cultivated the image by riding around on a creaky black bicycle with a beret on his head and a pointy white beard.

I spent a few weekends visiting Troup so he could get the measure of me. He had a complicated model train set in his back garden. Little trains went around through forests and hillside cuttings that he had created, pulling to a stop at a station next to a little model town. It was all a mystery to me. What was a man in his seventies doing playing with a train set? I wanted to ask him about the war, but he parried my questions. His house smelled of trees. He lived alone. He didn't seem lonely. These things interested me. But I hadn't yet found a way to ask questions that unlocked real answers.

After a few Saturdays, I stopped visiting. But I was offered a place at the school. Something must have worked. My parents were relieved and happy, and for different reasons, so was I. Boys' High was what I wanted, a big, potentially threatening new environment. It felt like I would be swimming in the open sea.

The school generated more university scholarships than any other in New Zealand at the time, in close rivalry with Auckland Grammar. One of my year-mates, Richard Loe, went straight into the first Rugby XV and later spent years as an All Black prop. The school generated cricketers, too, including the famous Hadlee clan led by the later Sir Richard Hadlee.

This was where I wanted to be.

As a small, garrulous redhead with a Pommy accent – and worse, as the product of a private school – I knew I would have to fight for my place in this big world. But I was up for it.

My first obstacle was Stephen A. Walker (the initial was needed to distinguish him from Stephen G. Walker, no relation, who was also in 3A1). Stephen A. Walker was the alpha male. At thirteen he was already six feet tall, blond, handsome, handy at rugby and one of the brightest in the class. He came from Westburn primary, the school my parents had pulled me out of to send me to Loreto. He was already established as boss dog of the Westburn kids and he was sizing up the ones who had come in from Heaton and Elmwood, and the other main feeder schools. A noisy pipsqueak from Medbury simply represented an opportunity to display dominance with no risk of getting a large chunk of his new classmates offside. Almost every day for weeks, my schoolbag would be emptied out across the schoolyard or my bike would be bent in some new, interesting way.

It was tedious and I got in trouble with my parents for repeatedly needing new schoolbags that they could ill afford. But this was what I had come to the big school for. I selected my friends on the basis of who I liked and admired. Consequently, Walker and I developed many friends in common. I also had a knack for distributing nick-names that tended to stick. I named Walker 'Wally' – friendly enough to be hard to reject but with a slightly disparaging overtone. Soon, three hundred kids were calling him Wally. Nothing he could do about it.

He once came up to thump me during a woodwork class. He was so confident of his physical superiority that, as he swung back his arm for a roundhouse swing, he left his midriff completely exposed. With nothing to lose, I sunk all my strength into a deep punch to his solar plexus and he went down like a sack of spuds. Didn't do me any good. He just belted me harder after school and distributed the contents of my schoolbag a little further than usual.

But resistance is not about winning. It is about resisting. I was holding my own socially in the class, had the mates I wanted, and on some level I enjoyed being this fella's irritant. By Year 10, most of us had driver's licences and some had motorcycles. Wally had a trail bike, a Yamaha 185 as I recall. Once, at a mate's place, he tried to pour a cup of piss over me – real piss, he had urinated into an almost empty plastic cup of beer. He missed, but the point was taken. A little later, when he was distracted elsewhere, I unscrewed the petrol cap of his Yamaha and refilled the tank with a little of my own unleaded. The motorcycle became mysteriously unreliable after that. When he challenged me about it, I freely admitted pissing in his tank. After that, a kind of truce descended.

Stephen A. Walker, last time I caught up with him, was a multi-millionaire mergers and acquisitions man with properties spread across a range of desirable locations. He was very cheerful and nice.

5

THE FIRST THREE SECONDS

NONE OF WHAT I HAVE REVEALED SO FAR IS TO SUGGEST THAT I WAS a young man overcoming crippling odds. Far from it. I knew even at the time that mine was a privileged upbringing. I still had memories of the crowded poverty of Sri Lankan towns. I had seen beggars lining the streets, some of them with grossly disfigured limbs or bulging sightless eyes. New Zealand in the 1960s was among the richest nations on earth on a per capita basis, and the cradle to grave social welfare experiment meant no unsightly poverty marred its neat suburban streets. Nor were there ostentatious displays of wealth – New Zealand, and especially Christchurch society, looked askance at such things. Everyone felt adequately well off and, in general, people did not feel much richer or poorer than their neighbours.

Notions of class were also déclassé. Christchurch undoubtedly had its own 'establishment', many proudly listing forebears back to the 'First Four Ships' which brought the initial English settlers in the mid-1800s. But no one imagined themselves upper class – or even, particularly, working class. There was Kiwi class. As migrants, ostensibly from Britain, we were welcomed without fuss into a community of friendly, if modestly reserved, people.

My parents stressed how lucky we were to be there. When Dad's sister Nancy visited from Jersey around 1970, she was appalled to find her nephews speaking in distinctly Kiwi accents. We were in turn indignant. How else should we speak? We were Kiwis. The pretensions and the anxieties of the British class system meant nothing to us.

And yet, as I marched into my middle teens, something happened.

Inexplicably, around my fifteenth birthday, a crowding darkness seemed almost physically to enter my head. I have read accounts of madness, where people feel pursued by the dark beat of wings, a sense of black birds or bats flapping at the edge of their vision. This describes my experience.

I started drinking in dangerous ways. There was another boy in my class who had bad breath. I decided that bad breath was the worst of things. I set out to avoid it by drinking a tumbler of whiskey – neat – every morning before school. It seemed to improve the morning. We had moved house and now lived close enough to Boys' High for me to get home for lunch. Mum would rarely be there. I would drink two or three coffees and sometimes take another nip of scotch to see me through the rest of the day.

My brother Paul left school about this time and took up an apprenticeship as a printer. This required a trip to Auckland for a few weeks at trade school. He returned with a new appreciation of cannabis and he was keen to introduce me to it.

I was keen to learn.

I took a holiday job in a hamburger bar in the city, back when hamburgers were a genuine meal. The cash helped fund my appetites.

I was still functioning on several levels. I won a school English prize for a short story. I was playing rugby for a good team. One of my friends, Bill Gregory, was a good ice-skater. He also owned a little two hundred dollar Morris Minor so we had transport. I took up ice-skating with him at the main Christchurch rink and gained some level of competency.

But I feared I was going mad. Visual hallucinations, and even auditory ones, came to visit. I never heard voices in my head. The sounds were more industrial, like the muted buzzing and clanking of machinery. At the same time, I was assailed by a deep sense of pointlessness. When I later saw the nightmarish David Lynch film *Eraserhead*, with its terrifying shapeless noises, it struck me with the force of documentary.

In the mid-1970s, the Cold War was at its peak and seemed unending. Films and books laden with imagery of a nuclear apocalypse were everywhere. It seemed impossible to imagine that something wouldn't happen to bring us down in flames. We were constantly told the number of nuclear warheads in the world would be enough to wipe out humanity twenty times over. New Zealand, with its ports, would be targeted to deny the US Navy safe haven. So we were told. Films like Peter Watkins' *The War Game* and written accounts of survivors from Hiroshima and Nagasaki left little doubt of what such a fate might be like.

It wasn't an optimistic time. The daily busy-ness of people seemed mere vanity – self-delusion, even – in the face of such annihilation.

This might have explained part of my mental state. But those were external factors. The crushing sense of unworthiness, of futility, were much more personal and internal. I can try to examine it from my adult perspective, to pick apart what was wrong now as I tried to then, but the short diagnosis was that I was dangerously depressed.

At fifteen, I tried to take my own life. I won't describe the technique I chose but I intended it to be effective and believed it would be. It failed because of a small error on my part. Even as I set it up, I examined my reasons for doing it. I felt that my feelings of pointlessness could only deepen. The phrase I used to myself was that I was bored. Whenever I see the heartbreak of parents as they ask in their anguish why their teenager took their life, I always think: perhaps their child didn't even know why. Perhaps they were just bored.

The attempt failed. My parents never knew of it. I lived on.

The fear that I was going mad stayed. There was a boy at the school a couple of years ahead of me who announced he was a Buddhist. No one at school even knew what that was, although I had heard a little bit about Buddhism mixed in with our Sri Lankan stories. The boy then began growing his hair outlandishly long, putting him at odds with the school. One day he rode past me in a neighbourhood park and stopped nearby to put his bike in a bike rack. I wandered over to chat because he had gained a bit of positive notoriety for his fights with the school authorities over his hair.

He seemed barely to notice me. He was saying something I couldn't make out and was fiddling with his bike in a way that seemed to have no purpose. Soon after, I heard he had been admitted to a mental hospital, diagnosed with schizophrenia. It struck me deeply. In my worst moments I feared I was going there myself.

I got through my sixth form year in reasonable order, though it was plain I was no longer counted among the bright young things. I had great English teachers, though. I had my first poet crush on Gerard Manley Hopkins, guided by a wonderful old teacher called Colin Macintosh. And, to my happy astonishment, I loved Shakespeare. I loved the feel of the words when they were spoken out loud. I loved the moral ambiguity. And I felt a particular sympathy with old King Lear, beseeching the heavens, 'Let me not be mad . . . oh, dear God, don't let me go mad!'

My concerns about my mental stability had one positive effect: I never took Class A drugs. I was well aware of the tragic tales of some of my musical heroes, like Pink Floyd founder Syd Barrett, or the brilliant early Fleetwood Mac guitarist Peter Green. The diet of LSD designed to expand their consciousness left them slow-blinking casualties, psychotic outcasts or empty husks. I felt certain that would be my fate if I went down that path.

Weed and alcohol were a different matter. The local cannabis – Akaroa Cabbage, as I liked to call it – did the job more than adequately. Most weekends I would be stoned to the eyeballs and drinking so heavily I would be physically sick. I found a drive-through bottle store that had a bin of two-dollar wines. They were barely drinkable. But I drank them. I found that if I restricted myself to two bottles of wine a night I would not vomit, so long as I tempered my marijuana intake.

In the middle of this malaise, I did a strange thing. I signed up with a local amateur theatre company. I knew no one there, which was possibly part of the appeal. For the first time, I was memorising and delivering lines on stage. Acting. I wrote a character scene for a play and performed it. As a pissed teenager in an op-shop overcoat, I fitted right in. I had no illusions I was a genuine actor but, in its own small way, that little theatre company probably saved me. It would bear odd and unexpected fruit. That small decision to join the Elmwood Players led to everything that followed. But I didn't know that at the time.

By my final year at school, teachers were warning other kids that I was best avoided because of my drinking problem. My cover was blown. But, strangely, I received no punishments at home. I am probably glad for that. One Saturday night I went out only to return home by 9 pm covered in my own vomit. I was out of control. My father met me at the door, gazed at me sympathetically and said, 'Leave your clothes outside and I'll get the shower running.'

I do remember coming home from school one day around this time, and walking into the living room. My mum came flying out of the kitchen and, without a word, began swinging punches at me. Bang, bang, bang, bang. She was intense and totally focused. I was seventeen by then and her punches couldn't hurt. My brothers watched mutely from their seats around the television. I retreated to the toilet, locked the door and waited for hours for my dad to get home from work.

Dad talked me through it. Nothing else was ever said about it. I can't even imagine the worry I was putting my parents through.

The teachers at Boys' High were good ones. Somehow, they nursed me through my final year at school. My drinking, dope-smoking and a few concussions put an end to my rugby playing – my enthusiasm for tackling had taken a toll. My Elmwood Players experience led me to try out for a role in the school musical. It was a joint production with a girls' school, Avonside. I was chiefly keen to meet some girls. I couldn't sing to save myself so the talented composer and playwright, Neil Pickard, wrote me into a single scene in which I would have a soliloquy. I am sure now it was calculated to require as little of me as possible, and timed to ensure I was all done before I had the chance to get too hammered.

I did meet a girl. Sue Perry. I approached her at a cast party when the show was finished. I had inhaled my two bottles of gut-rot red. The first words I ever consciously spoke to her were a declaration of love and a promise to marry her. She was sixteen. I was seventeen.

At that year's end I sat my final school exams. The marks came back.

I had gained entry to university. I was seven marks short of what was called an A bursary. I was a B student and that, I could acknowledge to myself, was a better result than my efforts deserved.

I was never made a prefect – or monitor, as they called them in New Zealand. The idea would have been laughable. I never made the top team in any of the many sports on offer. But for some reason, I was selected to make the valedictory speech at the formal leavers' dinner. It was a big deal. I would have to speak to all the staff plus the 350-odd students who were departing from the senior school.

The valedictorian's speech was traditionally reprinted in full in the school's glossy yearbook. I read a few from the back catalogue to see what might be involved. They all seemed to have been delivered by star pupils keen to show off a grasp – or at least, an awareness – of Greek and Roman orators or Shakespeare or Milton or pedagogical giants.

It did my head in.

The night before the big dinner, with no idea what I was going to say, I went off to a David Bowie concert.

The following morning, not only did I have no speech, I had shredded my voice. Vague tendrils of panic set in. One way to save the hoarse remnants of my voicebox was to shut up and get some work done.

With neither the time nor the inclination to build an address around homage to the ancient dead, I decided to write what I wanted to say about the school. I wanted to signal my affection for the teachers and the only way I knew how to do that was to take the piss out of them. The speech largely wrote itself.

By that evening, the grand old hall was full. I was at the top table, the kids – my mates – were lined up in rows facing me. The school reinforced our symbolic transition towards adulthood by freely allowing wine to be served to hundreds of kids aged sixteen to eighteen. On the top table, where I was the only person under forty, the flow was a torrent.

By tradition, I had to follow a distinguished old boy. In this case, he was a Rumpolian barrister called Mervyn 'Sticky' Glue who was best known to the kids as a character actor on New Zealand TV. He was well liquored up and loved a show. In mid-delivery he placed a chair on the top table, climbed onto it and stood there, swaying gently on one leg. Everyone was too transfixed to focus on anything he was saying. It wasn't clear Sticky Glue was attached to the concept of focus anyway but it all seemed to go over pretty well.

Then it was my turn.

I knew from debating that everything turns on the first three seconds. If you hear yourself sounding weak or uncertain, all confidence evaporates and you can never get it back. If you come out strong and clear, confidence follows – and with confidence you can do anything.

Would my voice produce anything at all?

I launched in. The sound that emerged was gravelly and . . . strong. Somehow, the top notes in my larynx had been wiped out completely, leaving me with the rough-edged baritone of a carnival barker.

My spirits intact, I proceeded to give thanks to the teachers in the guise of a merciless piss-take. The kids started laughing first. The teachers looked aghast. My final-year English teacher, Gillian

Wilkes, who I suspect put me up for the speaking gig, smiled on benignly. By the end, the kids were hooting and laughing and the teachers – even the tough old one-eyed headmaster Ian Leggat – were in on the joke or pretending to be.

We weren't privileged to go to the school, I finished up, we were just lucky.

I believed it.

And with that, the world awaited.

6

RAT-POO ALLEY

MY SCHOOL MARKS MIGHT HAVE BEEN UNDERWHELMING BUT NEW Zealand was a generous place. My B bursary was enough to get me into any university course other than medicine. Not only that, the government would pay for me to attend. And there would be no tuition fees.

This was the happy possibility facing most kids who managed to complete high school in New Zealand. Many, however, had little interest in university. Jobs at the freezing works slaughtering and trimming cattle paid a couple of hundred dollars a week. You could have a second-hand car in a month. Some kids took up those options or took trainee positions at banks, or apprenticeships in the building game, or went back home to the farm. University study was seen as a waste of time and a lost opportunity to make money, unless you wanted a specific job skill to become a lawyer or a dentist, teacher or engineer.

Kiwi heroes were people who just got things done. Like Ed Hillary, a beekeeper who climbed a bit before he went to the Himalaya, conquered Mount Everest and returned with a knighthood. He was later made an ambassador – the perfect representative of the New Zealand ideal. Who needs university when a life like that beckons? The main thing was to be – in the phrase immortalised by Kiwi humorist Barry Crump – 'a good keen man'.

34

Meeting Sue had steadied my self-destructive drinking. But I was still hammered, stoned and sick more often than was reasonable. I had a habit of falling off motorcycles, too.

At school, my best subject had been English. And people who were good at English became lawyers. But law school? That seemed way too grown up.

What I needed, I decided, was a job. Independence. Law school could wait a year.

And I had an opening. Dad told me to talk to a woman he knew about work as a hospital cleaner. So I entered that summer of 1978 with a part-time gig running a big floor polisher across the weathered linoleum of Christchurch Public Hospital. I got to do part of the neighbouring building too. It contained lecture theatres for medical students and some other rooms neatly crowded with obscure bits of equipment of a generally medical nature. All the rooms were empty by the time I went around well on in the evening.

One night, I was stretching my big spinning machine into the final corner of some sort of medical room when the polisher suddenly stopped with a bang. Never mind. I was pretty much done. I started rolling in the long electrical cord when I noticed a rupture in the rubber flex with a little flowering of melted metal poking through. I was curious. But, never mind, it was home time.

I packed up the machine and headed off without a second thought.

The next day I arrived at work. The lift doors opened. There was the stern-faced woman who had hired me and a grim-looking fella in a suit.

'Did you notice anything unusual as you went about your work last night?' she asked.

'Er, no.'

'Nothing?' the man said, peering down at me.

'Well, there was this little bang sound and my machine stopped working.'

'Really.' The woman's frown deepened. 'And did you tell Mrs Darby?'

Mrs Darby was the theoretical night manager for the cleaners but she spent her time gossiping with one of them who was an old mate, meaning I had to cover double the ground. And then Mrs Darby would head home early and leave me to it.

'No,' I said, with just a touch of innocent malice. 'I don't usually see much of Mrs Darby after about 7 pm.'

'Really?' the woman said.

It turned out my machine had shorted out when the electrical cord got caught beneath a huge industrial-size refrigerator. The fridge had shorted out, too.

And the fridge contained the back-up blood supply for the entire city.

While I was practising the 'deny and deflect' policy that had, broadly speaking, got me through school, surgical operations were being abandoned. The city's radio stations were broadcasting urgent appeals for all good citizens to come in and donate blood.

Not one of my proudest moments.

Oddly, I wasn't sacked. The protective powers of a unionised workforce. However, I was redeployed to a mysterious department that few of Christchurch's citizens knew about.

The teaching hospital did research experiments on animals. The poor victims of this science were chiefly rats, although there were mice, rabbits, and one lonely, agitated sheep. Some of the animals had been given things that induced cancer, others were being tested with things that might slow their cancer. Some had skin grafts being checked for rejection. I have no idea what the sheep was there for, inside her little cage. I chatted to her sometimes but she never responded beyond the frantic and desperate stamping of her feet.

Sheep counselling wasn't my job anyway.

I was paid to collect the square plastic trays from beneath the cages and wash off the accumulated poo, urine, occasional blood, plasma, and other mysterious fluids that collected on the thin coating of sawdust at the bottom. Once I had done this (into a giant grinding sluice), I refreshed the sawdust and put the trays once more under the unhappy animals in their cages.

As long as I didn't think about the animals' suffering, I didn't mind the work. The place smelled a bit when you stepped out of the lift but you got used to that soon enough. The pay was good and people left me alone. I was free to think my own thoughts, which frequently included speculations about a blonde lab technician who inflamed my fantasies despite – or, could it be because of? – her white overalls and gumboots.

Such was my station in life. And it wasn't a bad one. I had money to go drinking with my soon-to-be university student friends. I had a fine girlfriend, the good-natured, wise and steady Sue. I had the endlessly expanding free horizons of young adulthood. And every afternoon, rat-poo trays to keep me amused.

One day, I got a phone call from Gary Batchelor, a teacher who was involved in the drama production at school. His voice made me a little nervous. My valedictory speech had referred to him as 'The Bachelor Gay' – the kind of thing that couldn't be said out loud about a teacher forty years ago.

It seemed he bore no grudge.

'A radio station in town has got some funding to put on a radio play for young actors,' he announced.

'You want someone to swear you're still young?'

'Don't be smart. It's being run by a friend of mine. You should audition.'

'Really?'

'Got anything better going on?'

'I think I'm getting somewhere with a sheep.'

'You're an idiot. I'll send you his number.'

That December I found myself playing Scrooge in a radio version of Dickens' *A Christmas Carol*. The director was the station's main newsreader, Mike Lynch, a lovely man who believed passionately in radio and in training.

By the end of the play, he'd secured funding from the station to trial a four-week broadcasting course. He wanted me to apply.

The course proved to me – and to him – that I would never be a radio jock. I couldn't fake the sincerity necessary to segue smoothly from song to weather to community announcement to amiable joke in the style of the radio disc jockeys of the day. Reading news, however, seemed straightforward – simply channel the BBC World Service news announcers I had been hearing since early childhood. I remember one script contained the name of the then Zambian leader Kenneth Kaunda. I knew little about southern African politics beyond a staunch view that apartheid was bad. But I had heard this man's name often enough, thanks to the BBC, to pronounce it correctly as Kah-oonda.

Mike Lynch's eyebrows went up, approvingly.

During the course we received sessions from every important person on the radio station, from its founder and CEO to the star announcers to the advertising copywriter to the news director.

In the course's final week the more talented among the half-a-dozen participants were discussing job options. One, a beautiful Greek woman, was signed up to front a Christchurch tourism commercial. Others were looking at even more regional radio to get their professional start. After taking four weeks off to do the radio course, it wasn't clear that I would have a job back at the rat-poo factory. It was too late to change my mind and enrol at university. My best prospect seemed some warehouse work at a computer wholesaler.

Near the final day, I received a message.

Tom Clarke, the news director, wanted to see me.

Clarke had a somewhat fearsome reputation. He was in his mid-thirties, a powerfully built man with a thick head and beard of prematurely grey hair. He resembled a cave-dwelling animal. He was no social liberal. Every day at 8 am the station would broadcast an 'editorial' – usually by Clarke, although sometimes delivered by other senior reporters. The aim was to stir up our polite and sleepy town. His preferred technique was to rail against homosexuality in all its forms.

But there I was, climbing the three flights of stairs to the newsroom floor, walking through the door into the fug of cigarette smoke and announcing that Mr Clarke wanted to see me.

Clarke rose from his desk and summoned me into the newsreading booth.

He sat where the newsreader sat. I sat on the other side of a desk covered with volume controls and microphone switches.

He smelled of cigarettes.

'Why do you want to be a journalist?' he demanded.

I looked at him, his startling pale blue eyes, the mass of grey bristling hair, the sheer aggression that seemed to vibrate out of him. I didn't want to be a journalist. The idea had never crossed my mind. I just wanted to get out of that room.

But in the back of my mind was the prospect of shifting boxes around a warehouse, the long year of boredom before I could reverse my error and get off to law school. And I recognised that this uncomfortable encounter was some kind of job interview.

My instincts leapt into play. I said the first thing I could think of.

'Because it would be fun.'

'Fun!' bellowed Clarke.

'Well, isn't that why you do it? Because it's fun?'

By some stroke of luck, I had him. No one wants to admit they hate their job, and certainly not to a jumped-up kid. And I sensed he probably loved what he did.

I blagged on. He offered me a cadetship. It was forty-nine dollars a week after tax, half of what the warehouse job offered, but I didn't hesitate. I still planned to go to law school but I had something to do until then. As I walked to the door, I took in the rows of Adler desk typewriters, the chiefly bearded men sucking on cigarettes and pounding on the keys. Perhaps, I thought, I might learn something about how a city works.

I was seventeen.

7

HUGH RIMINTON, REPORTER

THE WORLD I ENTERED IS GONE FOREVER.

It is impossible to imagine now that a privately funded radio station serving a city of 330,000 people would maintain a newsroom with thirteen full-time reporters and a secretary/typist. Christchurch also had two daily broadsheet newspapers – *The Press*, a staid old city institution that was delivered every morning, and *The Christchurch Star*, a livelier rag that came out every afternoon so that returning workers had something to read during or after dinner (or 'tea' as the evening meal was then known in Kiwiland).

Television news was all but non-existent during my adolescence. The first news I saw on TV was at 5 pm in black and white, when the day's broadcasting began with five minutes of headlines delivered entirely without pictures. Sometimes, the newsreader would appear and announce that another Kiwi soldier had died in the Vietnam War. The screen would then go black. After a few seconds the name of the deceased and his unit would appear in white print on the black background. The name would be intoned by the newsreader who then fell silent again as the screen went back to black. After a few moments the newsreader would appear back on screen to read the rest of the headlines.

A national TV network in the true sense had only begun in 1973, six years before I stumbled into the game.

In time, TV would bring a sense of glamour to journalism. No such thing existed in the world I entered. Being a reporter was a disreputable trade and poorly paid. It was inhabited by some very bright people, but the type who were too troublesome – 'bolshy' was a favoured word – to fit into polite society.

A good example of the quality of the news team was Warren 'Go-Go' Grant. Go-Go, also known as 'Grunter', was a determined smoker. He was also a dedicated drinker. He lived above a pub and took his liquid meals downstairs. He vaguely resembled the Bee Gee, Robin Gibb, a skinny dude with long 1970s hair and an Adam's apple that bobbled around as he talked. Which he never stopped doing.

Not much actually happened in Christchurch but when it did, Go-Go would get very excited.

'Go-go-go-go-GO-GO!' he would bellow, when a house caught fire or a car crash carried the possibility of fatalities. On one very quiet Sunday, he had absolutely nothing to report. His solution was to walk a couple of blocks downtown to a pay phone. There he called police with a breathless, eyewitness account of an armed man stalking around on the roof of the Clarendon Hotel, the town's grandest hotel. The Queen, for heaven's sake, had stayed there.

The police did their duty and turned out in force to investigate.

Go-Go returned to the newsroom and waited half an hour before innocently calling the police to ask if there was anything going on.

'Well, we've had some report of an armed offender in the vicinity of the Clarendon Hotel.'

'You beauty!' Go-Go's manufactured story carried him all through that shift.

Everyone came to hear about the Clarendon gunman hoax, partly because Go-Go loved to boast about it. For some reason he was indulged but there were serious operators in the newsroom as well. Nevil Gibson, the deputy news director, was a cerebral gent who reviewed films and spent his holidays travelling behind the Iron Curtain in Prague or East Berlin. He became the long-time editor of New Zealand's serious business newspaper, the *National Business Review*.

Clare de Lore, who was barely a year older than me, finished up a Lady. She moved to Wellington and in time married the long-time foreign minister and later Secretary-General of the Commonwealth, Sir Don McKinnon.

Others were less fortunate. One reporter, whom we all loved, a gentle young woman with a lovely broadcast voice, went mad. And the young sports editor was shot dead not long afterwards by his girlfriend's jealous ex-lover.

Other characters came and went. One day an elegant young Englishman walked in looking for freelance work. He had come from Paris where he had fallen in love with a model. It turned out she was the daughter of a Christchurch diplomat and he had followed her home in the hope of marriage. He won her hand. The reporter was Adrian Brown, a fine foreign correspondent who became a big name in Australia and Asia.

Meanwhile, I was learning my craft. First, I took up smoking with serious intent. Every single person in the newsroom smoked – and, just to feed the fires, we regularly received visits from a cheery bloke with a big square briefcase. Rod Pascoe was the PR man from Rothmans. It was his job to know the preferred cigarette of every journalist in the country. He would appear in newsrooms to warm greetings from whoever was there. Up would pop the lid of his briefcase and he would hand out cartons of cigarettes precisely to the taste of each hack.

The first time I witnessed this ritual, he made a point of coming over, introducing himself, and checking my brand so he could be sure to bring it next time.

In those days, what you smoked said a lot about a man, or so we believed. To not smoke was considered odd, and certainly unmanly. Those were the days when some All Black rugby players still took a puff at half-time.

One day I was at work with a heavy cold.

'Not smoking?' inquired Mike Lynch.

'Terrible cold,' I rasped. 'The smokes rip my throat.'

'Oh,' he said helpfully, 'whenever I have a sore throat or the flu, I just switch to menthol – goes down a treat and you can keep smoking.'

Useful advice. I switched to menthol. For those too young to know, menthols are mint-flavoured cigarettes rumoured to be even more carcinogenic than normal ones.

Our station, Radio Avon, considered itself to be the bold, brash new face of broadcasting. We were so cutting edge, we had the very latest gadget in our lunch room – a Space Invaders machine. The station rated so strongly half the city listened to us. I recorded my first 'voice reports' within a day or two of getting there. A few days in, I was covering some story considered so important I was required to rush into the studio and deliver my report live. I have no idea what I sounded like over the roaring sound that suddenly filled my ears. I came out, a little stunned by the experience, to see the indulgent smiles of my colleagues. It hadn't been a disaster. I was on my way.

Soon, I was entrusted with preparing and reading bulletins at night and on weekends. When, a few weeks later, I went to open a bank account to deposit my pay, the teller looked at my ID.

'That's an interesting name – there's a bloke with a name like that on Radio Avon.'

'Er, that's me,' I said, my chest puffing.

'No. You're not him.'

'Er, yes I am. If you look, that's Radio Avon on the pay slip.'

She examined the slip. Then examined me. Her lip curled just a little.

'I thought you'd be much older, forty or something.'

I was acne-riddled, bespectacled, skinny and ginger. No wonder I was a disappointment.

—

Reporting in the 1970s was an unimaginably different task from today. No one had media minders or PR people. If you wanted to talk to someone you rang them or went around to see them. Every day, we rang almost every police station in the South Island of New Zealand to see if anything was going on. We were motivated by a legendary cautionary tale about two Auckland journalists in the 1950s. One decided he couldn't be bothered ringing every police station in the North Island on Christmas Day. The other stuck to his task. The next day, one paper had the full front-page splash about the Tangiwai disaster, where the packed Wellington-to-Auckland express train had plunged over a washed-out bridge. It happened at 10.20 pm on Christmas Eve in an obscure central part of the North Island. One hundred and fifty-one people died, the worst train disaster in Australasian history.

And the reporter who didn't make the call never lived it down.

At Radio Avon, we didn't just cover city council meetings, we covered council *committee* meetings. No discussion of by-laws was beneath us. For weeks, the city was gripped by a debate over whether ratepayers should fund a crèche. I was there for every twist and turn.

In my own way, I was getting an education. I was slowly grasping how a city worked. I was learning how to start a conversation with anyone, how to be patient with old folks, how to be ready to smoke and swear and spit on the ground to ingratiate myself with tow-truck operators, how to be properly attentive when power was speaking.

Something else was happening too. My marijuana intake had dropped right off. I once read a news bulletin while under the influence of the dreaded weed and it was terrifying. The dope interfered with the natural feedback loop. I could read the words but I had no way of knowing if I was going too quickly or too slowly, too loud or too soft. And the sentences themselves made no sense to me.

I emerged from the studio promising myself never to do that again.

I still drank more than was medically advisable – but from the day that I walked into Radio Avon, I was never again sick from alcohol.

Plenty of journalists have been alcoholics, including some of the best. I am a rare case. I was saved from alcoholism by journalism.

—

Radio Avon paid me rubbish money but they were generous in other ways. After a few months, they decided to subsidise me on a six-month journalism certificate course at the Auckland Technical Institute (ATI).

It is hard to believe in this age when universities crowd their halls with journalism and communications degrees but, in all of New Zealand at that time, no one offered such a thing. There was a one-year postgraduate diploma at Canterbury University, a one-year Polytechnic course in Wellington and the ATI's six-month crammer.

I was off to the big smoke.

Avon paid my basic wage. If there were any tuition fees, I presume they were covered as well. Sue joined me, to the loudly expressed displeasure of her mother.

'I brought her up to be a nice girl,' she shrilled.

'She is a nice girl,' I replied. 'That's why I want her to come and live with me.'

Sue had just turned eighteen so there was legally nothing her mother could do about it. Also her mother had already married off Sue's older sister at seventeen so age could not have been the defining element of her argument.

The six months in Auckland passed agreeably enough. There were twelve people on the course. Only four, including myself, were male. We learned how to touch-type and how to do shorthand. In the world before word-processing, fast, accurate typing was a core skill. We learnt practical reporting skills from seasoned old hacks: how to write an intro, how to build contacts on a round, the basics of defamation law and contempt of court. Our writing was belted into shape until we had the disengaged, neutral tone then expected while still opening with enough sizzle to keep people reading.

The time passed quickly. I made good friends. I enjoyed living with Sue, who took a job in a grocery store below our one-bedroom flat. We had a mattress on the floor, empty beer crates covered with a sheet for a table, and borrowed outdoor furniture for a lounge suite. We couldn't have been happier.

A couple of days before we pulled up stumps to head back to Christchurch, I felt wearied by the end-of-course parties and went early to bed. Around 9.30, I was woken by a knock on the door. It was a man delivering a telegram. In those times, when people did not necessarily even have home phones, it was possible – at great expense – to ring the telegraph office and dictate a message that would be priced out by the word. This would be relayed by telegraph to the target city and a telegram 'boy' would ride (or more likely drive) to the recipient's address and hand over the message.

This message read: 'Ring work urgent.'

I looked at it in confusion. It was a Wednesday night. Surely they meant for me to call in the morning. But 'urgent' has a certain . . . urgency to it. I found a phone and rang Radio Avon.

An Air New Zealand DC-10 passenger jet had lost contact on a sight-seeing flight over Antarctica. The official search and rescue headquarters was in Auckland. 'Get over there,' they said.

I thought it was a bit of unnecessary fuss. Bad things didn't really happen in New Zealand. The plane had some problems with a bung radio and would turn up sometime soon, I was convinced. It wasn't yet even overdue.

The search and rescue headquarters was in an anonymous office building in downtown Auckland. There were a couple of other reporters there but nothing to see and nothing to report. A handful of intense-looking people worked away behind desks. One came over to tell me the time at which the aircraft would be officially overdue. There was unusual sunspot activity, which may have interrupted radio communications.

There was a telex machine on the public side of reception. It blipped out random symbols and letters due to sunspot interference.

I filed reports across the New Zealand private radio network. I filed for the BBC; they had rung into the search and rescue centre and the harried co-ordinator simply handed the phone over to me. We waited. The deadline passed. No sign.

'Perhaps it has had to ditch into the sea,' I suggested to an old newspaperman. 'They could be in the water in those orange life rafts waiting to be picked up.'

'Those things are just to stop you panicking when you get on the plane,' he said. 'A plane that size hits the sea, there's no one coming home.'

It seemed impossible to believe.

We knew by then that 257 people were on that plane. Many had been given the tickets as early Christmas presents. One couple had won them in a raffle. The inflight guide was Peter Mulgrew, a mountaineering legend in New Zealand second only to Sir Edmund Hillary.

It seemed too hard to believe.

I went over, as I had done many times, to gaze at the hieroglyphics being spat out by the telex machine. There, among the random digits, was a line of words.

WRECKAGE SIGHTED. MOUNT EREBUS. NO SIGN SURVIVORS.

I had the grimmest of scoops. I called the search and rescue co-ordinator over.

'You might want to have a look at this.'

He stared at the paper.

'Give me two minutes before you report this.' And he went off to begin making the official calls.

It was my first experience of the actual out-of-body shock of disaster. I filed reports and updates throughout the night. An air force transport plane was being readied at Whenuapai base north of Auckland to carry search experts and body recovery teams to the ice. It was agreed some journalists should go and – in a grimly flattering turn – my name was put forward to represent radio. I was told I would have to be at the air base in a couple of hours to be fitted out with Antarctic clothing. Before I got there, it was decided to put more police victim identification experts on the flight and only one government journalist was cleared for the trip. Fine by me.

I walked out after dawn into a city devoid of people. Almost every adult in the country had been up all or most of the night following the news. The streets were empty. It was a beautiful subtropical Auckland morning in late spring. The previous day's newspapers were blowing unhindered through streets that would normally have been crowded with cars.

As well as a sense of communal shock and grieving, among the many sensations I experienced was, for the first time, a sense that reporting could be genuinely useful work – even necessary work in times of trouble.

I was eighteen years old. I made a decision. Law school would have to wait another year.

8

POLITICS AND SPORT

BY 1981, I WAS BACK IN AUCKLAND AND THE COUNTRY WAS IN FERMENT, split down the middle over the issue of racism in sport.

For more than a decade, a split had widened in New Zealand between two opposing moral and cultural forces. One was the national sport – rugby union. The other was opposition to the racist policies of New Zealand's fiercest rugby rival, South Africa.

South Africa was by law a racist nation. Its apartheid system was designed to entrench white rule and suppress the majority of the country's people on the basis of colour.

Nelson Mandela and the other main leaders of the resistance were either in jail, in exile, in hiding or dead.

But South Africa was also home to the Springboks, the only team with a positive winning record – at least, in 1981 – against the mighty New Zealand All Blacks.

In 1960, the New Zealand side had toured South Africa having left at home, at the South Africans' insistence, the Maori players who should have been selected. The All Blacks toured again in 1970, with a halfback of Maori descent, Sid Going, and an ethnically Samoan Aucklander, Bryan Williams, but only after the South African officials designated them as 'honorary whites'.

Even that was too much for South Africa's Prime Minister John Vorster, who lamented that letting brown-skinned men play on equal terms against whites was 'the beginning of the end for us'.

Meanwhile, calls for protests and a boycott against South Africa were growing.

In 1973, the Labour government blocked a planned Springbok tour to New Zealand after police warned Prime Minister Norman Kirk that protests would 'engender the greatest eruption of violence this country has ever known'.

By 1976, the recently elected National Party Prime Minister, Robert Muldoon, sent an All Blacks team to tour South Africa with his blessings, arguing politics had no place in sport. Bryan Williams toured again, along with five Maori players – again as honorary whites.

But the policy was increasingly tearing people apart. The 1976 tour happened at the height of the Soweto Uprising, when black school students rejected being taught in Afrikaans, the language – they said – of their oppressors.

Meanwhile, the 1976 Montreal Olympics had begun. South Africa had been banned from the Olympic Movement in the early 1960s. And now more than two dozen African nations boycotted the games because New Zealand, tainted by its sporting connection with South Africa, was taking part.

When Kiwi athlete John Walker won the 1500 metres gold medal in Montreal, it was to muted applause. None of the great black African runners showed up. The winning time was the slowest in years.

Every sensible instinct should have indicated that another South African rugby tour was madness as long as apartheid stood. But Prime Minister Muldoon was making other calculations. By 1981, he was in political trouble. He reckoned the election that year would be decided in the provincial towns. These contained rural conservatives as well as Labour voters. The one thing that united them was a passion for rugby.

Muldoon knew a Springbok tour would divide the country but he gambled it would win him support in the provinces. To the disgust of his Australian contemporary, Malcolm Fraser, Muldoon gave the tour the green light.

I returned to Auckland – New Zealand's largest and most Polynesian city – just as the Springboks prepared for their first visit there since the mid-1960s.

I had found work at an easy-listening radio station in the inner suburb of Grey Lynn. Its weatherboard houses now change hands for millions of dollars but in 1981 it was tired and poor, straddling the Great North Road with its bargain basement car yards.

Here, in a two-storey box, was Radio i. Other, more successful radio stations boldly stated their identity: Radio Pacific was a brash talk station; Radio Hauraki had history, beginning life as a pirate station pumping out rock from a boat in Auckland's Hauraki Gulf. Radio i played sleep-inducing soft pop to what I can only imagine were nursing homes and dentists' waiting rooms.

But it did have an interesting little newsroom.

At the time, music was in a growth phase. Punk had morphed into New Wave, reggae was moving on from Bob Marley into ska and dub, and the New Zealand post-punk pub scene was turning out dozens of reasonable bands. Watching every new release and every gig was a free weekly newspaper called *Rip It Up* – compulsory reading for every kid in the country.

And, weirdly, its best writers kept day jobs at sleepy old Radio i.

They were an eccentric lot.

Duncan Campbell looked like a suburban accountant with his three-piece suits and staid white Hillman Hunter car. But he was possibly the best music writer in the country and certainly the best connected. He would frequently jet off to Jamaica to hang out with his dub buddies or to the US to see what was going on. One day he came to work fresh from New York with an unmarked cassette tape.

'This girl is going to be bigger than Michael Jackson,' he said, pressing play. Out came an infectious post-disco dance track.

Months later, 'Holiday' was officially released and Madonna was on her way.

Radio i was also, to its bones, subversively, openly gay. AIDS and its associated prejudices had not yet been heard of. Here were men living as their gods intended, apologising to no one. It was new to me.

The news director was Nigel Horrocks, short, dapper, infinitely stylish. He lived in a harbourside house packed with records. Thousands of them. His parties were not to be missed. He wrote on jazz and the New York avant-garde, which sounds pretentious and unashamedly was.

He hired only young men, at least while I was there. But he hired well. John Clarke, the stepson of Tom Clarke who gave me my break at Avon; Jim Parker; Mark Everton; Glyn Jones; Eric Young and Ric Salizzo all went on to prominent careers in New Zealand or across the world. Whoever came under the spell of Nigel Horrocks came out better for it.

But there was work to be done. The Springboks were coming.

In July 1981, the South Africans arrived with plans for a three-test series against the All Blacks and thirteen other games, including one against an NZ Maori side. The Springboks had to fly to New Zealand the long way round, via the US, because Malcolm Fraser had refused them landing rights in Australia.

Their first game was a warm-up against lowly rated Poverty Bay on the remote east coast of the North Island. The Springboks were first given a formal welcome on a local Maori *marae* – or meeting house – a gesture that infuriated many Maori activists. A handful responded by driving onto the rugby ground before the game and scattering broken glass. They were arrested, the glass removed, the game went on.

But from the first it was clear some protesters were determined to break the law.

On the day of the game, thousands of protesters left the sanctioned route to cut across a golf course. They came up against rugby supporters heading to the match. Heads were bloodied. The creator of the *Footrot Flats* cartoon strip, Murray Ball, was there. The son of an All Black and a prominent former player himself, he nevertheless opposed the tour. Like many Kiwis, his family was split. Many a backyard barbecue ended early in those days.

'There was a feeling of hatred between both sides,' said Murray Ball. 'It was strange for New Zealanders to feel so aggressive towards New Zealanders.'

It was just the beginning.

Three days later, the Springboks were due to play in the city of Hamilton against Waikato. This would be a more serious rugby contest in a town of many more people. The ground was packed with spectators.

But the protest movement was becoming larger, better organised and tactically sharper. They tore down a perimeter fence and hundreds stormed the ground. There they stood, arms locked, while an outnumbered police force tried to remove them – while also protecting them from furious rugby fans.

Police Commissioner Bob Walton was at the ground when he received a blood-chilling intelligence report. A World War II Spitfire fighter pilot and determined anti-apartheid activist, Pat McQuarrie, had slipped surveillance and stolen a light plane from Taupo Airport 150 kilometres to the south. Walton feared McQuarrie was planning a suicidal crash into the packed stand.

Walton immediately ordered the game abandoned. McQuarrie, flying the plane with a transistor radio in his lap, heard the news and turned around. Nelson Mandela, in his prison cell on Robben Island, also heard of the cancellation and later remembered his emotion.

It was, he said, 'as if the sun had come out'.

Prime Minister Muldoon, who had done so much to ensure the tour would go ahead, was nowhere in sight during these dramas. He was in London, attending the wedding of Prince Charles and Lady Diana Spencer. As future Labour prime minister David Lange archly noted, 'There may be garden parties in London, but it is no garden party here.'

In Wellington, riot police took on protesters in what became known as the Molesworth Street incident. The demonstrators were mainly middle-class types with no idea of what they were up against. Many emerged with bloodied heads. From that point on, it was plain the tour would proceed amid open violence, with the police riot squads defending the tour, and protesters ever more determined to oppose it. In an act of flamboyant defiance, my mum, then aged in her fifties, borrowed my brother's motorbike helmet to attend a rally in Christchurch.

As young liberal, inner-city types, the sympathies of the Radio i news team lay strongly with the anti-apartheid movement. But Nigel Horrocks was a man of principle as well as style. As temperatures rose, he sat us all down and told us that every listener, regardless of their political views, was entitled to a clear, unbiased reporting of events. We would deliver it.

Radio i had one asset the other stations lacked. We owned a plane. Every day, a wonderful old bloke called Bill Mudgway took to the sky to report on Auckland's traffic. The 'i in the Sky' was an Auckland institution and probably helped explain why we had any listeners at all. The police force loved it. Bill would alert them to crashes and other mayhem before anyone else did.

The Springbok tour climaxed in Auckland with the third – and it turned out – decisive test. The All Blacks had won the first one, the visitors had dominated the second. In between, the contest against the NZ Maori team had ended in a hard-fought draw.

The week before the third test, the Springboks were down to play the Auckland provincial side, always one of the strongest in the country. Despite the continued violence, the match was a sellout.

By this time, police had successfully found a way to defend the sports grounds, but only by regularly beating protesters on the approaches to the stadiums. The police had also deployed a specially trained and equipped riot squad, whose most notorious element was the Red Escort Group, or simply 'Red Squad'. Internal documents later emerged revealing the police commissioner's concerns that the Red Squad had become reckless. He feared a peaceful protester could be killed.

On the day of the match against the Auckland provincial side, the police closed the airspace. But, thanks to the value of his traffic reports, Bill Mudgway was granted an exemption and I coat-tailed in on it. For the first time in my life, but certainly not the last, I found myself ad-libbing for hours about a big developing news story. We were flying at a thousand feet in a tight circle over Eden Park. I could see the protesters flowing and surging through the streets. I could see the spectators being allowed in through protected corridors. I could see the riot squads deploying, probing, holding the line.

My reports were blended with reports on the ground from Jim Parker, John Clarke, Eric Young and others. And then old Bill would interject with reports on the traffic. Completely secondary, but not ignored under the Horrocks' dictum, was the game itself. The Springboks won. We finished the day satisfied our system had worked. It had been an effective rehearsal for the real test the following Saturday. I was living, as it happened, in a house over-looking the Eden Park rugby ground car park. When I got home that night, there was razor wire on my lawn.

Saturday, 12 September 1981 dawned grey and gloomy in Auckland. I was up early to drive to the Ardmore aerodrome to the south to get ready for a long day. I had a bout of gastro and dreaded the prospect of hours in a light plane. Old Bill Mudgway presented me with a tube of condensed milk.

'Suck down as much of that as you can stomach and I guarantee you won't shit for a week.'

It was sound advice and a fine technique.

Others were up early too. More than two thousand police would defend Eden Park that day. Thousands of protesters were putting on crash helmets and padding and heading out. Thousands more rugby fans were off to see the deciding battle against their proudest enemy.

As our plane took its position in a circuit over the ground, we could already see the protesters and police facing off. Shipping containers and razor wire had been placed across all approaches to Eden Park. Again, the ticket-holders were fed through heavily policed corridors while protesters surged and probed for any weakness in the defences.

In all, 150,000 people took part in active demonstrations against those games, an astonishing number in a country of just over three million. They did so knowing that violence was all but inevitable. An even greater number turned up to watch the games.

Below us, as the lines grew tighter, three protesters dressed as clowns tried to lower the tension. The two men and a woman pranced between the lines, at one stage handing flowers to the Red Squad riot police. Within a few hours, all three of them had been violently assaulted. The riot squad never admitted liability but a court later ordered financial compensation. The bashing of the clowns symbolised the country's loss of innocence.

But all that would emerge later. The game kicked off, the protests ebbed and flowed.

And then suddenly another aircraft flew in fast and low, spearing towards the packed Eden Park ground. It dipped down to the level of the top of the stands and then pulled up, as protest pamphlets fluttered to the ground.

This was a stunning new development. From our plane, I reported what I saw. The rebel plane came round again. After the pamphlets came parachute flares. And then, on another go-around, a puff of white hit the ground. Flour bombs. One hit the powerful All Black prop, Gary Knight, on the head. As he was being attended to, the referee called the captains together to ask if they wanted to call off the game. Neither did.

Up above, the police ordered our aircraft into a wider circle and we had to climb from one thousand to two thousand feet.

A twin-engine police plane joined the circuit but there was nothing in practical terms they could do.

On the ground, smoke from flares thrown by protesters in the crowd added to the confusion. And still the protest plane circled round, each time seeming to get lower and lower. On a couple of passes, it was so low, the pilot tipped the plane sideways to get the wings through the uprights of the goalposts. The only injuries in the stands that day were to spectators hit by flying bottles as rugby fans tried to bring down the aircraft. But the slightest misjudgement by the pilot would have been catastrophic.

Suddenly, as the sun settled and the game came to its end, the protest plane broke from its circuit and took off, flying low to the north. We were close by and immediately spun off after it. I hoped to see where it landed and possibly land nearby to grab an interview. But we were not the only ones in the chase. The police plane passed just below us, swooping in on the villains and nabbing them as they landed on an airstrip north of Auckland.

The pilot, Marx Jones, and his teenage flour-bombing mate, Grant Cole, were charged and Jones was jailed. On the streets, the protests had descended into running violence, with criminal gangs joining in against the police. In total, some two thousand protesters were arrested, clogging the courts for months.

Muldoon got his victory. As he'd predicted, he won the election in November that year on a 'law and order' platform with strong support in the provinces. But the protesters claimed victory too. The Springboks had to wait until apartheid was dismantled before they ever got another officially sanctioned tour.

And at Radio i that night, we sucked down a beer and agreed that we had seen history. And, as reporters, we had done all right.

9

CROSSING THE DITCH

IN AUCKLAND, MY ADDICTIONS SHIFTED. I HAD ALWAYS LIKED running. Now I was at it all the time. I started doing ten kilometre fun runs, bringing my times down, clearing my head. Smoking didn't fit anymore, so I dropped it. My perfect distance was eight to ten kilometres but I set the goal of running at least five kilometres every day no matter what. That meant sometimes coming home with drink on board, lacing up the shoes and pounding the streets long past midnight. It kept me fit and keen.

I was also reading voraciously, as I always had. I had no university education. Hemingway, Fitzgerald, Jack London, Raymond Chandler, Le Carré, Graham Greene, Somerset Maugham and Evelyn Waugh were among my tutors. I read much more fiction than non-fiction but *Seven Pillars of Wisdom* by T.E. Lawrence (of Arabia) was huge with me. I also loved Ernest Shackleton's epic *South* about his escape from Antarctica after his ship was crushed by ice.

But no book had more impact than Jack Kerouac's *On the Road*. The King of the Beats' amphetamine-fuelled chronicle of endless restlessness in 1950s America struck every chord. So too did *Big Sur*, his searing account of alcoholic collapse. It should be read by anyone wondering if they are drinking too much.

But *On the Road* was the one. As I read it, I knew I could never be satisfied staying and working out my life in New Zealand. My Sri Lankan childhood meant I always knew of a world beyond. My favourite childhood book was Dad's atlas. One of my favourite childhood pastimes was drawing maps of islands and continents of my own invention. I would fill in my outlines with mountains and rivers, establish harbours and towns. I was doing SimCity long before computers.

Now Kerouac was urging me to move.

I had a British passport so London seemed more immediately possible than New York. But the Kiwi dollar was weak and my savings were scant. I could feel the slight tug of inertia so I did the only thing I knew that would signal my commitment to leaving New Zealand. I sold my record collection.

It was by far the most valuable thing I owned, well outstripping my 1955 VW Beetle. Guided by my own tastes and those of my music-reviewing mates I had gathered up hundreds of records – from Thelonious Monk to the Buzzcocks. And now it all had to go. It was a wrench. But when the last collector left and my shelves were bare, I knew there was nothing to do but to get moving. Sue, my steadfast girlfriend from high-school days, was up for it too.

But where to go?

My big brother, Paul, had headed off to Australia a few months earlier and was now in Perth. Out of the blue he mailed me a two-line job advertisement from a Perth newspaper. Radio 6KY was looking for a C-grade journalist. I rang the number. The bloke at the other end, Terry Spence, asked if I could read news. I was calling from work so I grabbed some scripts and read some down the phone line.

Spence took a punt.

'Can you start in three weeks?'

—

We flew into Sydney on a brilliant summer's day, 19 December 1983. From the window on approach to Kingsford Smith Airport, we had a perfect view of the Opera House, Harbour Bridge and the dizzying heights of Sydney Tower.

'That looks like a real city,' said Sue.

Two days later, though, we were heading west again. Everyone who comes to Australia discovers it in their own way. For me the flight to Perth provided the first sense of the size of Australia and its essential emptiness.

We got off the plane by the rear steps. My first impression was of the overpowering heat being blasted back by the jet engines. As I walked across the tarmac, it dawned on me the furnace-like temperature had nothing to do with the aircraft. This was Western Australia four days before Christmas.

My brother Paul and his wife, Donna, made us welcome in a thoroughly Australian way, by taking us to the beach. The sun went down over the Indian Ocean. The air was warm. The sea was warm. How good was this place?

It got even better when I started work. The radio station, 6KY, was owned by Alan Bond, then still in the glow of his America's Cup victory a few months earlier. The station was part of the Channel Nine TV affiliate in Perth and inhabited the same building as the TV studios in the northern suburb of Tuart Hill. It was so far from any shops, the building had its own café, so from the start I got to know some of the TV people. They included a couple of brilliant young talents, Michael Holmes – later a huge star at CNN – and Geoff Hutchison, who became a fixture on ABC Radio in Perth.

The most profound influence on me, however, was a jobbing journalist in the 6KY news team called Tom Needle. Tom was as true blue as they came. The son of a country copper, he had grown up in every back country town from Perth to the Kimberley. He was forty-ish, leathery, skinny and laconic. He had a cigarette always at his lips and, if the mood took him, a wealth of stories about how to know if your waterhole was hiding a croc or the dangers of cornering a big red kangaroo, and so on.

At the time I arrived, Australian shearers had a big scrap going on with scab labour. The pastoralists had introduced a wide-toothed shearing comb. It meant a sheep could be shorn of its fleece in fewer passes of the shearer's arm. The shearers' union said it put more strain on the worker, who had to drive the comb through a larger volume of fleece with each pass. The shearers had gone on strike. The sheep station owners had responded by bringing in contract shearers from New Zealand. The Kiwis were seen as scabs. Blows had been exchanged. The papers had been full of it.

When I turned up in the office in the first week of January, my immediate boss, Les Wheeler, made the introductions.

'Kiwi, are you?' said one of my new colleagues.

'Fuckin' Kiwis,' said another.

'Jesus,' chimed in another, 'you come over here, you steal our jobs, you take our women – you shear our fuckin' sheep!'

I knew a rite of passage when I saw one and could read the twinkles in their eyes. Frankly, I thought they were bloody funny.

Kiwis are polite. At the heart of New Zealand behaviour is decency. So Kiwi humour stops at the point where someone might be offended by it. Australians had no such qualms. Offence lay at the very heart of the joke. The only thing Australians couldn't stand was people taking the insults seriously. So I wore the banter, 'copped it sweet', chuckled to myself and got on with learning my job.

On the Thursday of that first week, as he was leaving, Tom Needle paused at the door.

'Look, we're having a barbecue this Sunday at our place. Would you and the missus like to come along?'

Sue and I turned up at his house and every one of my new colleagues turned up as well. That was the moment I fell in love with Australia and Australians. I was never close mates with Tom. He was nearly twice my age and his interests were hugely different. But he had quietly welcomed us in and our workmates had turned up to put a seal on it.

Kiwis, much as I loved them, would have taken far longer to extend that hand of friendship. I was touched. I have left Australia since to live overseas for extended periods. I still have a British passport – and a Kiwi one – somewhere in a bottom drawer. But from the day of Tom Needle's barbecue I have *felt* Australian and I have wanted to be Australian. It has been the longest love affair of my life. I have never stopped being grateful for it.

—

Becoming Australian had its issues, however, especially when it came to shedding my British-infused Kiwi accent. I was put on a shift to produce and read the news. The 6 pm bulletin ended at five past six, followed by a weather report. This required me to close off the bulletin by saying: 'It's six past six – 6KY.'

Few challenges in broadcasting have presented me with greater torment. Every Kiwi in Australia, especially in those days of fewer accents, was plagued with requests to 'say fush and chups . . . say sux'. There I was every evening gritting my teeth and stretching my lips wide to say – as it sounded to me – 'seeks past seeks, Seeks-KY'.

Eventually the phone calls of complaint dropped away.

Another challenge was the tour that year of the Pakistani cricket team. For me, the natural pronunciation was 'parka-starn' – as if the place was a nation of raincoats. Australians generally pronounce it as 'Pakka-stan' – as if it was owned by Kerry Packer. I strained to discipline myself to go with the latter until one day I heard the great Richie Benaud on the Channel Nine coverage. 'Parka-starn,' he called it – and I felt a wave of relief. If the former Australian captain could say it that way, I sure as hell could. Thank you, Richie. Wherever you are, here's cheers.

The station's on-air line-up was changing and included two big names in Perth – genuine 'Perth-onalities', in that they were not well known anywhere else. One was Howard Sattler, a race-baiting populist who would become WA's number one conservative cage rattler. The other was the self-professed 'egomaniac' Eoin Cameron.

Cameron was a larger-than-life character who a decade later became a Federal MP for the Liberal Party. When all that washed up, he became for many years the 'King of Breakfast Radio' on the ABC. He died, too young, in 2016.

Eoin was a man of Falstaffian charisma, with a booming voice fed on gravel and claret. We loved him in the radio station – and they loved him out there in listener land.

Suddenly, 6KY, the battling also-ran of Perth radio, started to rocket up the ratings. To celebrate, all staff were invited to a conference room where cases of vintage Moet et Chandon had been chilled for our arrival. Some of the staff had never tasted French champagne, let alone the vintage stuff. In Perth, this was still the age of Emu Export.

The chief of the station arrived.

'I am so fucking proud of you!' he announced. 'When I got this news I was in New York City and it was three o'clock in the morning. I had no one to tell. So I rang up and ordered a hooker. And she came to my room and I said, "I don't want to fuck ya, I just want to tell you that my radio station is going through the roof!"'

Images of a world far removed from ours crowded our minds. But hey – those were the high days of Bondy, the start of the era that would crumble into lawsuits, jail terms and the collapse of wealth summed up by the phrase 'WA, Inc.'. It was 1984. The world was rich with possibilities, begging to be taken at a gallop.

And who complains about vintage champagne?

Perth was a worker's paradise. Housing was ridiculously cheap. With my C-grade radio reporter's wage and Sue's salary as a practice nurse, we bought a newish brick and tile house with an in-ground swimming pool in Yokine in the northern suburbs. Our combined income was around $32,000 a year. The house cost $40,000. I cobbled the deposit together with a cash advance on my Westpac bankcard and we were in. None of it was difficult. We were twenty-three years old.

This is painful to read for someone starting out today, where a junior reporter and a basically credentialed nurse couldn't imagine buying their own home without family help or some other advantage. Make no mistake, we had the best of it.

We bought a Holden Kingswood from a bloke in a pub and took off to explore the tropical north. The first wild kangaroo I ever saw was just a fleeting blur before it took out the front of the Kingswood 180 kilometres south of Carnarvon.

Tom Needle had worded me up on what was required for a WA road trip.

'You need water, mate, at least two twenty-litre jerry cans. And you need a pair of pliers and some Bar's Leaks for when you hit a roo.'

Well, now I had hit one.

I was at the side of the road at the edge of the desert with a car with a mangled front end while the last contents of my radiator sizzled into the red sand.

A few minutes later a battered ute pulled up and a kid younger than me got out. His wild halo of hair was matted with dust and his skin seemed powdered with it.

'Okay,' he said, surveying the damage. 'Got any pliers?'

'Sure,' I said, going to the boot to extract the only tool I possessed.

He began twisting the shattered elements of the radiator, squeezing them to seal them shut.

'Any Bar's Leaks?'

'You bet.' I retrieved the plastic bottle of gunk with its miraculous claims about stopping any leak. He poured it into the top of the radiator.

'Got any spare water?'

I dragged out a jerry can. We topped her up.

'Don't go over eighty, but this should get you to Carnarvon.'

And with that he was gone. My entire emergency pack for a trip into the Australian desert had been expended but you couldn't argue about the efficiency of the packing or the wisdom of Tom Needle's advice.

I raved in letters back to my mates in Auckland about this dinosaur-stomping land where everything was empty and huge. Before long, both John Clarke and Jim Parker, my Radio i buddies, made the move to Perth themselves.

—

Perth was a great way to get to know Australian politics without being thrown too quickly into the thick of it. Most Sandgropers cared nothing about the 'wankers over east'. The state was run, to most people's apparent satisfaction, by a tubby former Channel Seven reporter called Brian Burke. His premiership would also end in disgrace and jail time but for most people it seemed fun while it lasted.

I was confused by the issue of race relations in Australia. In Auckland, there was active attention being given to land claims by the Maori. In New Zealand, on any normal day, an Anglo-Irish New Zealander would have interactions with a member of the *tangata whenua*, the indigenous 'people of the land'. White New Zealanders were generally quite comfortable calling themselves *pakeha*, the Maori word for white folk. Words like *mana*, which meant authority, dignity and power, were so widely used that it wasn't until I got to Australia that I discovered it wasn't English.

Issues for Maori and Polynesian New Zealanders were real ones, and much contested, but they lay at the very centre of New Zealand life.

In Australia, among my white colleagues and acquaintances, there appeared to be no Indigenous engagement at all. Aboriginal Australians I encountered seemed absolutely squeezed out to the fringes. When I asked in the newsroom what 'the Dreamtime' was there was an embarrassed silence. People didn't seem to know and, more to the point, it seemed a social gaffe to ask.

One bloke I interviewed many times was Rob Riley, a brilliant activist not much older than I was. He was the head of the

Western Australian Aboriginal Legal Service, chaired the National Aboriginal Council and helped negotiate the *Native Title Act*. But we talked almost entirely of politics and process. My own deeper questions I let fall silent, no doubt because I didn't want to reveal the depth of my ignorance.

I came to learn that Rob Riley was taken from his family soon after he was born – one of the Stolen Generations. He wasn't returned to them until he was twelve, by which time he had been sexually abused by older boys in state care. Tragically, he took his own life while still in his early forties.

Another mystery was gender politics. In New Zealand, I had many female 'friends'. It was entirely normal to chat with female peers with no agenda in play. It was well known, should they care to take note, that I was in a steady relationship. But even if I wasn't, it was just hanging out, having a chat.

This approach didn't work in Perth.

I turned up at a barbecue one hot summer's day through some connection with my brother. I didn't know too many people. There were a bunch of blokes outside. One of the women was preparing some food in the kitchen. I wandered in to help.

After a few minutes of small talk, she cut it short.

'You're not going to get a root, mate.'

I walked out, stunned.

I played squash with a bunch of blokes. Over beers afterwards, I commented on how strange it was that no blokes seemed to have female friends. One of these fellas put me straight.

'Mate, if I saw you talking to my girlfriend – that'd be it.'

I would be cut out of the brotherhood. The bonds of mateship have their limits. Even years later, in London, I went out with a large bunch of Australians. We finished up in a restaurant with a long table that placed me opposite a woman who happened to know a bunch of my old friends. I didn't know her, but it wasn't long before we were cheerfully gossiping and having a yarn. When she was momentarily distracted, the bloke to my left leaned over and growled into my ear, 'Mate, you're on a hiding to nothing – she's married.'

Back in Perth, it seemed depressingly Stone Age.

—

In 1984, Prime Minister Bob Hawke called a snap double dissolution election. Western Australian seats were in play. I was dispatched one blazing afternoon to a news conference with the shadow treasurer, John Howard. He was in the CBD, I was at the station in the northern suburbs and the call came in late.

The Holden news car had no air conditioning and had been parked in the sun. By the time I got into the city, I was running hopelessly late and, to make matters worse, I was drenched in sweat.

I burst into the news conference with John Howard already in full flight. Dripping sweat, I clambered up to the top end of the table to set up my microphone, trying to stay oblivious to the irritation and mirth of the reporter tribe.

Howard paused, looked me in the eye, gave me a friendly nod and a g'day, and held off his spiel until I was sitting back down again with microphone in place. I am always grateful for small mercies. I have known John Howard now on one level or another for over thirty years. Whatever his strengths and weaknesses as a politician, his capacity for personal courtesy has never changed. I was never more grateful for it than on that day.

That year also saw my first direct encounter with another giant of Australian public life. Paul Keating was forty years old, a federal treasurer driving momentous change, and the dark spirit at the heart of the Hawke government. After delivering his second budget, he went on the traditional round of selling it. Word came through that 6KY would be on his interview list. No one else in the newsroom wanted to do it. I swotted up all night, a crash course in Australian fiscal policy and budgetary dynamics. The next morning, I chucked everything I could at him. He swatted me off like a fly.

—

By my second scorching Perth summer, things were going swimmingly. In another year or two, the rental income on our house would cover the mortgage and we could revert to our original plan and head to London. But the thought brought a feeling of claustrophobia rather than joy.

Perth is the most isolated seat of government on earth. The world happened somewhere else. The people of my age that I was meeting seemed interested in marrying and settling down with kids. Almost everyone seemed to have bought – or were buying – a brand new car. A new Ford Laser was desirable. A new Holden Commodore showed you were heading somewhere. I have never cared what I drove. The cheapest practical transport was fine by me then and still is.

In Perth in 1985, everyone seemed in a race to be their parents.

Leaving would rob me of a chance to settle my finances to the extent that I had a bombproof base to fall back on if London didn't work out. But I had to get out of Perth.

6KY was part of the Macquarie Radio Network, linked to the titans of broadcasting on the east coast: 2GB in Sydney and 3AW in Melbourne. I rang the boss at 2GB, Charlie Cox. He listened considerately but had nothing for me. Before I had a chance to be despondent, however, I got a call from Melbourne.

Michael Frazer was another of those deeply eccentric figures who played a pivotal role in my life. He was a Vietnam veteran, a published novelist, a flamboyant drunk and a cheerful lunatic. His career would take a knock a few years later at Channel 7 when he waved a revolver in a colleague's face. Doutless he was intending a joke. When I first encountered him, he was news director at 3AW and he had got the tip from Charlie that I was keen to move on from Perth. He offered me a job, sight unseen.

I had never thought of Melbourne but I didn't hesitate. A little motto sprang up in my head that I have used many times since:

invest your money in your mental health. Perth's provincialism was getting me down. Boredom, I knew, could be fatal for me.

Like fools, Sue and I chose not to fly to Melbourne but to take a bus to enjoy the full glory of the Nullarbor Plain. Forty-nine hours after leaving Perth, the exhausted machine heaved into Melbourne and dumped us into a raw May morning.

It was too early to get a hotel room. We had no clothes for the frigid southerly and after two Perth summers had lost all resistance to an eight-degree morning. We walked aimlessly until we found the Princes Bridge over the famously brown and sludgy Yarra River. The office workers of Melbourne were spilling off trams and out of Flinders Street Station, clutching coats against the wind and heading off to work. My heart soared. Here were people, stories, anonymity, poetry, industry, Kerouac!

I've always loved Walt Whitman's poem 'Crossing Brooklyn Ferry', written as he gazed at the masses of people moving at the edge of Manhattan.

> Crowds of men and women attired in the usual
> costumes, how curious you are to me . . .
> (You) are more to me, and more in my meditations,
> than you might suppose.

So I felt that first Melbourne morning. I loved the city at the first ring of a tram bell, and I love it still.

10

THE RUSSELL STREET BOMBING

IN 1985, 3AW WAS ONE OF THE GREAT BROADCASTING HOUSES IN Australia. When I arrived its on-air line-up included comedian John Blackman and 'Uncle Roy', a former serious Channel Ten newsreader called Bruce Mansfield who found his true calling in making people laugh. They covered breakfast. The drivetime show was hosted by Mark Day. He was a mini media mogul in his own right, owning a bunch of regional radio stations and the trash newspaper *Truth*. He also hosted a nightly current affairs show on Channel Seven, *Day by Day*. But the unquestionable powerhouse of the place was Derryn Hinch.

Hinch has written so many autobiographies, I won't cover too much ground here. But he was a pushy lad who came from an even more obscure New Zealand town than I did. He got his start in journalism even younger than I did and went much further. He had a tabloid editor's gift for reducing any event to a headline.

Hinch was a braggart, a boozer, a womaniser and a brilliant radio man. At the time I arrived at 3AW's studios in their converted horse stable on Latrobe Street, Hinch was being paid $800,000 a year. This was when the median house price was $70,000. Where Mark Day, himself at the time a very wealthy man, drove around in a red Porsche Carrera, Hinch hired a tall blonde woman to chauffeur him around in a Rolls-Royce. He'd bought the Roller second-hand and it had cost less than Day's Porsche, but Hinch understood the theatrics of success and never lost an opportunity to put on a show.

The newsroom was in the first throes of getting computers. It still recorded interviews on reel-to-reel audiotape. Stories of national interest were played down a landline and shared around the Macquarie network.

Here I discovered a radio station with real power. The audience, both in Melbourne and across the Macquarie network, was so valuable to politicians and those seeking to influence events that they would call up to be interviewed. And the issues were not simply crime and car crashes and weather stories, but the actual affairs of the nation.

The Hawke–Keating government had just floated the Australian dollar, taking it for the first time out of the government's direct control. Wage rises were largely set through a centralised system, based in Melbourne, but the government and the union movement were working together in a so-called 'Accord' to reshape the way workers were paid. Compulsory employer-funded superannuation was being debated, along with reforms like the assets test on the pension. This was a lot of new 'stuff' for a reporter to get his head around, particularly one with only a high-school education achieved chiefly under the influence of alcohol.

I loved the challenge of it. I loved coming to work to bump into Paul Keating, slim-hipped and snaky in his soon-to-be notorious Italian suits, as he was preparing to do battle with Hinch on air.

Melbourne generated news. And lots of it. The main business lobbies were in Sydney but two of the four big banks were in Melbourne and Australia's biggest company, BHP, was headquartered there. In the same week, I might be subjected to a personal charm offensive from Sir Arvi Parbo, the Estonian coalminer who rose to head BHP, and Bill Kelty, the gnomic young secretary of the trade union movement who was helping rewrite Australia's political and industrial landscape.

Victoria's Labor premier John Cain took on the most thuggish of the unions, the Builders' Labourers' Federation (BLF) run by Norm Gallagher. Norm was an uncompromising Marxist and a crook. He used the labourers' capacity to shut down construction sites to extort great wages for them and a few kickbacks for him. His personal greed was modest compared with some of the corporate crooks doing business in those days. Norm's main pleasure was a holiday house on a drab Gippsland mudflat called McLoughlins Beach, paid for by what amounted to protection money extorted from building companies.

He was jailed for the crimes but not before I tracked him down to the holiday house to ask him a few questions. He wasn't pleased. His first instinct was to take a swing at me but his footwork was all wrong and he wasn't hard to dodge. His next option was more direct.

'I'm getting my shotgun and I'm gunna shoot you!' he growled, adding a few expletives. He shuffled off at maximum available pace towards a shed on his driveway. I didn't wait around to argue.

Crime stories were constant and could be tragically large.

By early 1986, I had been entrusted to host a newsy lunchtime current affairs show, *The 12.30 Report*. As I emerged from the studio at 1 pm, people were reacting to a loud noise that I had missed because of the studio soundproofing.

I grabbed a tape recorder and ran towards the chaos a few blocks east. It was a car bomb. The target was the busy Russell Street police station. Across the road was the Magistrates' Court. People were emerging from the buildings in obvious shock. A man carried a woman around the corner, blood pouring from her ankle, her face grey and her body shaking in his arms. Still held in her clenched hand was an unlit cigarette.

It was my first experience of being at the scene of something horrific before police had time to organise perimeters and 'Do Not Cross' tape. The ruins of a car were still burning with thick black smoke beneath the police building, where all the glass seemed shattered. One clearly distressed policeman yelled, 'Don't come here, there could be another bomb.' Admirably, despite such fears, he still held his ground. After a quick look, I retreated back out of direct sight of the burning car, taking shelter around the edge of the court building. I heard another deep explosion. It was just a tyre blowing up in the heat from the fire. But it was enough for me. The police were starting to get organised and were waving people back and I was happy to take their directions. I can't remember now what I reported or even how I filed but I will never forget the sight of that woman shaking in her rescuer's arms.

It was a long day, full of the disbelief that strikes a town when the unthinkable happens. It was longer and more difficult for the police. Twenty-one-year-old Constable Angela Taylor, who was crossing Russell Street to get lunch when the bomb exploded beside her, lingered for twenty-four days. It was her sad distinction to become the first Australian policewoman to be killed in the line of duty.

11

THE HOLIDAY COUP

THE RUSSELL STREET BOMBING WAS A REMINDER THAT BIG NEWS comes without warning. It came again one late autumn morning in 1987, when the wire services chattered out a single line:

'URGENT:: BREAKING:: Military coup in Fiji. More to come.'

It seemed as improbable as a coup in New Zealand. Fiji was for holidays. It conjured images of palm trees, beaches and smiling locals with hibiscus flowers behind their ears. Not guns.

The 3AW news team took to the airwaves and hit the phones. Colin Tyrus, the boss, stuck his head up – there was a direct flight leaving at 1 pm, less than three hours away.

'Anyone got their passport with them?' he shouted across the newsroom.

Sheepish looks.

'I could make it home and get that flight,' I offered.

'You're on your way, son.'

And so, thanks to an inner-suburban address, I began my life as a foreign correspondent.

The sun had already set over Western Fiji as the Qantas flight approached Nadi International Airport.

The pilot came on the PA.

'As you know, there has been a military takeover in Fiji,' he began, 'so here is what I plan to do. I will do a pass over the airport.

If I see anything I don't like the look of – anything at all – I will not be landing. We'll divert to Auckland. If it looks okay, we land.'

If anyone had any objections, now was the time to tell the cabin crew.

The plane was full of journos. There were no objectors.

The plane did a pass, low and slow.

'Looks okay,' declared the pilot. 'We're going in.'

An army troop truck was parked on the tarmac. They paid no attention to the pack of newshounds crowding into the terminal. A connecting flight took us to the capital, Suva, landing near midnight in an airport so sleepy and abandoned it was hard to imagine anything had ever happened there. A cab driver confirmed the basics. A breakaway group of army rebels, led by the third-ranked Fijian officer Lieutenant-Colonel Sitiveni Rabuka, had seized the parliament. The entire government had disappeared. No one knew where they were.

The cab progressed through the silent streets of the capital. It all seemed unreal. I knew Suva slightly. My uncle had been the chief magistrate there in the early 1970s. As a ten-year-old I had stayed with him at his large colonial bungalow behind the governor-general's mansion.

Armed with this very limited local knowledge, I checked into a hotel on the waterfront opposite the parliament and set off for a stroll. The seaside path went past the front of the governor's place. Perhaps from there I could gain some clue as to what was going on. If challenged, I would try to pass myself off as a tourist with insomnia.

Nothing stirred. The night was starlit. The Pacific Ocean in the broad and sheltered curve of Suva Harbour lapped peacefully against the stone sea wall. There was no sign of activity. Nothing.

What in God's name was going on?

Suddenly, a couple of hundred metres ahead, a motorbike approached. Its headlight caught in silhouette an electrifying image. A roadblock. Two armed soldiers. They turned the motorcyclist back. For a moment, one of the men was lit up in the sweep of the light. He was wearing a black balaclava.

I turned back, a little shocked. Next, I set out to probe the grey stone bulk of the parliament. Creeping through the ornamental gardens, I worked my way around to the side of the building until I saw the outline of an army truck. Three or four men were hunched over a low fire.

I backed out unseen and retreated to the hotel. The coup was real. I filed reports for the breakfast bulletins and waited for daybreak.

If the coup was a shock it was not absolutely a surprise. Fiji was a complex place, containing many of the intractable problems of the postcolonial world. In the nineteenth century, Britain had shipped in labourers from India to build a sugar industry. A hundred years later, the descendants of those Indian semi-slaves controlled much of Fiji's business and industry. They had become almost exactly half of the national population and were increasingly asserting their political rights.

In April 1987, a political newcomer, Dr Timoci Bavadra, led the Fiji Labour Party to a shock victory. Bavadra was ethnically Fijian but his government was dominated by Indo-Fijians, and it was Indo-Fijians voting en masse who had delivered the victory.

It was too much for ethnic Fijian hardliners, who feared the Indians' aim was to seize control of not just politics and commerce, but of the land itself. Despite Bavadra's assurances to the contrary, a volcano was building.

Enter Sitiveni Rabuka. He was everything the mild-mannered Bavadra was not. Swaggering, charismatic, a former Fiji rugby forward, Rabuka projected power and a hint of violence. He was a decorated officer, a former battalion commander, who had served with distinction in the Middle East. Tellingly, he had also written a paper on how to conduct a military coup while on study leave in Canberra.

He had walked into parliament as business opened the previous day. With armed troops at his side, he took the government MPs prisoner.

Less than twenty-four hours later there were still more questions than answers. Where were those MPs? Had any harm come to them? What were Rabuka's intentions? What might the reaction be?

As a lone radio reporter with a national network hungry to be fed, I needed allies. I found one in Leon Gettler from the Melbourne *Sun-News Pictorial* (later, the *Herald-Sun*). I found another in a somewhat shady character who had flown in from Auckland. Andy Shenton was an ex-heroin addict and convicted armed robber from Perth. I had reported from court when he was jailed, the judge brushing aside character references from the Premier Brian Burke and shock jock Howard Sattler.

Having served his time, Shenton was looking for a new start in New Zealand as a journalist and I was happy to have him on my side.

Rabuka, meanwhile, was tightening his grip. He started with the media. Masked soldiers already controlled the radio station. By lunchtime on that second day, they'd shut down the two Suva newspapers. I was with the Fijian journalists, interviewing them, as they were being ordered out. With no local TV network, information control was now in the plotters' hands.

Rabuka had been too slow to block the airports on the first day but on the second a scheduled flight from Sydney was turned away. A chartered Lear jet packed with Sydney journalists was also refused permission to land. This was a boon to me. I was originally sent just to hold the fort until the heavy hitters from Sydney turned up. For the Macquarie network, with an audience size that rivalled the ABC, the story, now, was mine. And with TV unable to file and newspapers limited to daily editions, this was a radio yarn.

Rabuka's goons, however, were not done yet. They wanted to catch *all* media. It was soon clear they were at the hotel listening to every outgoing international call, physically pulling the plug on anything they didn't like.

'I reckon they're going to chuck us out,' said Gettler.

I thought he was probably right.

I remembered the enclave of expatriates around where my uncle used to live. As night fell, I walked there, knocking quietly on the door of a solid white bungalow.

To the couple in their thirties who answered, I laid out my plan.

'I believe we are about to get expelled,' I explained. 'If I could lie low here, I could still cover the story.'

They listened seriously. They couldn't help.

'We have a young child,' said the mum.

They wished me luck.

A similar response came at the next place I tried. I was also having second thoughts. It would be almost impossible to hide out without being sprung by someone. These properties came with domestic servants. If they were sympathetic to Rabuka's cause, I would be given up and the family sheltering me exposed. Would these gunmen punish my protectors? They were holding an entire government hostage so anything was possible. What was the balance between covering a story and putting people at risk? These were questions I was asking myself for the first time.

I abandoned the plan and walked back into town hoping to find a phone box that was not being monitored.

It was approaching midnight when I found a payphone at a boarding house not far from parliament.

I dialled through to Melbourne and prepared to file a bunch of voice reports and some interviews, including those with the newspaper staff.

A young woman, apparently the daughter of the boarding house operator, came to check me out.

'You're not doing anything bad, are you?'

'No, no. Just making a call.'

She disappeared. I got down to business, twisting the mouthpiece off the handset and attaching electrical alligator clips to the phone terminals. By plugging these into the tape recorder I was able to send close to studio quality sound.

The young woman returned, looking a little more agitated.

'I hope you are not doing anything bad.'

I gave her a reassuring smile, but nothing about what I was doing looked remotely normal. I was hunched over a disembowelled handset with wires hanging out all over the place and earphones on my head. She scurried off. I returned my focus to the job.

A clomping sound came down the hall. Perhaps the lads from the boarding house were coming back from their night out, I surmised, still listening intensely to the output. The clomping stopped. A silence settled around me. Turning my head a few degrees, I saw a row of brown polished boots glowing in the low light. Something else was closer to my eye. I refocused. It was the muzzle of a gun.

In that instant of realisation, a vast hand grabbed my shirt between my shoulder blades and hoisted me to my feet.

'What are you doing?' growled the lead soldier, a giant of a man.

He started tearing away at the wires on the phone.

'It's okay,' I said, 'I'll fix that.'

I unclipped the wires that were left and screwed the handset back on, bringing it momentarily past my mouth.

'Sorry, mate, gotta go. I'm being arrested, I think . . .'

With a furious growl, the lead soldier slammed down the phone and I was marched out into the night, past the wide eyes of the girl who must have given me up.

My heart was racing. More soldiers emerged from the shadows. I was pushed up a dirt path. My thoughts were like a compass, spinning, with no sense of north. This was a coup. There were no rules. In Central America, in South East Asia, in East Timor, journalists got shot. But this was Fiji, surely not.

The soldier behind me leaned forward.

'It's okay, man,' he whispered. 'You're cool.' His reassurances meant nothing but I was grateful for them anyway.

Of all the ironies, I was taken to the loading bay of the *Fiji Times* newspaper, now some kind of patrol base for the rebel troops. I heard the patrol leader report back to someone, describing me as having 'transmission equipment'. Perhaps he had taken me for a spy. There was nothing to do but stay calm and wait it out.

During the night, other journalists were brought in as they were sprung across the capital. Sometime before dawn, we were marched down a hill to a police lock-up and put in cells.

As light filtered in, I heard raised voices from outside. An Australian voice shouted out, 'Is a Hugh Riminton in here?'

My colleague back at 3AW had heard my message. He rang the boss who got onto Foreign Affairs and the good folk at DFAT swung straight into action. My 'gotta go, I'm being arrested . . .' clip was running on every TV bulletin and across the Macquarie network. 3AW even took a full-page ad in *The Age* with a picture of a phone hanging down under the headline: 'Fiji As It Breaks'. That strangled message, designed simply to explain why the feed was being cut off had proven useful.

Other colleagues were less fortunate. Rabuka was particularly incensed by Radio Australia and the BBC, which were able to broadcast back into Fiji on the shortwave band. This gave Fijians their only independent reporting. Fiji's domestic radio was now dominated by Rabuka's message, declaring the constitution void and railing against the lies of the foreign media.

One morning the veteran BBC reporter Red Harrison walked through the lobby of the Suva Travelodge, ashen-faced. He went straight to the bar, ordered a whiskey and drank it hard. It was 8 am.

The day before, Harrison and the ABC's Peter Cave had scored a big scoop, a smuggled taped interview from the imprisoned Prime Minister Bavadra.

After it went to air, broadcast back into Fiji on shortwave, the two correspondents were in Cave's hotel room when masked soldiers kicked in the door. The reporters were ordered to take off their shoes and belts and forced into the bathroom while the soldiers ripped the room apart and upended their luggage. They were looking for the Bavadra tape.

In charge was a very tall lieutenant who kept his face obscured with a balaclava and a mesh scarf. He was aggressive, shouting at Cave and Harrison that they had endangered the coup and the rebels' lives.

The reporters were forced down a fire escape to a basement area. They were stood up against a breeze block wall. Orders were being given in Fijian and English.

'Several of the soldiers formed up and aimed their rifles at us,' says Peter Cave. They appeared done for. The reporters were outwardly calm. Frozen. But Peter Cave recalls a fever of calculation in his brain: 'if they shoot maybe I can throw myself through the brick wall and get away.'

A sergeant argued with the lieutenant. The other hotel guests had been rounded up in the foyer. There were too many witnesses.

Cave and Harrison were roughly bundled outside and into separate trucks. They were taken into the bush, far from witnesses and totally at the rebels' mercy.

'I realised they were deadly serious,' recalled Cave many years later. 'I thought we were sunk.' Part of his mind felt the rebels were just trying to scare them but his over-arching feeling was 'Oh, shit!'.

'They stood us against two trees and again cocked and pointed their weapons, yelling at us not to turn around.'

Again, the sergeant argued with the lieutenant. He wanted written orders.

The officer was in a fury, shouting at the sergeant and the soldiers to 'do as you're told'. But the sergeant prevailed.

'They threw us back in the truck and took us to the central police station and told the police they would shoot them if they let us escape.'

The soldiers then went off to get written orders for the execution.

'The police kept bringing us bowls of kava,' says Cave. The officers said the mildly sedative Fijian national drink would 'ease our pain when the soldiers came back to shoot us'.

During the night, the hard-working Australian consul arrived and convinced the police to release the two reporters. 'But as we left, several truckloads of soldiers arrived yelling and screaming and threw us and the Australian consul back in the cells until morning when we were released without explanation.'

Hence Red Harrison's early-morning scotch.

The word went around that the murderous lieutenant was a bloke called Ratoki. He had been seen by some with a red bandana around his forehead, Rambo-style. Military discipline was collapsing. Ratoki had reportedly been seen ordering around higher-ranked officers.

Rabuka was determined to shut down independent reporting and this Ratoki fella seemed to be the main agent of his fury.

Some reporting was dodgy. The TV networks in Australia were in knots of frustration at having no pictures. One evening bulletin dressed up its report with pictures of tanks rolling through the streets. Fiji had no tanks. The pictures came from an uprising in Africa. When vision did start filtering out, often smuggled by compliant passengers once flights resumed, TV executives were disappointed to see no obvious evidence of physical destruction. Instead, they used images of a building site in downtown Suva where a banking complex had been demolished for redevelopment. The rubble was entirely innocent but it was now being pressed into service as evidence of a shattered capital.

At the other extreme, tourists returning home were mobbed on arrival by camera crews. They hadn't seen anything, they said. Everything had been fine on their coral atolls hundreds of kilometres from the capital. It was all just a beat-up, they said.

Newspaper columnists with space to fill shifted their headlines from the inevitable 'Trouble in Paradise' to 'The Holiday Coup'.

It was no holiday on the ground.

With little reliable information for the Fijian people, rumours washed the land. Thugs were coming with machetes to kill all the Indians. The Australians were sending ships, they were going to invade. The Queen was about to intervene (the Indo-Fijians' faith in the powers of the Queen was touching, if wide of reality).

Someone discovered the prime minister and his cabinet were being held in buildings with barred windows on a hillside behind the capital. I raced there to join a mob of government supporters, most but not all of Indian background. Soldiers in balaclavas stood guard behind a line of army trucks. From the buildings behind, an arm emerged through a barred window to wave at the crowd, which responded with cheers and shouts. The mob began spontaneously singing the Fijian national anthem. They sang it over and over. I could sing it myself today.

Looking around, I saw other journalists leaving. Rabuka had called a press conference, his first. Gettler and Shenton headed there. I stayed with an increasingly emotional mob.

They were not rabble-rousers. For the most part, they were the softest of civilians.

'Let's storm in and get them out,' shouted a balding middle-aged man.

'They can't shoot us all,' yelled a woman.

The eyes of the soldiers glowered through their facemasks. The previous year, a 'People Power' revolution in the Philippines had toppled the dictator Ferdinand Marcos. Crowds of people then had stared down the army and the army had refused to fire.

But that had happened in the full glare of international cameras. Looking around, I couldn't see another journalist. The soldiers, meanwhile, had spotted me.

On the strength of some command, the trucks began inching forward into the mob. Some people threw themselves at the wheels, but others as quickly pulled them out. The shouts and screams were intense. On the trucks rolled, an inch at a time.

It was time to go. My ride had gone. A young Indian man stepped forward and offered to get me out of there. I accepted.

Born to high privilege that war would soon end.
My dad, circa 1938, Jersey, Channel Islands.

RAF flying officer Jacqueline Donegan,
my mum.

The senior staff, Tangakelle Tea Estate. My parents are in the centre of the seated row.
I am at the front left.

A constant of my childhood, Dad poring over a map. Not for the last time, the camera has caught my eye.

Junior Kiwis: Paul, Adrian, Sean and me (far right).

Inelegantly wasted in my mid-teens. A danger to myself and others.

Head full of poetry, lungs full of smoke – the teenage cadet, complete with feeble moustache to help me look older!

My first foreign adventure. Covering the
1987 Fiji coup for Macquarie Radio.

Photo: Leon Gettler

Smartening up the crew car.
Kosovo crisis, 1999.

With Peter Watts in Moscow as the tanks roll and the parliament burns.

Checking out *qat*, the Somali drug of choice, with cameraman Drew Benjamin. Baidoa, 1993.

In the dying days of South Africa's apartheid era, white supremacists launched multiple car-bombings. Whether it was in Johannesburg or in Britain with the IRA, my early terrorist bombs were set by white 'Christians'. Photo: Cameron Bennett

Tahiti's main airport just before it went up in flames in the independence riots of 1995.
Photo: Rob Hopkins

The looks of a mercenary, the soul of a giant: photojournalist turned aid worker Steve Levitt.

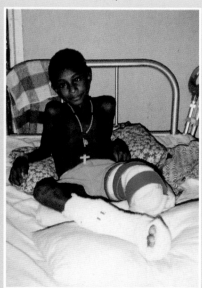

Nine-year-old Sebastian Alosi, saved by an Australian army surgeon, contemplating life as an amputee.

Abducted and raped, with twin girls as the result, 27-year-old Abuk Lual Athurum was one of 876 slaves we helped free in southern Sudan, 1999.

Mountains have taught me much about decision making under pressure and the joys of good small teams. This is from a Himalayan climbing trip in winter 1991. Photo: Susan Aitkin

On my first trip to East Timor, Indonesian-funded militias terrorised the land. By 2001, these Australian troops had the borderlands secured. The cameraman is Tim Hawkins.

With Malcolm Fraser on the Rwanda–Tanzania border, 1994. Photo: Richard Malone

A palpable tension as tens of thousands of armed youths flood out of Soweto to greet their hero, Nelson Mandela, 1994. Photo: Cameron Bennett

ABOVE: Reporting one of innumerable pro-Saddam rallies in Baghdad in the days before the 2003 invasion. George Gittoes is second from right at the rear.

Photo: Richard Moran

LEFT: The unending misery of the Gaza Strip. The kids at the rear had just launched a hail of rocks at us. An old bloke walked over to tell them to stop.

Lost in the crowd as imams swear their allegiance to Saddam Hussein. Pre-invasion Baghdad.

Photo: Richard Moran

Rabuka, meanwhile, had announced that he was going to seek approval for his coup from the Great Council of Chiefs, the traditional leadership of the ethnic Fijian population.

The ousted prime minister was released. He was dropped off at his Suva home around 2 am. Rabuka's coup had obvious support among ethnic Fijians but Bavadra seemed unable to read that play. He declared Rabuka guilty of treason. It was a capital offence. Bavadra urged all Fijians to meet at a park next to parliament (and directly in front of the main media hotel) at 11 am the following morning.

It was the same morning that the Great Council of Chiefs was due to begin its meeting a few hundred metres down the road.

Having been up all night preparing reports on Bavadra's release, I wandered down with Leon Gettler to where the chiefs were gathering. A vast crowd of ethnic Fijians was building on the grass outside the hall. Most of them were young men from outlying districts. Rabuka turned up and was greeted with a roar, which he acknowledged with a pump of his fists and a beaming smile.

The meeting began in closed session. With the Polynesian love for consensus, it could take days for it to end.

Leon and I started strolling back to where Bavadra's supporters had been urged to gather.

We stopped at a shop along the way, picking up spare notebooks and pens. (Whenever coup soldiers stopped us, they always demanded our notebooks. We had become very circumspect with names.) It was a moment of relaxation. We were dog tired after days of little sleep. To do something as simple as buying pens and paper was a welcome reminder of normal life.

As we stepped outside, we were surprised to see the Indian staff frantically putting up cyclone boards in front of their windows.

'What are you –' I began.

The young Indian man looked past me, over my shoulder.

I turned. There, twenty-five metres away, from one side of the street to the other, was a wall of young Fijian men. Some were carrying cane knives. Others had wooden clubs.

They were coming fast.

'Go!' I yelled at Gettler.

Some instinct told me not to run. I had a reasonable turn of speed – I suspect Leon a little less so – but running would be the flashpoint. It would be a bold man who backed his speed against an army of young Fijians.

We walked as fast as we could, but already the leading edge was onto us.

'Why are you telling lies?' shouted a lean boy, dancing along beside us, all but spitting in Leon's face.

I was silent. Head down, walking as fast as I could. No one had touched us. The first swung punch, I sensed, would bring it all on.

Leon, bless him, began explaining quite reasonably how we were covering all aspects of what was happening in Fiji, puffing as he spoke and trying to keep the pace.

More faces were jeering around us. But still no one had touched us.

And then, by some indefinable process, the confident violence of our challengers flagged. Our pace had taken us just a few metres in front of the main mob. The youths trying to incite the first violence were suddenly not one of a thousand. But one of five. They were not a mob anymore, they were just individuals. They lost their power.

The perimeter of our hotel loomed ahead, with security guards watching from the grass verge. We sprinted to get inside as a vast roar arose behind us and the mob broke into a run. We were not the target. They had spotted the Bavadra supporters gathering in the park. And their blood lust was up.

Racing into the hotel, Leon and I went upstairs to the first floor rooms which had a clear view of the park. Print photographers were standing on the bed (so they were not visible on the balcony) taking snaps of the melee. The Bavadra supporters stood no chance. I saw women and families, some of whom had brought picnic rugs, go down under the flailing crowd. An army truck stood nearby, its troops simply watching.

A photographer turned to Leon. They were not from the same paper but the snapper thrust a roll of film into Leon's hand. The photographers had set up secret dark rooms across the city, moving them constantly to stay ahead of the goons. Leon was given the name of a boarding house and a room number and was begged to take the film there.

'You've gotta be crazy,' I said. 'You're not going to survive out there.'

Leon didn't say a word. He didn't ask me to go with him. He simply set off for the door.

The violence in the park that day broke the spirit of the government supporters. Leon turned up back at the hotel the following day, covered in blood and with a deep, roughly stitched gash in his head.

He had found an Indian taxi driver trying to flee and had somehow convinced him to take him along. But the mob had blocked the way. Pieces of concrete torn up from the edge of the road rained down on the car, smashing the windscreen and Leon's head. The driver, in panic, had floored the accelerator, running over a couple of people in the crowd. He went to the hospital, where the wounded being brought in from the park were starting to fill the corridors. Someone stitched Leon's head while he sat on the floor but when a doctor realised a foreign journalist was there he ordered Leon outside. He feared Leon's mere presence might invite an attack.

The holiday coup was losing its power to entertain.

As trying as violence – and the threat of violence – had become, it was lack of sleep that was really hurting. Running around in the tropical heat took its toll, as did dehydration and the lack of regular food, but sleeplessness was the killer. It robbed me of judgement. Was my fear that the mob would swarm our hotel reasonable or insane? I was a reasonable swimmer. If the mob came would I be better trying to barricade my room or take my chances leaping from the balcony and swimming into Suva Bay?

Filing reports out of the hotel was getting increasingly difficult with the disruption to the phone service. I quietly obtained rooms in two other hotels. I was in the second of these with Leon when the goons came again. It was late morning. I was filing for the midday news. Two thickset men simply walked into the room. They had a key. I hadn't latched the door. Both wore sunglasses and bright, touristy floral shirts.

'You come with us,' said the one in the blue shirt. Leon and I started a torrent of bluster. Blue shirt took it impassively for thirty seconds or so.

'You come now,' he repeated.

We went.

'You guys are in trouble,' said the red-shirted guy as he drove us through the town. Somehow doing all this in daylight seemed less threatening. An unworthy thought crossed my mind. I was exhausted. A couple of hours break from reporting and filing might be just what we needed.

We were taken to the downtown police station. A police inspector intercepted our progress.

'Who are these?'

A conversation followed in Fijian. Some sort of power tussle was going on. The inspector seemed to win.

'You come and wait in my office,' he said.

His name was Moses Driver. He was smaller than most Fijians, lean and intelligent. I liked the look of him. I knew there was a deep split between elements of the army and the police over what Rabuka had done, as indeed there were splits in the army itself. I hoped Inspector Driver was one of the good ones.

His office was not empty. A Melbourne newspaperman, Peter Coster, was already there but his news wasn't good. Apparently we had been picked up on the orders of the notorious 'Rambo' Ratoki, the man who had been carrying out mock executions.

Still, for the first time in days, there was nothing to do but rest. I might even have nodded off for a while.

The afternoon shadows were lengthening when a new goon walked in, a huge, blank-faced man, with pockmarked skin.

He ordered us to come.

'I'll take them,' said Driver, in English.

We crossed the courtyard in the centre of the multi-storey block. Glancing up, I saw a tall, lean man watching us from an internal balcony three storeys up.

'That'll be him,' said Coster.

As we entered the building again on the far side of the courtyard, I could see an internal staircase leading up. But there was also the main door to the outside world.

'Go out here,' said Driver. 'Keep going. Get out of the country as quick as you can.'

We didn't need to be told twice. We bolted. A passing taxi never had more eager passengers.

But we didn't leave Fiji. We dug in and got smarter.

During this time, I met my first true international correspondents. American journalists had turned up, including a photographer from *Time*, skinny and intense. This was an altogether new version of what a journalist could be – permanently on the move from one coup or war or disaster to the next.

'Imagine doing this all the time, nothing else,' mused Shenton.

It was something to think about.

But the *Time* man was already bored with Fiji.

'What's bigger than this right now?' I asked him.

He gave me a somewhat condescending look.

'No one's getting killed and no one cares about a place with half a million people.'

'Where will you go instead?'

'El Salvador,' he said. 'It's going off.'

12

TOUGHENING UP

WHEN I FINALLY GOT HOME TO MELBOURNE EVERYTHING FELT SUBTLY changed. I was hyper alert and the *Time* photographer's words nagged in my head. Daily news seemed suddenly dull. At the same time, my status within the network was higher. Managers and stars knew who I was. Journos sought me out for a chat.

What if Fiji wasn't the only international story I ever covered? I knew I had done some things poorly in Fiji. But I also felt, in an environment of stress, threat and fatigue, my native instincts had generally been solid. How could I retrain myself to retain the good elements of my coverage while improving on my errors?

I was fit. I was still running five to ten kilometres a day and going as hard as I could. If I wasn't running, I was swimming. I picked it up on the advice of a physiotherapist when I injured an arm. Now I easily burned off an old-fashioned mile. I had also bought a little racing catamaran, *Rising Damp*, and spent my summers competing at the little Port Melbourne Yacht Club. My mental health was solid. My near-fatal adolescent blues had lifted. Perhaps I simply grew out of it. Importantly, I was getting a sense of purpose from my work. And adrenalin seemed to work for me. It was time to up the pressure.

In New Zealand, I had been intrigued by the courses run by Outward Bound. Based on the teachings of German educationalist

Kurt Hahn, Outward Bound grew out of the need to build resilience among merchant navy seamen. During World War II, many would find themselves in lifeboats after their ships were torpedoed by German submarines. The British War Office discovered something unexpected. The sailors who survived prolonged exposure to the elements in the North Atlantic tended to be the older ones. The young and the fit died first.

Hahn, a Jew who had been an early public opponent of Hitler, was dedicated to the British cause. The future Prince Philip was one of his students. Hahn's intuition was that the young sailors died because they lacked experience in overcoming hardship. His answer was to expose them to sustained – but not fatal – levels of stress. And Outward Bound was born.

I thought an OB course would provide me with stresses similar to covering a coup, so that I could examine and improve my responses.

There was a month-long course that December in the mountains west of Canberra. I signed up.

Before I got there, though, another opportunity arose. Channel Seven was in dire straits. The previous year, Rupert Murdoch had gained control of the Herald and Weekly Times (HWT) group. The rules required HWT to divest its TV channel. Seven was picked up by the Fairfax empire, a Sydney-based institution that displayed little insight into Melbourne's proud rejection of Sydney influences. Long-time newsreader Mal Walden was sacked. As he read his final bulletin, he farewelled his audience with great dignity and with a tiny tear glinting in his eye.

Melbourne went ballistic. Seven's news audience plunged so low it was represented in the official ratings by an asterisk – a number too small to be measured. Seven's news reporters started desperately looking for other opportunities. And that opened a door for me.

In Perth, I had tried to liven up my professional life by applying for a reporting job at Channel Seven. The news director was John

Rudd. I was sent off with a cameraman and instructed to do some pieces to camera, ad-lib about a subject that was in the news, and generally walk around and nod.

Rudd called me up a couple of days later.

'Well, you weren't as bad as I thought you would be.'

'Thanks.'

'But you can't wear a beard on TV.'

'That's no problem,' I assured him. 'It's only a bit of holiday fuzz. It can come off.'

'Hmm,' grunted Rudd. 'Your glasses are a problem, they create glare.'

'No problem,' I said. 'My eyesight's basically fine, good enough to drive. I can leave the specs off when I'm on camera.'

'Hmm,' grunted Rudd again. 'Your red hair is a bit of a problem. The camera doesn't like the colour red . . .'

'I get it, I get it,' I said, laughing. I was reminded of the *Two Ronnies* comedy skit, where Ronnie Barker tries to find polite ways to tell Ronnie Corbett that he can't be a TV newsreader. When all else fails, Barker bellows out: 'You see, you're just bloody hopeless.'

'Oh,' replies Corbett. 'Well, if it's just a technical problem I do understand.'

John Rudd was doing his best to break it to me gently that TV was never going to be my thing. Yet, here I was two years later about to be hired by Channel Seven Melbourne on what the news director assured me (and I was easily enough flattered to believe him) was the best contract he had ever seen offered to a rank TV novice.

I was taking advantage of Seven's desperation. With me, they were scraping the bottom of the barrel. But with their news being out-rated by re-runs of *Inspector Gadget* on the ABC they were not in a position to be precious.

A few weeks later, Seven took another punt and hired Derryn Hinch. Hinch called me up and invited me to be a reporter on his new nightly current affairs show. 'If you can swing it past the news bosses,' I said, 'I'd be happy to.'

So I set off to the Outward Bound base at Tharwa, south of Canberra, not knowing exactly what I would be doing when I returned but confident it would be an adventure.

The Outward Bound course was all I could have hoped for and more. Forty-eight people aged between seventeen and twenty-seven set off in groups of twelve. I was one of the oldies, at twenty-six. Of my dozen, five would be medically evacuated off with a variety of injuries, including hurt backs and blood infections from unhealed wounds.

It was tough.

But I learned plenty. The group was evenly mixed for gender. As time went by I observed the fittest young men break down. Their sense of self was too heavily invested in their physical strength. When that started to fail them under the deliberate conditions of the course, they had nothing in reserve. The women, in many ways, were far tougher. They endured the bumps and found ways to keep going. Because they were not expecting their physical strength to conquer all, their spirit was more resilient. Their humour was much more reliable.

The most inspiring example was a tiny Singaporean-born Queenslander called Coreen Lim. In the weeks before Outward Bound she had been quite sick. As the course began she was unable even to break into a jog. But her good nature endured through everything.

Coreen couldn't swim. One section required a descent of the Goodradigbee River. We went over the rapids on inflatable mattresses which we had reinforced with rubber offcuts. Our packs lay beneath our chests as we paddled as best we could between the rocks.

After plunging over a cataract, I was resting in a downstream pool when I saw an air mattress floating empty on the surface. Deep in the water beneath me, to my horror, I saw Coreen drowning. Her hands were gently flailing, almost like seaweed in the tide. I plucked her to the surface, where she coughed and gasped.

Then she thanked me with a smile, allowed me to help her get back onto her air mattress and tackled the next set of rapids. It was one of the most courageous displays I have ever witnessed. Since that day, whenever I have been in danger or stress, I have drawn on her example and challenged myself to match it.

Cancer was to claim Coreen, far too young. She dealt with that bravely, too.

I finished the Outward Bound course intact and with a new confidence that I could tough things out under difficult conditions. But whether I'd survive tabloid TV was going to be a different kind of test.

—

Derryn Hinch had won the right to my services. He made a virtue of doing something different, with people new to television. All of the Hinch team, from Derryn to his executive producer, Paul Barber, to reporters like Margaret Peacock and me, were newbies. The only reporter who had a clue was the redoubtable Jackie Quist, who at twenty-two years old was a three-year television veteran. Had it not been for the professionalism of the long-suffering camera crews and editors, the show would never have got to air at all.

I imagined I had some idea of what television was about. I had watched enough of it. I had seen news crews hard at work for years. It was alarming how ignorant I was. Television journalism, and especially current affairs, required a story to be *made* as much as told.

After a few harried weeks, the executives decided it was time to muscle up. A streetwise young news reporter, Rob 'Mad Dog' Muir, was added to the list. Margaret Peacock went off to radio. Paul Barber, a gentle-natured former seminarian, was replaced by Dermot O'Brien, the proud embodiment of the cynical, hard-nosed journo.

Mad Dog did a story one week on an Australian cameraman who had spent years travelling to the hardest places on earth, reporting on wars and upheavals for American TV networks and *Time* magazine. His name was Steve Levitt.

Muir's story presented Levitt as the inheritor of the legend of Neil Davis, the Australian Vietnam War cameraman who had been killed covering a coup in Thailand just a few years earlier. Whether the comparison was fair on either man, Levitt was plainly an impressive dude.

With the story done, I managed to tag along as Levitt and Mad Dog took off to the Botanical Hotel for an afternoon of refreshment. Levitt made a phone call and his good mate Tracy Grimshaw turned up. At the time, Tracy was the most glamorous party fixture in Melbourne as well as a damn fine journalist.

I felt like I was in good company.

Levitt would spend months at a time in awful war zones that no one else could be bothered covering. For example, the Eritreans were fighting for independence from Ethiopia. It was trench warfare. Hundreds of thousands of people died. Levitt spent six months in the trenches. Much of the coverage the world saw of that atavistic contest came from his cameras. He shot stills and video.

Levitt reinvested the money he made directly into his next adventure, to the next war that had caught his sympathies and his eye. He was a vivid raconteur, funny, lunatic, and oddly shy. The afternoon passed in what the Irish call 'great *craic*'. I noticed Levitt's blue denim shirt was all but threadbare. He had no interest in anything but life and the next yarn.

Those early months in TV also gifted me with one of those tremendously powerful encounters that journalism provides. I met Elie Wiesel.

Wiesel not only survived the Nazi Holocaust, he had coined the word. He was one of the few figures to have been seriously in contention for the Nobel Prize in *two* categories. He was awarded the Nobel Peace Prize in 1986 but it was as a literary figure that his reputation towered.

Wiesel had been invited to Australia. It was his first visit. I suggested to Hinch we interview him because, in 1988, Australia was having a new argument over refugees. Perhaps a former refugee of his prominence might have something useful to say.

Seeing Wiesel was relatively easy. Getting to him was a little more difficult. He had been put up at one of the big Melbourne hotels. A news conference was organised but it was hijacked by elderly Melbourne Holocaust survivors who wanted to see their hero and were not going to be denied. Who could interrupt people carrying such weights?

The news conference became more like group counselling, conducted partly in Hebrew and partly in a range of other European languages. Wiesel accepted the role of consoler and counsellor with depthless patience.

When, finally, someone urged the session be brought to an end, the literary editor from *The Age* asserted his right for extended time with the great man. Wiesel's deceptively small little memoir of life as a teenager in Buchenwald and Auschwitz, called *Night*, had established his literary reputation when he was still in his early twenties. He had written many dense and weighty volumes since. *The Age*'s literary man seemed intent on taking Wiesel through every paragraph.

Then there was ABC radio and an interview for ABC TV.

And finally, Elie Wiesel looked up and saw only one obstacle left between him and a chance to sleep off his jet lag: the reporter from the *Hinch* show.

Wiesel was clearly exhausted. But he did something I have never forgotten. He looked at me with great warmth and respect and asked me about my life. I was embarrassed. I answered, parried and tried to put my questions to him. But Wiesel persisted. The more I ducked, the more serious and searching and personal his questions became. My relationships . . . Did I have children . . . Were my parents alive?

My resistance crumbled. I answered his questions. I asked questions of my own – the stuff I really wanted to try to understand.

'In the concentration camp,' I asked, 'what was the worst of it – the fear, the hunger, the exhaustion, the humiliation, the grief for the people you had lost . . . what was the worst of all?'

'It was all of it,' he replied. 'All of it.'

By showing such deep interest in me, he had given permission for a deeper conversation with him. I asked him about Australia's 1988 version of the refugee debate. The hardest thing of all, he said, wasn't feeling abandoned during his time in the camps – because he assumed the world had no idea. It was afterwards, with his home in Hungary gone forever, when everyone knew what the Nazis had done, and yet still no one would give him a place to live. That was when he felt most betrayed, most rejected by humanity.

Have an immigration policy that brings in the people you need for your national economy, he said, but spare some room for people who need your shelter.

Only a tiny clip of the interview – the news 'grab' – made it to air, but in all the thousands of interviews I have done, my encounter with Elie Wiesel counts among the most precious.

Back in the *Hinch* newsroom, it was quickly apparent that nightly commercial current affairs was not for me. Now that the show was becoming 'professionalised', the illusions dropped away about what might be involved. I was castigated for not making the family of a recently deceased truck driver cry. Another story from the Brisbane office was a set-up designed to make a family photographer look like a paedophile. There was no evidence at all of anything improper. Indeed, the photographer insisted that he could never be in a room with children without the parents being present. He had no police history. He was a guy making a living in a specialist niche and being very careful about how he did it.

The set-up, though, involved the journalist springing out from a hiding place with two cameras in tow, demanding to know what he was doing with the children. The bloke was so alarmed that, after a few stammered words, he realised he was being set up and headed for the door and his car parked on the street. Another camera was waiting for him, capturing him bug-eyed and terrified as the journalist continued to screech defamatory questions.

'You're destroying this bloke and he's done nothing wrong,' I objected.

'Mate, this will rate its tits off,' growled the senior story producer.

'Who cares about the ratings if you're destroying a man who hasn't done anything wrong?'

'Mate, you might not care about the ratings. I do.'

Eyes met. The stare was held. I realised I had to get out immediately.

The story wasn't run in the end, but only because it breached a then sensitive law about the use of hidden microphones.

I went to the newsroom and asked the boss if I could serve out the rest of my twelve-month contract there. Hinch gave the move his blessing. He was a strangely admirable man. He has done some unconscionable things, particularly with his impulse to smear the name of famous people who had recently died. But he went to jail for defying court rulings that allowed a notorious paedophile priest to continue having access to children, safe in the knowledge his name was being kept secret by court order. Hinch was brave and right. He took on the paedophile cover-up industry when everyone else looked the other way.

Everyone in Seven assumed I had been sacked and was being 'sent down' to the newsroom, a perceived humiliation for a television greenhorn who had briefly touched the heights of national current affairs. I couldn't have cared less. But Hinch understood how things worked. On my final Friday, he took me down to the Channel Seven pub. He bought two bottles of champagne and sat yarning until the message was received loud and clear by the people I would be working with on Monday: Hinch valued me. In Chinese terms, Derryn was protecting my 'face'. I've always kind of liked him for that.

13

DRUNK BY NOON, RESCUED BY NINE

I THREW MYSELF INTO NEWS WORK. I LIKED THE BASIC HONESTY OF it. Seven still barely rated but it was clawing its way back off the bottom. Many of the long-term staffers were demoralised, however. They had a huge chip on their shoulder about Channel Nine.

'They might have the ratings, but we're having the fun,' one cameraman told me. But they didn't look like they were having fun.

The news job I had been hired to fill before my detour into the *Hinch* show had been taken by someone else. The news director, a courteous and decent man called Bob Kearsley, told me he would have nothing for me when my contract ended at Christmas.

Where to? There was a job going in Darwin. Alternatively, I could try my luck in London. By this point, Sue and I had married and she was up for it, even though we had just bought a place at Port Melbourne and had a mortgage to manage.

While these thoughts crowded my head, a huge flood came through Lara, between Melbourne and the old port city of Geelong. I went off and covered it and thought no more of it.

A couple of days later, I received a call from Tom Bennett, the chief of staff at Nine.

'The boss liked your work at Lara,' said Bennett. 'He wants you to have lunch with him tomorrow.'

'Er, sure. Where?'

'Grand Hotel, Richmond.'

The boss could only be John Sorell, a brilliant, ferocious ogre of a man who had come out of newspapers to make Nine the dominant news station in the city. Just his nicknames gave the clue: 'The Admiral', 'The Bear'. Massively powerful both physically and in his hold on the city, he had a reputation for being permanently drunk and a hideous sleaze. He was the best raw newsman I have ever met.

I fronted up at the Grand Hotel in my best suit.

Sorell, blue business shirt unbuttoned halfway down his massive chest, gazed at me for a couple of seconds, his glasses halfway down his nose.

He grunted.

'Beer?'

I drank a schooner. He drank a schooner.

He drank another schooner. I drank another schooner.

So, I thought, the interview is going well.

After a couple more wordless schooners, small electrical currents were flashing red lights in my brain: keep doing this and you're a dead man.

'I might just have a light beer, or sit on this one,' I said.

'Oh?' grunted Sorell. 'Don't you drink?'

Two of his news producers turned up to the 'lunch' (I later learned there was no food when Sorell went to lunch). Tom Bennett was there too. One of the producers, Colin Paterson, came to my rescue, asking me a few questions about what I had been doing.

Sorell, his interest now completely gone, gazed off elsewhere as beers continued to sizzle down his throat. From my perspective, the whole exercise was looking increasingly pointless.

After a while, I circled around to Sorell again, hoping to find some clues to navigate me through the process.

'So, are you setting up a short list?' I ventured.

'Nah,' grunted Sorell. 'I thought I might hire you.'

With that his gaze returned to a distant corner of the ceiling.

'What are they paying you?'

I told him.

'You don't want more than that, do you?'

'No.'

He grunted again. The interview was over.

I left.

Tom Bennett rang that night.

'So what did he say?'

'He said he was thinking of hiring me.'

'Did he!'

'What does that mean?'

'It means you've got the job.'

I would like to say I started at Nine on a handshake agreement, only there wasn't even a handshake. Sorell, though, was as good as his grunt. Not only had I dodged unemployment, I was going to the dominant network in the land and arguably the best TV newsroom in the country.

Sorell, bless his roguish heart, was giving me the break of a lifetime.

—

Channel Nine in Melbourne – GTV9, to give the official station name – was a young reporter's dream. The camera crews were probably technically no better than the people at Seven, but at Nine they were motivated to be their best.

Every night at six o'clock the reporters and editors gathered in Sorell's office to watch the news. Drinking was mandatory. Sorell's fridge was well stocked and the grog was free. The monitors showing what Channel Seven and other outlets were doing were left on mute.

Sorell's obsession was his own product. He didn't care about anyone else. As the news opener rolled and the great Brian Naylor began his read, Sorell's reaction could be interpreted by the tone of his grunts. He missed nothing. Every night he took as much interest as a Broadway impresario watching opening night. In Sorell's world, he wasn't just putting out a news bulletin, he was putting on a show.

He wasn't a man given to lavish praise. A grunt with a satisfied tone to it would signal to the journo he or she had done okay. A 'nice job, Hughie' was a rare event but it was like being mentioned in dispatches. Sorell's rages were rare but when they came they were volcanic.

At the end of the sports break one night, Naylor ad-libbed some quip to the sports presenter. The sports guy ad-libbed back, but 'Nails' was not expecting it and for just a moment seemed off-balance.

Sorell was waiting for the sports presenter as he left the studio.

'You c***!' spat Sorell. 'Don't you ever f*** up my newsreader again.'

The words on the page cannot capture the venom and barely suppressed violence of the scene. The sports presenter had been a professional athlete in his youth and was still muscular and fit. But he quailed at the sight of Sorell. He soon found himself working in regional radio. An innocuous quip, and Sorell's fury, had done him in.

Sorell's day would begin with the 9.30 am editorial meeting to set up the day. Then he would go to the gym, where even as an alcoholic fifty-something he held records for the leg-press. By midday, he would be back in the office to check in on how the day was going. Then to the pub for a three-hour foodless lunch. By four o'clock he was back, satisfactorily lubricated, and ready to play havoc with his desk producers. If rain fell on his windshield on his way back from the pub – yes, he drove – he would arrive on the news floor declaring that the bulletin would lead with 'the flooding'.

'There is no flooding, John.'

'We. Are. Leading. With. The. Flooding.'

The chief of staff was adept at dispatching crews to the two or three locations around Melbourne where a railway underpass would reliably fill with water at the slightest hint of rain. With any luck, some hapless tourist would have driven in and got stuck. It is amazing how little rain you need to create a ninety-second report on flooding.

Sorell would be satisfied. Melbourne people, he reasoned, loved nothing more than a grizzle about the weather.

The Admiral's unique combination of gym warrior and alcoholic worried his doctor, who interrogated him about what he drank.

'Beer and whiskey,' said Sorell.

'Well, you'd better knock off the beer and the whiskey.'

The next day, Sorell staggered back from lunch more intoxicated than anyone had ever seen him.

He subbed my script, grumbled that it was 'wankey-woo' and proceeded to scribble illegible lines over the top of it.

'Got it, Admiral, I'll fix it,' I said, retrieving the script and scurrying away.

'What on earth has got into the Admiral?' I whispered to one of the senior producers.

'Patto was with him at the pub. Apparently the doc told him to go easy on the beer and the whiskey, so he tucked into some wine.'

'Is he allergic or something?'

'No, but he never touches wine so he drank it like beer.'

'Jeepers!'

'Six bottles of red wine for lunch.'

When the show went to air, we gathered as usual in Sorell's office. Long sofas dominated one wall. Three of the female journalists sat side by side.

Sorell leaned back in his big recliner and bellowed at his favourite foil, the chief editor Grahame 'George' Loutit.

'George!'

'Yes, Admiral!'

'GEORGE!'

'YES, ADMIRAL!'

Sorell swung a leery eye at the women on the couch.

'Which one would you fuck first?'

By any measure, even then, this was intolerable behaviour. So why did so many smart young men and women put up with it? One answer is that Sorell's thunderclaps bonded the people who worked underneath him. Great friendships were made because we were all in the trenches together.

The other reason is harder to explain. Sorell was a fine judge of what worked on television and, for all his boorishness, was most intensely proud of the women he discovered and turned into stars. When he died, Jo Hall – a Melbourne television institution – credited Sorell with teaching her 'about journalism and life'. Tracy Grimshaw, another of his proteges, gave a tender eulogy at his funeral.

Sorell would not survive in a newsroom today. Many might argue that would be no loss. But good work got done and most people survived. And he did learn one lesson from the six bottles of wine disaster. He went back to whiskey and beer. The doc could get stuffed.

14

THE VOCATION

ON 9 NOVEMBER 1989, THE BERLIN WALL FELL.

That simple sentence cannot begin to capture the drama and historical importance of the event. The hold of Soviet communism across Eastern Europe and the world was broken. The dreadful fear of a nuclear exchange was suddenly lifted.

In Berlin, Nine's stylish London correspondent, Robert Penfold, stood on the wall as the East German border guards kept back and did nothing. Coming just five months after the Chinese Communist Party had crushed demonstrations in Tiananmen Square, here were new grounds for hope in the world.

I was far too junior to be considered in the coverage plan but I wasn't going to miss out.

That night Sue and I schemed to get over there as fast as we could. East Germany was still a legal entity so we had to apply for visas through the communist bureaucracy but the papers came through and, within weeks, we were in Berlin.

On a frigid winter's night, I joined teams of youths bashing away at the wall with sledgehammers. For them, it was less the joy of freedom now, than the desire for filthy lucre. The bits of smashed concrete were being painted up with instant graffiti and sold for good profits to the tourists flocking in.

No matter. I walked across no-man's-land into the East German lines. The communist side of the wall was a free fire zone. Blank cement fields ensured no one could hope to make a run for it and live. I clambered up into one of the abandoned machine-gun towers, now burnt out and vandalised. Suppressing a population was an expensive business. And, as I shivered in the tower, it seemed to me a cold one. A little museum on the western side memorialised the many who had died trying to make the crossing. It also celebrated those who had somehow escaped – by hot air balloon, or smuggled out in false petrol tanks, even the circus star who erected a high wire and tiptoed to freedom.

In the East German countryside, we pulled over for a column of Soviet tanks. They were heading home.

There were still theoretical dangers. In Dresden, I was on a suburban street when a car pulled up and a man stepped forward to open the boot. Within moments, hundreds of copies of a Frankfurt newspaper were pulled out and rushed away by accomplices. Under statutes that still existed, they were risking jail. But it was another reminder of the value people place on a free press.

Dresden still carried the scars of the Allied firebombing that levelled the city in the last weeks of World War II. The once magnificent cathedral on the banks of the Elbe had been left as charred ruins, as both memorial and accusation. The opera house, where Wagner premiered *Tannhauser*, had been rebuilt. We bought tickets to Mozart's *Cosi Fan Tutte*. As we left, drably dressed East Germans headed home in their notorious little two-stroke Trabant cars with sour little sidelong glances at the West Germans who had come over for an evening's entertainment in their furs and Mercedes-Benzes. The propaganda that asserted East Germany was not only equal but superior to their capitalist cousins was being exposed.

Two things struck me about the communist system.

One was how the lack of a profit motive retarded innovation. South of Dresden, I picked up three young hitch-hikers as it started to rain. One spoke good English. He was at technical college.

He spotted my camera and asked politely if he could examine it. Much serious chatter followed. When I asked him to translate, he explained that they were amazed to see a telephoto lens.

'Have you never seen one?' I asked, astonished.

'I have read about them in technical papers,' he replied, 'but I have never even heard of anyone having one.'

Without a commercial impulse, East Germany's technical and consumer advances had atrophied.

The other inescapable conclusion was that communism was bad for the environment. There was no geographical barrier distinguishing East Germany from West Germany, particularly if you approached from the south-west. But within a few kilometres of crossing the border, there was no escaping the levels of air pollution. Pulling into the city of Erfurt, where our visas required us to stay the night, I wound down the window to stare through the winter fog at a street sign. Immediately, my eyes started stinging. The fog was pure industrial-grade pollution. Appalling. In a western democracy, any mayor or state leader presiding over such degradation would be voted out within a term. But no such mechanism existed under communism.

It was a useful lesson I would see repeated two decades later in China.

Most starkly, I also visited Buchenwald concentration camp, where Elie Wiesel had laboured and from which he alone of his family emerged alive. A bare, wintry landscape held the remnants of the camp, its ovens and the rooms where medical experiments were conducted on human beings. Not a bird sang.

In the centre of the camp was a large memorial to the Soviet prisoners of war and the German communists who had been murdered there. You had to go looking for the much smaller memorial to the Jews, who were slaughtered there in far larger numbers. Lest we forget.

—

We spent a few more weeks driving through Czechoslovakia, Austria, northern Italy and France, before a quick trip to London and Ireland. It was an education. And one I would draw on sooner than I'd imagined.

Another education was waiting for me when we got back home.

In late 1990, I got a call from the newsroom chief of staff, Geoff Wilkinson.

Wilko was chewing on a problem. There were reports of a shooting in New Zealand, at a little seaside hamlet outside Dunedin called Aramoana. Officially, there was a report of one person wounded, but the Kiwi police, according to Wilko's contacts, had been unable to raise a police officer at the scene. Wilko, who had worked for the police, knew officers did not simply go off radar. He took a punt and barely an hour later I was on a flight to Christchurch with a connection to Dunedin.

Wilko's instincts proved tragically right. An Aramoana local, David Gray, had gone nuts after arguing with a neighbour about a dog. A gun collector and a loner, Gray killed thirteen people including four children as young as six. Two other children, one just four years old, were shot but survived.

The following morning, having killed a police sergeant who went to investigate, Gray was shot dead as he charged at police from a hiding place in a shed.

In echoing silence, I walked through the tiny town with a police escort. A little beach house was still smouldering where Gray had set it alight, killing two young girls who were trapped inside. A shot-up ute remained in place where Gray had gunned down well-meaning locals who had come to help put out the fire. A child's bicycle with training wheels lay on the ground, a spray of arterial blood glistening in the spring sunshine. The only sound was the gentle thump of the sea on the other side of the dunes, and the calls of the seagulls wheeling overhead.

I attended the funeral of two of the children. The coffin of one seemed barely larger than a shoebox. The parents displayed astonishing grace, talking about their kids and what they had meant to them.

It was heartbreaking.

Days later, on the flight home, I scrawled a poem in the corner of my notebook. It ended:

I, *who wanted everything to see,*
Want no more of mother's tears
Or boxes carried toy-like
Down the stairs.

The Aramoana massacre remains New Zealand's worst. It was my first exposure to such a thing. It was the first time I was confronted by the callous destruction of children. Who could ever get used to that? The gunman's rage was so absolute, and the suffering and death of the kids so pointless. One of my climbing partners at the time was a psychologist, Chris Trafford. We spent a day clambering up rock faces in the Cathedral Ranges, north-east of Melbourne, while he listened and I tried to make sense of it all.

Chris suggested I go and see a partner in his psychology practice. I already knew Tim Watson-Munro. He was a high-profile forensic psychologist, frequently in the media talking about the criminal mind. Tim would spectacularly crash and burn nearly a decade later when a monstrous cocaine addiction came to light. But he was a fabulous counsellor. He listened to my story of agitation, grief and depression at the murder of the Aramoana children. His insights lifted and calmed my mood. His simple, clear advice was to fortify me for many years against deeper stresses that were still to come. So good was he, that I only needed to see him once.

There was no doubt, however, I had come up against one of the invisible barriers in a journalist's life. It was no different from that of a doctor, a paramedic, a police officer. I could choose to end my exposure to soul-tearing events by simply shifting focus to other journalistic fields: business, sport, politics. But if I kept going as a general reporter, I knew these distressing shocks – what psychologists call 'moral injuries' – could only pile up.

Those sad little coffins nagged at me but this was the world. Straight, honest reporting was a genuine calling. People needed to know.

But if journalism had started as a happy escape from rat-poo alley, with Aramoana I felt its burdens. I saw for the first time the price of the ticket and I recoiled. It was not danger to me, but the sadness and futility of an act of evil to others that had me questioning whether I wanted to go on. But violence, callousness, was also part of life. Wiser, and with an inward sigh, I signed up for more.

15

LONDON CALLING

LATE IN 1990, SORELL ASKED ME IF I WOULD LIKE TO FILL IN OVER Christmas for the Los Angeles correspondent. It was a dizzying prospect but it came to nothing. The correspondent changed his holiday plans. As a cameraman reminded me, 'A trip is not a trip until the Dunlops have left the tarmac.'

I decided to head to Nepal for six weeks of trekking, topped off with a minor mountain, the 6189-metre Imja Tse, or Island Peak. My climbing partner would be my Outward Bound instructor Susan Aitkin. For an extra degree of difficulty, we aimed to summit in December, in the Himalayan winter.

About a month before we took off, Sorell sidled up to me in the newsroom.

'Still interested in LA, Hughie?'

'Sure boss, any time.'

'Well,' he said, tilting his head back, smirking through his bifocals, 'I'm not sending you.'

'Okay, Admiral, whatever you think.'

'I'm sending you to London instead.'

No interview process, no selection panels, no clawing together of CVs and showreels. Without letting me know he was doing it, Sorell had pushed my case in Sydney and one of the prized jobs in Australian television, European-based correspondent for the Nine

Network, had simply fallen into my lap. It wasn't a holiday fill-in, it was for a minimum of three years. That the network executives were willing to take a punt on a kid with just a couple of years' TV experience, whose red hair and glasses had been judged impossible barriers only a few years before, was testament to the enormous trust the network placed in Sorell's judgement. My job now was to live up to it.

—

I got in my Himalayan climbing adventure before Sue and I arrived in London a few days after Christmas 1991. Oh, the magnificent bleakness of it. The Old Grey Lady, dark and shrouded in mists until 8.30 am, the darkness falling again by mid-afternoon. The English, muffled in hats and scarves and layers of coats, walked their trembling little housedogs in all-embracing gloom.

We stayed initially with friends from Melbourne who had made the move a couple of years earlier. My old mate John Clarke from Auckland and Perth was living a few suburbs across. He was at the start of the career rise that would see him become global head of Reuters Television, based in New York. I set out to catch up with another old colleague from the *Hinch* show. She lived at Golders Green, not such a huge distance on the map. But after two hours of driving through sludgy roads in barely moving traffic, it slowly dawned on me what a vast and creaking beast London really was. My friend and I never quite managed to catch up again.

The Channel Nine bureau occupied a shed at the back of the growing Sky Television complex. Based at Isleworth, we were directly under the flight path to Heathrow airport. At the Sky canteen at lunch one day, I wasn't sure if I was more impressed by Manchester United legend George Best sitting at the next formica table, or the rows of jumbo jets lining up to land at the world's busiest international airport. At 6 pm each day, a louder roar would signal the arrival of Concorde, the supersonic luxury jet on its daily service from New York.

I joined a team led by the redoubtable Robert Penfold. He was about forty-two and wore easily the nickname 'The Elegant Veteran', bestowed by the foreign editor, David McCombe. As well as being one of Australia's finest reporters, Penfold possessed inexhaustible charm. He needed it. I tested him in every possible way. But as he did with others before me, and many more afterwards, the Elegant Veteran gave me a master class on how to understand a story, how to manage the moving parts, write it usefully and deliver it on time no matter what the obstacles. He taught me skills in small-team management that were largely lost on me at the time, but which drove my thinking when I ran a political bureau twenty years later.

I had so much to learn.

To welcome me to the bureau, we headed to a pub on the south side of the Thames. It was the watering hole of the bureau's current affairs reporter, Mark Llewellyn. His nickname was 'Ordo' – short for Mr Ordinary – which he plainly was not. A manic lunatic and a brilliant maker of television, Ordo would later rise to head Nine's news and currents affairs. Also present at the pub was the ABC's London correspondent Max Uechtritz, who would become head of news and current affairs at both the ABC and Channel Nine, at various times.

Penfold presented me with a pint of beer. I knew the reputation of English ale: warm undrinkable swill. But this muck was so awful I was convinced it was a joke on the new boy. I was certain my new colleagues had got the publican to fill a glass from the drain-off beneath the taps.

Penfold convinced me it was the real deal. I slowly became a fan of British pints and Victoria Bitter was never an option for me again. So much to learn.

On a personal level, it was a big year. We had barely arrived when we discovered Sue was pregnant. Our daughter, Caitlin, was born on 5 October 1992 at Queen Charlotte Hospital where my mother had worked decades before. I also met up with cousins and other connections from my parents' former lives. Channel Nine supplied a generous and extremely vague 'entertainment allowance', which I spent largely on tickets to the Royal Opera and serious-minded theatre. Wherever you go, I figured, enjoy what the locals do best.

So, I saw Pavarotti at Covent Garden in *Tosca*, I saw Shakespeare performed in the West End and Stratford. I patrolled the antiquarian bookshops of Charing Cross and art galleries all over the city. I was the old cliché, the provincial Antipodean filling my boots with the cultural glories of London.

But in news terms, nothing much was going on.

'I've come too late,' I lamented to Penfold. 'Thatcher's gone, the Berlin Wall has fallen, the Gulf War is over, the Soviet Union has collapsed . . . all the history has already happened!'

'Well,' said Penfold, who had covered all these momentous things, 'stick around.'

The collapse of Yugoslavia had begun. Penfold narrowly missed being shot up in Slovenia in the first weeks of the war. He had made some compelling television out of an attempt to get a badly wounded Slovenian independence fighter to hospital, laying him out in the back of the rental car during a desperate rush for help.

This experience convinced Nine it was too dangerous to send crews to the worsening siege of Sarajevo, particularly as Australia was not directly involved. New Zealand, however, had sent peace-keepers and observers under the United Nations mandate. We shared the bureau with a fine Kiwi reporter called Cameron Bennett and he made several trips to Bosnia with the Nine bureau cameraman, Richard Malone. The stories they came back with were sobering. A young Aussie trainee cameraman quit our bureau to sign up with a British freelancer to cover the siege of Sarajevo. In a convoy trying to get into the city through a snowy pass, his mate in the vehicle ahead of him was blown up by a Serbian anti-tank gun.

Every generation has men and women who go off to war for adventure. Innocence is always the first thing to go and it was being stripped off fast as autumn turned to winter in 1992.

Ruled out of such things by company policy and my junior status, I had other things to amuse myself with. Britain was heading into an election. Margaret Thatcher had been toppled by her own party in 1990. The Iron Lady's chosen successor was a mild, almost gormless-looking former insurance clerk called John Major. He outraged the pompous end of the Conservative tradition by wearing shirts bought at Marks & Spencer with – heaven forbid – buttons instead of cufflinks on the sleeves. Major left school at sixteen. His youthful ambition to become a bus conductor was reportedly thwarted when he failed the height test.

Still, there he was after just three years in cabinet being backed by the mortally wounded Thatcher to replace her, primarily to scuttle her sworn enemy, Michael Heseltine.

After thirteen years in power, by 1992 no one expected the Conservatives to be returned, least of all the Labour Party. Under the red-headed Welshman Neil Kinnock, Labour set up a US-style campaign designed to showcase their man as prime ministerial material and ready to govern. Vast halls were hired. Crowds were bussed in.

John Major, in a move widely mocked, took a different approach. He turned up in every town and village square with a wooden soapbox. There he stood, in whatever weather, delivering a modest stump speech and then taking whatever questions or complaints the public had to throw at him. It made for unscripted moments, as the great unwashed of Britain stepped forward to give him a piece of their minds. It was exactly what modern campaign managers hate, uncontrollable exposure to punters. Major, however, was an affable man. Nothing much fazed him. Bit by tiny bit he started gathering little mossy tendrils. The tiny green shoots of public respect.

In its last big campaign event before polling day, Labour staged a massive show in Sheffield Arena. Ten thousand supporters were there for a blockbuster more than a year in the planning. It reputedly cost a six-figure sum to stage. Neil Kinnock strode out to be greeted by a wall of noise. The cheering was so loud and so sustained that Kinnock could do nothing but stand, grinning awkwardly, while repeatedly shouting 'Well, all right! . . . Well, all RIGHT!'

Watching it left me feeling queasy. He was being hailed as a victor without the first vote being cast. Everything about it jarred.

A week later, John Major's Conservatives swept home with an eight percent majority. It was one of the most stunning upsets in British electoral history and a lesson in the political value of authenticity over hype. It would take a new kind of Labour man, Tony Blair, to finally put the Tories to the sword five years later.

Historically, that was all interesting enough, but the appetite from Australia was modest. The insatiable hunger was for Princess Diana.

Less than a month after the British election, a tabloid journalist, Andrew Morton, published a book called *Diana: Her True Story*. It revealed the sensational news of Prince Charles's long-standing affair with the married Camilla Parker Bowles. Diana's relationship with her sons' riding instructor, James Hewitt, also emerged. What made the book a bestseller was the lack of any convincing denials and the widely held view that Morton was little more than a ghostwriter for Diana herself.

Worse followed. Two recorded phone conversations, one involving Diana with a paramour James Gilbey, and the other purported to be an intimate conversation between Charles and Camilla, appeared in the tabloids.

Few other things were being discussed in hair salons and cafés across the far-flung former British Empire. I delivered many reports outside Buckingham Palace or Kensington Palace during this time of torment for the British monarchy – hell! For our monarchy, too.

As winter closed in over Britain, the prime minister formally announced to the House of Commons the intention of Charles and Diana to 'amicably separate'.

It was as if night had fallen. Sir Edward Heath, the former prime minister who at nearly eighty years old was the 'Father' of the House of Commons, levered himself to his feet.

This, he declared, was 'one of the saddest announcements made by any prime minister in modern times'.

Heath had served under Churchill, when there really were some tragic announcements to be made. But as doubts grew about the future of the monarchy itself, the old stager's sense of gravity reson- ated. All of it was lapped up back home.

Not long before the formal announcement, with even the conser- vative broadsheets finding ways to discuss the royal couple's obvious difficulties, I went to see *La Boheme* at the Royal Opera House. Just before the curtain lifted, a frisson ran through the crowd. Diana, magnificent in a jewelled ice-blue evening gown – and magnificently alone – took her seat in the dress circle. The crowd, once they saw who it was, rose as one and applauded. It was proper, muted, under- stated British applause, much of it conducted by women in gloved hands. There were no cries of 'Bravo!' or 'We love ya, Di!'. After fifteen seconds or so, as Diana graciously nodded, the audience turned again to the stage, sat down, and settled in for a satisfying evening of consumptive beauties dying for love.

Gotta love the Poms.

In those early London days, I had another encounter I treasure. Nine was home to a splendid program called *Sunday*, which blended award-winning investigative reporting, with Laurie Oakes' penetrating political interviews, and a middle- to high-brow view of the arts.

The show phoned our bureau one day. Sir Sidney Nolan was going to be the subject of a special feature to mark his seventy-fifth birthday. At the time Australia's most internationally celebrated artist, Sid Nolan lived in a grand set of apartments overlooking the River Thames at Whitehall. With no one else available, it fell to me to do the interview.

The truth is, I knew bugger all about Sid Nolan except that he had painted the Ned Kelly series. There was no internet then to help me become an instant expert, and a quick scramble around arty bookstores produced precisely zero that had anything to do with him.

'I hear he doesn't mind a glass of red,' suggested Robert Penfold. 'Pop around to a decent wine store and spend a couple of hundred pounds on some very good Bordeaux. That'll get you through the door.'

I did as he suggested and Sir Sidney was indeed well pleased.

His apartment was magnificent. Art worth millions of dollars hung from its walls and was even stacked half-a-dozen wide in the corridors. Richard Malone took some lovely shots of the great man as we walked by the Thames and as he did some work for us in his paint-strewn studio.

We sat for the interview and I conceded my ignorance on matters art and Nolan. To my great luck, he was in an expansive mood. He uncorked one of the wines and reminisced about his father and his St Kilda childhood, and explained the themes and motifs in his paintings. He caught me out many times for my sheer artistic witlessness but his mood was generous and forgiving.

The only difficulty was the constant reappearance of his wife, Mary, a tiny bird of a woman with piercing light blue eyes. Mary was the sister of Sir Arthur Boyd and an artist in her own right. She had also been married to the notoriously alcoholic painter John Perceval.

'She doesn't like me drinking,' explained Sid, having reassured her yet again that the interview would soon be over if we were left on our own to do it.

Finally, Sid had to go. He had an opera to attend. He had designed the set.

'Thank you,' he said with a big grin, shaking my hand. 'I enjoyed that.'

I thanked him back.

He died a few weeks later.

16

A NECKLACE

SUDDENLY A TRIP WAS ON, BUT IT WASN'T WHERE I WAS EXPECTING to go and the terms were unusual.

South Africa had freed Nelson Mandela two years earlier but white rule still held. Frustrations were building. But for South African business, Mandela's release spelled opportunity. Sanctions were lifting.

And so it was that, in a plush office a short walk from Buckingham Palace, I found myself waiting to meet Sol Kerzner, a somewhat notorious character. It was mid-afternoon.

'Would you like a drink?' asked a dull-eyed PR woman. 'Mr Kerzner only ever drinks Johnnie Walker Blue Label.'

I had never heard of Blue Label. I declined.

A few minutes later I was ushered in to meet Kerzner. There was no sign of whiskey, making me gladder that I hadn't accepted one.

Kerzner was a scrapper who had made good. The son of Russian Jewish migrants to South Africa, he first drew notice as a welter-weight boxer before building up a hotel business. His real gift was for reading the play.

South Africa's Dutch Reformed Church gave religious cover for apartheid. With its heavily bearded Old Testament–style patriarchs, known as *dominees*, the church laid down religious law in a highly conflicted Christian state. South African church leaders used the Ten Commandments to justify the notorious statute criminalising sex between people of different colour. Such activities, the *dominees* decreed, broke the commandment to 'honour thy father and thy mother'. It takes a particular kind of genius to come up with such a thing.

The Calvinists also disapproved of gambling.

But in order to give itself the fig leaf of caring about black development, the apartheid government had established theoretically autonomous 'homelands' within South Africa's borders and put black leaders in charge.

Sol Kerzner saw his chance. In the 'homeland' of Bophuthatswana, he negotiated rights to build a casino and golf course complex that would make his name. His resort, Sun City, allowed gambling – and opportunities for sex across the colour line – for the white bogans who flocked in from Pretoria and Johannesburg. Kerzner had then sought international legitimacy, inviting global stars to perform for huge fees, in defiance of UN sanctions. Frank Sinatra, Rod Stewart, Elton John and Queen were among those who took the money.

In 1985, 'Artists United Against Apartheid', led by Bruce Springsteen's guitarist Steve Van Zandt, released an anthem '(Ain't Gunna Play) Sun City'. It was a hit in Australia. It was banned in South Africa. As activism, it worked. Big-name bands stopped going.

Mandela's release gave Kerzner new opportunities. He wanted to update his resort to attract global tourists. He created a new fantasy resort at Sun City called 'The Lost City'. It capitalised on the imagery made popular by Indiana Jones movies. At regular intervals jets of fire would erupt into the air and every few hours the entire resort would shake as if it was being hit by a minor earthquake.

Kerzner was willing to fly me and a crew to South Africa to report on the official opening of this place. We would fly first class. He expressed his revulsion for apartheid. He had been a big donor to Mandela's African National Congress, he said. I checked and he had, indeed, given more than one million dollars to the ANC. (Later, the ANC even asked him to organise Mandela's inauguration.)

I was not impressed, however. I left thinking there was no way I was going to take a junket from a sanction-busting beneficiary of apartheid economics.

Robert Penfold took another view. South Africa was on a knife's edge. Channel Nine was unlikely to fund a trip there. But if Kerzner accepted that we would have full editorial control and if he allowed us to book a return flight two weeks after The Lost City shoot, we would have time to report some genuine news about what was going on in South Africa.

I allowed myself to be convinced, the only reporting junket I have ever taken. And I am glad I did.

I filed a piece for the *Today* show on the opening of The Lost City and scuttled off to Johannesburg to get some real reporting done.

On the city's south-western fringe lay Soweto. The name itself signalled its artificial origins, standing simply for South West Township. It was a dark triumph of apartheid's social engineering. Millions lived there, mostly in the deepest squalor, banned from establishing businesses or industry except within extremely tight limits. Only two roads led in and out, allowing the South African Police (SAP) and South African Defence Force (SADF) to bottle it up if trouble broke out.

The population existed to provide labour for the mines and the other enterprises run by white money. It was a polyglot community, dominated by the Xhosa, of which Mandela was one. But the South African security apparatus was adept at destabilising the people it feared. They brought young Zulus in from Natal to provide extra industrial labour. Those men's families were forbidden to join them. So, within the 'township' were these young men, called 'hostel dwellers', from a rival tribe, without the moderating influence of family, engaged in constant low-level warfare with their neighbours. All of it was being stirred by a white regime that preferred to have black people fighting each other than fighting them.

Mandela might have been free, but there was still no date for an election. Security forces and some politicians were behind what Mandela called a 'Third Force', determined to make South Africa ungovernable, to prompt martial law and force the retention of apartheid.

From 1990, the inter-tribal violence accelerated. Not only did police do nothing, they were frequently caught supplying weapons to gangs. The most feared street-level tactic was 'necklacing', where the victim would have a tyre hung around his or her neck. Petrol would be poured into the bottom of the tyre and set alight, guaranteeing an agonising death. The 1991 Pulitzer Prize for Spot News Photography went to Greg Marinovich, a member of the so-called 'Bang-Bang Club' of South African photographers. He captured a hapless Zulu man being hacked at with machetes with his body already in flames from a necklacing.

At the time, most people would have said the most dangerous city in the world was Sarajevo, besieged and under constant artillery and sniper attack. But Soweto's Baragwanath hospital dealt with more war trauma every night than even the Bosnian capital.

I went to Baragwanath with cameraman Peter Watts. We spent a night in 'Blood Alley' where an endless flow of the beaten, stabbed, burnt and shot were brought in. The head of surgery, Dr Bokkie Rabinowitz, was proud of what they did.

'If you can get to us alive, there's a ninety-five percent chance you will leave us alive,' he boasted. Unlike most hospital emergency departments, the patients were generally young. Strokes, heart attacks, the complications of ageing barely featured. Young doctors from all over the world competed for internships at Baragwanath, knowing they would see a greater concentration of traumatic wounds than at any other hospital on earth. Treatment techniques were also being developed faster there than anywhere else.

One of the few forms of business black South Africans were allowed to take up was running minivan 'taxi services' around Soweto and between the township and Johannesburg. A train service also linked the cities. To drum up business, the thugs who ran the minivans would hire people to go to the train stations and shoot a few passengers. Long-suffering Soweto folks would then abandon the trains for the minivans.

But there were rival businesses. So as commuters waited at their minivan stop, they could be shot up there as well, to encourage them to use a different minivan service. When all the minivan operators were shooting up the passengers of their rivals, the poor workers would flee back to the trains. At which point, the trains would start being shot up again.

We saw direct evidence of this as an ambulance raced up to the front of the hospital. 'Ambulance' was too grand a word – it was simply a Toyota HiAce van with all the seats removed. The patients were thrown in the back without any medical care while the driver tried to get them to hospital. It was too late for one young man. He lay in his blood, glassy-eyed and ignored, as orderlies grabbed a middle-aged man in a tweed suit and threw him onto a gurney. The victims had been waiting for a minivan when someone had come along and shot them. The tweed-suited man was still semi-conscious when the ambulance pulled up, despite being shot five times with an AK-47.

Peter and I trailed the gurney into the operating room as a visiting German intern took over. One of the bullets had gone through the man's lung. The effect was to release air into his chest cavity. With every breath, he was filling his chest with air, which in turn was collapsing his lungs. The German raised the man's arm and plunged a piece of sharpened steel into his side just below his armpit. The man groaned pitifully. There had been no time for anaesthetic. But the measure allowed him to breathe again. The team started getting to work on him, with Rabinowitz dropping by to supervise.

Later, the young German doctor sought us out to show us the X-rays. Three bullets had gone through the man's chest, one through an arm, and the fifth had shattered the top of his femur.

'What are his prospects?' I asked.

'Oh, he'll be fine,' said the doc breezily. 'We bring them back from far worse than that.'

Still, it seemed a terrible price to pay for just trying to get home from a day's work.

—

Wattsy and I made several trips into Soweto. We stopped in an open space one rainy afternoon shooting some general vision to give a sense of the place. On what looked like a picnic table, two women were selling a high pile of guts. A little boy was with them, running around the table leg. On one pass, he misjudged the distance and hit the table. The guts slid into the mud. One of the women thrashed the boy while the other collected the produce from the dirt and piled it back up again, ready for sale. Deep poverty, it struck me, was a struggle for dignity against heavy odds.

Our guide in this was Aubrey. He had been born in Soweto but fled after twice being shot by police during the 1976 Soweto Uprising. He was back now, with high hopes for the future. Aubrey was a dedicated Buddhist. He had tried all other religions, he told me, including a conversion to Islam complete with circumcision. He gave that up, he said, because there were 'too many rules'.

Now he made a living acting as a guide, or 'fixer' for journalists and other visiting foreigners. It was dangerous work but he had some protection. His nephew was 'the biggest car thief in the township'. I briefly met him, a huge man with pitiless eyes, driving the very latest model BMW.

Aubrey's self-imposed exile had allowed him to pick up many South African languages.

'Very useful,' he said. And so it would prove.

We were nearing the end of our trip. Our final story was pretty much written. All it needed was a piece to camera, a 'stand-up', in Soweto. Ever since the mob in Fiji, I had anxieties about crowds of young men in volatile times. Driving around a corner, I saw bare ground on both sides of the road. Not a soul in sight. A row of drab four-storey accommodation blocks stood one hundred metres off to the right.

'Let's do it here,' I said, slowing down.

'Don't be mad!' said Aubrey. 'Keep driving. Don't stop here.'

He explained the road marked the border between the hostels and the township.

'If we had got out of the car, they would have been on us in a minute,' he said. 'That's if they didn't shoot you from the windows.'

That explained why there was no one in sight. My instincts were so poor I had mistaken danger for safety.

We drove on for another kilometre until the road curved and the hostels were no longer in view. There was an open space with a couple of trees. A few people were milling about. It seemed relaxed. Low houses crowded up a gentle rise.

'How about here?' I asked.

Aubrey seemed uncertain.

'All right,' he said. 'Let's be quick.'

I parked the car in the open. Wattsy pulled out his camera. I leapt out of the driver's seat.

Within seconds we were surrounded. People came running. It was as if hundreds of bored youth suddenly had something to play with. They shouted questions at Aubrey. They threw a few at me, in English.

'Australians,' I announced cheerfully. 'We're here to ask you, um . . . what you think of this government? How long do you think you will have to wait for an election?'

A quiet, bearded young man appeared at the edge of the crowd and pushed through.

'What do you want?' he asked, calmly.

I started to run my line, that Australians wanted to know about conditions in Soweto (not entirely untrue), and that we had travelled here to talk to people and find out their concerns.

The crowd was restive.

The bearded man called out across the noise. I hoped he was calming them down. For a moment, it seemed to be working. Then another voice was raised, more raucous and angry. I turned to look at a boy no more than fifteen. I was struck by the dead coldness in his eyes and the top-quality black leather jacket on his shoulders. A kid didn't get to keep a jacket like that unless people were too scared to take it from him.

I exchanged glances with Aubrey. There was fear in his eyes.

I looked at the car, fifteen metres away, the keys in my pocket. No chance.

'Wattsy,' I said, 'let's interview this bloke over here.'

I sensed the mob had two poles. The more energetic surrounded the boy. But the man with the beard seemed to have some status too. A television camera gifts authority to whoever it is pointed at. Our best bet was to enhance the man with the beard.

Wattsy framed up on the man and I began asking him serious questions, as if it was a political interview with a major player. Aubrey was right on to it, translating my tricky English and urging the crowd to be quiet so we could hear.

For perhaps sixty seconds, the tactic worked. The man answered seriously. A few in the mob tried to shush the others. But it didn't hold. The boy with the leather jacket suddenly started shouting orders. A group of kids broke off and ran away. Aubrey caught my eye again. His look told me things were grim. The bearded bloke had fallen silent. He had lost the battle and so had we. The boy was now mob leader, and he was shouting out a speech, swaggering and pumping his fists. We were getting jostled. The crowd was growing.

Suddenly, at a shout, they all broke and scattered. Over the hill came a bright yellow 'Buffalo' – the armoured shooting platforms used to notorious effect by white police in the townships. To me, they were figures of oppression and loathing. But I have never been so glad to see a white supremacist in my life.

The machine roared up to where we stood, suddenly alone in the middle of the intersection. From the firing step, a South

African paramilitary stared down at me from behind his pump-action shotgun. He was blond, sunburnt and astonished. I held his bright blue eyes for a moment. They kept driving. We dashed for our car, fired it up and raced away.

With adrenalin firing the accelerator beneath my foot, I listened as Aubrey explained what had happened.

Our instincts had been right. The bearded man was a representative of the ANC Youth wing. He had some semi-official status. The boy with the leather jacket was a street tough. He had been pulled in by security forces and – in Aubrey's word – 'bastardised'. He had sworn to kill the next white person who came into his hands. We were it. He had dispatched some kids to get a tyre and petrol. We were minutes away from being necklaced.

There was so much to reflect on. The nearly fatal level of my ignorance. The irony of being saved by people I had spent my life despising. The sense of powerlessness in the face of a mob. But also, the effectiveness of our efforts to buy time – if only a couple of critical minutes – by trying to work the crowd psychology towards the non-violent leader in the group.

The fact was, though, we were saved by dumb luck.

A couple of days later I was sitting in the front of a South African Airlines jumbo jet heading home to London. It was a daytime flight. I had a large window. For hours I watched Africa unfold beneath me, its rivers and vast lakes, the orange and olive-toned savannah, the deep green-black of equatorial forests. For all the continent's population, there was little visible evidence of human impact from 35,000 feet. Only once did I see, amid dark green hills, a dense concentration of villages.

Where was that place, I wondered, turning to the little real-time map that marked our progress. Ah, yes. There we are. Rwanda.

How peaceful it looked.

17

OPERATION RESTORE HOPE

THROUGHOUT 1992, AS SARAJEVO'S NIGHTMARE DEEPENED AND Charles's and Diana's extra-marital flirtations occupied the British press, another disaster was unfolding. Somalia was falling apart.

Through the Cold War, the desert nation in the Horn of Africa was sustained by the Soviet Union. As the eastern bloc collapsed, Somalia was left to its own devices. It had no natural sources of wealth but it was awash with guns. BBC and ITN reporters game enough to venture into Mogadishu, the capital, filed stories of an armed-up, medieval hell. Food was scant. People were dying in horrific numbers.

'Shouldn't we go there and see for ourselves?' I ventured to a senior network hand.

'What for? All you're going to get is skinny blacks.'

There was not much you could say to that. The UN Secretary-General Boutros Boutros-Ghali could rail at the west for 'fighting a rich man's war in Yugoslavia while not lifting a finger to save Somalia', but no one yet cared.

By the time I got back from South Africa in late October, that was changing. In his final significant act as US president, George Bush Senior signed the US up to lead a multinational force into Somalia. Its mission was to secure a failed state and ensure food reached the starving. It had the lofty title of 'Operation Restore Hope' and Australia agreed to provide a full battalion of troops.

Suddenly, the news bosses in Sydney were interested.

—

I flew in from London via Nairobi, conning my way onto a UN flight for the final leg of the journey. The plane tracked north over an endless white sand coastline, the waves curling in to waste themselves on a shoreline devoid of life.

Mogadishu airport could hardly have been a greater contrast. It was like a Hollywood film set. Blue UN flags flicked in the sea breeze against an equally blue sky. The busy clatter of helicopters and the roar of incoming transport planes spoke of the mighty scale of American industry and purpose.

I had landed just ahead of the Australian press pack, who tumbled out of a C-130 Hercules, blinking in the stark light. Naturally, I greeted them with the casual but seasoned air of someone who had been there for weeks.

We set up to capture the arrival of the advance party of Australian troops. For some reason, the defence force had seen fit to charter a Qantas jumbo. The gleaming red and white aircraft with the kangaroo artwork made an incongruous sight carving through a mosquito swarm of Black Hawk helicopters.

The diggers danced down the staircase onto the tarmac, all in good cheer. Civil aviation rules banned all weapons from the cabin of the aircraft. So we stood grabbing interviews while the cargo hold was emptied. The troops were still unarmed when a sniper opened fire.

The first thing I saw was all the soldiers diving for cover behind some freight pallets. I didn't hear any shots over the noise of the plane. But the Qantas pilot had also seen the army's reaction. Eyes wide, he put the engines into a screaming roar and started a hard right-hand turn to get the hell out of there.

I was standing with Tony de Cesare, a young Tasmanian cameraman from the ABC. He was lining up for a shot of the sprawling Aussies when I bellowed an instruction to get a shot of the plane. Tony hesitated for just a moment before complying. I put my body between Tony and the likely source of the shots, feeling a brief flush of heroic virtue for doing so. In fact, it was a daft reaction. We should have been on the ground with the troops. If the snipers were using AK-47s, which would be most likely, my unarmoured body would barely slow down the rounds. My idiotic instructions also meant we finished up with a shot of a plane turning. No bullets lit up the side of the plane. By the time Tony got back to what he knew was the best shot – our soldiers sprawling on the ground – US marines on air perimeter duty were racing for the fence line and the moment was gone. The diggers quickly sprang back to their feet, the Qantas pilot made a quick and no-nonsense departure, and everyone was saved from having the moment recorded by my over-excitable treatment of the cameraman.

My embarrassment at my greenhorn error couldn't settle for long. There was too much to do.

With the diggers reunited with their weapons, we joined a convoy heading to the vast US embassy compound, our base for the next couple of days. Just outside the airport perimeter we passed a large stony field. The stink was indescribable. It was a vast gravesite, a cemetery without headstones or names. Here lay just some of the tens of thousands of people who had died of starvation or violence over the previous few months.

The searing stench was a reminder of why we were there.

That night, behind the embassy compound walls, we stood in the redemptive cool of midnight, watching tracer bullets arc across the city and hearing the ragged morse of the small-arms fire.

US marines, vast in their body armour, read the play.

'That's AK . . . that's fifty-cal . . . Yeah, Mama, git some!'

Our news bosses, and we presumed our audience, were interested in stirring tales of Aussie troops on a difficult and dangerous deployment. To break it up a bit, stories on heroic aid workers – preferably Australian – would also be useful. Given the language difficulties – we had no access to translators – we had no insight at all into the complex horrors of life for ordinary Somalis. They were reduced to stereotypes, either grateful recipients of our generosity or armed thugs we were there to subdue.

Not all threats were human. In Baidoa, a spitting cobra struck a marine in a neighbouring tent. That ended his tour.

Equally feared was the tumbu fly. It was known to seek out urine residues in underpants, resulting in maggot invasions of the penis.

The greatest dangers, however, were man-made. Somali men were not only generally armed. They were also off their heads. They chewed a straggly leaf called *qat*, a euphoric, mildly hallucinogenic drug that induced feelings ranging from invincibility to paranoia. In the name of science, I tried some. The sun-hammered pallor of the landscape gradually became rich with pink and golden highlights. The greens seemed luscious and cool. The underlying background tension that was part of being in Somalia floated away, replaced with a sense of wellbeing and ease.

That was after just a few stalks. Some Somalis ate the stuff by the kilo.

We flew into Baidoa, the City of Death. At the height of the famine, thousands of people were dying every day in this flat and broken desert town. The battalion commander was the rising young Lieutenant-Colonel David Hurley who would go on to become Chief of the Defence Force and, ultimately, Governor of New South Wales. On the first major operational deployment since the Vietnam War, Hurley and the mission's overall commander, Colonel Bill Mellor, had a problem to solve.

The Australians were outnumbered. The militia gangs owned the province. They drove around in what were known as 'technicals' – stripped-down vehicles worthy of *Mad Max*, bristling with machine guns and anti-aircraft weapons. The Australian commanders had little option but to bluff. Their first act would be a 'show of force' – to tell the warlords and militias that a new mob ruled.

So half-a-dozen Vietnam-era armoured personnel carriers rumbled through town like suburban hoods with a particularly brag-worthy car. The effect was somewhat muted by the pile of journos trying to hang on to the top. Colonel Mellor was worried about snipers and insisted that journalists wore their helmets and flak jackets. Once up there, riding the big steel elephant, I dumped both. The helmet felt ridiculous and the flak jacket was too light to stop a bullet anyway.

Naturally, all the other TV journos recorded a piece to camera in their battle gear 'on patrol'. I didn't. Over subsequent days, everyone else received letters from viewers worried about their safety and praising them for being so brave. I received messages from my office, wondering what I was thinking. Why had I appeared on camera with my sweaty hair glued to my forehead and why was I not wearing military gear like everyone else?

Looking macho has always been a bit beyond me.

Soon we had no time to concern ourselves with competitive vanities. There was much to try to understand. We went out on foot patrols or on food distribution convoys to areas that still had received no relief. Mass starvation is a horrific sight. I think we all felt – soldiers, aid workers, journalists – the urgency of the work.

The days were long, hot, dusty and dry. Our camp could only produce enough water to give us each three litres a day. In Mogadishu, the best we had averaged was thirteen litres. Before long, some soldiers and journalists were collapsing, with the headaches and nausea of dehydration and heat exhaustion.

From the start of the Baidoa mission, Australian troops were being shot at. Initially, it was a tactical ploy, to see how the Australians would react. Soon, though, the shots came with deadly intent. Corporal Wayne Prosser, who I would meet again in East Timor, felt three shots pass by his ear as he manned an observation post.

The Australian zone included the town of Buur Hakaba, ninety kilometres to the east. Its water supply was a foul-smelling green pool at the base of a huge rock, somewhat reminiscent of Uluru. Bodies of the dead lay stacked up nearby, a wall of cadavers lightly covered with rocks.

The army chose a spot a couple of kilometres away to organise a food distribution. I trekked along to watch.

Only the women were given food. The head man from each village identified how many mouths each woman must feed, and wheat sacks, stamped 'Gift of Australia', were opened up and the appropriate portions of grain were measured out.

The soldiers were keyed up, expecting a militia raid. Food was power and the Australians were carrying a lot of it.

The food distribution process took forever. The aid agencies were all about accountability. Every woman had to have her name and the amount given to her recorded in a book. The women, tall and impossibly thin, sat on the ground, mustered behind coils of razor wire in the blazing heat, making their own calculations. Most of them, they quickly realised, would still be waiting long after the sun had gone down.

The women became agitated. The diggers had been issued long wooden staves for crowd control. They were taught Somali words for 'Sit down!' and 'Stay!' But the women didn't want to sit down and stay. They wanted food. They started pressing against the razor wire. Nineteen-year-old Private Ken 'Polly' Farmer was one of those gamely trying to hold order. What part of this teenager's previous Australian life, I wondered, prepared him for this moment – waving a stick over the heads of frail and desperate women who knew they and their families must eat soon or die.

The temperature advanced into the forties. There was no shade. Some of the women could no longer endure the heat. I saw the eyes of first one, and then several women, become glassy. Pressed in on all sides, their bodies stiffened and slackened, their lips peeled back from their teeth. Women began wailing, an unnerving, piteous sound.

Soldiers were starting to fall over. Some were helped to the shade of a troop truck. I went to check on them and took a moment to nibble a muesli bar and take a slug of water. A woman saw my water bottle and beseeched me to give her some. I had half a litre left. Would I be able to get it to her, one arm amid a forest of need? Could I spare it myself? Would the mere appearance of the water bottle trigger a stampede?

I put the bottle away.

A soldier, tending to one of his stricken colleagues, caught my eye. 'We're not going to hold this.'

He was right. The women had taken the measure of these big white soldiers. They had not fired their guns once. They had not even hit them. The women were plainly ready to risk whatever these strangers might do, rather than starve and thirst hopelessly in the open sun.

I made another survey of the crowd. I felt sick. The woman who had begged me for water was now lying on her side.

With a sudden crescendo of yelling the women at the back pushed forward. Women were pitched onto the razor wire and others ran straight over them. They trampled over a soldier standing with his arms wide, as if this was the kind of traffic you could stop.

'Free feed! Free feed!' bellowed a sergeant, as someone else ordered 'Back to the trucks!'

Soldiers were running. My instinct was to go with them but the vision was too apocalyptic not to record. Cameraman Geoff Carroll held his ground as tiny women fought over twenty-kilogram sacks of grain stencilled with a cheerful image of a kangaroo. One bag tore in two. In clouds of dust, women launched themselves at the fallen grain.

A thick arm came through the murk and grabbed my shoulder. 'We gotta go! Now!'

We pulled out, leaping onto the final truck as it was already moving away. We were hoisted into the open tray to fall among grimy, hollow-eyed soldiers. Private Farmer was swearing, watching the scene as we jolted off. Women were trying to run, matchstick legs beneath their sacks, falling, having the sacks torn from them, trying to get home before hands clawed away their winnings, or the militias came in to seize it all. We were so shocked, so breathless, so grateful to escape, we weren't sure what we were even seeing.

The dust cloud hung above the thornbush scrub. Soon it looked like just a smudge of smoke. And then it looked like nothing at all. We drove on under the pitiless African sky.

—

Somalia was a mess.

A heavy transport helicopter delivered another load of aid. The target village had received no help and the only road in was said to be heavily mined. Twenty tonnes of food was delivered, with the helicopter brought up from Mogadishu and Australian troops riding shotgun.

But, as it was being unloaded, the soldiers found they weren't being mobbed. No one, in fact, seemed much interested. They had landed in the wrong village. This one, the locals told them, had received a big food drop just two days before. By the time all this became clear, the chopper was halfway back to Mogadishu.

The real target village was ten kilometres away linked by the heavily mined road. The aid worker in charge, an Irishman, came up with an idea. The first person who could get to the other village and tell them that food was here would get a whole sack of grain just for themselves.

A convoy of fleet-footed adolescents raced for the start of the track and disappeared from sight.

'What about the mines?'

'They'll know where they are,' said the aid man.

The soldiers, meanwhile, now found themselves protecting a big pile of food in an open field. They prepared their positions against a militia raid.

Hours later, an ancient and misshapen truck wheezed into view. The grain was loaded up and the truck headed back up Landmine Road. It was a case study in the haphazard and dangerous realities of the new world of armed humanitarianism.

The difficulties mounted. Within months, US forces were drawn into a shooting war. An attempt to seize the warlord Mohamed Farrah Aidid ended with the disaster captured in the film *Black Hawk Down*. Eighteen US troops were killed on that mission, along with two from Pakistan and one from Malaysia who went to the Americans' rescue. In the fifteen-hour battle, perhaps 1000 Somalis were also killed.

A captured US helicopter pilot Michael Durant was paraded on television and the bodies of US troops were dragged through the streets. Bill Clinton, the newly installed president, had seen enough. He ordered the Americans out. Somalia collapsed back into civil war and disarray.

It remains in that state today.

—

Getting out of Somalia was a simple process. One day we were ordered to pack up, a plane was coming. A lumbering Hercules transporter thundered onto the dirt strip. We heaved our gear on board and I was asleep before the wheels left the ground.

After hours of droning flight, I was shaken awake and told to buckle back in. I doubt any of us even asked where we were landing, and the Herc's tiny windows were too high to give us a view. As the plane came to a halt, the rear loading door descended to reveal a view too ridiculously beautiful to be credited. The sun was setting behind palm trees. Little islands dotted a tropical bay. A soft warm wind washed over the rank-smelling journos in the cargo hold.

We had landed in the Seychelles. The Indian Ocean Islands remain sealed in my memory as the most perfect vision of paradise.

The rest of the news teams were heading back to Australia. I had to find my way back to London. I turned thirty-two on a flight to Nairobi and decided to mark the moment by spending a few days on a game park on the Maasai Mara.

It was an important time. I was exhausted, more spiritually than physically. In the previous three months I had seen some of the worst that Africa had to offer, from the everyday violence of Soweto to the intense suffering of Somalia. Deepening my anguish was the recognition that my marriage was ending. I felt assaulted by wounds both global and deeply personal; the personal ones due to my own carelessness and absence.

I took a light plane onto the high plains of western Kenya to find the game parks almost empty of tourists because of a threat of political violence associated with the Kenyan elections. My only fellow travellers were an American TV crew who were taking a few days leave out of Mogadishu. One of their colleagues had been shot dead by a teenager on the street. Oddly, they were good company as we talked out our experiences.

I also found myself restored by long walks that began before dawn with a park ranger. He was a white Kenyan. Accompanied by a bloke armed with a very large calibre gun, we walked for hours across the plain, hearing the roar of lions and the movements of many other animals in the savannah grass. It was useful therapy. But my mood was depressed. The scale of African suffering seemed irredeemable.

More than any other continent, Africa has shaped my views about what matters. But after those first encounters, bleak of soul, without the tools to see it squarely, I would have had no complaint if the entire land mass had sunk into the sea.

18

HOTEL UKRAINE

THROUGH THE NORTHERN HEMISPHERE SUMMER OF 1993, TROUBLE was brewing in Russia. The Soviet Union had collapsed after the fall of the Berlin Wall. Russian satellite states from the Caucasus to the Baltic had asserted their independence and most had achieved it.

The charismatic former Moscow mayor, Boris Yeltsin, had succeeded President Mikhail Gorbachev, the reformist who had effectively called an end to the Cold War.

But Yeltsin faced a parliament stacked with lifelong Communist Party hacks, neither ideologically inclined nor temperamentally suited for democracy.

For months, an arm wrestle played out between President Yeltsin in the Kremlin, and the deputies who controlled the Russian Parliament, the Duma. In March, the Duma fell just short of the votes needed to impeach Yeltsin. The deputies then organised a national referendum which essentially amounted to a motion of no confidence in the president.

The voters rejected it. Yeltsin was popular. The deputies were not.

On 21 September 1993, Yeltsin acted, issuing a decree that dissolved the Congress and the Supreme Soviet, effectively the parliament.

All of this had rumbled on as background noise while the international focus remained on the misery of Sarajevo. But suddenly, the Yeltsin decree had set Russia on course for a decisive clash.

From London, I started trying to find ways to get into Moscow. The London embassy had stopped issuing visas to journalists. My friends at Sky were flying to Dublin, in the hope that the embassy in Ireland might be more accommodating. I couldn't justify the trip on spec. Head office in Sydney was still not convinced Russia was going to become a story.

I worked the problem over with our trusty travel agent, Glenn. The Russians issued seventy-two-hour transit visas on arrival in Moscow if the traveller could provide proof of an ongoing connecting flight to another international destination. Perhaps we could devise a scam.

We found a service that connected Moscow with Anchorage, Alaska. I booked it with cameraman Peter Watts. Suddenly, the TVNZ reporter Cameron Bennett was interested. Very quickly, *A Current Affair's* correspondent Mark Llewellyn wanted in, too.

The tickets were booked but we needed a cover story. There was still no effective internet to make this easy, but somehow we discovered there was an environmental conference being planned in Anchorage. That would be our story. We were on our way to cover a bunch of Alaskan greenies.

Even as this was happening, the anti-Yeltsin forces had taken control of the parliamentary building, known confusingly as the White House. Crowds of their supporters were thronging outside, some of them armed. They included a fruit salad of nostalgic communists, proto-fascists, anti-Semitic nationalists, even some who waved the flag of the old Russian monarchy which had been slaughtered to a man, woman and child by the Bolsheviks in 1918.

We had to travel light. Any checked-in luggage would wind up in Alaska, where we had no intention of going. There were five of us, Llewellyn, Bennett, Watts and myself, plus a smart young sound recordist called Brendan Donohoe.

We arrived in Moscow's sprawling Sheremetyevo Airport near midnight. With no visas, we immediately attracted police attention, especially with our stripped-down camera gear. We trotted out our story. The hard-faced Russian officers looked unimpressed. Deportation by the next plane looked likely. Then Cameron Bennett stepped forward with our last and riskiest play.

'Look, I know this is all very inconvenient for you,' he began with his best Kiwi/British tones. 'Is there anything we can pay to cover any administrative expenses?'

He let it hang, his eyebrow politely raised.

The danger in this trick is that the official sees it for what it is – an outright offer to bribe. Such offers carry their own penalties, or at the very least the threat of punishment to extract an even bigger bribe.

But these blokes were uncomplicated in their demands. For US$100 each, a total of $500 in cash, we were in.

For children raised in the Cold War, as we all were, bribing your way into Moscow carried its own frisson of delight. We scurried through the airport to find people scattering in all directions. There were no taxis, just one car oozing smoke that was already moving off.

I threw myself bodily in front of it. The cabbie was reluctant to have anything to do with us. Most unusual behaviour, I thought. When does an airport cabbie knock back a fare? Within seconds, though, he had four Australians and a Kiwi piled in his car and showing no signs of wanting to be evicted.

'The Hotel Ukraine,' I ordered, naming the splendid Gothic landmark on the banks of the Moscow River where I knew Reuters kept an office. We had no way of knowing what had happened while we were in the air and a local news office with its own satellite point was a good place to start.

The driver objected, waving his arms and complaining but we spoke no Russian and simply, rudely, insisted he get going.

Grumbling, the cabbie headed into town. There were surprisingly few vehicles on the street, and those that were seemed to be large official limousines travelling at speed. The night was cold, the windows were wound up, and if the driver was unhappy, his passengers were gripped with glee at having scammed our way in. Moscow – bewdy! A shit fight – all the better! Where else would you rather be!

The cabbie suddenly pulled over to the side of the road. He seemed angry now. He wound down the window and gave an urgent, agitated speech that meant nothing to us. Outside we could hear what sounded like a busy freight marshalling yard, with trains moving urgently up and down the line.

'Keep going!' we chorused. 'Hotel Ukraine!' We waved US currency and made unsafe promises about how well he'd be looked after.

The cabbie swallowed hard and drove on, travelling much faster now.

After a couple of kilometres, he pulled over again, now almost beside himself with frustration. He wound down the window once more, waving at the dark night. The same noise invaded the cockpit of the car. The same restless trains . . .

'Hey fellas,' said Brendan. 'That's machine-gun fire.'

And indeed it was. A constant shuddering exchange of heavy-calibre guns.

Suddenly, we paid attention to the driver.

He struggled with his frustration, looking for words. One word he kept on repeating: 'Coffee . . . coffee . . .'

What was he on about?

'Curfew!' shouted Cameron from the back.

'Da!' said our cabbie. 'Coffee!'

He pointed to his watch, showing well past midnight. The curfew was already in force, hence the scattering of people from the airport as we arrived. We were driving into who-knows-what at an hour when the army was allowed to shoot anything that moved.

We had no option. We had to keep going.

The driver now picked his route. As we neared the city centre we passed armoured vehicles securing intersections. Troops stood alert. Gasoline drums had been set up as bonfires against the deepening chill.

We crossed a bridge across the Moscow River. There, a kilometre away, was the White House. The top two or three storeys were ablaze.

We made the hotel and felt it best to try to get a couple of hours sleep. There was none for Brendan, though. He had copped the short straw and the pleasure of hosting our driver, who immediately drank dry the minibar and turned the volume up loud on the hotel's in-house supply of hardcore pornography. For Brendan, the new day couldn't come soon enough.

—

We had come too late. By daybreak, the battle for Moscow was over. The machine guns we had heard were the efforts of defeated rebels to break out of the encircling armour of the Russian army, and the army's reply. Hooking up with our affiliates from Britain's ITN, I entered their building to the heartbroken wails of a woman being consoled by a weeping man. It was a French TV crew. Their cameraman, Ivan Scopan, had been killed as rebels attacked the Russian TV headquarters at Ostankino. The rebels had already seized the Moscow City Hall. At the TV centre, they put all but one network off air (the other, RTR, kept broadcasting from an emergency location across town).

Five journalists died during the ferocious assault on Ostankino. Among them was Rory Peck, a redoubtable Northern Irishman whose name lives on through an international award for conflict cameramen and women. Peck was probably killed by shots fired by Yeltsin loyalists.

The rebels' next move was to attempt a takeover of the Kremlin. The army remained loyal to the president, however, and once that became clear the revolution was doomed.

The unfiltered grief of the friends of the fallen Frenchman was a reminder of how real the stakes were, not just for Russia, but for those who were seriously involved in covering it. Two more journalists were killed the following day.

For us, however, it was an anti-climax. We had come after the crux. Huge crowds milled in streets still guarded by tanks but the sting of anger was gone. They gazed at the smouldering remains of their parliament, a symbol of another of the great struggles in the life of Moscow. The tanks rolled out, we filed our yarns. We bought kilos of black market caviar and flew back to London.

Yeltsin held power, popular in the west until his drunkenness and his decline into chicken-dancing embarrassment left him nothing but another footnote. His final act of significance was to choose an obscure spy, Vladimir Putin, to replace him. But that was still years off.

The personal significance of my first Russian adventure was the realisation that walls were not immutable. I had found a way to get in there, with the help of the travel agent and the smooth-talking Cameron Bennett. Perhaps I was developing some instinct for this foreign reporter game.

19

SKASE CHASE

NO ACCOUNT OF A LONDON REPORTER'S LIFE IN THE EARLY 1990S would be complete without mention of Christopher Skase, the creator of hundreds of journalistic holidays to the Mediterranean. The smooth-talking former finance journalist was one of the great villains of the age.

He built a company up from nothing into a multibillion-dollar empire of TV stations and tourism assets. He siphoned shareholder wealth into his own private accounts and then saw it all collapse with $1.5 billion in debts.

Skase was arrested in Queensland, bailed and then fled. He set himself up in a mansion in Majorca, despite claiming to have less than two hundred dollars to his name.

My Nine colleague, Mark Llewellyn, tracked Skase down to an upmarket Majorca restaurant and memorably bailed him up with a camera. It was great television. Skase was the fat cat who ratted out on his shareholders, the mums and dads who had trusted him. Now here he was fleeing an Australian television camera in a taxi while Llewellyn, in a moment of spontaneous genius, convinced the cabbie he was part of the same fare and climbed in with him. Laugh! We certainly did. And all of Australia was in on the joke.

Skase, in company with his loyal wife, Pixie, their daughter and her husband, was shacked up in fine style in the little port town of Andratx. He resisted extradition with claims of ill health. He had himself wheeled into the courtroom while sucking on an oxygen mask. The first court allowed his extradition but he immediately appealed to a higher court in Madrid, the *Audiencia Nacional*. In the meantime, he took up residence in a hospital in the island's main town, Palma.

The Spanish legal process was opaque. All we knew was that the *Audiencia Nacional* only made decisions on Fridays. It would not reveal which cases were up for decision. If your case was not announced by 2 pm Friday from Madrid, you could come back again a week later to see if anything had changed.

Oh, the glorious absurdity of it.

The only way to get into position in Majorca on a Friday should the court make a decision was to take a Thursday flight from London's Heathrow. The Australian contingent would then have a Thursday night to hit the bars, nightclubs and restaurants of this ancient and charismatic island. And hit them we did. The company credit card covered all contingencies. The weather was spectacular after the grey curtains of London and the women were languid and lovely – if utterly out of reach for a bunch of *no hablo espanol* hicks from Australia.

If, by Friday afternoon, the word from Madrid was 'no word' the carousing would hit epic heights. The decision came too late for any flight back to London that day. We would have to take one on the Saturday afternoon. And so, Friday night would glide seamlessly into Saturday as we experienced some of the best clubs and restaurants in the world.

This went on for months.

Majorca has a reputation as the Kuta of Europe, groaning under the weight of sunburnt drunken Poms on their first overseas trip trying to liven things up by picking fights with bogan Germans on the same mission. The Spaniards are no fools, however. They funnelled the package tourists into purpose-built hellholes where they could be with their own kind. They kept Palma for themselves. It was the richest city in Spain. And one of the loveliest and most stylish. We did our best to keep up.

Forget the war zones of Europe. Majorca nearly killed us. One evening, after researching some of the Skase tribe's favoured haunts in Andratx, I found the wheels of our rented car locking up on a gentle corner back to town. A stone wall that appeared to have been there since medieval times chose not to yield to the thin metal of the Citroen. My slackness with seatbelts was not in my favour either. Someone from a neighbouring hacienda took pity on us – it helped that he was a former NBC cameraman who had retired after decades in the Middle East. With a quick glance at our written-off wreck, he drove us back to town while I assured him my arm was fine, just a little sprained.

By 3 am I was in agony, my forearm swollen to the size of my thigh. I have a quaint ritual. When in pain, I try to avoid painkillers and shave instead. I like to think it has something to do with self-mastery. Stupidity, more like it. It was a shaven, but deathly white face that presented itself to the public hospital emergency room sometime before dawn. My hand was shattered in complex ways. It was four months before it finally re-emerged from the cast.

Personally, I blame Skase.

Nothing wonderful lasts forever, of course. One somnolent Friday, as we were struggling to hold off the temptation to nap before the night's adventures, word came through that the *Audiencia Nacional* had finally made a decision. And they'd found in Skase's favour! Too dangerous to move him, they said. We scrambled to the hospital in time to see the rogue being transported out in an ambulance, still sucking on his oxygen mask.

An unseemly chase then followed across the south-western corner of the island until Skase was deposited back at his mansion. Twenty minutes later, he appeared in front of us, arm around Pixie, grinning broadly, with neither wheelchair nor mask. He had scammed Australia and now he had scammed Spain as well. To put himself even further out of reach, he then took out citizenship with the impoverished Dominican Republic. All while staying in Spanish luxury.

In the end, it wasn't the Australian liquidators or John Howard's attorney-general Amanda Vanstone who got Skase. Cancer did that. He died in Spain, his sources of wealth officially unexamined, his thumb firmly to his nose against the Australian business, legal and political establishment.

My one regret is that I was never able to pull him aside to get a little financial advice for myself. Anyone who can stretch two hundred dollars so far, plainly had a gift.

20

FREE AT LAST

AS 1993 DREW TO A CLOSE, I SENT INCREASINGLY URGENT MISSIVES back to Sydney. A date had been set for the South African election. If the vote was not rigged, it would mark the end of apartheid. An issue that had sparked riots and bloodshed, global boycotts and sanctions would finally be laid to rest. I had come of age in its shadow. I had lost friends over arguments about it, and I had tasted the life and death consequences of the policy.

The Sydney news bosses seemed unmoved. Hotel and crucial satellite bookings were filling fast. I sent yet another plea for a decision.

Early in 1994, network executives finally made one. Nine would go at the story full bore. We would spend whatever it took to cover the election across all our news and current affairs shows. We would gamble that Australians cared enough about South Africa to watch whatever we produced.

Our chief commercial rivals, Seven, took a gamble the other way. They calculated the audience had only a passing interest. Instead, they would go lightly on reports out of South Africa and focus heavily on local content instead. They would blindside us.

And so I flew to Johannesburg at the start of April knowing the network's expectations were high, while the prospects of a peaceful election were low.

In the London bureau, cameraman Richard Malone, editor Mark Douglas and I packed for a civil war. The company had invested in state-of-the-art bulletproof vests with ceramic plates for armour. They weighed a tonne. They were streets ahead of the light flak jackets the TVNZ team had been taking into Sarajevo but they came with their own disadvantages. There was no way you could sprint in the new helmets and armour. I feared mobs more than snipers. Even as I packed the vests, I made a promise to myself never to use them.

The fears of war were real, however. The head of the Zulus, Chief Mangosuthu Buthelezi, withheld his Inkatha Freedom Party (IFP) from the electoral process. He demanded constitutional recognition for a Zulu kingdom with its own security apparatus or he would go to war. He had long been a rival of Mandela's African National Congress (ANC). He would not accept a new South Africa in which Zulus were subordinated to a new tyrant, albeit a black one.

It was a sobering time.

The best journalists and photographers in the world were descending on South Africa. The first to die, however, were locals. Just south of Johannesburg, the township of Katlehong and its neighbouring suburb Thokoza were the scenes of almost daily violence. As usual, it was the ANC supporters against the Zulus of the IFP. A new paramilitary unit had been sworn in, a national peacekeeping force made up of anti-apartheid guerrilla fighters who were now being enfolded into the South African Defence Force. It was important that these people had jobs in the new South Africa.

But the peacekeeping force's training and discipline were poor. On the front line of the battles of Thokoza and Katlehong, they were a danger chiefly to themselves. In a long day of lunacy and crossfire, two of South Africa's most famous photographers – members of the legendary Bang-Bang Club – were hit. Ken Oosterbroek died almost instantly. Greg Marinovich, who had won the Pulitzer Prize for his coverage of the township wars, was shot in the chest but survived.

It was a grim reminder that death was ever-present in South Africa and even the most seasoned survivors could fall.

A week short of the election, Nelson Mandela and President F W de Klerk held a meeting with the Zulu leader Buthelezi at the seat of government in Pretoria, the Union Buildings.

Along with almost every other journalist in the country, I crowded into the building to witness, after many hours of waiting, Mandela emerge with Buthelezi and de Klerk. They had cut a deal. Their six-point peace deal included the rejection of violence. Buthelezi would later emerge as Minister for Home Affairs in the new ANC government. In the meantime, he agreed his Inkatha Freedom Party would take part in the election.

The threat of war was over, at least from that source.

The white supremacist peacocks of the Afrikaner Resistance Movement (AWB) were threatening their own war of resistance. These odious bullies summoned the world's media to a little frontier cottage that was once the home of the nineteenth-century Boer independence hero Paul Kruger. Paramilitaries stood guard while we were all prayed over by the Dutch Reformed *dominee* and then subjected to a sneering lecture by the thug in chief Eugène Terre'Blanche.

It was an awful diatribe. The Dutch had brought civilisation and the bible to South Africa. The Boers had tamed the land. The blacks were an uncivilised race who, to the degree that they had been raised up at all, owed that advancement to the benevolence of the God-fearing and sturdy Boers. And so on. While Terre'Blanche spat and growled, his goons made constant threats of violence to the camera crews whom they had invited. Pressed in near the front, trying to catch the audio on a short boom pole, I couldn't see or hear anything going on behind me. However, a long rant from Terre'Blanche in Afrikaans sparked a shiver through the crowd, followed by shouts of 'No!' from some of the journalists.

'What's he saying?' I asked a blonde South African reporter beside me.

She shook her head, clearly upset.

The cries from the rear were building up.

'Seriously, what is he saying up there?'

She relented.

'He's saying, "The cameras can stay, but there's a slave at the back, get rid of the slave at the back."'

One of the reporters was an African-American from the *New York Times*. Sure enough, he was rough-handled out of the media scrum and expelled.

'We should all just walk away,' urged one woman.

But journalists are impossible to herd and never take instructions from each other. The story remained with the racists. I stayed to cover them and so did most of the rest of the pack, reporting the expulsion of our colleague.

The white resistance movement would have been comical had their tactics not been so murderous. They set a series of massive car bombs in and around Johannesburg. One was just around the corner from our city hotel. Nine's *Sunday* host, Jim Waley, was close by and was badly shaken by the blast. Nine people died.

The second bomb went off in the racially mixed suburb of Germiston, just to the south-east of the CBD. I was with Richard Malone and Cameron Bennett on a nearby highway when we heard the news and, within minutes, we were on the scene.

There were no police tapes or any sign of order. The blast had happened where minibuses picked up and dropped off passengers around a train station. The streets were named after World War I battlefields – Somme, Vimy Ridge and so on – and the titles seemed grimly apt.

A row of trees had been shredded of branches and leaves. In the top of a solid plane tree were the remains of a minibus, bizarrely upright as if it had been placed there. Survivors were reeling in shock. I heard no screaming or wailing. It was oddly quiet. We didn't dive in with Richard's camera to the heart of the carnage. We spoke to bewildered people, whose incoherence was more eloquent than words. We worked almost as automatons. As we shifted position I noticed that a metre from where I stood was a severed human foot. Ten people died that lunchtime in one of more than a dozen bombings in a right-wing campaign to discourage voting. A caller rang a conservative newspaper to claim responsibility, warning that the blasts so far were a 'picnic' compared with what would come.

As we left the bombsite that day, Richard Malone and I had a blazing row. It was out of nowhere and about nothing, and totally unprecedented in our working relationship. Psychologists talk of 'moral injuries', profound disturbances to our core sense of what is proper and right. Our stoush was doubtless symptomatic of such things but we had little psychological awareness back then.

What we'd seen simply shook us all. It was an act of terrorism, with the victims – as always – blameless ordinary folk getting about their day.

Despite these terrorist attacks, Buthelezi's decision to enter the election fray had cut the tension between the Zulus and everyone else in the townships. It was possible, with a little care, to wander quite freely around Soweto, where less than two years earlier it had been all but fatal. I spent a couple of hours drinking rank spirits in a shanty shebeen, an unlicensed grog-house, at the raucous insistence of the patrons. They gave lively, if not particularly profound, assessments of how life might be under Nelson Mandela.

On another trip down a highway fringing Soweto we came upon a horrible car crash. A heavily laden minivan had spun off the road and rolled into a cyclone-wire fence. Inside the van was a poor white Afrikaans family. At least one man was plainly dead, others were in various states of injury. I concentrated on a middle-aged woman who had been flung from the vehicle, hitting the fence so hard she'd left an imprint on the wire. She was drifting in and out of consciousness. Some young men from the black shanties on the other side of the fence clambered over to help. Their concern was genuine and their care tender. As the woman drifted back to wakefulness, her look of horror at realising she was surrounded by black faces was as great a tragedy as the accident itself.

As a bare-bones ambulance rolled up from Baragwanath hospital, we withdrew from the scene. Just down the road we saw streets neatly laid out for a new subdivision. Where plots had been marked out for houses, ragged tents and shanties had sprung up. It was such an odd image, we pulled over to have a look.

This fresh-born settlement already had its neighbourhood ANC official, a chest-puffing braggart of a youth. With sufficient obsequiousness towards him, we earned the right to talk to some of the people.

The poorest, it appeared, was a lean, bearded bloke called Zacariah who had come up from Bloemfontein in the hope of gaining labouring work for twenty rands a day – about a dollar. It was better than anything he could get back home in the Orange Free State. He lived in a torn scrap of white woven plastic, like those red-white-and-blue zip-up bags that are so often seen around Asia. He appeared to possess nothing else but the ragged clothes he wore. His great hope was to make enough money to allow his wife and young son to join him.

The vote was by now just a couple of days away.

'What do you hope will come from the change to black rule in South Africa?' I asked him on camera. I hoped for some poetic statement of what freedom meant, some earthy expression of the long-hoped-for goal of liberation.

'Oh, well . . .' he began shyly. 'I don't want to expect too much.'

'Surely you hope it will bring some change,' I pressed.

'Well, what I really hope for . . . what I would really like . . . is some corrugated iron.'

I was moved by the modesty of his ambitions. I shook his hand and wished him well. As would happen so often, I felt drenched in an awareness of my own ridiculously privileged existence. I felt Zacariah, with his patience, hard work and optimism, was by far a better man than I.

As a postscript, I returned a year later to report on the first year of the country under ANC rule. I raced down to this little place, more modest even than the township shanties. I encountered again the ANC street official, slightly chubbier but just as swaggeringly rude as the year before. I asked if Zacariah was around. No, Zacariah was back in Bloemfontein organising for his family to join him.

'Did he ever get any corrugated iron?'

'Yes! He has a house.'

I asked to see it, and was taken to the best house on the little cluster of streets, a two-room shanty of unlined corrugated iron carefully washed with thin white paint. Neatly aligned scrap metal marked out a tiny front garden. Modest as it was, it shone with an owner's pride. I met Zacariah just once, for a few minutes. I think of him more often than he could ever imagine.

—

During this time, I got to see Nelson Mandela in action. I had encountered him first in 1990 in Melbourne when he visited Australia soon after his release. I saw him again at the Union Buildings in Pretoria announcing the peace deal with Buthelezi. At both events, Mandela had been generally unsmiling and austere, the unquestionable grown-up in the room. Now, in Soweto on the eve of the election, I came to a deeper understanding of his power.

The Soweto football stadium rose like a spacecraft out of the hard-baked dust at the edge of the township. All day, youths streamed out of the slums and the squatter camps, the shanties and the hostels. They came as warriors, tight units of young men covering ground fast in the half-jog, half-dance known as the *toyi-toyi*. In their hands, held high, were homemade weapons – axes, knives, machetes and clubs.

Cameron Bennett, Richard Malone and I watched from a small rise, not unhappy to have a row of armoured vehicles behind us. The men came in their thousands until the dust from their feet obscured the stadium. Judging the risk worth it, I walked down to find these men almost in a trance from their chanting and rhythmic movement. They gave no sign of noticing I was even there and I was able to go right up to them to take photographs.

Richard and I had indulged in a little camouflage, buying cheap baseball hats with the ANC and South African Communist Party logo on them. Grinning widely, we made our way through the security checks and took a place in the stand to await the great man's arrival.

The deepest fear, here on the very eve of the election, was that Mandela would be assassinated.

Eventually, he turned up, taking his place on a podium set up on the grass. The stands erupted. Gunfire broke out. Somehow, despite all the precautions, people had smuggled in weapons. Mandela didn't flinch. These were shots of joy, exuberant firings into the air, though no one in the instant of hearing them could be certain.

Mandela raised his hands and finally settled the crowd.

At that moment, he could have said anything. He could have ordered the multitude to go from that stadium into the homes of their race enemies to rape and murder and the mob would have done it without hesitation.

Mandela's first act was to address those who had fired guns. His voice was stern, as full of patriarchal power as an ancient prophet. Those who had brought in guns had shown immaturity and a failure of discipline, he lectured. The new South Africa had no place for such failings. Those people had let the crowd down, they had let themselves down, they had let him down.

A shamed silence fell upon the crowd.

Mandela then launched into his speech. We must never forget, he said, the sacrifices made by Indians under apartheid. They too had been excluded from the fruits of the land. They too had struggled to be free. He named South Africans of Indian extraction who had helped him along his journey. He reminded them that Mahatma

Gandhi had begun his campaigns of civil disobedience here in South Africa against white rule.

Mandela went on and on.

There was not a single Indian in the crowd. Their population base was hundreds of kilometres away in the cities of the eastern coast. Had he brought the wrong speech? The crowd which had begun by cheering his every gesture fell silent.

After twenty minutes, Mandela wrapped up. There was no lap of honour, no pumping of the mob. He simply left. The thousands of people there went quietly home.

What other leader could have denied themselves the thrill of riding all that adulation? Who else could have said no to the temptation to have that crowd in their hands, to play to their passions, to feel that uplift? It wouldn't even have been wrong to do it. These people of Soweto had waited so long. Why not give them the show they wanted?

But Mandela had another purpose. The new South Africa would have a leadership that looked like the people. Their skins would be, for the most part, black. That victory was assured as long as the election was held and wasn't rigged. What Mandela wanted was for the new victors to understand the responsibility that came with that power. He asked them to consider a group about whom they had probably never passed much thought. He wanted not triumphalism but empathy.

Like the crowd, I felt a little disappointed. I would have loved a soaring speech that sent roars of power circling around the stadium. I would have loved rhetoric as memorable as Martin Luther King's on that autumn day in Washington more than thirty years earlier. Mandela gave no quotable quotes, no sound bites to be replayed through the generations but never had I admired him more. Demagogues are far too common, true leaders all too rare.

—

The day of the vote came: 27 April 1994. From before dawn, people who had never been able to vote for anything in their lives queued patiently for their chance. The day passed peacefully on a cloud of something that felt like a national euphoria. As Mandela had long argued, this was the day of white liberation too, the sloughing off of a long burden of sin and shame.

All things seemed possible.

I wandered through Soweto with Richard Malone. We stood and watched children performing gymnastic feats in the dirt lanes, showing off and shouting. A man in his fifties called Seymour wandered up and we shook hands.

'From today,' he said, 'I can come to your house and we can eat dinner together.'

'Yes,' I replied, 'and I can come to your place and eat dinner with you.'

Let there always be a place for Seymour at my table.

The gamble to go heavily on South African coverage had more than paid off. Nine's news ratings went up and stayed there. One executive reckoned the South African story proved the financial value of foreign bureaus so effectively they were safe from the accountants' knives for years afterwards. As a foreign correspondent, it is enormously gratifying to know the audience is interested in what interests you.

It took several days for the vote to be counted. Speed mattered less than the integrity of the process. As April tipped into May, rumours swirled that an official declaration would be made in the next twenty-four to forty-eight hours.

The ANC had set up a VIP space in Johannesburg's downtown Carlton Hotel. As luck would have it, we were staying there. As security became increasingly tight, we had the best possible excuse for entering the building whenever we wanted to.

The VIP ballroom had its own security cordon, but we had a secret weapon on our side. Mandy, our South African 'fixer', was one of those absolute gems that luck sometimes sends your way. An

Afrikaner – and a Mormon – she had a gift with people, as well as long and deep connections within the ANC. Through her, we got one of the priceless passes into the ANC victory-party-in-waiting. The first night, nothing happened. There was no announcement from the electoral commission. We amused ourselves by spotting some of the lions of the anti-apartheid struggle: Tanzania's president Julius Nyerere and the Zambian leader Kenneth Kaunda (whose name – properly pronounced – had gained me the approval of the radio course director in Christchurch more than fifteen years before). There were white figures from the struggle, too – the Lithuanian Jew Joe Slovo whose activist wife had been murdered by the South African security forces. Slovo had risen to lead the armed wing of the ANC – an extraordinary position for a white man – as well as heading the South African Communist Party. Jobs had to be found for such figures and Slovo became housing minister in the new government until cancer claimed him just a few months later. Also there was Albie Sachs, a human rights lawyer who lost an arm and an eye to a car bomb set by a government hit squad.

Cyril Ramaphosa was there, a younger generation leader who had built his power base through the unions. Many felt he would be Mandela's choice for prime minister but the party went instead for Thabo Mbeki.

The following night we returned. Mandela hadn't been seen for days. There were rumours he was exhausted and sick. The ballroom filled again with the great and the good of the anti-apartheid movement. There was still no word on when the election results would be declared – or by whom. It was quite possible this historic announcement would go to some nameless electoral commission bureaucrat.

Sometime, late in the evening, with a band playing up on the stage, the music suddenly went ragged and stopped. From stage left, picking his way over the electrical leads, came Mandela himself. He was wearing a chocolate brown patterned shirt, buttoned at the throat, as was his style. Not even the VIPs seemed aware he was coming. The room fell suddenly silent as he took a place behind the microphone.

'I wish to inform you,' he began, his reedy voice more raspy than usual, 'that twenty minutes ago I received a phone call from the head of the electoral commission . . .'

He proceeded to detail the results of the count. His face throughout was expressionless, his voice flat and serious. He concluded with the key figure. The ANC had won with more than sixty-two percent of the vote.

'Now,' he said, 'we know the true meaning of the words: "Free at last, free at last, thank God Almighty we are free at last."'

They were the words that closed Martin Luther King's speech in Washington, words that themselves were sung in a Negro spiritual from the age of slaves. And with them, Mandela suddenly smiled, and a woman burst into a shrill ululation, and everyone in the room who was not a sober and dispassionate journalist jumped up and down like they were punks pogo-ing to Johnny Rotten, so urgent was the need to leap in the air and scream for joy. It was unforgettable.

The band struck up and, for a couple of minutes, Mandela held the stage and danced – the little two-step *toyi-toyi* – beaming with pleasure. And then with a raised clenched fist that softened into the wave of his arm, he disappeared.

We had the story of our lifetimes – or so it seemed at the time. We were there at the very moment Mandela told those closest to him that the struggle had been won. His twenty-seven years in jail, the piled corpses across townships and fields, every sacrifice seemed justified at last.

Freedom. It is a hell of a word.

But we still had to get it to air.

I raced up to get something from my room, bursting through the door. As I grabbed notebooks and tapes, a noise like a faulty air conditioner needled me. It sounded like out-of-service machinery, wheezing and roaring, rising and falling. I realised it was coming from outside. The window, well over twenty floors up, opened as if it was a suburban home. As I swung it open, the roar burst in like a tidal force. There in the streets below me were hundreds of thousands of people, pressing in to the heart of Johannesburg, to the place where Mandela was. The word had reached them. Even from my height the sound was astonishing. There were no cars I could see, just countless black heads and black faces in the dark night, dancing and surging, beating drums and blowing horns.

In the lobby, security was in a panic. There was no way they could have held a surge through the main hotel doors. The guards looked at us in disbelief as we signalled we wanted to get out. We had to file the story. I was willing to gamble that the mob would be friendly. I certainly wasn't going to give up without a try. The head of security clearly thought we were mad.

We were immediately engulfed by the dancing crowd. The mood was ebullient, but edgy. Posters of the Zulu leader Buthelezi were being set on fire. There was no such contempt directed at de Klerk or the National Party but, in a sense, they were already history.

Behind us, the gates to the basement car park opened and a canary yellow Porsche Carrera emerged. Plainly the driver, a thick-set middle-aged white guy, had no idea what he was heading in to. His face went shades paler as within seconds he was surrounded. Richard shifted his camera to catch whatever was about to happen. And then the driver, thinking quickly, lowered his window and stuck a meaty forearm up into the air. Clenching his fist, he bellowed 'Amandla!' – the cry of black defiance and solidarity – and bellowing it for all he was worth he edged through the crowd unmolested until he disappeared from view.

When people ask me what was the biggest story I ever covered, I like to quote the one I filed that night. It probably wasn't the biggest, whatever that means. But news tends heavily to favour the awful. This was a night radiant with freedom and joy, a night of biblical promise, when the yoke of an enslaved people was finally thrown down. In life – in history – there are few moments of such power.

Since that night, South Africa has fared better than many people predicted but it has also been a disappointment. Far too many people still live in poverty as gruelling as ever existed under white rule. A racist police state has been replaced by a corrupt one. And it is getting worse. Violence remains constant, striking rich and poor alike. Yet it is still better now than it was back then because race is no longer a weapon to keep people disempowered and poor.

There remained only Mandela's inauguration. Australia was given two seats. Prime Minister Paul Keating insisted his two predecessors, Bob Hawke and Malcolm Fraser, should have the honour in acknowledgement of their efforts in the long fight.

The day dawned sunny, with 100,000 people crowding the lawns in front of the seat of government, the Union Buildings in Pretoria. Armoured vehicles were stationed on streets blocked and managed with razor wire. But the mood was serene. Late in the afternoon, as I walked out to retrieve our car, a black limousine swept up alongside me. The door swung open to reveal the Pakistani Prime Minister, Benazir Bhutto. She left it open as a flunky stepped out from the other side and crossed in front of me to a Pizza Hut, returning a few minutes later with piles of pizza. It was that kind of day.

The sun was setting by the time we pulled up outside the Australian ambassador's residence. Hawke and Fraser were guests of honour for celebratory drinks.

Bob turned up first, well lubricated and cranky.

'Ahhhhh . . . are you going to ask me stupid fucking questions like you always do?' he demanded. I was a little taken aback. I hadn't asked him many questions at all outside routine press conferences and I suspected my queries were generally pretty run-of-the-mill.

Anyway, I pressed on and as soon as the camera was rolling he was Statesman Bob, reflecting on the meaning of the Mandela inauguration and Australia's role in this moment.

Malcolm Fraser was a different type. I knew him slightly, having spent a day with him once at his farm at Nareen. I had also – I admit this now – rung his wife Tamie on the day news broke that Mr Fraser had been found trouserless in the lobby of a Memphis Hotel.

To my surprise, Mrs Fraser had answered the phone herself.

Her husband had told her he had been robbed by a woman he had met at a bar. He suspected she had spiked his drink.

'And do you believe him?' I asked.

'What other explanation could there possibly be?' said Mrs Fraser. An unimprovable answer under the circumstances. She politely put an end to the call.

Now here was Malcolm Fraser towering over me.

'Do you want to talk about South Africa or Rwanda?' he asked politely.

I had been focused on South Africa's election for so many weeks, I knew nothing about what was breaking in Rwanda beyond a few snippets on car radios as we'd moved about.

'It is genocide,' said Fraser. 'The biggest and fastest movement of refugees since World War II.'

I felt ashamed I knew so little about it.

'I am flying up there tomorrow,' he said. 'Do you want to come with me?'

One of the happiest events of the century was over. The pendulum was now swinging hard towards the darkness. And I was riding on it.

21

GENOCIDE

WITH A QUICK CALL TO CHANNEL NINE'S NEWS SUPREMO, PETER
Meakin, in Sydney to get the nod, I boarded a flight to Nairobi
with Richard Malone. Malcolm Fraser was up the front of the
plane. I was on a crash course to catch up with events in Rwanda.
I fell into conversation with Matthew Fisher, a reporter from the
Toronto Sun. He had hopes of getting a UN flight into the Rwandan
capital of Kigali as the airport was being held by a tiny force led
by his fellow Canadian, Roméo Dallaire.

Fisher understood what was going on and had a plan. I was flying
north in a state of abject ignorance. Remember – there was no
Google. I snatched at whatever newspapers I could find, spoke to
whoever I could. The reports suggested a nation slaughtering itself.
It appeared to be an ethnic or tribal conflict conducted in a frenzy
of annihilation. Even those clues, however, told a false tale. It was
not conflict, but genocide. The majority of the Rwandan population who identified as Hutus were hacking with machetes their
neighbours who were Tutsis. Any Hutus who objected to what was
going on, risked being murdered alongside the Tutsis they hoped
to protect. Many were.

Malcolm Fraser was at the time the head of CARE International,
a US-based aid agency. I presume it was their money that was used

to charter a light aircraft at Nairobi Airport. We were soon heading west across the magnificent Rift Valley and the plains of the Maasai and the Serengeti. After a brief stop at Mwanza at the southern edge of Lake Victoria, we took off again to land soon afterwards on a dirt strip surrounded by towering grasses.

A crude chain-driven ferry took us across a river to a waiting four-wheel drive. We ground our way up a rutted track and found ourselves on a narrow shingle road slicing through a mixture of forest and open grassland. This was the central African plateau, close to the equator but high enough to take the raw heat out of the sun. We were crossing western Tanzania, bound for the Rwandan border. For many kilometres we saw no signs of life.

After an hour or so, we crested a rise to see a low, broad hill blanketed with people. We drove into what had become, almost overnight, the second largest city in Tanzania. A city without a building. It was impossible to see the crowd from beginning to end. People were clustering in family groups wherever there was space to collapse. The trail in from the north-west was alive with more people walking in from the Rwandan border.

In this human river, I met a man pushing a wheelbarrow containing a sack of rice and a little girl, about three years old. Her eyes were gummed with pus and her breathing was raspy and laboured. She was desperately sick. The father's effort in getting her so far spoke of the endless, nameless acts of quiet human heroism. Nearby was a woman, vastly pregnant. Her husband had been 'lost' on the journey, she told us. She had been walking for seven days. The ragged, crowded hilltop represented her hopes for safety.

Malcolm Fraser strode around the lower edge of the hillside seeking briefings from the various agencies busy establishing tent warehouses in the hope some food would come. A couple of truck-loads had arrived. Surprisingly to me, there was no panic in the crowds, no evidence of acute desperation – certainly nothing on the scale I had seen in Somalia.

'These people are not starving,' said a Tanzanian Red Cross worker. 'Don't feel too much sympathy for them – these are the Hutus. These are the ones who have been carrying out the genocide.'

Suddenly, I saw what I had missed before. At the fringes of the crowd were bands of young men dangling machetes. Some seemed to be organised. Others simply stood in clusters of sullen menace. One prowled by a few metres away, sustaining eye contact as he passed with his machete propped upon his shoulder. His look conveyed contempt and arrogance. 'I've got you if I want you,' the eyes said. 'You are nothing to me.'

Malcolm Fraser strode up. He was worried. People were drawing drinking water from a muddy and stagnant dam. That was the best of it. There was no sanitation, no shelter and nowhere near enough food.

We drove the short distance to the border itself. A bridge crossed the Kagera River. On the other side was Rwanda. A Tanzanian soldier lazed in the burnt-out ruins of a car. The refugee flows were avoiding this bridge, crossing at a ford lower down. The soldier blocked us from driving into Rwanda but had no objection to us walking across the bridge.

The Kagera River was swollen from seasonal rains. As we walked out onto the bridge we realised the river was thick with corpses.

Like a brown, rushing conveyor belt, dozens, scores, hundreds of bodies flowed beneath us. All appeared naked and hideously bloated. They stalled for a moment at the crux of a cataract, the Rusumo Falls, and then tipped over into the roaring water to bob and eddy and resume their journey downstream. An endless, piteous soup of lost humanity, silent proof of the horrors taking place upstream. Malcolm Fraser and I stood a little distance apart, saying nothing, trying to absorb what we were witnessing.

The genocide would continue for another two months. But the crowds on the nearby hill were proof the tide was turning. They were fleeing the Tutsi-dominated Rwandan Patriotic Army (RPA), which was sweeping in from bases in Uganda. The Hutus who were fleeing south and east, and who were now occupying the hill behind us, would soon be dwarfed by the numbers fleeing west into Zaire (now the Democratic Republic of Congo). Cholera and internecine warfare would claim more until the UN calculated five million people had died in what some have called Africa's World War.

(I had many further encounters with Malcolm Fraser and interviewed him on many subjects. In 2011, I was covering the Commonwealth Heads of Government Meeting in Perth. Fraser was on a panel at a seminar attached to the summit meeting. I dropped in to listen and to catch up with him afterwards.

Just as we parted ways, I turned back to him.

'I don't expect you necessarily to remember,' I said, 'but I was with you in –'

'The bridge,' he said, cutting me short.

'Yes,' I replied. 'The bridge.'

We looked at each other for a few moments, both stirred again by indelible images.

I never saw him again.)

—

The afternoon was passing and there was work to be done. Fraser took off with the four-wheel drive on business of his own while Richard Malone and I continued filming. We agreed to meet up at 6 pm to get out of there.

At 6 pm there was no Fraser and no car. I had packed a survival kit in our brief time in Nairobi – a couple of blankets, water, medical kit, some emergency food – but foolishly I had left that in the car. We were now without food, water or shelter at the edge of a seething refugee camp where an epidemic was being predicted at any hour. Those things were mere inconveniences. More pressingly, we had no means to charge our camera batteries. More pressingly still, the lads with their machetes had noticed us. We were being watched and talked about. We were starting to feel uncomfortable.

Where the hell were Fraser and the car?

With no other options, we stood at the side of the track and hoped to thumb a lift. If need be, we could try to impose on the aid workers for a corner of their tent but we didn't want to bring them unwelcome attention. Their lives were tenuous enough.

The road remained resolutely empty of vehicles.

Africa sank towards twilight.

Richard and I shared a cigarette. 'Dickie' was a cameraman of great talent and deep eccentricity whose left-field humour had redeemed many a bleak moment. It got a good run now. We had a couple of laughs. After a while, we had another cigarette.

Just when the mercy of the aid workers seemed like our only option, a Toyota ute rattled up the road from nowhere. It stopped, as if hitch-hikers were routine.

'Where do you need to go?' The accent was French.

'Anywhere will do.'

We threw our camera gear into the back and clambered on board with an 'up yours!' grin towards the machete boys.

The sky turned a deeper blue. The few high clouds took on ever richer colours. The vehicle roared along the rough track through fields of high savannah grass shining with gold in the green. Without food, Dickie and I dragged merrily on his cigarettes – a habit I try to avoid but which seemed, on the evening of this strange day, like a perfectly agreeable diet.

In the back of the truck with us was a beautiful Spaniard with long dark hair that blew in the African air. She laughed freely. The focus of her attention was an equally beautiful Frenchman who sat with his back to the cabin and bantered in return. Both were doctors with Médecins Sans Frontières (MSF). They were flirting with keen, concentrated intent.

Watching them, I was struck with a question: what on earth is real?

The pregnant refugee labouring that night in the wretched camp? Was she real? What of the gaspings of the child in the wheelbarrow? Or the last despairing moments of the people whose bodies, even in the darkness, were still floating down the thick brown Kagera River?

But was the serenity and perfection of a high country African evening not equally real? Or the careless delight of these two lovers, far from home and alive in their freedom? How could a human imagination balance this blend of sweetness and evil?

Somewhere in these questions lay the perplexing nature of a reporter's life. How could I sit in London enjoying a beer with friends, knowing people were starving to death where I had been just the day before? I was aware of a pattern. At times in Somalia I felt like a fraud, like a mere tourist exploiting the pornographic extremes of what I was seeing. But, with more time in Africa, the horrors started to make sense. At that point, my comfortable life between the trips felt like a fraud.

But on the back of that ute, I had a moment of enlightenment. All of it was real. No moment displaced the others. The good was real. The bad was real. The killers. The lovers. The machetes. The soft night. Nothing was everything. At any moment in the world there is always both horror and joy, grief and laughter, fear and boredom. So – and people might groan at the platitudinous nature of my great discovery – you can do nothing but live as completely as you can with whatever is in front of you.

It may sound simple. It certainly doesn't sound like much. But such serenity as I have found has stemmed from what became clear to me that night.

We were in luck. In the now moonless dark, muted lights appeared at the side of the road ahead. We farewelled the MSF crew and stumbled towards the source. Suddenly, an old man rose from the darkness and thrust a spear into our faces. He looked at us without expression. Behind him a generator thrummed.

We stood.

He decided.

He turned and we followed him towards a large canvas tent. I flung open the flap.

'Rimmo!'

'Jigga!'

On a nameless hillside in the middle of Africa, I had stumbled onto a tent occupied by Peter Gigliotti, who had worked with me as a sound recordist years before in Melbourne. He was now with an international satellite dish operator called Newsforce, based in Cyprus. Nothing like an old mate when you need one.

Suddenly we had food to eat, a corner of a tent for shelter, a means to charge batteries and – unbelievably – a system for filing a story back to Sydney.

A couple of days later, we found our way back to Nairobi and got a seat on an overnight flight back to London. We had one more story to file. We could do it from there. Treating ourselves to seats in business class, we were at the front of the plane when a man stumbled in just as the doors were closing.

It was Matthew Fisher, the Canadian journalist I had met on the way up. He was wearing the same tan suit, now stinking and stained. In fact, he was wearing the same blue checked shirt. I caught his sleeve. He was unshaven, hollow-eyed and agitated.

Yes, he had got into Kigali. He had been on patrols with the Canadians. Artillery fire was more or less constant, he said. He saw people being hacked to death with machetes in full view of the UN troops and tortured in ways too hideous to describe. They found some people hiding in a building, who ran towards them but were shot or chopped down before they could reach the vehicle. Across the capital there were bodies in their thousands. The dogs feasted. The hospital had been abandoned except by one Dutch nurse who was trying to treat the wounded with few dressings and no pain-killers. It was stinking, screaming bedlam. Many people had had their feet cut off. Those still living dragged themselves around the streets in agony and terror, or simply gave up. Any passing killer was free to dispatch them.

The passengers in the cabin were transfixed. Fisher seemed not to know where he was. An air hostess took his elbow and began to urge him to his seat.

'Look!' he cried. 'I've got photos.'

He dredged from an inside pocket a roll of photographic proofs.

They were taken in the hospital. A young girl sat at the edge of a cot. Her legs were missing below the knee. The stumps were bandaged. She stared at the camera. Her mouth, as she screamed, formed a perfect O.

22

THE CHAMPAGNE COCKTAIL THEORY

I RETURNED TO LONDON IN MORE THAN A LITTLE TURMOIL. WE HAD missed the Rwanda story. I felt we had been close to it without really telling it. We should have stayed, found a way in. I had no doubt Rwanda was so huge, so dark, it would reframe thinking about peacekeeping missions for years to come. How could so many people, half a million . . . more than a million – who knew? – be slaughtered in a matter of weeks and so little be known about it?

I knew there was a deliberate desire for it *not* to be talked about. The world had piled into Somalia and it had ended with the bodies of Americans being dragged through the streets. The people behind the Rwandan genocide were hideous beyond belief, but they weren't fools. The first thing they did was capture some Belgian peacekeepers, torture them and murder them. They had seen Somalia. They knew the west had plenty to say about peacekeeping efforts when the casualties were slight and the public relations good. They had also seen how the west packed up and fled the minute their troops were killed and their bodies desecrated.

So that was what they had done. And sure enough, the world had kept its distance.

My newsroom bosses seemed indifferent to the story anyway.

The main 6 pm bulletins went to air as middle Australia sat down to dinner. There was only so much horror you could feed to people at dinnertime before they switched channels. This calculation, second nature to the seasoned producers at Nine, was still a shock to me. I worked to slightly different arithmetic. The bigger the human story, the closer you should get to it, the more loudly you should tell it. But I was wrong. Who is to blame someone for not wanting to be confronted with the whole awful truth about something that they can't change anyway?

Over time, I developed my own method of telling stories about confronting events. I call it 'The Champagne Cocktail Theory'.

Once upon a time, *The Bulletin* magazine ran a cover story on alcohol. Amid the pages of discussion of policy and practice in a keen drinking nation like Australia, there was a little break-out article about how the body takes alcohol in.

It put the question: what was the fastest way to get drunk? Apparently drinking straight spirits was not the answer. Above about twenty-two percent alcohol, so the article explained, the body treats alcohol as a poison. The stomach moves automatically to slow down its absorption. Gargling down beer or even wine is not the fastest way to get hammered for the obvious reason that the alcohol concentration is too low.

The perfect combination is a drink with twenty-two percent alcohol content, which is slightly sweet and ideally effervescent. The bubbles help the stomach relax, further speeding the absorption. The drink which does all this perfectly is the classic champagne cocktail.

Into a chilled flute, place a cube of sugar lightly coloured with Angostura Bitters. Add a splash of brandy or cognac (enough to raise the overall alcohol content a little, but not too much). Top the glass with champagne and, the article explained, you could understand why this little drink was famous as the perfect party starter.

It is also the perfect metaphor for a foreign correspondent trying to engage an audience with deeply distressing news.

You can't write the full horror. People recoil as if it were poison. You lose them. But nor can you soften it so much that the audience gets no sense of the truth. You must concoct your own champagne cocktail – strong enough to leave no doubt what is going on, light enough to give the viewer permission to keep watching.

As a journalist, I have been trying to mix that cocktail for most of my adult life.

My return to London also marked the final departure of my long-suffering wife, Sue, back to Australia, taking with her my beloved daughter Caitlin. The inevitability of this parting did not make it any less dismal or sad. A few days later, extracting a heavy tripod from the boot of a taxi, I wrenched my back leaving me with agonising spasms. The London cabbie, who had experienced back problems of his own, very generously helped me into my cold and empty home. I collapsed onto the bed, shot through with pain.

It was a useful moment.

I realised that I was done with pessimism. Miserable, bereft, alone and hurting, I recognised that optimism was the only state of mind of any damned use. I have been an optimist ever since. And it has generally been a more accurate predictor of the future than despair.

I became more than ever a travelling man. Channel Nine was generous in allowing its foreign crews to take days off after extended periods in the field. On a whim, I would take off, to Scotland, the west of Ireland, to Jersey where my father was born and where his sister still lived in well-seasoned elegance. My ambition after my first visit to Paris was to go there more times than I could possibly remember. I achieved that goal and then some. The Greek Islands, the Amalfi coast, countless picturesque towns across England, I filled my gaps with restless movement. I lost all friends who required reliability. I cemented friendships with those who did not. Two Aussie journalists, Dennis and Miri Broadfield, lived in grand style in Kent. They welcomed me to their table there and to their retreat in the south of France. I made friends with a Serbian soprano

– a sentence my former Christchurch schoolboy self could never have imagined – and my knowledge of the opera rapidly improved.

Something about London makes things possible. I have none of the instincts of a socialite and yet I found myself at parties with figures of the moment – there was Boy George, oh, look that's Pierce Brosnan between outings as James Bond. When the Australian musical *Tap Dogs* hit the West End I was invited to the show and the after-party. I was yarning with the ferociously fit young Aussie dancers when slender fingers worked their way into my hand and I turned to find Paula Yates in extremely close proximity. She was then still married to Sir Bob Geldof and was yet to have her famous fling with Michael Hutchence. I had met her once before, on the set of her TV show. This is not a story about my wild affair with one of the most notorious – and tragic – *femme fatales* of her times. It was quickly clear she wanted an introduction to the young dancers, with whom she was soon flirting as if it was an Olympic sport. Paula Yates received terrible press in the end as her life spiralled into grief and addictions. I prefer to remember the woman of irrepressible mischief and presence who stole the hearts of two of the most eligible men of her age and who briefly – I admit it with a glow – held my hand.

There was a sleepless week in the south of France, where a friend had secured me an access-all-areas pass to the Cannes Film Festival. An American scriptwriter invited me to the MTV party on the beach. Tina Turner was the main act. She came down a staircase more than a little wobbly on her feet, disappeared into a screened-off area and wasn't seen again. That was okay. The warm-up act was Freak Power, the vehicle that launched Norman Cook (aka Fatboy Slim) onto the world. So they played all night.

All of this was well and good but my mind was constantly away in other places. I felt in exile from that darker reality I had touched on in Africa. Trips to Northern Ireland and to Russia on assignment for the *Sunday* show tested me in various ways. The great Robert Penfold had been recalled to Australia. The biggest yarns going around were now mine.

Not all the great stories were grim. I spent a week with Richard Malone in Bordeaux ahead of a Wallabies test match against France. Some very good wine was drunk. I think the Wallabies won. I do remember it was the first 'run-on' test match for a rising young fullback called Matthew Burke. He gave a perfectly poised television interview, an on-camera skill I would see up close when we shared a news desk for Channel Ten in Sydney more than twenty years later. His rugby career was not too shabby either, kicking twenty-five points to win the World Cup in 1999.

Another unforgettable privilege was covering, in 1993, the return to the Western Front of fourteen Australian veterans of World War I. Their average age was ninety-five. With them were seven war widows. They were a great bunch, a living link to one of the most inexplicable human calamities of a blood-soaked century. Ted Smout was probably the liveliest of them. As soon as they landed in Paris he was sporting a beret and flirting and charming whoever he met. He had grown up a barefoot Queenslander. In the filth and mud of flooded trenches, he developed sophisticated drainage systems that probably saved his life. He became so much in demand for his skills that he was called behind the front lines to explain his methods just before one engagement that wiped out most of his mates.

We only expected to do a couple of stories at the beginning of their trip and then leave them to it but every day they charmed their way deeper into Australians' hearts.

'You're making my mum cry,' a senior producer told me one night from Sydney. The tour became far more than a quaint historical curiosity. It became a national phenomenon. One day outside Arras, as I clambered onto the bus, I noticed a newcomer. John Howard had joined the tour. His father and grandfather had both served in World War I. By late 1993, his political career appeared finished and he had time on his hands. If a genie from a bottle had popped up to tell him he would end up the second-longest-serving prime minister in Australian history, I think even he would have laughed.

Every day would bring at least two visits to the vast war cemeteries dotted over Belgium and northern France. To walk the old battlefields with men who were there all those years ago was profoundly moving. One veteran, Howard Pope, asked permission to make a side trip to a much smaller graveyard a couple of hours' drive away. I went with him.

In a pretty little cemetery beneath a massive oak, Mr Pope stood at the graveside of his older brother. He stood there a long time, dignified, erect, impassive. His brother had joined up first. Howard Pope had rushed to join him. They met for an afternoon in London when they were both on leave before Howard's first deployment into battle. He told me how much he'd idolised his big brother, how much he'd wanted to be like him. But he never saw him again.

Now, here he was at the gravesite, a man aged nearly one hundred remembering a youth who had not grown old. What thoughts must have flooded his mind.

By the end, the old diggers were exhausted. At the final event, as the Australian anthem played, they struggled to rise from their seats in the honoured row. Arms stretched out from the strongest to lever the next man in line a little higher, who then did his best to lift up the next. The spring-heeled men who had leapt from the trenches into the fire were being asked to call on all their reserves again. There is the courage of youth and the courage of age. They had known them both.

I have wept only twice while writing a script. Once was at Port Arthur. But the first time was there, feeling the precious, fading, fragile link between these men and the times they had known.

HOTEL RWANDA

I WAS IN LONDON. SPRING WAS FINALLY HAPPENING. I WAS PACKING a bag for South Africa for a one-year anniversary story on how the Rainbow Nation was faring under Nelson Mandela's rule. I got a call from an aid agency contact in Brussels. Something awful was happening in Rwanda – a new massacre, only this time Australian troops were caught up in the middle of it.

As happened so often, I called Peter Meakin in Sydney. Yes, I could go to investigate, but only if I could still make it to Johannesburg for the Mandela anniversary.

A rapid change of flights and I was on the overnighter to Nairobi. We scrambled a charter plane to get us into Kigali, the Rwandan capital. The airstrip was empty of life. The pilot kept his engines roaring as we heaved out our gear. He had taken off again by the time we'd hoisted it to our shoulders.

The airport had been besieged during the genocide the year before. Shattered windows spoke of the battle, as did the pockmarks of bullets and residue of blood stains.

Improbably, in all the ruin, a man and a woman materialised to demand twenty dollars for an entry visa. They had a stamp pad and a stamp. Few thieves come so well equipped. The man pressed a crimson smudge into our passports and we were in.

The latest massacre had been at a place called Kibeho, in Rwanda's south-west. By all accounts, most of the killing had been done by the Tutsi-led Rwandan Patriotic Army (RPA). It was the same mob who had come in from Uganda the year before forcing the architects of the original genocide to flee.

First stop, find the Australians.

The Australian army medical support team was based in a military training facility in town. I hoped to get a briefing and advice on how to get to Kibeho. We arrived at the base at the same time as a bunch of wild-eyed Australian men and women. They appeared both agitated and exhausted. And they stank. They had just returned from Kibeho.

From many strands, I started to assemble their story. Some of the soldiers spoke freely and eloquently. Many seemed tired beyond redemption, eating mechanically in the mess, staring blankly, or lying on the floor with arms draped over their faces.

Most vocal was George Gittoes, an artist and photographer who had been at Kibeho. His photographs are the lasting record of the massacre. His account was shocking.

There is no way to apply the champagne cocktail rule to the Kibeho massacre. A variety of accounts exist, including three by men who served in Rwanda. Kevin 'Irish' O'Halloran wrote *Pure Massacre* and the official Australian military history *Rwanda: UNAMIR 1994/95*. Terry Pickard wrote of it in *Combat Medic* and a vivid account can be found in my friend Paul Jordan's book *The Easy Day Was Yesterday*.

The bare bones were these. The Australian contingent was there primarily to provide medical support to the UN mission that had been set up after the genocide the previous year.

By 1995, most of those involved in the genocide had fled into neighbouring countries to avoid the revenge of the RPA. Those who had not fled were clustered in displaced people's camps inside Rwanda. The largest of these was Kibeho, where perpetrators of the genocide were hiding out among more than 100,000 civilians.

Thirty-two Australian troops, a medical team with a few infantry soldiers for protection, were at Kibeho as the RPA set out to 'clear' the camp. At first it was relatively orderly. But it was soon clear that any Hutus the Tutsis suspected of being involved in the genocide were being separated out. Many were simply bayoneted at the edge of the lines. Realising they would soon be exposed, those involved in the genocide started killing their own Hutu compatriots to discourage them from leaving.

There were some two thousand RPA soldiers at Kibeho, almost all of them men who had lost relatives to the genocide. Australian troops watched many of them gather in and around a church at the top of a hill, where for hours they sang and chanted. The next day, they suddenly opened fire on the massed refugees. It wasn't just bullets. They used mortars, machine guns and rocket-propelled grenades.

It was pure slaughter. The Australian troops were forbidden under their rules of engagement to fire back to defend the people now being torn apart. As Irish O'Halloran later wrote, 'it was the orders I wasn't given that hurt the most'. If they had fired, they wouldn't have lasted long. They were outnumbered sixty to one. And any Australian soldiers who did survive could have been charged with murder for exceeding the mission brief.

The rules did allow them to tend to the wounded. So repeatedly, and often under fire, the small infantry team went out into the carnage to carry in those who were not yet dead. The medical team under Captain Carol Vaughn-Evans was overwhelmed. As well as wounds from bullets and shrapnel, many had horrific machete wounds. I will spare you the descriptions that were given to me.

It is a sign of what that team confronted over three or four days, that four of the thirty-two were later awarded the Medal for Gallantry, the military bravery award that ranks just two down from the Victoria Cross. Among them was Captain Vaughn-Evans.

The Australian team was able to get some of those they saved back to their base clinic in Kigali. Army nurse Lyndall Moore showed me a little boy, swathed in bandages. He had been sliced open with a machete, from above his sternum to below his navel. A male military nurse had sung to him to calm him on the long journey to the capital. As I watched, from behind his oxygen mask, the little boy began a rhythmic kind of groaning. He was singing the song back to us.

The male nurse was in tears. 'We decided we were going to save this one boy,' he said. It appeared as if they had, though his long-term future was far from clear.

In Kigali, the troops were not just traumatised. They were furious. When the guns finally went silent, an Australian counting party walked out into a field of bodies. Using a military 'pace-counter' designed to click off distance during infantry manoeuvres, the party recorded 4050 dead bodies before they were ordered to give up on that exercise to concentrate on saving more of the living.

'We wouldn't have counted half of them,' said Gittoes, who was with the counting team. Others had the same opinion.

But the RPA was saying there had been no massacre at all. Any dead, they said, had been killed by the Hutu militias in the camp.

We slept a few hours that night in Kigali in a concrete block building that had been heavily blasted by machine-gun fire on its eastern side. It overlooked a main route into town – a road snaking around the foot of a hill with a river on the other side. It was a prime sniper position. It had also plainly received a lot of incoming fire. We had hooked up with Ian Robbie, a famous South African cameraman for ITN and Sky. He wrinkled his nose at the strange, dense smell.

'Lots of bodies,' he opined. 'And left to rot for quite a while.'

We were up early. A satellite dish had been set up at the Hotel des Milles Collines, the notorious 'Hotel Rwanda' of the Oscar-nominated movie. We set up with plenty of time to hit the 6 pm news back in Australia. And we had a scoop, of sorts. There were no other Australian journalists in town.

As the deadline neared, we received increasingly frantic calls from Sydney that they weren't seeing our satellite signal. Desperate calls were made to Intelsat in the United States to check the co-ordinates. We were assured they were correct. At the third time of asking, the disembodied voice seemed as perplexed as we were.

'Where did you say you were sending from again?'

'Kigali!'

'Oh, KIG-ali . . . where's that?'

'Rwanda.'

'Rwanda? Where's that?'

'Africa.'

'Damn! Sorry about that. I thought you said *Tig*-ali.'

'Where the hell is Tigali?'

'Oklahoma.'

We missed the slot. The story never made it to air. And for the life of me, even in the age of Google Maps, I have never been able to find a Tigali in Oklahoma.

—

Missing a feed is always a blow. With a story we felt an urgent need to tell, it was doubly so. We had little time to indulge our frustration, however. The UN's top official in Rwanda had called a news conference and I was determined to challenge what I already suspected was a cover-up of the death toll.

As we pulled up at the central army barracks, I was approached by Sam Kiley, the excellent Nairobi correspondent for *The Times* of London. He also smelt a rat.

'What are your Aussies saying?'

'Eight thousand plus. More than four thousand by direct count.'

Kiley looked thoughtful.

'The RPA is saying no more than three hundred dead, most of them killed by the *interahamwe*,' he said, referring to the largest Hutu militia.

I believed the Australian number. They had no reason to lie.

The UN, however, had a problem. It had failed the previous year to prevent a genocide that had killed roughly one million people. Most of those victims were Tutsis. Now, a Tutsi army was being accused of a massacre of Hutus.

The grandly titled Special Representative of the UN Secretary-General, the Maharajah of Bhopal, Shahryar Khan, took his seat. Behind him stood a powerfully built Rwandan in a black suit. He was introduced as the information minister.

Mr Khan announced that inquiries indicated two thousand people had died at Kibeho.

When I queried that figure, quoting the Australian numbers, he explained that some estimates of the death toll had been inflated through confusion or over-excitement. The official figure was a matter for the United Nations to decide.

'What is the point of having United Nations observers in the field,' I pressed, 'if you are not truthful about what they observe?'

So it went on. Finally, the maharajah all but begged the furiously scribbling reporters in the room if anyone *else* had any questions, while the information minister fixed me with a look of rage.

'Yes, I have a question,' said Sam Kiley. The maharajah turned to him with relief.

'What part is it of the United Nations mandate to cover up a massacre of Rwandan civilians?'

Every outlet there wrote a story about a UN cover-up. It was picked up by American CBS, on CNN, on Britain's ITN and it ran prominently, thanks to Sam, in *The Times*.

I quickly wrote, voiced and cut a story, including some of the interviews we had secured for the previous story that had failed to make it. Editor Mark Douglas and I had to get out of Rwanda to cover the one-year anniversary in Johannesburg. I left our tape with the satellite operator at the Hotel des Milles Collines. I knew him and trusted him and I also knew the American satellite guys would know where we were this time.

We bolted for the airport. Alas, the one scheduled flight out, via Uganda, failed to turn up.

Night was falling. A storm was building up in high fists of cloud over the capital. The taxi that had dropped us at the airport had disappeared. We were on our own in an insecure building with our only company being a cluster of young men who were watching us through the shattered glass of a former feature window.

At least we were confident our story would get out and something of the events of Kibeho and Australia's role in it would be told.

Suddenly, a German television crew bustled in. The producer was a man I knew slightly. He agreed to let us hitch a lift in his charter flight. We clambered on board, and were soon clawing our way into the sky in the middle of a violent thunderstorm. The little twin-engine plane tossed in the turbulence. My German friend offered a wan smile.

'Like Wagner, huh?'

I take an irrational delight in violent air travel. It was the best flight of my life.

Finally, we came in to a hairy landing in Nairobi. The plane was met by a British ITN reporter, Mike Nicholson, the wind whipping at his tropical linen suit. His face fell when he saw none of his people on our little flight.

'They didn't give you a tape, did they?'

'No,' I replied. 'Why?'

'Well, apparently some clown gave the UN fella a roasting at the press conference. The RPA was so pissed off they've shut down all the satellite dishes. Not a damn thing is getting out.'

And so it was that I failed – twice – to get out a single word on one of the most gruelling engagements Australian troops have endured. To this day, the official UN death toll for the Kibeho massacre remains at two thousand.

The Australian troops who were there suffered mightily. Over the years, I have caught up with quite a few of them. Not only have they had to process images of utter human degradation, they have had to endure the sneers of some who say they should have gone down swinging in defence of the civilians in the camp.

Twenty years later, I met a senior officer at the Lavarack army base in Townsville who all but called the Kibeho veterans cowards. It was both ignorant and deeply unfair. The troops sent to Rwanda dealt with appalling things. Most of the young diggers, in the words of one of them, Paul Jordan, had never seen a dead body before they were pitched in to slaughter. More importantly, they had never encountered the reality of matching restrictive rules of engagement – the legal limits to their ability to operate – to chaos that stretched well beyond the imaginings of the bureaucrats working at their desks. Some of those sent to Rwanda have never really recovered.

24

A NUCLEAR BLAST

A FEW DAYS AFTER THAT AFRICAN TRIP, I RECEIVED A CALL FROM Sydney. The bosses were pleased with what I was doing. The London job was mine for as long as I wanted it. I put down the phone and felt a wave of relief. I had not realised until that moment how much I feared I was no bloody good at all. To be effectively offered tenure in one of the most prized jobs in Australian journalism was the best endorsement I could have hoped for.

I felt euphoric. Now when I travelled around London, I looked upon it as home. In fact, I thought, I should buy a place. I started looking at the real estate pages.

The feeling lasted a couple of weeks. Then it left me.

If I stayed in London, I would probably stay for good. One day, inevitably, Nine would call time on my excellent adventure. That didn't trouble me unduly. I had a British passport and I had good contacts already at the BBC, Sky and ITN. I would find another job.

But did I really want to wake up one day, forty years old with a house in Fulham and discover that I had become a Pom? Britain was what my parents had escaped. Far more to the point – and the compelling element for me – was that I would wake up and realise that my daughter was growing up in Melbourne and I would not know her and she would not know me.

Over the course of a day, I reflected on this. Before the sun had set, I knew I had to return home. On one level, I couldn't believe I was doing it. On another, I knew I had no choice. To do otherwise would have been to lay in regrets I could never assuage. I might only have one child. I was delighted with the one I knew. I missed her.

As so often, Peter Meakin, the crusty, wise old boss in Sydney, took my call.

'Let's find something worthwhile for you to come back home to,' he said.

I had no ambition for a job on one of the current affairs shows, *A Current Affair* or *60 Minutes*. I liked the simple verities of news. Meakin came up with a nebulous new job title as 'Network Reporter' – essentially a roving reporter on stories of national interest. I would be based in Sydney. My daughter was in Melbourne. From the distant view of London, the two cities looked close enough.

As a sweetener, Meakin promised my first assignment would be in French Polynesia, covering the resumption of French nuclear testing in the Pacific. I had already been in Paris covering protests by the French left against the nuclear program.

The deal was done. I went out into the streets of London, the city in which I had journalistically grown up, the Old Grey Lady who had given me so much experience and so much of the world. Was I mad to leave? Perhaps. But after the dark night with my damaged back in an empty house, I determined I would only live my life forward, not looking back, not harbouring regrets. And I have never regretted that return to Australia.

I had a girlfriend in London, a really wonderful woman. She had no interest in Sydney but she flew with me to New York to start my journey home. We spent a week there. On the day of our parting, she had a lunchtime flight back to London and I flew in the evening for Australia. I ordered a limousine to take her to JFK Airport. As she waved a languid goodbye, I wondered if I would ever see her again.

I never did.

—

After fourteen years under the Socialist president François Mitterrand, Jacques Chirac won the election in France in 1995 determined to reinvigorate the country's nuclear deterrent by resuming the testing of nuclear weapons. As before, it would happen a safe distance from France itself, on the other side of the world in the central Pacific.

From the start, this assertion of nationalism and patriotism started to go off the rails. Chirac's announcement came just a few days before the tenth anniversary of the bombing of the Greenpeace vessel, *Rainbow Warrior*, by French agents in Auckland Harbour. Acts of state terrorism by western powers have rarely been so flagrant. That it happened in peaceful New Zealand, a fellow member of the broad western alliance, was even more clumsy.

The attack on the *Rainbow Warrior* was the work of the Mitterrand administration but the anniversary made it Chirac's problem. Another awkward date approaching was the fiftieth anniversary of the atomic blasts at Hiroshima and Nagasaki.

The resumption of tests was divisive in France. In the Pacific, the mood was unremittingly hostile. The shadow foreign minister, Alexander Downer, started running hard on the issue. He forced the somewhat complacent Keating government, then on its last legs, to make a show of dispatching Foreign Minister Gareth Evans to Paris to urge the tests be canned.

Chirac, newly installed, could hardly back down on his first foreign affairs challenge.

As Meakin promised, I received a call from the foreign editor, David 'Mullet' McCombe.

'We've booked you into a hotel, the . . . er . . . Park Royal Tahiti Beachcomber,' said Mullet.

'Those are four of my favourite words,' I replied.

After some rugged travel around Africa, I was ready for Tahiti. The job seemed straightforward, if a little out of the action. The test would take place on Moruroa Atoll, where the French had conducted atmospheric nuclear tests in the 1970s. The new tests would be underground. Greenpeace would try to get its new *Rainbow Warrior* into the test zone to disrupt it. Nine's excellent Canberra-based reporter Janet Gibson would go on board the Greenpeace ship along with cameraman Rob Hopkins, a man who would play a key role in many coming adventures.

The prospects of Janet being able to file from the high seas, amid probable disruption by the French military, were slight. My Tahiti deployment was to ensure we had secure coverage from the region when the bomb went off.

The French would not name the precise date of the test. Every network sent journalists to Tahiti. We all holed up at the same hotel, with its infinity pool gazing across the Pacific at the dramatic silhouette of Mo'orea Island some twenty kilometres away. Some cocktails were drunk. A little snorkelling might have been done.

Tahiti was administered as a province of France. Its civil service was run by French bureaucrats who, astonishingly, were paid an extra margin over what they would earn in Paris. Nice work if you could get it. The indigenous Polynesians did a little less well. The nuclear testing plan had reinvigorated a local French Polynesian independence movement but the mood initially seemed fairly bucolic and contained.

Then things started to change. French commandos boarded the *Rainbow Warrior II* and the *Greenpeace* as they entered the exclusion zone. Rob Hopkins and Janet Gibson were able to get their vision out, revealing the uncompromising violence the French authorities were willing to use. They flew into Tahiti and Rob became a major player in recording what was to follow.

Amid rising tensions, a rumour went around that the French Polynesian leader Gaston Flosse was about to fly back to the Tahitian capital after consultations in Paris. A plane did land at the international airport next to the village of Faa'a. It seems unlikely Flosse was on it. Certainly, he denied being on the plane.

It made no difference. A crowd of people surged out of the village of Faa'a and began attacking the plane. The airport was close to our hotel and we ran onto the tarmac just in time to hear a series of loud bangs as mobs of people ran for the steps attached to the front of the aircraft. Suddenly, I saw what looked like a mortar round falling towards me.

'Incoming!' I bellowed, a word I knew only from war movies. There was absolutely no cover on the tarmac and the projectile was tumbling now almost to my feet. Knowing what I know now about mortars, I would have flattened myself on the ground. Being more innocent in those days, I could only watch it and hope that the explosions I was hearing were not the real thing. The French military had a poor reputation for restraint but, in this case, the projectile simply spouted out tear gas that quickly dissipated on the brisk sea breeze.

The French had an armoured vehicle and troops from the Foreign Legion along with a contingent of armed paramilitary police. Despite the confusion, the tactics started to become clearer. The French were using tear gas and stun grenades to manage the crowd, but they were outnumbered. The stun grenades were essentially harmless if you stayed away from them. They would land, skittle along for a second or two and then explode with a lot of noise but not much mischief. They were not entirely benign, however. A protester who grabbed one before it exploded had his hand blown off.

Rob Hopkins and I instinctively followed the well-known rules: keep together and stay behind the police lines. The journalist's job at these times is to protect the cameraman, who – with his eye to the lens – is essentially blind to any threat that is not within his narrow field of vision.

It soon became clear that the French security forces were not using lethal weapons. The rioters, however, were flinging large rocks with force. After a couple of narrow misses we changed tactics and took up position among the rioters.

We quickly gathered a lot of dramatic vision. Tahiti being far to the east, this mid-morning outbreak of violence could still make it onto the *Today* show, Nine's breakfast program. But we had to get to a satellite dish.

Once again, we crossed between the lines, with rocks flying all around us from one direction and tear gas and explosions coming from the other. Our car was out the front of the terminal. We were jogging around the main building when we saw a mass of young men coming to reinforce the rioters. French paramilitaries had formed up a line in front of the airport building. But with their main force still battling on the tarmac, they looked hopelessly outnumbered.

We paused for a moment as both sides sized each other up. Then suddenly cars started exploding into flames in the car park (including, as we later discovered, our own). Pelted with rocks, the paramilitaries withdrew from their exposed position into the terminal itself. We took cover with them. The major danger was from the rocks coming in like a horizontal hailstorm. The troops started firing off their tear gas and stun grenades but they chiefly just gassed themselves. The mob outside had the benefit of wind to disperse the chemicals.

Inside the terminal, with windows shattering from the onslaught and with the air thickening with choking gas, I delivered a fairly ragged piece to camera trying to explain what was going on. Rob, bless him, with no head protection against the missiles, kept his focus with admirable sangfroid. We got the hell out of there, found our way to a satellite point and made the cross into the *Today* show.

Within a couple of hours, the terminal was fully aflame and the rioters had made an international scene. Some were angry over the nuclear testing, more were simply sick of French rule, and others seemed chiefly motivated by the chance to cause a little mayhem.

The rioters set up roadblocks that made it impossible to return to our hotel. Somehow, the technicians found a way to extract their bulky satellite equipment and set it up again at the Sheraton Hotel, perched on a promontory on the far side of the capital, Papeete.

At the end of a long day, everyone managed to file their stories. I found a room in the hotel and my first priority was to wash my skin, which was raw from hours spent in the tear gas. I made a beginner's error. I put the shower on warm. Never do that. The pores opened further and the chemical residue simply dug deeper until my skin blazed with the pain of it.

The hotel was not only comfortable and safe, it provided restorative food and a cold beer. And more besides. That night I watched from my open window, as a gentle Pacific breeze cooled my skin, while most of the central business district of Papeete burned in the fires set by the rioters. To watch a capital burn, even a provincial backwater like Papeete, is not something easily forgotten.

—

The riots and the international condemnation about the tests shocked the French, who announced they were cutting their program in half. Within a year they had signed the Comprehensive Nuclear Test Ban Treaty (CTBT) and they have never tested again. The Tahitian Independence movement, however, failed in its goals. The violence of their response unnerved many Tahitians. The beautiful islands of French Polynesia remain French.

There was one other postscript. A few months later I had the honour of collecting the Logie Award for 'Outstanding Achievement in News' on behalf of the Nine Network. Rob Hopkins also won the Walkley Award for his camerawork. I had never been to a Logies night before. I accepted the award from the political reporter Paul Lyneham, a truly great figure in Australian journalism who had just joined Nine and was a colleague of mine on the late news program *Nightline*.

The following morning, I popped the Logie into a backpack and took a tram to Richmond to catch up with old mates from the Nine newsroom in Melbourne. Several people on the tram congratulated me on the Logie. I was perplexed. My initial thought was that the statuette was hanging out of my backpack. It wasn't until I got to the newsroom that I learned the Logies were televised live and was one of the most watched programs of the year. I didn't know. I had never watched one. The most mortifying thing was realising my stumbling speech had been to an audience larger than the room.

25

PORT ARTHUR

THE WORST STORY I HAVE EVER COVERED IN AUSTRALIA CAME A FEW months later.

I was flying from Sydney to Melbourne one Sunday afternoon to deliver Cait back to her mum when my mobile phone started ringing as the plane landed. The devices were still new and the etiquette not yet firmly established.

It was Jim Carroll, the head of *Nightline* and one of my bosses.

'Where are you?'

'Landing in Melbourne.'

'Grab the next plane to Hobart,' he ordered. 'I'm sending Rob Hopkins from here – there's some kind of shooting going on in Port Arthur.'

I knew Port Arthur. My first holiday after moving to Melbourne was a campervan trip around Tasmania. But a shooting . . . ? It seemed so improbable.

I handed Cait off to Sue and made another couple of phone calls. Two more reporters would be heading down from Nine's Melbourne office. One was a man I knew and admired very much, a stately former RAF fighter pilot called Charles Slade. The other was a brash youngster called John Vause. They each had different strengths. I knew I would be carrying the main network story – the 'What happened?'. Charles, a dignified and decent man, was best suited to seek the stories of the survivors and the bereaved. John Vause could unleash his energies on finding out whatever he could about the gunman.

All of this was agreed and decided before we even landed in Hobart, allowing each reporter and crew to concentrate on their angle.

I met Rob Hopkins and Nine's beloved Tamil soundman Ilankovan 'Frankie' Frank at Hobart airport. We set off immediately for the Tasman Peninsula, the south-east tip of Australia, where the convict ruins of Port Arthur attracted multitudes of tourists every year.

Night had fallen. The late April air was cold. We drove on through a black night with little idea of what lay ahead. Pictures had already emerged of gunshot victims being helicoptered into Hobart hospital but the death toll was still unclear and the gunman was still at large.

In those days, terrorism was almost unthinkable in Australia but we'd had a few firearms massacres. The question everyone was asking, stranger to stranger, was 'Why?'. Something awful had happened at Port Arthur. Every update seemed worse than the last. The 'What?' was still only slowly coming clear, the 'Why?' remained an utter mystery.

A little over an hour from Hobart airport, a police officer loomed out of the darkness and told us to stop. They had blocked the road. The killer, they believed, was holed up in a bunch of buildings just around the corner. He was still firing off occasional bursts of shots.

The following morning, smoke could be seen rising in a thin line to the south of the roadblock. Martin Bryant had set fire to the Seascape Cottages. This was both his last hold-out and the place from which he had launched his murder spree by killing the two owners. Soon afterwards came word that Bryant, his clothes on fire, had fled the building and been arrested. The worst mass killer in Australian history had taken his last steps as a free man.

While Bryant was contained and besieged at the Seascape Cottages, the police and medical emergency response had bypassed him to get into Port Arthur itself. What they found were horrendous scenes. Thirty-five people were killed that day. Nearly two dozen more were wounded.

In the early afternoon, some very sombre police officers shepherded a small group of journalists and news crews around the historic Port Arthur site. We were part of that grimmest of tours. The Broad Arrow Café, where Bryant had massacred people (after first eating lunch) was still off-limits. Twenty people were murdered in that small space in a matter of seconds. A tourist named Barry Turner was a little distance across the grounds recording some home video when the shooting began. Unaware of the nature of the sudden patter of loud reports, he kept filming, even maintaining a steady frame on the golden stone of the historic prison. Two things were striking. One was the rapidity of the shots. Mr Turner recorded twenty-one shots in twenty-five seconds, before he stopped filming. In a small space among unsuspecting holidaymakers, Bryant killed or disabled twenty-six people. Some had time to stand or dive for cover, though seeking cover did not always save them. One man, Anthony Nightingale, had time to say 'No, no, not here.' Another visitor, Ray Sharpe, said 'That's not funny!' Within seconds, both men were dead. Another died with the café cutlery still in his hand.

The other striking thing was a sound that I will forever associate with the massacre. The video caught the distinctive alarm cry of the masked lapwings, or plovers, as they reacted to the sudden, unusual noise of the gunfire. The rising, panicky 'kerk-kerk-kerk' of the plovers rang out above the sounds of mass murder. The plovers were still disturbed when we walked through the following day, calling their raucous alarms above a scene now funereally hushed. I sometimes hear plovers today in the parkland near my Sydney home and I cannot break the association. I hate the sound.

On that afternoon walk through the site, we got a sense of Martin Bryant's movements. The twenty-nine shots he fired in the café in approximately one and a half to two minutes accounted for more than half his victims. He was using an AR-15 semi-automatic .223 rifle with a thirty-round magazine. All the shots in the café were at point-blank or very close range.

Bryant reloaded as he walked outside the café, shooting at people in and around the cars and tour buses in the open-air car park. He fired towards the ruins of the prison and towards people running up the road in the direction of the visitor information centre and the entrance. It appears all of these shots missed although, as the prosecutor Damian Bugg later pointed out, 'certainly the weapons he used were capable of hitting people at the range he was firing'.

This detail is important because the small conspiracy industry that has grown up around the massacre argues that only someone with military training could have killed so many people in so short a time. Bryant's marksmanship was so freakishly good, so the argument goes, he was either a plant carrying out a massacre to provoke a toughening of gun laws, or there were several gunmen involved on the day. The plain fact is he was staggeringly lethal in a tiny enclosed space with targets who were either seated or cowering on the floor and who had been taken utterly by surprise. In open air, with people racing for cover, the super-marksman theory falls apart.

People in the car park area were starting to cotton on to the desperate peril they faced. Many tried to shelter in or around the tour buses. Bryant chased many down and shot them. He shot some on board the buses. He returned to some he had wounded to shoot them dead. Just before shooting one man, Neville Quin, at point-blank range, he told him, 'No one gets away from me.' In this case he was wrong. Mr Quin pitched forward as he was shot and was struck a non-fatal blow to the back of his neck. His wife, whom he had been trying to rescue, was shot dead.

During this phase, Bryant went to the back of his car to swap his AR-15 for a military-style FN assault rifle. He also had a semi-automatic shotgun. Each of these weapons he had been able to obtain with no apparent difficulty under the slack Tasmanian gun laws of the day. Bear in mind that this was a man of such low intelligence that at twenty-nine years of age he could neither read nor write. His IQ was rated at sixty-six. Put another way, if tested alongside a group of eleven-year-olds, ninety percent of them would score higher. Yet it was within his capabilities to obtain not one but three semi-automatic weapons. He also carried two sets of handcuffs and a hunting knife, as well as a length of rope and some cans of petrol.

After his slaughter at the café and around the car park, Bryant returned to his yellow Volvo with the surfboard on the roof and drove back towards the toll booth at the entrance. Along this road, he came upon Nanette Mikac, the wife of the local pharmacist, Walter. Mrs Mikac had her three-year-old daughter Madeline in her arms. Her six-year-old, Alannah, was running beside her. They knew there was a gunman further down the road because they had encountered two other couples who were fleeing towards the toll booth.

When the Volvo came up the road, Nanette Mikac and at least one other person approached the car hoping it would take them to safety. A woman nearby, Caroline Boskovic, heard Mrs Mikac say to Alannah, 'We're safe now, Pumpkin.' Bryant stopped the car and ordered Mrs Mikac to her knees. 'Please don't hurt my babies,' she pleaded.

Bryant killed her and little Madeline. Alannah ran for her life. Bryant fired two shots at her and missed. He pursued her. She tried to find cover behind a tree. Bryant stepped up to her and shot her dead. The specific details of this murder are contained in the prosecution statement of facts to the Supreme Court of Tasmania. I will not repeat it here. Enough to say that the final moments of Alannah Mikac's life contained more terror than anyone should have to face.

I came through these scenes a few hours later, with the physical evidence still visible under blankets laid on the ground. My daughter was the same age as Madeline Mikac. The horror of it swarmed in my head. Up until that point, the question was – 'Why?' Looking at that bloody spray, I formed my answer.

Bryant continued to the toll booth where he abandoned his car to steal a BMW after killing its four occupants, including two tourists from Switzerland. They had just driven up and had no idea what had taken place at the site. There was panic as other cars arrived, saw Bryant killing the occupants of the BMW, or saw bodies being dragged out of the car or lying on the ground. At least two vehicles made a desperate attempt to get out of there, with Bryant firing two shots into one of those cars.

His focus was elsewhere, however, as he transferred one of his two spare firearms from the Volvo to the BMW. (He left behind the semi-automatic shotgun, which he later told police was a weapon that 'scared him'.) He also transferred his handcuffs, at least one drum of petrol, the rope and a knife.

Driving the BMW a short distance on the road towards Hobart, Bryant pulled into a service station. There he forced a young man, Glenn Pears, out of a Toyota Corolla and into the boot of the BMW. Mr Pears complied, possibly hoping to divert the gunman away from his girlfriend, Zoe Hall, who was in the Corolla. It made no difference. Bryant shot her too.

He then drove the few hundred metres to the entrance of the Seascape Cottages, where his murder spree had begun. For a while he simply stood at the side of the road, firing at passing cars from a distance of just a few metres. He killed no one with these shots, but that was pure luck. Several people were hit and suffered horrible injuries.

Bryant then retreated to the Seascape Cottages, taking Mr Pears with him and securing him with handcuffs before returning to set the BMW alight with petrol. When two local police officers turned up, he fired shots at them. Inside the cottages he had found, and was using, weapons that the owners kept there, including a semi-automatic assault rifle.

Around this time, ABC Hobart–based TV reporter Allison Smith was heading to Port Arthur with a cameraman. She was making calls as he drove and she tried the number of the Seascape Cottages. The man who picked up the phone was, she said, laughing hysterically.

'Who am I talking to?' asked Smith.

'You can call me Jamie.'

'It's the ABC calling – what's happening?'

'What's happening,' said the male voice, 'is that I am having a lot of fun.'

There was a pause before the man went on. 'But I really need a shower. If you try to call me again, I'll shoot the hostage.'

He also rang the home number of the local police constable, talking to the officer's wife and implying that he had the officer as a hostage. Again, he identified himself as Jamie.

As police teams swarmed in from across Tasmania and Victoria, a secure line was established into the Seascape Cottages. Bryant demanded a helicopter to take him to the airport so he could fly to Adelaide. He said his hostages were all alive and he had fed them. In fact, the owners of the cottages, Sally and David Martin had been killed before Bryant went to Port Arthur. It appears likely that even as Bryant went through the motions of 'negotiating' he had already killed his remaining hostage, shooting the young Melbourne lawyer Glenn Pears twice as he sat handcuffed to a chair.

Between the phone conversations with police, Bryant continued to fire towards those who had him besieged. He fired about 150 shots throughout that night.

Just before 8 am the following morning, Bryant set the main building ablaze. Within minutes it was well alight. Bryant waited until the building was almost consumed before running out, his clothes on fire. He disappeared from view before re-appearing, naked. He staggered on a short distance further before collapsing on the ground.

The Port Arthur massacre was over.

Most of the details would emerge over time, to be collated for the prosecution brief.

On that Monday afternoon, I had a story to write from what I knew. Charles Slade had covered the story of the survivors and the relatives of those killed. John Vause had dredged up a fair picture of Bryant's former life. Both did a fine job. But I had to tell the main story and I was finding it hard to think past the image of the dead children at the side of the road.

We were getting close to the deadline. I knew that when big news happened Australians tended to turn over to Channel Nine. It was an honour that people felt that way about our product but it only added to the terrible responsibility to get the story right.

I also knew that the news coverage would include interviews with survivors. How else could it be? And yet survivors, by the very fact of their survival, can only tell part of the tale. I remembered something the Auschwitz survivor Primo Levi had written, that the Nazis' true witnesses were no longer speaking. And I thought of Alannah and Madeline, hunted and murdered with a malevolence beyond all reason.

Between Port Arthur and our affiliate studios back in Hobart was a mobile phone shadow. Just before I lost contact, I took a call from the production desk in Sydney. They had a picture of a man, filmed through the window of a car. He was visibly upset.

'Can we use it?' I asked.

'I think we have to,' came the reply. 'It is a powerful image but it is also softened by the reflections on the glass. It seems respectful.'

I scrawled a script with pen and notepad as Rob Hopkins drove towards Hobart. The body of the script was factual and direct, the events too stark for adornment. At the end though, I sought to address the question everyone was asking – 'Why?'

I had in mind the last seconds of Alannah Mikac's life.

'There is no why. There are no reasons. There are no words.'

The final shot was of the unidentified man writhing in grief through the windscreen of a parked car. I had not seen the shot.

I didn't learn until later that this was Walter Mikac, who had just learned his entire young family had been blown away. To this day I feel gutted, at his loss and for our use of that image.

I was so choked up that day that when it came to putting my voice down I could barely get out the words.

The Nine Network veteran Charles Wooley, a Tasmanian, later wrote of the particular pain of an atrocity against his tribe. But all Australians were part of this tribe. And all felt that day a terrible wound.

I felt guilt afterwards that I had let my emotions get to me. My last three sentences scarcely qualified as reportage. Meakin sidled up to me at the Channel Nine bar a few days later and we had a brief discussion about the story. 'You said what all Australia was thinking,' he said, which was kind of him. Many years later, I was startled when a young journalist wandered up to me and recited my entire script from memory. Apparently, his journalism lecturer had required the class to study it.

My own sense was that I lost control of what I was there to do: to deliver a dispassionate factual account, as best as we could know it, of a profoundly awful event. I knew the viewers' emotions would be triggered by the report. How could they not be? But my job, particularly on such an unremittingly grim day, was to deliver the news dead straight. And I had failed to do it.

—

The massacre happened just weeks after John Howard became prime minister. He visited the site and met some of those who were there and who had lost loved ones. It was a cold autumn day. One of the bereaved reached forward from the line and raised her arms to be hugged. Howard, after a fractional hesitation, allowed himself to be embraced and held the woman for long seconds.

John Howard was an entirely proper man, stout in his Methodist plainness. Being hugged by a grieving stranger was a challenge for him but he met it. I think he realised in that moment that the prime minister, at times of national hardship, symbolically becomes Australia. The woman was reaching for the embrace of a nation and Howard, to his credit, gave it.

His far greater act was to defy his party's base and drive through gun law reforms that have spared Australia the drumbeat of massacres that so blight the United States. It is true, as gun advocates point out, that mass murders have still occurred through the use of fire, vehicles and other devices but we have had no gun massacres since that awful Sunday in Tasmania.

My involvement in the story continued throughout Bryant's court appearances. He insisted to his lawyers that he was not guilty. The Director of Public Prosecutions began the process of preparing witnesses for a long and painful trial.

Bryant was ultimately persuaded to admit guilt. His mother, who also urged him to do so, later argued that he had been denied a trial. She told Charles Wooley on *60 Minutes* that she believed he had not done it. Conversely, she also said that if Bryant's attentive father, Maurice, had not earlier committed suicide the massacre might never have happened.

In his initial police interview, Bryant offered a fairly garbled account of going surfing that day and dropping into the Seascape Cottages to visit the owners, but finding they were not home.

The Martins' property was only a kilometre or two from the Port Arthur historic site. Police spoke to six hundred witnesses, many of whom placed Bryant at the main murder scene. Two people had caught him on their video cameras. Yet Bryant apparently believed he could brazen it out.

'I haven't been in Port Arthur (in) probably six or seven years,' he told the two senior detectives at his most extensive interview, about ten weeks after the massacre.

He then claimed to know nothing about the carnage there.

Officer: 'Do you know what's happened on that day?'

Bryant: 'What's happened on that day?'

Officer: 'On the twenty-eighth of April?'

Bryant: 'No.'

Officer: 'You don't?'

Bryant: 'No.'

Officer: 'Are you sure about that?'

Bryant: 'Positive.'

But Bryant took an intense interest in the numbers killed and wounded. He also begged to be allowed to look at police photographs from the scene.

Bryant: 'Have you had other trouble like this, dramatic?'

Officer: 'Not on this scale, no.'

Bryant: 'No. Suppose it happens, doesn't it?'

Then, in the course of the interview he suddenly admitted, out of nowhere, stealing the BMW at gunpoint and taking a hostage. It came as Bryant was explaining that he had stopped on his innocent 'surfing trip' for a toasted sandwich at the little hamlet of Nubeena.

Officer 1: 'What did you do then?'

Bryant: 'Then I left and drove around past Port Arthur and went, and went in to see the Martins.'

Officer 1: 'Was there anyone else there when you called in?'

Bryant: 'No, I umm, unfortunately I held up a car, I took ahh, I saw this car I liked and got ummm, held up the person in the car and kidnapped him.'

Officer 2: 'Kidnapped him?'

Bryant: 'Mmm.'

Officer 1: 'So you drove away in the BMW?'

Bryant: 'Yes.'

Officer 1: 'With another male person?'

Bryant: 'Yeah, he was in the boot. I put him in the boot of the car.'

Bryant was plainly willing to admit a serious crime. But he didn't want to be held accountable for the larger one. His attempts to distance himself from the slaughter in and around the Broad Arrow café were taken as signs of 'consciousness of guilt'. His denials were inept but, importantly, they ruled out an insanity plea. They proved he knew what he had done was wrong.

Bryant's responses might have failed to convince police of his innocence but they were devastatingly effective in exposing the flaws in Tasmania's gun laws.

He bought two of the three firearms he took to Port Arthur at the local gun store in suburban New Town. He could see it from his house. Guns and Ammo was run by a bloke named Terry Hill. Bryant also bought hundreds of rounds of ammunition from him. Bryant asked the police officers if Hill was still in business.

Officer: 'Why do you ask that, Martin?'

Bryant: 'Because I didn't have a licence. I had no gun licence . . .'

Officer: 'So, just let me get this straight. You didn't have a gun licence?'

Bryant: 'No.'

Officer: 'Did you make out you had a gun licence when you purchased them?'

Bryant: 'No. Never.'

Later in the interview Bryant explained, 'When you got the money it helps. People pass things over if you've got the cash.'

So whatever gun laws Tasmania had in place, a licensed gun dealer felt there were no unacceptable risks in selling military-style weapons to a man, who had a local reputation as being weird or worse, and who never offered and was never required to show a gun licence.

The firearms lobby hated John Howard for acting but they had left him with little choice.

—

Even more than two decades later, the police record of interview remains an astonishing document. In some ways it is a masterwork of dialogue. Trainee playwrights would do well to study it. In the simple language of a child, in response to the deceptively bland questioning of two experienced detectives, Martin Bryant revealed the full nature of his character.

He was by turns boastful, deceitful, cunning and vulnerable.

At one point, in a phrase worthy of *King Lear*, Bryant suddenly bursts out a madman's lament.

Bryant: 'I lose track of the days. I'm losing, I'm losing my mind.'

Certainly, his grasp of his circumstances appeared delusional.

Bryant: 'I just want, I'd love to just get out of here now. Live a norm . . . a normal life. Will I be allowed to do that?'

The court ultimately sentenced Bryant to a separate life term for each of his victims. He is due for release in a little over a thousand years.

He did not express remorse and never has. A forensic psychiatrist who examined him said the concept was outside his emotional range. At his final hearing, prosecutor Damian Bugg, QC, noted that Bryant had not 'given any reason for why he did it'.

To that extent, I had been right. There was no why and there were no reasons. Thirty-five people died, more than twenty were wounded, hundreds of families were shattered, the sweet potential of children and the dignified age of adults were laid waste in the name of nothing at all.

I attended every single minute of every one of Martin Bryant's court appearances. As the representative of one of the major national networks, I was assigned a seat in the press box. The levels of interest were enormous and the courtroom was not large. Scores of people watched from screens in nearby rooms. Bryant appeared behind a specially built bulletproof screen. The main body of the court was allocated to survivors of the massacre and relatives of those slain, people revisiting their worst moments in the hope of what people describe as 'closure'.

They got precious little from Bryant.

Most of the hearing time came after Bryant pleaded guilty to all charges. Mr Bugg recited in painstaking details the murders, trying to establish their sequence and flow. Furiously taking notes, I would glance up from time to time to see if there was any sign of recognition from Bryant, or any sign of disturbance inside the court. Many people sobbed and clung to relatives. Bryant looked at various times bored, skittish and mischievous. On a couple of occasions, I looked up to see him gazing directly at me, eyes wide, trying to hold me for a staring contest. I didn't indulge him.

Towards the end of the descriptions of the murders, Mr Bugg came to the fate of Glenn Pears, on holiday with his fellow lawyer girlfriend Zoe Hall. The horror of his final hours was awful. The prosecutor dispassionately described Mr Pears, handcuffed to a chair and further secured to the wall, being tormented and then shot by this malevolent man-child whose behaviour sat so far outside normal human conception. As the description went on, I looked up to find Bryant laughing, as if the account was triggering recollections of a high school prank.

He was a pathetic and hopeless man, sent out into the world ungifted by nature. But by his own actions he rendered himself unworthy of compassion by anyone other than a mother or a saint. And I was neither of those.

26

THE HOLY LAND

IN NOVEMBER 1995, THE ISRAELI PRIME MINISTER YITZHAK RABIN HAD been assassinated in Tel Aviv. His killer was not a Palestinian terrorist but a young devout Jew opposed to Rabin's efforts to make a lasting peace with the Palestinian people.

Two years earlier, Rabin had stood on the White House lawn and shaken hands with the Palestinian leader Yasser Arafat. Both were awarded the Nobel Peace Prize for the handshake. A young Bill Clinton stood in the middle beaming at them. The deal he had helped broker was meant to bring lasting peace to the Middle East.

But Rabin's death had shaken Israel as had the continued sporadic violence against Jews.

Rabin's deputy Shimon Peres took over the prime ministership and an election was set for May 1996. Despite the vocal complaints of right-wing Jews, it seemed all but inevitable that the Israeli people would endorse the peace process. How could they not, having come so far?

I set off in mid-May with a perfect reporting team. Jim Carroll, the boss of *Nightline*, came along as field producer. Gary 'Disco' Fidelia, a cameraman of Mauritian background and an old friend, joined us from Melbourne. Disco possessed both talent and an unquenchable sense of fun, lightening up any assignment. Also along as a fixer was a brilliant young man, Guy Spigelman, the nephew of former New South Wales Chief Justice Jim Spigelman. Guy had already served in the Israeli Army. He would return to make a run at the Israeli Parliament, the Knesset. He was well connected and smart.

Nightline had its own budget. The main 6 pm news desk was not interested in the story and the highbrow *Sunday* program only committed to stay in touch in case anything happened.

Once we got to Israel, however, the sheer drama of what was happening changed their minds. In ten days, we filed two full-length *Sunday* cover stories, seven *Nightline* features and at least seven separate news pieces.

Disco, Guy and I raced around the country. We looked at the disputed city of Hebron, an Arab town built around the Cave of Machpelah. It was here, according to tradition, that the great early patriarchs of Judaism – Abraham, Isaac and Jacob – were buried, along with the early matriarchs, Sarah, Rebecca and Leah.

For Jews, there are few places more sacred. But Abraham was also revered by Arabs, who drew their traditions from his first-born son Ishmael, who was cast into the wilderness with his slave-girl mother to be comforted by the voice of God.

The caves were home to both a Jewish temple and a mosque. A small, embattled settlement of Jews was dug in a couple of kilometres from the tombs, surrounded by Palestinians who frequently had them under attack. The Israeli Defence Force (IDF) committed vast numbers of troops to protect them.

Two years earlier, a Jewish doctor and fanatic, Baruch Goldstein, attacked the mosque at the Cave of Machpelah, shooting dead twenty-nine Muslim worshippers and wounding more than a hundred. Until Martin Bryant's attack at Port Arthur, it was the largest single-gunman massacre on record.

Survivors overpowered Goldstein and beat him to death. He was buried at the nearby fortified Jewish settlement of Kiryat Arba where he lived. It is Jewish tradition that mourners place a stone on the grave of the dead as a sign of respect. The more stones, the more respect. When I visited Goldstein's gravesite, it was piled high with stones.

The peace deal Rabin had made with Arafat, and whose hopes were now being carried by Shimon Peres, was supposed to bring a lasting peace to disputed places like Hebron. While we walked Hebron's streets, however, it crackled with tension.

It was my first trip to Israel. Like so many before me, I was struck by the sheer charisma of the old stone town of Jerusalem. Here were so many places I knew from my brief Catholic schooling. To walk among ancient olive trees in the Garden of Gethsemane, as Jesus had walked before his betrayal and crucifixion, was powerful indeed. On the road to Jericho to interview the Palestinian negotiator Saeb Erekat, I passed a Bedouin man heading up to Jerusalem on a donkey – a scene unchanged in two thousand years.

The pictures were so powerful, the stories so strong, that they all but wrote themselves. I would return from the Golan Heights, or the Jordan valley, or the wealthy suburbs of Tel Aviv, or a joint patrol with Israeli and Palestinian police along the Green Line, pound out my script, record a voiceover, and leave it to Jim Carroll and a local editor to cut into shape.

It was exhilarating work.

The political contest was fundamentally about an idea. Could Israel be rendered secure through a peace deal with the Palestinian Liberation Organization (PLO), the organisation they had fought for decades?

Shimon Peres believed so. He was an utterly uncharismatic man, a politician of deep if undemonstrative conviction. In his long mournful face and careful language, he seemed to carry something of the old patriarchs of his tribe, a profound sense of history and the duties of office.

Against him was the brash and showy Benjamin Netanyahu. With his American accent and punchy turn of phrase, the young leader of Likud projected the counter-argument. Israel could only know peace if it did not weaken itself in the face of an implacable enemy.

Helping his argument was Hamas. Funded by Iran, Hamas was a small but rising player in the alphabet soup of factions operating in Gaza and the West Bank. Whereas Arafat's PLO was a substantially secular movement, Hamas was unabashedly religious. That did not necessarily fit with many hard-pressed Palestinians, whose primary interest was in trying to make a living. But unlike the PLO, Hamas had not been debased by corruption. It funded local welfare operations and health clinics and it largely kept its promises.

Peace was not its plan.

As the election approached, Hamas sponsored a series of bombings that killed more than sixty people in Israel. With two big bombings in Tel Aviv, Hamas blew away the strong lead Peres held in the polls. Israelis' sentiments were shifting inexorably from hope to fear.

A few days before the election, Palestinian gunmen killed a Jewish teenager on the occupied West Bank. Photos showed a chubby, innocuous boy with the hat and distinctive hair of an orthodox religious student.

The boy's mother appeared fleetingly on television, shouting in Brooklyn English 'This is not peace!'

It was a powerful argument that resonated with Israelis, and with me. When I mentioned this to Guy Spigelman, he suggested we go and visit her.

'After the death of her son?' I asked.

'Why not?' said Guy.

We found that she lived in a settlement on the outskirts of Jerusalem and it was here that I got my introduction to the Jewish system of mourning known as *shiva*. For seven days after the death of a loved one, the family leaves its door open. Friends and neighbours bring all the food the mourners need. They also bring their ears. In the week that the principal mourners 'sit' *shiva*, they speak to whoever comes about the person they have lost. No sincere person is turned away.

So we walked into this woman's apartment with our camera and, taking our turn, sat and asked her about her son. Her grief was on full show and her anger was undimmed. She blamed Shimon Peres for her son's death. Israel was ambling towards disaster. The country was trading down its strength for an illusion. Benjamin Netanyahu got it, she said. He had come to visit her after her son's death. From Peres, she had heard nothing.

It was a powerful interview. For the first time, I sensed that the Oslo peace deal secured with the Rabin and Arafat handshake was crumbling. I also got an insight into the value of ancient traditions. At the end of seven days, the family members are all talked out. The door closes again. The family starts to grope forward towards the life they must live in their bereavement. But by then they have had the love of many and they have spoken of their regrets, pride and pain.

The ritual has some parallels in the Maori *tangi*. Under the New Zealand tradition, mourners of all kinds are encouraged to step up and speak to the deceased as if they were still alive. Siblings settle old arguments and voice old resentments. Lovers speak their love. No one is abridged. When all is done, the griefs and complex emotions are purged – at least in their first urgent flamings. Life limps on.

Both systems seem much more psychologically satisfying than my own Anglo tradition of stiff upper lips, of silences and solitude and the deadening demands of dignity.

During this phase I also met, through Guy's connections, one of the senior Israeli negotiators through the Oslo period. He had a clear-eyed sense of the dangers to the peace process. He and his Palestinian counterpart both had doctorates in conflict resolution from western universities. When they bumped into each other at international airports, they greeted each other as true friends. They inquired about each other's children. They wished each other well.

Negotiators from both sides knew the parameters well and knew what needed to be done.

On both sides, though, they knew the difficulty was in carrying their own population. Every concession agreed at the table was a sign of weakness to their own support base, never mind that it might lead to a better world. It was always easier to revert to a hard line and enjoy the cheers of the home crowd.

And so it was.

On the night of the election, we went to Peres's Labour Party headquarters in a vast hall near the Mediterranean seafront in Tel Aviv. The late polling indicated Peres, and the peace accord, would get up by a narrow margin.

As the first numbers came in, a group of young Labour Party volunteers leapt onto their seats, singing and dancing. Many around them were also on their feet. As more numbers progressed, the youthful glee club kept up its celebrations but the older heads became increasingly subdued.

Soon, although all announcements were in Hebrew, it became clear from the body language that the cause of Oslo was lost. Israelis had voted against the peace deal. Netanyahu's victory was as tight as it could get. His Likud party was outvoted by Labour. But with religious parties joining his cause, he got up. In the direct vote for the prime ministership, Netanyahu's win was so slight that it would have gone the other way had just fifteen thousand people out of more than three million (or 0.5 percent) chosen differently.

But a win is a win.

Netanyahu was Israel's youngest prime minister. He lasted just three years before Labour returned under Ehud Barak. But the Oslo peace deal never recovered. In the coming years, as I would see for myself, Hamas would grow in power while the Palestinian Authority (the rebranding of the PLO) grew more impotent. Palestinians still live largely in misery. Israel, however, has marched more towards the Likud version of reality. The people most often defeated in the Middle East are those who trust. That's a sad thing to have to say.

The experience brought home to me how easy it is to become one of the many people intoxicated by the Middle East. The issues are real, the people fascinating, the history as deep as anything our culture provides. As for the future? In the Book of Exodus, Moses dies and Joshua leads the Hebrews to the Promised Land, blowing his trumpets until the walls of Jericho fall. And for the next two hundred pages of the Old Testament, there is virtually nothing but a record of conflicts met and enemies vanquished.

The old pale dust of the land of Abraham and Ruth, of David and Solomon, of Jeremiah and Lot – and yes, of Jesus – has seen much blood and many sorrows. Why should we suppose it ends now?

27

ENTOMBED

IN THE DARK OF A WINTER EVENING, A RESIDENT AT ONE OF THE SKI lodges crowding the steep southern bank of the Thredbo River noticed the ground around a stairwell was unusually muddy. It was the first and perhaps the only clue to a coming disaster.

The New South Wales mountain resort was busy with skiers and snowboarders on 30 July 1997. By 11 pm most had taken to their beds, especially those who worked on the mountain. They could look forward to early starts checking or staffing the chairlifts, or keeping all the other human and physical machinery of Thredbo in order.

When the landslide hit, not long before midnight, it swept away two complete lodges chiefly populated by staff. Nineteen people were buried under mud, rocks and concrete.

It seems clinical to speak of disasters like that. A bare recitation of facts. There was nothing clinical for those involved. Of the nineteen buried, ski instructor Stuart Diver would lie entombed and unnoticed for fifty-five hours. He was sleeping when a rumbling sound woke him, his eyes shooting open as he was suddenly thrown around amid the explosive noise of windows shattering and walls collapsing. In the pitch black, choking on dust, he heard his wife Sally, screaming, screaming . . .

Stuart Diver estimated it took thirty seconds for the movement to stop. The ceiling settled three centimetres from his nose. He was able to wriggle sideways, falling off his bed onto a space filled with shards of glass which lacerated his hands and knees. He could see nothing. He could barely breathe in the dust-thickened air. He could find no way out.

Sally was conscious and screaming. Her head was pinned beneath the bedhead and a concrete slab lay heavily across her body.

'I can't feel anything from the waist down,' she said.

Stuart tried to reach her. He was able to feel the obstacles on her face and her body.

'It's all right, Sal. We'll be okay.'

And then another rumble. This time it was a freezing cascade of mud and water. Sally started screaming again.

'Stuart! Stuart!'

He put his hand over her mouth to try to stop the water getting in. But he could not stop it. He felt her face contorting beneath his hand. He felt her go limp. He felt her drown.

Stuart Diver then forced himself up until he was touching the concrete above him. The water lapped at his lips but there was a tiny air pocket. He was all but naked, shocked with cold, stunned by the loss of his young wife. Stunned by his inability to save her. But alive.

And there he would remain as the world turned. Buried. Unnoticed. Waging his own private battle against the deadly winter cold, against his shock and grief, fighting to win the conflict between his desire to live and his desire to die.

—

Thredbo is a small place. The vast alpine wilderness rises around it, with Mount Kosciuszko just to the north, a pleasant stroll on a summer's day. In winter, Thredbo village huddles in its valley, offering food and fun and comfort and rest for the thousands who go there for the sport.

On the morning of 31 July, people gathered on the little all-weather walkway on the northern side of the Thredbo River. The path gave a view directly onto the landslide, where several buildings were damaged and tottering and two had been completely swept away.

Gathering in silence were people who lived and worked at Thredbo. Those who were not part of the regiment of volunteers already working on the other side of the valley, watched in mute disbelief. They had work colleagues buried in that shambles. Thredbo holidaymakers also came to watch. Some, powerless to do anything and self-conscious about being rubberneckers, did what mountain people did and went skiing. They were condemned by many for doing so. Not me. I knew from experience that mountains clear heads and give space for emotions to find some room.

Also gathering were TV cameras and reporters. The path and the grassy slope just above it gave an unobstructed view of the catastrophe. We were out of the way of the rescue workers but could show the work being done and the nature of the challenge. But we could not stay out of the way of the little clusters of people who arrived through that first day and the next. These were the family members of those missing, presumed lost. They wanted the same view we wanted, a chance to understand what had changed their lives so suddenly and with such force.

Most of the journalists, reading the anguish in the body language of these visitors, gave them as much respectful distance as was possible. But not all of them. I have never quite forgiven a reporter from a rival network who, seeing me, boomed out, 'Ah, Hughie! Remind you of Port Arthur, eh?' I put my head down and walked past him without a word.

There were many reasons for anguish in the village.

In the first hour after the landslide, people from neighbouring buildings scrambled out onto the still-shifting wreckage of the shattered Carinya and Bimbadeen Lodges. They could hear people screaming for help. The first police officer on the scene, Paul Hoyer, also heard voices – a man and a woman calling 'Help'.

Two ambulance officers who had raced up from Jindabyne, nearly forty kilometres away, crawled beneath the rubble in pursuit of voices they had heard. One, John Bartley, believed he was only a metre away from them but was blocked by a wall of debris. In my colleague Simon Bouda's later account, Bartley had to be pulled out by his ankles as the rubble continued to move.

The police ordered everyone away, insisting no rescue effort should be attempted before daylight. It was solid policing practice. Don't lose more life. But the shouts and cries died down until dawn was met with total silence from the wreckage. Many fumed that they had been prevented from saving mates and colleagues, or from even trying to.

Specialist emergency teams were on their way within hours – urban search and rescue experts, paramedics trained in treating people as they lay trapped, and mine rescue teams. The police presence multiplied.

But by the first major daylight news conference, the senior officer on the site admitted, 'The chances of anyone being alive in there are very, very negligible.'

Grief and anger made a volatile mix.

I knew the symptoms and was sensitive to them. The sudden hand of disaster brings terrible loss. After the initial shock, anger hits hard. People in this state are experiencing emotions they might never have previously encountered, at least not in such circumstances. Their lives have been changed utterly and they don't like it at all. They will rail against police or other emergency workers – but even then, they know these are merely professionals trying to help. But the media! The cameras become a symbol of what has changed. Even if not one lens is aimed at them, they feel intrusion mounting on all their other emotions.

I feel for them.

In every disaster, I urge a demeanour of quietness and respect. We have a job to do. If the people railing at camera teams as 'bloodsuckers' and 'vultures' were at home that day and unconnected with the disaster, they would have turned on their TVs to find out what was going on. That is our job.

At the Christchurch earthquake in 2011, I saw a police officer with foam flecking from his mouth raging at a camera crew. The crew was standing precisely where emergency scene controllers had told them to gather. The stress of sudden loss is no small thing.

At Thredbo, some journalists went into the village one evening to have a meal and a drink at the pub. They were called out by people living in the village and it almost came to blows. Some of those journalists were indignant at their treatment. I wondered how they imagined it would be different. I found a lodge that would have us and we cooked up rolling vats of spaghetti bolognese.

Criminologists talk about 'community policing'. I like the idea of 'community reporting'. You are of your community, not merely reporting on it. A little empathy goes a long way.

As the hours passed and the grim recovery of bodies began, it was interesting to note the contrasting styles of some high-profile journalists and presenters. One insisted on being flown home every night after the bulletin, to be flown back the following morning. She looked magnificent in her snow-gear as she took her place in the village until it was time to deliver her emotive account of the day's events.

There was no bigger star than Channel Nine's Ray Martin. Coming out of our lodge after taking a pee, I saw Ray perched on the metal grille where people kicked the snow from their boots. Notebook in hand, brow furrowed, he was working on the precise words he wanted to say to capture the day's developments. Ultimately, that is the core task of the reporter, especially when emotions are troubled: what are the words that will do justice to this?

For all his wealth and fame, Ray Martin was a reporter's reporter. Doing the work, not simply sucking up the prime-time glory. He was the real thing.

—

As rescuers crawled over the face of the landslide, they were in constant danger of a new slip. Again and again, work stopped because sensors stationed in the unstable rubble picked up shifts and movement. The collapse of the multi-storey lodges had left slabs of concrete stacked on each other at outlandish angles. Compressed between them were whatever muck, mud and furniture had fallen with the cement.

Nineteen people were missing. As hours passed there were fewer and fewer prospects that anyone would emerge alive. But the scene was alive with threat. The rescue workers searching out void spaces, exploring where reports of voices had come in the first hours, were in danger of being sliced by shifting slabs. There was bravery afoot.

On the opposite side of the valley, the Nine camera teams had determined that one camera would be permanently trained on the site. If anything moved or shifted, if a voice was heard, we would have the shot.

Every so often the work would stop so rescuers could call for survivors and listen for any sounds. With the generators off and the heavy equipment silenced, a deep quiet settled on the mountain valley. The very air seemed colder and more still.

Nothing.

The work resumed.

All of this, for hour after hour, was watched by a young cameraman, Ben Hanson. He had volunteered for the mountain-watch job. This was due to his junior ranking – he had only just become a 'graded' cameraman. It was also a consequence of his unassailable good nature.

Every so often, I would walk up to see how he was going and to check if there was any shot I needed to know about. Around 9 pm, he confessed to being a little cold.

'It's mainly just my feet.'

For the first time I glanced at where he was standing, in a stamped-down patch of wet snow. He was wearing simple canvas tennis shoes. They were soaked through.

As a kid on my schoolboy mountain courses in New Zealand, it was drilled into me that hypothermia came from a combination of any of two or three things: wind, wet and cold. His feet were literally freezing.

Like many young Sydney cameramen, Ben could pick out a rip on a surf beach from half a kilometre. But he had never been in snow before and knew nothing about how to manage intense cold. Uncomplainingly, he had placed himself in genuine danger.

As it happened, my New Zealand mountain training had been augmented by a climbing trip to the Himalayas on my way to London. With my former Outward Bound instructor, Sue Aitkin, I had spent extended periods above eighteen thousand feet in the Himalayan winter, with temperatures below minus thirty degrees Celsius. I had a better than average grasp of what cold could do.

That training kicked in and we got Ben into the nearest lodge for some repair work. No lasting damage done. But I knew I was going to have to watch out for the team.

I also looked across the valley at the scene of ruin. If anyone had survived the first hours after the landslide, I thought, surely the cold would have got them by now.

In his tiny void space, Stuart Diver was, indeed, cold. He could no longer feel his feet or legs. He was drifting in and out of sleep. Both his dreams and his waking states were filled with hallucinations. Increasingly weak, he hit a metal pipe rhythmically against the metal bars of his bedhead. He could hear rescuers moving above him. He could distinguish the sounds of chainsaws from excavators and other machinery. In utter darkness he had investigated the space around him. He knew he could do nothing to get himself out. He would have to rely on the efforts of others. The thought displaced his terror, anger, fear and frustration. He became passive and calm. He had to hang on and stay hopeful. Beyond that there was nothing he could do.

By Stuart Diver's own judgement he was on his last legs when a New South Wales firefighter, Steve Hirst, thought he heard something above the racket of cranes, excavators, concrete-cutting saws and other equipment. The frequent periods of silence when the rescuers listened intently, using specialist equipment to detect any sound, had brought them nothing. But in the squall of noise, something had got through.

Or at least, that was Steve Hirst's belief.

He lowered himself onto a shattered concrete slab from where he thought the sound had come.

'Quiet on the site!' went up the call.

Hirst yelled out, 'Rescue party working overhead. Can you hear me?'

A faint human sound emerged from the layers of wreckage.

Hirst called again and this time the words were unambiguous. 'Yes, I'm down here!'

Both above ground and below there was a sudden powerful jolt of euphoria.

It was just before 7 am.

Within a few minutes the police officer in charge of the site, Charlie Sanderson, was addressing a hastily gathered press conference.

'A miracle has occurred,' he said.

Privately, the rescue teams calculated it could take three hours to cut through the layers of debris separating Stuart Diver from daylight.

In Sydney, Channel Nine's production teams were being scrambled. In very little time we were live on air with no script and no plan other than to stay on air until it was over. Thredbo was our studio and the story we had to tell was a drama of almost exquisite tension.

Tracy Grimshaw, my old mate from Melbourne days and one of the finest broadcasters I know, took over the chair in Sydney.

'There's every chance this won't happen quickly,' I counselled her, and the producers, on air. I was getting tremendous information from the fire brigade, which ran the urban search and rescue teams on the mountain. The ambulance service also had its crack rescue paramedics on the scene, the Special Casualty Access Team, known by its acronym SCAT. It was led by the calm and experienced Paul Featherstone. Ambulance officials came repeatedly to our live position to bring us up to date with their methods and progress.

My mountain training again came in useful. I had had hypothermia recognition and treatment ground into me so often I could talk about it all day. I pretty much did. We were on that mountain broadcasting live without a break for more than nine hours that day. That's a lot of air to fill. These days, twenty-four-hour TV news is run-of-the-mill stuff. But we had never seen a spontaneous news broadcast of such length before from a single site.

Little by little, we got a picture of what was going on. We learnt that it was Stuart Diver. We learnt a little bit about him – that as a ski instructor he had knowledge of cold and how to survive it. We learnt that his wife had not survived – a delicate piece of information to work around. We learned how the rescuers hoped to get him out and the dangers of the task. They had not discerned the physical state of their patient. Hypothermia was inevitable and frequently fatal. But, given the state of the buildings that had collapsed on top of him, fractures, crush injuries, internal bleeding were all at least possibilities and all would narrow his chances.

First, rescuers had to find him. The sound of Stuart Diver's voice was being filtered through so many layers of rubbish, it wasn't clear exactly where he was. For more than three hours, they tried to reach him believing he was between two particular concrete slabs. They were wrong. He was actually beneath the lower of the two slabs. The rescue effort had – effectively – to start again.

Finally, the rescuers were able to get a remotely controlled light through the gaps in the rubble until Diver could see it himself. He realised there was a larger cavity than the one he had been lying in and he was able to edge himself into it. When he reached the light, a wave of relief ran through him.

'In twenty minutes,' he thought, 'I'll be out of here.'

His hopeful time frame was very wrong. The light had come through a crack in the slab. Diver's rescuers were lying on top of it. Diver reached up and his fingers emerged through that crack. Rescuer Geoff Courtney saw the fingers, blue with cold and trembling, and gripped them with his own.

But the hard bit of the rescue had only just begun.

The moment-by-moment struggle to get Stuart Diver out deserves a book of its own – and it has one: Stuart Diver's own account *Survival*, written with the help of my Nine colleague Simon Bouda.

From our live spot, we were getting continued excellent briefings on progress. I was also getting pulled to one side for off-the-record updates on specific details of the rescue to give me a deeply informed idea of what was going on.

But there were some things they didn't say.

Stuart Diver was a remarkably resilient personality. But with his own rescue possible, if not yet certain, he had time to reflect more deeply on the death of his wife.

'There were plenty of tears,' he later recalled, 'but they weren't tears of joy.'

Little by little, the rescuers opened up larger gaps in the concrete until they could get an oxygen mask to him and a tube that directed warm air to counter-balance the still-freezing conditions. Paul Featherstone, the paramedic, was able to monitor Diver's heart rate and respiration. Diver was still on the very edge. Twice Featherstone thought he was about to lose him.

They managed to get a tube to him so Stuart could suck down a specially concocted mixture of electrolytes and nutrients. But the first attempt to get a drip into his arm failed because they couldn't find a vein. In hypothermia, the body goes into an emergency state, retaining such warmth as it can for the core functions of the heart and brain. The extremities, starting with the fingers and toes but ultimately entire limbs, become starved of blood and oxygen. They go blue as the circulation ceases to reach them. They become as cold as the outside conditions. Slowly they die.

After hours determining exactly where he was lying and how the debris was structured, rescuers settled on a plan to access the void through a slab lying above his feet. Clearing a mattress lying above the slab and then cutting a hole through the slab itself took well over another hour. Cutting through a couch lying compressed beneath the slab took another hour.

Even then, they were not quite there. A rescue worker, Warwick Kidd, had his hand in the hole trying to clear away loose debris when he grabbed something as frigid and solid as every other bit of rubbish. It took him a moment to realise he was gripping a foot. He called in Paul Featherstone. The paramedic saw clear evidence of frostbite.

I later learnt, though I was not surprised, that people were crowding in streets outside electrical stores to watch the rescue on TV, in scenes last witnessed in the very early days of television when only the wealthy could afford sets. People didn't want to go home in case they missed something. As Stuart Diver was sucking on his oxygen mask, the country was holding its breath.

Several times, parts of the mountain moved. The rescue workers were ordered away. But after the first time he was dragged off the hillside, Paul Featherstone determined it wouldn't happen again. He was monitoring Diver's emotional and psychological wellbeing as well as his physical health. The sense of abandonment could undo all the work the rescuers were attempting.

So Featherstone stayed there, his fate tied to the man he hoped to save. Two brave men, one conscripted against his will into this fierce drama, the other a volunteer.

It was eleven hours after Diver was discovered before a doctor was able to cut into his foot deep enough to find a working vein in order to get in an intravenous drip. For half an hour this liquid link warmed Stuart Diver and went some way to correcting his body's biochemistry, full of toxins after so many hours trapped.

Finally, nearly twelve hours after his voice was heard, sixty-five hours after the landslide, Stuart Diver was pulled up and out, into the daylight. He was surrounded by the rescue team and, for a moment, it wasn't clear from the opposite side of the little valley what was going on.

But then, with the sun settling over the back of Dead Horse Gap, came the sign of a stretcher being moved. Tracy Grimshaw was relaying the news that Stuart Diver's release was imminent when I broke in.

'There he is,' I shouted, 'a cheer is going up around the mountain.'

And lifted by willing hands, the one good thing to be extracted from that awful tragedy was carried up the broken slope to a fleeting reunion with his parents and brother, before an ambulance took him to hospital.

In broadcasting terms, it was a unique experience. Across the nation, word spread of the survivor being located and of the complex and uncertain business of winning his release. Australia was utterly united with just one wish. By the time this brave man, this sole survivor, had been lifted clear, there could have been few people in the country not absorbed with the drama and the tension. To be able to call it, to be able to announce that news on the most-watched network in the land was both humbling and powerful.

The only other time I have seen Australians so utterly united in one wish was when Cathy Freeman made her gold medal run at the Sydney Olympics. And even that great day was not a matter of life or death.

Stuart Diver's survival was due in no small part to his own incredible resilience and determination. He could not have made it without his physical fitness and his knowledge of surviving cold conditions. He had acted again and again in that drenching, freezing tomb, to improve his chances of survival – for Sally's sake, as he put it, and so he could explain to Sally's mum what had happened.

But it was bittersweet. Gathering on the hillside alongside the cameras were the family members of others who'd disappeared that night. Their joy was tempered by the knowledge that it wasn't their son or daughter coming out. That confusion of feelings was perhaps strongest for Sally Diver's family.

Still, the nation celebrated. The tireless work of rescuers and volunteers had gained a reward beyond anyone's hopes. But every time I return to Thredbo, as I have done many times, I always think of the silence that fell on that scarred corner of the hillside. I think of the rescuers and the volunteers who did work that fully earns that exhausted adjective 'awesome'. I also think of the eighteen lives that ended in shock and trauma. For me, the beautiful mountains will always carry that mark.

28

SEBASTIAN'S EXAMPLE

THE EVENTS OF THREDBO MARKED A CHANGE IN HOW I WAS SEEN AT
Nine and – in a modest way – around the country. For a while,
strangers would routinely stop me to talk about and relive that
compelling day. Even today, two decades on, people want to talk
about Thredbo more than any other single story.

At Nine, I arrived back at the Willoughby studios to be presented
with a car. Newspaper features were written calling me Nine's 'go-to
guy'. Brian Henderson, the greatest of all Sydney newsreaders, took
to calling me 'The Master of Disaster'. It was all heady stuff, causing
me to remember Kerry Packer's great advice: 'You are never as good
or as bad as they say you are.'

I was assigned newsreading shifts and back-up hosting duties
on the *Today* show. Rather like when I was told I could stay on in
London, I felt I had passed another stage in the endless, lifelong
apprenticeship that is a reporter's life. I was not merely reliable and
useful but also, in some small way, recognisable.

I also began doing more news feature stories for *Nightline*. The
longer three- to four-minute duration allowed a little more depth
on issues that were running across Australia. *Nightline* was at that
stage the most-watched single news bulletin in the country. The
Nine News bulletins at 6 pm had a larger overall audience when
taken together but each of those was a distinct show for each state

market. *Nightline* was a national bulletin and routinely attracted audiences of over one million people.

It had serious firepower. Jim Waley was the anchor, the credibility of his mahogany voice further polished by his presence on the highly respected *Sunday* show. Paul Lyneham, a restless, trouble-making inquisitor, led our national political coverage. The show was run by Jim Carroll, later a very effective head of news and current affairs at the Ten Network and a senior executive at SBS. Mark Barlin was a fine features reporter and the production desk included stalwart figures like Fiona Pie, Ramon Dale and the irrepressible surfie scribe Wes Hardman.

It was a happy crew.

Late evening news has fallen out of fashion in Australia – even though it remains the standard for flagship programs in Britain and the United States. It is a shame. I always felt that a 6 pm bulletin was forced to compete with all the noise of people's busy lives – getting the dinner on, sorting out the kids, etc. A late news, so I hoped and believed, was a place for people who genuinely wanted to know what was going on. It was a more thoughtful time of night. The link between news studio and armchair seemed more intimate.

I have always worked best when I am doing several things at once. Boredom was my bogey. On top of studio work, feature stories and daily news, I had also become, in a fragrant term 'the shit fight specialist'. If it was complicated and uncomfortable, I was likely to get the call.

On Friday 17 July 1998, a sharp earthquake struck off the northern coast of Papua New Guinea (PNG). Minutes later a series of tsunamis, with waves up to fifteen metres high, hit the coastline. The first reports emerged around midnight and by first thing in the morning I was on a plane to Port Moresby. We filed from the capital that night, using patchy vision shot from the scene by Nine's PNG affiliate, EMTV.

There was still little clarity about the scale of the disaster when cameraman Ralph Cook, soundman Mick Tolman and I took a scheduled flight over the spine of PNG to the northern coastal city of Wewak. From there a charter flight took us north-west towards the little town of Vanimo where a rescue operation was starting to get organised.

We flew along the coast at five hundred feet. At one point the unbroken line of sand and palm trees gave way to a large circular lagoon. Over the headphones, the pilot indicated this was the place hit by the tsunami.

Gazing down, I felt that coldly embarrassed feeling when you realise you're on a mad goose chase. The coastline appeared innocent of trouble, a postcard image of palm trees alongside a placid, sparkling sea. Then I noticed rows of rectangles partly covered by sand. I realised with shock that these were concrete slabs marking buildings that no longer existed. An entire town had been wiped from the earth.

We landed further up the coast much sobered.

Over the next couple of days, the little town of Vanimo became the centre of an international operation. The PNG highlands had a variety of mining operations and other enterprises running helicopters and light planes. Many of these businesses donated their aircraft to the rescue mission. There was no road access to the disaster zone so reporting the story involved going from pilot to pilot at the little airstrip, seeing who had room to take us in.

I spied a big Russian helicopter with two flight crew sucking back a last cigarette before taking off. I greeted them in Russian and their eyes brightened a little. Their chopper was loaded with sacks of rice from a government emergency store.

'Where are you heading?'

'Wherever we can land.'

'Any chance you could fit us on board?'

'No, we are way overweight.'

'What's your carrying capacity?'

'Two tonnes.'

'How much have you got?'

'Already six tonnes.'

I looked at them to see if they were joking. Apparently they were not. Russian fatalism: what would be, would be.

I mooched off to try my luck elsewhere.

A few minutes later one of my Russian friends jogged up to me. The big rotors were already spinning.

'We can take you if you want.'

We were getting nowhere with the other pilots. We decided we would be Russians for the day.

The only way to fit on board was to lie flat on top of the sacks of rice, in a tiny envelope of space beneath the roof. The chopper laboured, shuddering, into the air. We barely cleared the palm trees before the pilots pointed it south-east along the coast and we flew a couple of hundred feet above the shore break. The helicopter was plainly at its limits. I knew enough about helicopters to know that if they hit water they flip upside down – all the weight of the machine is at the top where the engines are. If the pilots had to ditch it, I would be crushed beneath six tonnes of rice before I even had a chance to drown. Still . . . Russian fatalism.

The shaking of the helicopter caused thousands of weevils living happily in the rice to emerge through the weave of the sacks until I was lying suspended on a vibrating mass of beasties.

The chopper landed heavily but it had done its job. We were at the edge of Sissano lagoon near the former town of Aitape. Nothing remained of any buildings of substance. A man wearing only shorts, with fresh scars on his arms, was picking his way through the remains of a wooden hut. It was his home. He had been away. His family was gone. He extracted a tin of golden syrup from the wreckage and tossed it to the ground, Then, with a second thought, he retrieved it and put it to one side. That, and some salvageable planks of wood were all that remained of any value. In places, putrid-smelling water stood in large pools. The body of a boy, about four or five years old, lay at the edge of one of them. No one was around to identify him or to bury him. A dog had survived. And a pig. When the dog came skulking around the boy's corpse, a fit young man appeared from nowhere with a bow and fired an arrow at the animal. He missed, but the dog got the message.

About two thousand people died in the tsunami. Some survivors had been swept from the narrow beach right across Sissano lagoon. They had fetched up on the landward side, and were now emerging from the jungle into little villages above the flood line. Cadging a lift from another plane, Ralph and I landed on a tiny bush airstrip and walked into a little settlement now crowded with bewildered and stunned survivors.

Most, understandably, spoke little or no English, but I met one gentle figure, a school teacher, who told me eleven members of his family had been swept away.

I gazed into eyes that conveyed a measureless pain.

'You are lost,' I said quietly.

'I am lost,' he said.

The Australian Defence Force had flown in a variety of support equipment, most notably a tent hospital. It was, to use the language of an earlier age, a 'M.A.S.H' – a Mobile Army Surgical Hospital – like the TV series of yore. The waves had deeply scored the seabed, churning a dense mixture of broken coral. Many survivors had nasty coral cuts, which were easily infected. Much of the military medical unit's work was in cleaning wounds. There were broken limbs as well, and nasty head wounds, and a woman in labour. Beneath its jungle green canvas, the medical teams worked non-stop.

After a few days the worst of it seemed over. The patient load reduced. The CNN reporter, John Raedler, told me he'd been ordered to pack up and leave.

Suddenly there was a new influx of patients. The hard-pressed local nursing clinic near Aitape had treated the first injured survivors. They had put plaster on broken limbs. But over-run with casualties, they had not managed to clean out all the dirt and coral beneath the dressings. Nearly a week on, the Australian medics found themselves facing a gangrene epidemic.

Around 9 pm one night, I saw a little boy brought into the tent for surgery. Both his legs had been broken. His name was Sebastian Alosi and he was nine years old. I watched quietly as one of the surgeons finished up his examination and approached the boy's father.

'There is poison in the boy's legs,' said the surgeon, through an interpreter. 'The only thing that will stop your son from dying is to cut off his legs.'

The agony on the father's face confirmed he understood. It was explained to him that he would have to consent for the operation to go ahead. I cannot forget the look on his face. After a while, he gave his assent and little Sebastian was taken inside.

I stayed up that night outside the tent flap and in the morning, still hours before dawn, the doctor emerged to say the operation was complete. They had managed to save one leg but the other was gone. I entered the recovery tent and there was Sebastian semi-conscious as he emerged from the anaesthetic. I returned to PNG some six weeks later and found out that Sebastian had been taken for further recovery at Wewak hospital. His stump was still heavily bandaged but his spirits were solid and his father was still there looking after him. My heroes are not generally massive men with deep chests. They are people like my Outward Bound colleague Coreen, and that uncomplaining little nine-year-old. Courage takes many forms.

I spoke to Sebastian's father, who had taken weeks away from the rest of his family to be with his son. His spirits were somewhat lifted. I tried to encourage him further with talk about developments in prosthetics that might benefit Sebastian. Mr Alosi listened politely and then summed it up in a single sentence.

'My boy will never run,' he said. And with that, the subject was closed.

29

CROSSING THE NILE

SOMEHOW, THROUGH ALL OUR SEPARATE TRAVELS, I HAD STAYED IN touch with Steve Levitt, the hardcore cameraman I first met in 1988 when Channel Seven was shooting a story on him. The more I got to know him, the better I liked him. He looked like a mercenary with his wolfish grin, short-cropped hair and permanent stubble.

Nothing about him, though, suggested boastfulness. His conversation always turned to the people struggling on the planet. He had seen things no one else in our little world had seen and he told the tales of the things he knew.

Steve Levitt had grown up with an older brother who had learning difficulties. His childhood had been spent wading into fights with bigger boys to protect his brother from being bullied. Perhaps Steve became conditioned to risking his skin in the name of just causes.

For years he had lived in a world that was precarious on two levels. He would spend months at a time in obscure war zones like Eritrea or southern Sudan. His material reward was the hand-to-mouth existence of a freelance operator. He had some solid paydays along the way but would always reinvest the money on his next mission.

By the late 1990s, though, family life beckoned with his French anthropologist wife, Isabelle. It was time for a regular job. He became an aid worker, taking a senior role as adviser and film-maker for World Vision.

He and I had often spoken about an assignment together. Our only joint project had been covering demonstrations in Paris against nuclear testing, where the bar crawl afterwards was the most dangerous part of the venture.

Then, one Saturday morning, he was on the phone.

'It's getting grim in southern Sudan,' he said.

Sudan was in a state of civil war even before it gained independence in 1956. Apart from a break in the 1970s and early eighties, southern Sudan had known nothing but conflict. There was a deep cultural divide between the Muslim, Arabist north and the nominally Christian south. It was a war of medieval hopelessness fought with Kalashnikov rifles and famine.

The official government in Khartoum used terror raids and crude bombing attacks to disrupt the planting and sowing seasons in the south. In a place where successful cultivation was hard enough at the best of times, the consequence was famine.

In 1998, hundreds of thousands of people in South Sudan were on the edge of starvation.

Steve was going there with World Vision's chief executive, Dr Lynn Arnold, a former Labor Premier of South Australia. We cooked up a plan. If I could find a way to join them, Steve would shoot stories for me. Nine could hardly object to me going off on a frolic of my own, especially if it was essentially 'off the books' with none of the costs of sending a cameraman.

Notwithstanding the grim nature of the mission, it was an exciting prospect. I was going with a legendary figure of Australian photojournalism on a mission deep into an African war zone. What could be better than that?

Levitt was an excellent travelling companion, full of stories and limitless sound advice on the politics and culture of the southern Sudanese. We flew together to Nairobi and from there to

Lokichokio in northern Kenya, just a couple of kilometres short of the Sudanese border.

Lokichokio was a village of huts built from mud and saplings, but it had an all-weather airstrip, a Red Cross hospital and a UN food store. Almost all international aid agencies working in southern Sudan had a presence there. It was the launch-pad for dangerous flights through hostile airspace to deliver aid or carry out intel missions like ours.

Lynn Arnold was already there waiting. Also getting ready to go was Bruce Menser, a big unflappable American whom I had first met in Somalia some years before. I remembered that first meeting well. Menser was living in a compound in Baidoa dangerously exposed to all kinds of bandits and killers. I had tracked him down for his take on how things were going. As we were wrapping up the interview, his American instinct for hospitality kicked in. He groped around in a cluttered storeroom to re-emerge with a can of warm Coke. We solemnly shared this token of a different world before I took my leave.

Now he was head of World Vision for all of East Africa, taking in the complex troubles of not just Sudan but Ethiopia, Somalia and Eritrea.

The major cost of travel into southern Sudan was chartering a plane. The place was at war and the north considered itself within its rights to shoot down any unauthorised flights. Khartoum looked especially unfavourably on aid flights, given the support they brought to the very people the north was trying to crush.

Pilots willing to take on the work were either thrill-seeking eccentrics, people whose flying record was so spotty no one else would hire them, or those out to make quick money.

Our mission had two official purposes. One was to allow Bruce and Lynn to see for themselves the extent of the famine. Their goal was to visit an emergency feeding centre that World Vision had set up in a village called Panacier, in the front-line county of Bahr-el-Ghazal. The second purpose was to examine a dirt airstrip at a place call Malual Chaat, to see if it was safe for a twin-engine transport plane to land with emergency food aid. We could not stay in-country overnight. The charter costs were prohibitive. We were going to have to get in and out in a single day.

Steve and I drew away and conferred. We could do interviews with Lynn and Bruce back in Lokichokio on our return. Our time at Panacier was so short we had to concentrate on getting the pictures we needed, with such interviews as we could grab with people on the ground. We figured we were likely to be there for just a couple of hours. Our plan was to get material for a news story and for a separate news feature for *Nightline*.

We took off at dawn the following day, just as the African sun hit the tabletop promontory to the north-east of the airstrip. The little prop plane banked right, to the north, and soon we were crossing the Sudanese border. Below us, I noticed the wreckage of a plane that hadn't made it. I was later told – I don't know if it is true – that the smashed fuselage was the aircraft that had crashed a few months before carrying the great Mike Willesee and Australian cameraman Greg Low. It was his survival from that crash that propelled Willesee towards his deep Catholicism. But I knew nothing of that as our little Cessna Caravan clawed into the brightening sky and began its journey into a place of unceasing suffering.

We crawled across a blue sky between a blazing sun and the broad savannah. Occasionally thin tracks marked the sunburnt earth, linking little villages. We avoided the major towns, many of them garrisoned by government troops, and so the landscape seemed little changed from the days of the first men and women.

After a while, sharp glints of sunlight reflected back between breaks in the foliage. This was the Sudd, the largest wetland on earth, where the mighty Nile lost its momentum in the flatlands below us, forming an immense swamp. Finally, this too was behind us, and we flew on, the single engine thrumming. Our pilot was a New Zealander called Chris. He was trim and crisply dressed, which seemed a good sign, but he also seemed tense and unfriendly. No matter. He kept the plane headed north by north-west and after three hours or so he throttled back and we landed on a broad expanse of hard-packed earth seemingly in the middle of nowhere.

Some boxes of supplies, medicines and high-protein cereal mixes were off-loaded from the plane and piled in the dust. In the mysterious way of Africa, people started arriving out of nowhere.

The first evidence that we were near the feeding centre came when I gazed across flat country to the north. Here, out of the heat-haze, emerged the flickering forms of people, immensely tall, achingly thin and deeply black. They looked like Giacometti statues on the move.

Soon a couple of battered four-wheel drives turned up. The supplies were loaded into one. We clambered into another. Conscious of the limited time we would have, Steve and I were anxious to get to the feeding centre just a few kilometres away.

As we approached, we saw more and more people walking with the efficiency of exhaustion towards our goal. In the dust lay the bodies of some who had not made it. Some lying on the ground were still evidently alive, if only just. And some, I saw with shock, were children. The aid workers, all Africans, hurried on. The sight of children in the dust reminded me of a famous photograph which had been taken in Sudan just a few years before. It was a small child unable to hold up his head, curled in a fetal position in the dust. Behind him stood a vulture, waiting. I cut that picture out of the paper and pinned it next to my desk in London. I saw the child in my own newborn, Cait. The image shook me. The photograph garnered a Pulitzer Prize for the man who took it, Kevin Carter of South Africa. But he took his own life soon afterwards, saying he wished he had picked up the child.

Now I was seeing similar images all around me. The sheer number of people collapsed near the feeding centre was shocking. I didn't order the vehicle to stop. The aid workers could see it all as well as I could. They pressed on.

Soon the vehicles pulled to a halt and we entered a crudely fenced compound crowded with naked and starving people.

It was overwhelming. Only Steve's busy example and our own pre-planning enabled me to keep focus. A worker from the feeding centre walked around with us. It was soon clear there was organisation at work within this huge crowd. Most had been living on bark and leaves for days or weeks. They were getting food here, two meals a day of a starchy gloop thickened with protein supplement.

In a separate area, children who were hanging on with stick-thin limbs and swollen bellies, their hair turned red from malnutrition, were being fed a special rescue porridge developed and sent from Australia. A little boy I guessed to be eighteen months old, two at the most, was in fact six. He was hoisting porridge with his fingers out of a handmade wooden bowl.

'What are his prospects?' I asked an aid worker.

'Oh, he'll be fine, he's going well,' he said. 'Come with me.'

I followed him into another hut with a thatched roof against the blazing heat.

'These are the children who can no longer eat,' he said.

I looked at him sharply. He understood the question in my gaze.

'There is nothing we can do for these ones.'

Some of the children were all alone, left on mats woven from thin strips of wood or on blue plastic sheets. Through some of the tiny rib cages I could see the fluttery evidence of a heartbeat. One little girl was incontinent in the last hour of her life, a thin stream emitting from her withered body. A little boy, called Riek Matar, was lying on the ground in front of his mother. She was so emaciated, there was no flesh to her at all. But her eyes were clear and they watched me. I have never felt so helpless.

While I watched, little Riek died. The little girl, all on her own, died too.

There are no words for the helplessness. I felt all sorts of utterly useless emotions. I felt a choking grief for all of them. Somewhere anger was raging too, for these deaths had been deliberately contrived. There is no blunter instrument than famine. It carries off the weakest, the smallest, the most deserving of care and love and support.

Something happened in that compound. I looked into the faces, the curves of necks and shoulders, the tired movements of exhausted people and I felt like everyone I was seeing was someone I knew. That woman there, bent over her child, I could see her at a dinner party in Sydney. That woman seeking shade beneath a tree, with wiry grey in her short hair – she could be a grandmother in my suburb.

Steve, bless him, had seen all this many times before. He kept working. And my years of performing the simple tasks of reporting kicked in and I worked alongside him, like an automaton.

I had seen people dying before. I had seen victims of violence with horrifying wounds. I had seen the bodies of the recently dead stacked like firewood. I had seen African famine and African violence and I thought, after nearly a decade of looking for trouble, that I had seen it all and had my protective veneers in place against any shock.

But my defences were worthless at Panacier.

I was there for no more than three hours but the man who arrived and the man who left were different men. The more time that has passed, the clearer to me are the lasting changes that were wrought by the emotions of that day. Even more than Rwanda, or Somalia or South Africa, something boiled in me for justice even as I knew there could be no justice for a blameless boy dying in the sight of his blameless mother. It was as if I had stumbled into Belsen but I wasn't a liberator, I was simply a gawker, a hideous tourist. I would leave and my presence there would have made no difference. I knew telling stories could make a theoretical impact, that every sentence that was written would link with others being written and ultimately people would have to know. Maybe some-time, all of this might add up to pressure, and perhaps one day all of this would be over.

But my presence would not help one child in that straw hut. My body weight in porridge would have made a far better passenger in that plane.

Obscenely, even the feeding centre was not safe from attack. Two weeks after we left, government aeroplanes bombed it.

While we were there, everyone was on guard against a land attack as well. The poorly defended front line was just a few kilo- metres away. The aid workers each had 'run-bags', a backpack containing survival essentials. If government troops came, the aid workers would flee into the bush and simply try their luck along with any of the people still strong enough to move.

We needed to flee too, not because of immediate danger but because the precious charter time with the aircraft was running down and Bruce and Lynn still had work to do.

We returned on the rough track past the most recently fallen – could we have done more? It haunts me still. We were soon airborne. But the day hadn't done with us yet.

—

Our homeward journey should have been simple. We needed a quick stop at Malual Chaat to see if the dust airstrip was suitable for a hardy twin-engine Buffalo aircraft. The plan was to build up an emergency supply base within reach of the worst-hit areas but less vulnerable to attack.

We touched down in baking heat on a bouncy earthen strip. Lynn Arnold and Bruce Menser used the time to greet some of the locals, who included an ancient Italian nun and a monk of similar vintage whose beard made him look like a feral Santa Claus.

Malual Chaat had also been famine struck. A few children came by to examine the plane and us strangers, as did a grey-haired woman of indeterminate age. She made it as far as the thin shade of a leafless tree where she sat down, arranging her long, painfully thin limbs as comfortably as she could.

The monk was excited to see us because two young men of the village had been caught in a grass fire the previous day. They had serious burns across their bodies. A call went out for them to be collected so they could be taken in the back of our plane to the Red Cross hospital in Lokichokio.

While we awaited their arrival, I chatted with some of the kids, with the old nun acting as translator. Many of the children were afflicted with guinea worms, which they would have sucked up in larval form from stagnant water. Inside their human host, the worm could grow to two metres long. At a certain point in its lifecycle, the worm broke the surface of the skin and its head would emerge. For the human host, this would result in a horrendous burning pain. The overwhelming instinct for the human sufferer is to cool the pain by putting the affected part of the body into water, at which point the worm would suddenly burst, expelling thousands of eggs back into the water to continue the cycle.

Guinea worms, the nun explained, were a particular torment in this region where the dry season shrank all watercourses to the Sudanese equivalent of billabongs. If the sufferer tried to ease the agony by pinching off the head of the worm, the body of the creature would die inside the human host, bringing poisoning and death. The only option was to roll out the worm, millimetre by millimetre, like twisting a piece of fettuccine around a chopstick. It was a delicate process, attended by constant pain. If the worm broke at any stage, the consequences were fatal.

Many of the people we saw had little cylinders tied around their necks. These contained filters to enable them to suck in water without taking in the parasites. A surer system was to dig wells deep enough to reach ground water even in the dry season. Well-digging was a major focus for many international aid agencies.

My conversation with the kids was interrupted by the arrival of slender youths carrying the two severely burnt men in woollen blankets. The men were laid out with as much care as could be

managed in the now-empty cargo space behind the seats in the
Cessna Caravan. They were in terrible shape, their deep black skin
torn open with rosettes of full thickness burns. They offered no
complaint at all, simply gazing at the ceiling of the plane.

We needed to move.

Chris, the pilot, had locked the lower half of the cargo door,
leaving the upper section open to help cool the suffering passengers.
He had also left the windows to the cockpit open. We were making
our farewells with the Italians and the locals when Chris suddenly
issued a shout.

Some children had been hanging at the door of the cockpit.
Suddenly they scattered. Chris strode to the cockpit door to see
what they had been up to and noticed his camera, left lying on the
seat, had been stolen.

He let out a bovine bellow of rage. He took a few quick steps
to try to chase down the kids, but they were scattering fast in all
directions. He shouted a torrent of abuse after them and stamped
back towards the rest of us standing, concerned now, in the thin
shade of the tree.

The very thin, old woman sitting on the ground was watching
him, as we all were. Something about her must have aggravated
him because he interrupted his progress to stand right over her,
his fists clenching.

'What's so funny?' he shouted. He was genuinely foaming.
'What's so fucking funny?'

The woman recoiled.

The threat of violence directed at such a fragile and innocent
party galvanised the rest of us. Lynn Arnold was raised a peace-
loving Quaker. He would ultimately retire from aid work to become
– in his sixties – an ordained Anglican priest. Every instinct in his
body propelled him forward to soothe the pilot and find out what
had suddenly brought about this change.

Chris was so angry, he was barely coherent.

The stolen camera was not expensive, but it contained pictures of his son. He could barely stand still as he gave voice to his pain and rage. The trim, intense professional pilot had disappeared. In his place was a man plainly on the edge – if not in the full grip of – an emotional and psychological breakdown. His shirt was drenched in sweat.

Somewhere in his telling it emerged that his marriage had ended, his son was his life, the photos were all he had of him. It was as if in stealing the pilot's camera, the kids had killed the thing most precious to him.

He demanded the thieves be caught.

'The kids will be far away,' soothed Lynn Arnold. 'Would it help if we were to chip in and buy a new camera?'

This elicited a stream of oaths. Chris suddenly announced he was going to get the little bastards and started striding off over the sandy savannah in the direction of the mud-hut village.

'Those poor sods in the plane aren't going to survive this,' said Steve Levitt. He and I trotted to the back of the plane where the men lay in a rapidly heating capsule. The lower gate to the cargo hold was locked making it impossible to get them out. We could do little more than offer them water. One seemed semi-conscious and beyond caring but the other accepted the water and drank deeply.

Lynn and Bruce had chased down Chris and convinced him that the village would have its own system of law enforcement with a better chance of retrieving the camera. The word was sent out and two tough-looking characters turned up, one with an AK-47 dangling from his shoulder. The old monk translated the difficulty. The two 'police officers' took in the information and the nature of the complaint in muted disbelief.

Eventually, hands were waved and some naked boys were dispatched to find the thief. Bruce Menser, meanwhile, was raising another point. The landing strip at Lokichokio had no lights. If we did not take off soon, we would be unable to land before darkness closed the option. And if we did not get there tonight, the men with their terrible burns would almost certainly die.

Chris was beyond reach of reason, however. He took himself away to the edge of the strip and squatted down. He remained drenched with sweat and knelt on the ground sobbing.

A boy jogged back to the 'police officers' who duly made their report. The thief was a lad from the next village. He had already run off in that direction. We would not reach him that night.

Lynn relayed this news.

'We have to go,' he quietly urged.

'All right!' Chris said. 'We'll go – but those men have to be offloaded from the plane. I'm not taking them.'

Bruce tried to talk him down, but Chris was unyielding.

'Fuck them – they don't care about anyone but themselves. They can fuck themselves.'

He began a long rant listing all the things he had done for the South Sudanese, which chiefly seemed to involve making a living flying them around.

Lynn Arnold strolled over to where Steve and I were trying to keep out of it. TV teams make poor diplomats, especially when compared to dedicated humanitarians. Steve, gentle soul that he is, was fuming at the treatment of the injured men and was building up a head of steam to go and clock Chris.

'If he insists on unloading the injured men, we can't fly,' said Lynn. 'Agreed?'

'Agreed,' I said.

'Absolutely,' said Steve. 'Agreed.'

Lynn went back to deliver our position to Chris. He knew full well that a pilot returning to base with none of the passengers in his care was finished.

He suddenly stood and, without a word, turned for his plane, pulling keys from his pocket. He unlocked his cockpit door and clambered in. With a quick exchange of glances, we followed him, took our seats and buckled in. We could do nothing to secure the injured men.

If Chris did any pre-flight checks he was quick about them. What I noticed were his shoulders shaking as he sobbed and gasped as the engine fired up.

The Cessna Caravan, more laden now than when we'd arrived, began a long rumbling acceleration across the dirt, the single propeller grasping at the thin, hot air as we laboured into the sky. The Santa Claus monk fell away behind us. More of the village became visible through the trees. The plane seemed to be struggling to gain height.

Suddenly, at about one thousand feet, Chris wrenched over the joystick and the plane tipped on one wing, spearing down to the right. We plunged towards the ground. There was no sound on board, no shouts. We were heading to death, collateral damage in a broken man's misery.

The joystick was twisted again. The plane began to respond but we levelled out so close to the ground we were below the canopies of the scattered trees.

Again, the aircraft began a painful, shuddering ascent. The treetops were cleared, the village raced by, the inhabitants watching gape-mouthed at the spectacle. At one thousand feet, he did it again, this time on the opposite wing. Once more we were spearing down towards the village. This time, surely, he meant it.

Again, he pulled the plane out with a deep, groaning shudder at the level of the trees. Chris was making a grunting, barking noise. The plane levelled, struggled again for height, and began to claw for altitude. He brought us up to ten thousand feet and set our course for the south-east and Kenya. We flew with barely a word and in the very last glimmer of light landed at Lokichokio.

Our two injured passengers were gently extracted by a Red Cross team. As we watched one of the men groaning in pain, I had to talk Steve out of smashing Chris's lights out.

From what I hear, a quiet word was put out and he never flew again in Kenyan skies.

We had had one day in southern Sudan. I tried to imagine what a lifetime might be like.

30

THE SLAVE TRADERS

OUR BRIEF TRIP TO SUDAN HAD NOT BEEN ENTIRELY WORTHLESS. When our stories went to air on Nine's 6 pm news, *Nightline* and the *Today* show, World Vision received a flood of cash – more than $100,000 in the first twenty-four hours. They had to put extra volunteers onto their phones. Other agencies also saw a rise in donations.

Lynn Arnold said the cash was put to immediate use, purchasing more supplies and buying more charter flights to get food to where it was needed most. Perhaps, together, we did save some lives.

Steve had been a pleasure to work with. We began making plans for more stories out of Africa. Both of us were fired by the same zeal to bring to life stories that captured the nuance and complexity of African lives. Steve saw Africa as the most essential of continents and the most poorly understood. Inspired by his passion, I found myself re-examining my earlier dismay about the place. It was an insult to the people's resilience for me to indulge myself with despair at the challenges they faced.

If they weren't crippled by despair, it was indulgent of me to be so.

And so I felt a calling that was somewhat in sync with Steve's. With his knowledge and contacts, and my platform at Nine, I felt we had a moral obligation to see how far we could go.

Steve was tuned into the chatter emerging from the Sudan war in a way that I could never be. He knew that, in the shadow of constant warfare, the ancient slave trade was being revived.

The regime of Omar al-Bashir in Khartoum was broke. Sudan had great potential oil wealth but most of it was in the fiercely contested borderlands between the two rival halves of the country. No one could get at it. With a war to fight, and little cash to sustain it, Bashir turned to his spiritual adviser Hassan al-Turabi. Turabi was a strange character. He was an Islamic scholar and intellectual. He spoke good English. He was known for his easy and enthusiastic laughter. But he was also an uncompromising fundamentalist with no shortage of Koranic arguments for visiting violence on the unbelievers of the south.

With Turabi's encouragement, Bashir declared the civil conflict a holy war. This mattered. As a religiously sanctioned fight for Islam, anyone who signed up gained certain rights. Along with death becoming elevated to martyrdom, any goods and chattels seized from the non-believers could be kept.

Suddenly, Khartoum had a means to fund its military ambitions. Rather than keeping and paying for a large regular army, the Sudanese government could make use of the traditional tribal militias roaming around western Sudan on the edges of the Sahara. These included the fierce Darfuris, who combined Islamic faith with a keen interest in cattle raids on their southern neighbours.

And that is how it began. Sanctioned, and to a large degree armed, by the government in Khartoum, Darfuri raiders stepped up their old habit of riding into Dinka country in northern Bahrel-Ghazal, shooting down any resisters and heading off with as many cattle as they could herd along with them.

Before long, they found people were a more mobile and better-paying booty.

In small numbers initially, and as a by-product of the cattle raids, the horsemen of the north started carting off women and children. Any girl between nine and the mid-twenties was fair game.

They were tradeable as domestic slaves and concubines. Boys were more problematic. They were useful up to the age of fourteen or so. After that they were too likely to resist and were more trouble than they were worth. The slave raiders killed any adult men they encountered.

Steve had researched all of this. He had also found a way to get into the story.

A couple of Christian activists had made connections with some of the Arabs involved in the slave trade north of the unofficial border. They had begun making payments to buy some of these enslaved southerners back, so they could return to their homes and freedom.

But there was a problem. Their activities had not gone unnoticed. Khartoum had put a price on their heads. The slave 'redeemers', as they styled themselves, did their work in the shadows, fearful of being identified, even more fearful of their movements becoming known. They were managing to combine Christian idealism with the habits of French resistance fighters or Cold War spies.

Steve, using his contacts and the trust he had built up over many years, tracked down their names and their numbers. At first they weren't interested. But Steve was dogged. He knew some of the people the Christian activists knew in the Sudan People's Liberation Army, the SPLA. Slowly, he convinced them of his trustworthiness. And then he began the work of convincing them that a little publicity might help them shame Khartoum into cracking down on the slave trade.

It took months of work but eventually I got the call.

'We've got 'em,' said Steve. 'Can you get some time off work?'

I had a strange arrangement with Nine. My bosses didn't want to sanction these adventures. They carried too much risk. But they were happy enough to run my stories when I returned. Or, at least, have a look at running them.

If we were heading back to Africa, there were other stories to look at too. Steve and I were both keen to find out more about the

Lord's Resistance Army, a terrifyingly violent cultish militia that preyed on children in the lawless borderlands of northern Uganda, southern Sudan, the Central African Republic and north-east Zaire.

We co-ordinated with the activists. We made some calls into northern Uganda. We booked our flights.

A couple of days before leaving Sydney, I was walking home from the shops when I suddenly cramped up with a feeling of overwhelming dread. Fear gripped me like a choking force. My internal dialogue went something like this:

You barely survived the last trip to Sudan.

You are going back with men with a price on their heads.

You'll be there for longer and deeper in bandit country.

You don't have to do this.

You have a daughter.

Channel Nine doesn't even want you to go.

The reasons for saying no crowded my head. My spirit shrank. The benign breath of a Sydney breeze blew around me. What was I thinking?

I don't want to make light of this feeling of terror. Several times in my life I have been in immediate mortal danger, but those moments kick up quite different sensations. Adrenalin, arousal, a heightened sense of clarity, the phenomenon of time standing still – all these instincts fire up. They are deeply embedded, primitive responses that displace the more common sensation of fear. And yet, here I was with time to think, with options available to me, almost unable to breathe for dread while in the safety of a suburban street.

Old warrior wisdom says fear comes and goes in its own unbidden time.

I got home. I knew I couldn't let Steve down and I couldn't *not* do the story. Proving a slave trade in Africa? Hell, yes. Slowly the terrors faded.

By the time I boarded the plane with Steve, I was as happy as a lamb.

—

There was a secret squirrel element to hooking up with the activists. It was a reminder of the stakes involved if our movements were signalled too widely. There were spies aplenty in equatorial Africa and killings came cheap.

Having arrived in Nairobi, we awaited instructions. When they came, they were unexpected. We had to go to an airstrip. The pair from Christian Solidarity International (CSI) was waiting for us.

Clive James once made an observation about *Star Trek*. The writers, he noted, had split humanity's essential nature into two separate characters. Captain Kirk was all passion and emotion. Spock was pure, cold reasoning.

There was an element of that in our two Christian activists. John Eibner, an American, was the stronger personality. He was wiry and intense, all business. He brought a strategist's insights to the battles facing the South Sudanese. At the time, Sudan's civil war was all but unnoticed by the outside world. Eibner believed that by stressing the religious nature of the conflict, he could attract the interest and sympathy of Christian conservatives in the US Congress.

African civil wars might cut little ice in the US but saving Christians carried weight. And when slavery was thrown in, you had issues that resonated in America – or at least in American politics.

Eibner was made for the task. His strategic vision was allied with a good grasp of the media and a willingness to take enormous personal risks.

Gunnar Wiebalck was a different fish. Where Eibner had the lean intensity of the fanatic, Wiebalck looked like a village accountant. A cartoonist would see circles, with metal-rimmed spectacles popped on his nose. From his comb-over hairstyle to the soft lines of his jaw, nothing about him suggested passion or courage. But those looks deceived.

Gunnar was the soul of the operation, a man with almost saintly levels of empathy for the people he met and the struggles they faced.

'We'd like you to come with us,' said Eibner. 'But we can't tell you where we're going.'

'Oh . . . kay,' Steve and I chorused.

It was as good a way to start an adventure as any other. We clambered onto a light aircraft and were soon heading west, over Lake Victoria. The French pilot revealed mid-flight that his career back home had been ruined by a nasty crash in which he had had to ditch into the sea. Some pre-flight check he had failed to make, apparently. The waters of Africa's biggest lake glittered up at us as we took that information in.

We were soon touching down at Uganda's Entebbe airport, where the rotting ruins of an Air France passenger jet remained at the edge of the tarmac from the famous terrorist hijacking and rescue of 1976. At the Sheraton in Uganda's capital, Kampala, we waited. Eibner was being mysterious. Wiebalck assured us it would be worth our while.

It was not until the following morning that a car turned up. We were driven in what seemed like circles for over an hour until I had no idea where we were. We finally stopped at a rundown compound in a suburb of rolling hills. Two T-shirted men with AK-47s checked us out. A gate swung open. Strolling over the lawn to greet us was Colonel John Garang, the leader of the South Sudanese rebellion and the man whom above all others the Khartoum government wanted dead.

We shook hands, fully aware that John Eibner was making a point to us. He was seriously connected. His slave-buying missions were controversial but clearly the leader of the hard-pressed South Sudanese wanted them to happen.

Garang was a man of African contradictions. He held a PhD in agricultural economics from a university in Iowa but his life had been dominated by the dirtiest of wars. He was no Mahatma Gandhi. His human rights record was as bleak as his enemies'. But if South Sudan was to gain independence, Garang was the best hope of holding its disparate factions together.

We interviewed him on plastic lounge chairs in the garden, while a skinny mongrel dog went to war with its fleas on the nearby grass. Garang spoke of slavery as being just one pernicious element of the long war.

I took care to have my photograph taken with him. A snap with the leader of the SPLA might one day save my life, though I would have to be careful where I flashed it in case it had the opposite effect.

Garang farewelled us with an easy-going wave. It took many more brutal years but he would, finally, win his war. In 2005, he was made president of the government of South Sudan with the task of moving it to full independence in 2011. He held that job for just three weeks before he was killed in a helicopter crash. Since independence, South Sudan has unravelled. As I write this, it is as miserable a place as it ever was, as the government and army splits and the UN warns of another famine.

But all of that was still ahead as we gathered that night in the garden bar of the Sheraton and leading members of Garang's team joined us for a drink. I had hoped for insights into the state of the conflict. But these senior figures were chiefly interested in throwing back Nile Lager and lamenting old colleagues killed by homemade spirits in long ago drinking binges in Egypt. If this was the political cream of the movement, they were unimpressive. They seemed disillusioned, demoralised and increasingly drunk. The one whose company I enjoyed most, Arthur Akuen Chol, would later be jailed for corruption by the newly independent authorities – otherwise known as his drinking mates that night in Kampala.

The next morning, nursing our hangovers, Steve and I joined the clear-eyed Eibner and Wiebalck to fly to Lokichokio in northern Kenya.

Enough of the preliminaries. We had slaves to buy.

—

Once again, I was flying north-west from Lokichokio over the threadbare landscape of southern Sudan. It was a more broken journey than the one Steve and I had made just a few months earlier.

Eibner and Wiebalck had business to attend to, intelligence to gather, war lords to appease. We camped one night in Marpel, a village guarded by children with weary eyes and the ever-present battered Kalashnikovs. Steve's shortwave radio picked up the BBC World Service reporting that Médecins Sans Frontières was pulling all forty of its staff out of northern Bahr-el-Ghazal because of security concerns.

That was where we were heading.

The following day, we pressed further north, making a forward base for the slave purchase at a more substantial mud-hut town called Malual Kon. There was a certain nervousness afoot. A large body of government troops was less than fifty kilometres away. They could be on us within a couple of hours.

Travelling with us on the plane was Luol Ding Wol, a brigadier in the SPLA, who was greeted with great reverence. It was his first visit back to his hometown since he stood beneath a big tree and announced he was heading to Ethiopia to get guns to fight the north. That was in 1983, when the second phase of the civil war began. One thousand men followed him into the bush. Very few returned.

There had been many battles, he told me. Some had been so horrific that afterwards he said, 'My boys would not eat meat.'

The sight of the old warrior returning seemed to cheer the people of Malual Kon. The fierce old man stalked around in his splendid uniform discussing tactics with the ragtag defenders.

'What does South Sudan need most from the world?' I asked him.

'Ammo,' he replied. 'And maybe some artillery.'

The nights were moonless. Prayer meetings were held in a dark so deep nothing could be seen but the shine of teeth or a white cotton garment. Songs of praise rose up strong and urgent, Dinka hymns in a call-and-response dominated by the voices of the women.

The following morning, Eibner came to us early. There had been a slave raid in a nearby village, Warawar.

We took some four-wheel drive utes, with a few men with AK-47s riding in the back, and went cross-country.

We arrived just before noon to find the still-smouldering remains of a mud-walled commercial town. Local leaders came forward to tell their story.

There had been rumours of a militia strike aimed at another village and all the armed men had gone there to set an ambush.

They had been fooled.

Just after dawn the previous day, about a thousand slave raiders had ridden in to the defenceless village on horseback. They were riding two to a horse. Some of them wore uniforms.

The raiders torched the thatched roofs of the huts and shot any adult men they could find. They rounded up women and children and drove them off to the north. The whole thing took no more than an hour, by which time forty-nine villagers were dead or dying. About four hundred people had been enslaved but no one knew the final number for sure. Some people might still be hiding in the bush.

One of the men killed was the new husband of a young woman who had been taken. Married in November, widowed and enslaved by February.

While we spoke to the head man, a seven-year-old boy called Atak Majok Ayok was led into the village. He was one of those seized by the raiders. The elders gathered around to hear his story.

In the fear, confusion and smoke, Atak had been herded away along with many others. A boy who tried to escape was run down and killed. After the first, exhausting rush, there was a brief pause. The attackers re-organised themselves. Atak and some other children were assigned to one man who was responsible for driving them onward. Night fell and still they moved. The captor dismounted to relieve his bowels, threatening to kill the children if they tried to run. But Atak ran anyway. He ran and hid, ran and hid. He kept heading south. He listened out for the sound of horses. The night was dark but somehow he kept heading south.

Nearly eighteen hours later, barefoot and naked apart from a pair of red nylon shorts, he had made it home.

The old men of the village thought this was a great tale. Atak had told it without fuss or tears. He looked weary but otherwise fine. Someone was instructed to find the boy water and food.

While John Eibner settled into a long, intelligence-gathering conversation with the village head man, Steve and I explored the burnt remains of the town. Warawar had been an important crossroads. The village markets had sold everything from food and cooking utensils to blankets and radios. It was famous for the fabrics that traders brought from the north. Somehow that commerce had survived the bitter war.

Now all was gone. There was not a roof on any building. With the thatching burned to whitened ash, the mud walls rose only to chest height and the village looked insignificant. We could see the full length of the place, empty but for the occasional survivor searching for something to scrounge.

Victor Akok, the district commissioner who had come with us, estimated up to two thousand people had been carried off in slave raids in eastern Aweil county in just the previous few weeks.

To these people, Eibner and Wiebalck were heroes. They had begun their slave 'redemptions' during more conventional aid work, when they had first encountered people desperate to recover loved ones who had been carried off by the raiders.

Across the porous front line, sightings would be reported back of a wife or a child still alive and in the service of this or that (relatively) rich Arab. Recovering them by force was out of the question – but if the 'owners' could be enticed to sell their slave perhaps there was a mechanism to free them.

So it began, with ad hoc payments to go-betweens who posed as legitimate buyers and traders. In ones and twos, the enslaved would be smuggled back into the perilous freedom of their former lives.

At first, Eibner and Wiebalck had facilitated targeted ventures to recover known individuals. By the time we got to them, however, Christian Solidarity International (CSI) had scaled it up. On the northern side, slave brokers flourished just like sales agents for any other commodity. It did not necessarily raise suspicions for someone owning slaves to be visited by someone trying to sell them more – or perhaps offering to buy some that they already possessed.

CSI decided it would pay for any slaves who their traders could buy.

As the slave redemptions grew, the risks increased too.

Khartoum seethed at what Eibner and Wiebalck were doing. It understood the PR problem. It offered a reward of twenty million Sudanese pounds – about AUD$35,000 – for the capture of any northern slave traders who were dealing with the Christians.

The United Nations hated what they were doing too. They publicly denounced the slave 'redemptions', saying any trading in human beings was abhorrent regardless of the motivation.

John Eibner was unmoved.

'I have never seen a family member call it abhorrent when they get their loved ones home,' he said.

Gazing across a town now largely stripped of women and children, I could see the point. Already, the surviving men of the village were imploring Eibner for help.

Steve and I completed our interviews and filming. The heat was a physical force. My metal water bottle blistered my lips when I went to drink from it. The resilience of the South Sudanese to hunger and thirst staggered me. As a ginger-headed Anglo-Irishman, I knew I wouldn't last long in a Dinka world.

Back at Malual Kon, I was the recipient of Dinka hospitality. Arthur Akuen Chol invited me into a mud hut where he and the old warrior Luol were set up around a battered aluminium stockpot. Inside, along with warm greasy water, were bits of grey and gristly meat. Goat was my guess. It was a decent feast. Other old comrades arrived. A bottle of Johnnie Walker Red Label – an unimaginable luxury – was broken out. In the close heat of the mud-walled hut, toasts circled around to long-dead brothers in a war that seemed without beginning or end.

—

We were on a track barely more than a scuffing in the threadbare earth. The day was new. Our spirits were high. We were on the adventure we had been planning for months. Again, we were in two battered Toyota four-wheel drives with an armed escort.

For a long time, we saw no one. Finally, a smudge of dust resolved itself into a dozen longhorn cattle guarded by a pubescent boy with a weathered Kalashnikov across his narrow shoulders. The eyes that watched us pass had no childhood left in them.

A little past mid-morning, we came to a small village called Yargot. Armed youths stood around as Eibner briefly conferred with the head man. Money had been sent for a store of food to be waiting. The head man confirmed the arrangements had been met. There was a sense of tension about the place. Just to the north was the Lol River, the de facto front line. If all went well, Yargot's population would soon be swelled by escaping slaves.

From here, we walked. The onward track was mined. Some local kids, tough and serious, were sent with us as guides.

It was a beautiful morning for a stroll in Africa. I have often noticed how intense times make the world seem especially lovely. Danger arouses the senses. The day was not yet punishingly hot. The air was desert clean. There is no freedom like the sense of being ready for whatever comes.

Levitt and I had stripped the camera kit to bare essentials. Steve had a lightweight Panasonic. I had a little Sony. We had ditched the tripod for a simple monopod. Stable, long distance shots would be hard but we would not be too much encumbered if we had to run for it.

Eibner was the most heavily laden. Hanging from his bony shoulders were the straps of a canvas hold-all that was bulging with cash. The agreed price was fifty US dollars per person – the cost of a healthy goat. But the transaction had to be settled in almost worthless Sudanese pounds. Beneath the straining zip of the bag was the equivalent of US$4500. More than four million Sudanese pounds, carefully tied up in the equivalent of fifty US–dollar bundles, added up to a fair volume of dosh.

Eibner was a practical man and an uncomplaining one. He would not entrust the hold-all to anyone but himself. He measured his pace along the sandy track, carefully following the path of our mine-watching guides, and settled in for the hike.

The countryside resembled parts of inland Australia. Grasses and head-high scrub were broken every twenty to thirty metres by small trees rising to three or four metres. Every so often, however, would stand one of the huge *agook* trees – named for the Dinka word for monkey – that dominated the landscape like a bull elephant dominates a game reserve.

As we walked, an unusual stand of three of these mighty trees appeared ahead of us in a space the size of a cricket oval.

The two Christian activists consulted with an older Dinka man who had come from the village.

'Okay,' announced Eibner. 'We wait here.'

A silence fell, an inland quiet alive with the buzzing of insects. The air seemed suddenly too thin for speech.

If the Christians' mission had been betrayed, or the Sudanese government had caught on to what was happening, we could be in nooses. At any minute the horsemen could arrive.

The young men from the village fanned out to keep watch. Levitt, ever alert and restless, went with them.

The stillness settled again, broken only by the arrival of two sweating youths from the village carrying jerry cans of water.

At last, there was a muted call and one of the young lookouts came jogging back.

And suddenly, there they were.

First came a tall man in a white Arabic *jalabiya* robe. He wore a turban with a strand held loose to cover his face. And behind him, in single file, came hundreds of women and boys. They walked in a snaking line into the open ground between the trees. Some of the women carried babies. One was heavily pregnant. They were dressed in rags with the women mostly bare breasted. Of the children walking, some were barely more than toddlers.

It was such a staggering sight. I felt I was a witness not to the present, but to history. Some of the young men were wearing Muslim clothing and headdress. Some of the women looked anxious. Most kept their eyes downcast, or looked at their surroundings – including us – only furtively, to catch a glimpse.

The traders sat their groups in distinct lots. They needed to ensure they got the credit – and the payment – for each one they had brought.

For their part, the 'slaves' had no idea what was going on. Gunnar Wiebalck said this was deliberate. It only needed one to let slip a loose word, or to make too passionate a farewell, for the whole project to be endangered along with everyone in it.

So here they sat, eyes downcast, as they awaited the next transaction in their bonded lives.

John Eibner stepped up to make a speech.

After greeting them in the Dinka language, Eibner told them they should not fear. 'Today is going to be a very good day.'

People across the world, he went on, were concerned about them and had prayed for them.

He was about to talk to the traders, he said, and they would all soon be free.

No outbreak of cheering greeted this speech. People seemed just as fearful but now more confused. A small murmur of conversation broke out.

While the people beneath the trees surreptitiously checked with each other to see if they had heard right, a count was in progress.

There were 876 'slaves' beneath the trees. The number included the smallest infants.

Each of the traders had presented Eibner with a list of names. He then conducted what he called a 'spot check'. He would call a name at random. The person called was asked to stand up to have their photograph taken by Gunnar. The first people being called looked quite terrified. But before taking the shot, Gunnar greeted each one in Dinka: 'Cibak, yin apuol? – Good morning, how are you?' and he shook their hands, the little children and all.

He recorded their name, took their photo after urging them to look into the lens, and thanked them in Dinka – apath apai – before politely directing them to sit back down. Such elaborate courtesies were so bizarre, a few of the bolder ones sitting on the ground began to smile. As the ritual continued, some even giggled. Gentle Gunnar had achieved what John Eibner could not.

The 'spot check' had two purposes. One was to keep the traders honest. The other was to provide CSI with a database for their advocacy work and to prove they were keeping their own promises. Not every name was checked off the list. There wasn't time for that.

The traders quickly gathered in another patch of shade. A piece of fabric was laid on the ground and Eibner got down to business. Each of the traders had his numbers checked off. Eibner then counted out the fistfuls of packaged Sudanese notes and handed them over.

The traders kept their faces covered. They complained the price was too low. The task of gathering the slaves for the Christians was becoming too dangerous. Also, the Sudanese pound was devaluing. To make the same profit they had to gather more slaves.

Eibner explained that CSI would not raise the price. If the price went up the value of slaves would rise, creating a motivation for more to be seized. The traders grumbled but took their money.

Eibner shook each hand. 'Shukran,' he said in Arabic, thanks. Each trader in turn quickly disappeared back into the bush.

While this went on, I spoke to some of the people being freed. They still seemed a little bewildered by what was going on.

Achol Angok Angok was twenty-three. Her hair was braided in cornrows and her face and forehead were marked with beauty scars. She had been a slave for five years. She had been beaten and raped. She had had a child by her 'master' but the baby died.

Some of the boys had taken Arabic names and had converted to Islam. They would have been beaten or starved if they refused. Atem Deng Thou was eighteen and had been taken in a slave raid seven years earlier. From the slavers' point of view he was a success story. He had attended Koranic school. From the age of twelve he had gone on slave raids himself, attacking his own people. All the time he felt shame, he said. He had done what he had to do to avoid being beaten.

'Just give me a gun and I will go back there and get them,' he said.

Ajak Atem had been enslaved for five years. At her breast was Mohammed, her son by her master. Her master had been happy to sell her and the boy on. She would now change the child's name to Adup, a Dinka name.

All were terrible stories delivered as simple statements of fact.

Under a tree I found Gunnar speaking to a young woman. Nyibol Malek Makuei also had the facial scarring of a traditional Dinka woman. When the raiders had come a year earlier they had captured her and her husband. They quickly shot her husband. She saw him fall. She was pregnant, just three months gone, and she had two other children. They were driven off with her. She was raped. She saw another woman killed.

When she was seven months' pregnant, her master said she should be circumcised in the Arab way. She refused and was beaten and starved. Finally, she agreed to submit. Five men held her down. The genital 'excision' was performed with a small knife. There was no anaesthetic. For a week the pain was agonising. She was given a rag for the bleeding and left to look after herself in her hut with the animals.

Steve gave her a bottle of water. She gave most of it to her bright-eyed child, Atuk.

When I asked what would happen to her now she said, 'I will live as a widow.'

I asked her if it was good to be back. 'Yes,' she said. Her face displayed no sign of joy, just a profound fatigue. She was probably twenty-five years old.

'You are free to go,' announced John Eibner to the crowd. 'Go back to your homes, go back to your families.'

There was a small clatter of applause. Some of the women embraced each other, some walked hand in hand as they went for water at the jerry cans. There were signs of joy, some laughter and celebration but many seemed a little lost.

Already village lads were guiding them around the mines on the track back to Yargot, where food was waiting. After that they were on their own. Their futures were hardly less perilous than their lives as slaves. Already we had heard that among the four hundred taken at Warawar were some who had been 'redeemed' by CSI on earlier trips. A cycle of capture and – if they were lucky – release.

And if they made it home, it would be to families with other gaps around the tables. After years enslaved in the north, whole families back home might have gone. Southern Sudan was full of the disappeared and the holes they left behind.

My joy at seeing people savouring their unexpected liberation was muted by the knowledge of the complex layers of their loss. And by the nagging thought that perhaps by taking people out of the slave market in the north, we were simply creating vacancies to be filled by future raids.

Many years later, on a wintry day on the shores of Canberra's Lake Burley Griffin, I discussed the matter with a senior academic economist.

He told me it boiled down to the principles of economics. Unless supply of a commodity was infinite anything that reduced supply would increase demand and, therefore, all other things being equal, prices.

So, on one level, our slave-buying exercise had only made matters worse. Far from freeing people from slavery, we might have been ensuring that others, unseen, would in future be enslaved.

It was a disheartening thought. I can only hope the publicity from the slave-buying – the story made a fair splash – added pressure on Khartoum in a way that reporting mere famine had failed to do.

31

THE LORD'S RESISTANCE ARMY

STEVE AND I HAD A PLAN FOR ANOTHER STORY WE HOPED WOULD HIT as strongly as the slave-buying.

We headed back to Uganda but this time boarded a small prop-plane to the north of the country. The sense that we were headed for the badlands was reinforced by the drunken fellow passenger complaining about having to hand over his pistol before takeoff. It was 6 am. He was one of three men travelling together. The other two, Robert and David, seemed like nice blokes. They told me they were 'revenue collectors'. I got the feeling they weren't from the tax office.

The plane landed in a dusty little town to let them off. After that, Steve and I went on alone.

We were heading for Gulu, a small city not far short of the Sudanese border. It was one of the epicentres of a conflict that was brutal and senseless even by the standards of Africa. The Lord's Resistance Army (LRA) arose in northern Uganda in the late 1980s. Its leader, Joseph Kony, claimed direct contact with God and announced a plan to recreate Uganda on the basis of the Ten Commandments.

In fact, he launched numerous raids on his own Acholi people, typically seizing children whom he would mercilessly convert into conscripted recruits. We were on our way to meet some children who had escaped the LRA and to hear their stories.

Steve's World Vision contacts led us to a barracks-like school. It was like no other educational institution on earth. The students were of school age but all the boys, and many of the girls, were killers.

Nighty Akello explained how it worked. She had been captured just nine days earlier when LRA soldiers attacked her village. As they were being rushed off into the bush, three young boys were killed when they tried to escape and run home. One boy was stabbed and the other two beaten to death in front of Nighty and the other young captives. Despite that terrifying example, she also ran away during the night. She had been brought into this compound just that morning. She was ten years old.

A youth called Charles Nyeko told me the LRA came in the middle of the afternoon when he was sitting with his uncle. His uncle, he said, was weak. Charles was forced to watch as his uncle was stabbed to death. He joined a column of other young captives. One boy, a friend of his, said he was hungry. The LRA gunmen killed him just for asking for food. Another boy became too weak to walk. All the boys were then forced to stamp on him until he was dead.

Charles did what he had to to survive. He became a fighter for the LRA. He went on raids himself. He fought five pitched battles, three in Uganda and two in southern Sudan.

Good fighters were rewarded with the girls who were captured.

One of those girls was Margaret Akoko. She was eleven when she was abducted. The children, she said, were forced to kill kids or be murdered themselves. She was the fourth child in her family to be taken. Her three older brothers were all now senior soldiers with the LRA. She survived by being given as a 'wife' to an LRA commander.

I discovered the rehabilitation centre was partly funded by Australian aid money. The children were taught basic numeracy and literacy, and life skills like how to run a sewing machine or fix bicycles. Much of their time was spent playing ball games, singing and dancing. Trying to be kids again. They also were encouraged to do drawings. The walls were covered with childish pictures of firing squads and stabbings. It was better, the centre's managers believed, to get children to externalise their nightmares.

But still the nightmares came. One girl had broken her hand the night before trying to fight off an attacker who existed in the memories that infected her dreams.

'It is hard on the boys but much harder on the girls,' said Teo van der Weele, a psychiatrist. There was a cultural expectation among Acholi boys to become warriors and kill. For the girls, he said, the shame of sexual abuse came with no cultural escape route.

We were chatting over a meal of curried goat in the single-storey Acholi Inn, which had been partially burnt down in an LRA raid.

Van der Weele had his own nightmares to settle. He was born in the 1930s to a father who was a leading figure in the Dutch Nazi party. When Teo was seven, fighters from the Dutch resistance broke into their home and demanded to know where the old man was. They put a gun to Teo's head threatening to shoot him if he did not tell.

'I had seen children killed, people machine-gunned,' said Teo. 'I was just a boy but I chose death. I wouldn't tell on my father.'

At war's end, Teo's father was jailed and the boy was sent to reform school where he 'learnt about paedophilia from the lower end'. Psychiatry and his work trying to help damaged kids was his penance for his father's sins.

The girls who escaped from the LRA were considered unmarriageable. Everyone knew the life they had had. So their trauma was compounded by loneliness. A centre volunteer, Santa Lanyero, had been seized at the age of fourteen when the LRA raided her Catholic boarding school and marched two hundred girls into the bush. When one girl tried to escape the rest were ordered to form a circle around her. Each had to step forward and stab their friend. Anyone who resisted would also go in the middle.

Santa became a 'wife' assigned to one of the LRA officers. She was soon pregnant. When she was six months gone, she escaped at night. She made her way home wanting to abort the child but the doctor said it was too late. She named her unwanted son Rubangakene, which meant 'made by God alone'. It had taken a long time, she said, but she loved the boy now. He was nine years old, always the first in his class, helpful and good.

Santa was twenty-four years old. She deserved a lot better from life. They all did. But her life was not empty. She had been spending a lot of time with a young girl who had been abducted with her sister. She told Santa the LRA ordered her to stab her sister with a knife.

'Kill her or we will kill you.'

The girl stabbed her sister to death.

'She has been here nine months,' said Santa. 'Sometimes for three days at a time she will not eat or sleep. She just cries.'

Santa had been speaking with the girl's mother. The mother had recently agreed, after much initial reluctance, to take her daughter back. By these small advances, Santa measured her work.

In the evening, thousands of people crowded into Gulu from the surrounding countryside, hoping for safety in numbers against an LRA raid. The Ugandan army kept forces in the town but the local people were ambivalent about the army's activities. If the army took on an LRA unit and killed the kids, they would be killing the children of the area. The villains and the victims were the same people.

Somewhat recklessly, Steve and I borrowed a car and went out to the edge of the forest, which by dusk was LRA controlled. In the lengthening shadows, we found a very lean man walking across a scorched field next to some burnt-out huts.

Henry Okello-Gama was fifty-nine. The LRA had burnt down his house eight times. In 1997, they abducted two of his daughters and a son in a single raid. He had not seen them since. Another son had been killed in an LRA raid.

'I am tired,' he said, gazing down at his son's grave. 'I want to retire.'

He spent his mornings tending his fields and rebuilding his home, though he no longer slept there because it wasn't safe.

'You must rebuild,' he said, 'otherwise you just become a madman.'

Night was approaching.

'Any time from now they come,' he said. He was anxious to get into town. And happy to accept a lift.

I felt myself deeply moved by these people's struggles. On my first trips to Africa, I saw only the violence and horror. None of that was diminished, but now I saw much more clearly the resilience and courage and optimism of people who I had come to realise were far stronger than I was. I felt moved by the example of Santa Lanyero, as I had felt moved by the stoicism of Nyibol Malek Makuei, the young Sudanese woman who had been widowed, raped, mutilated and enslaved and yet who still found a way to keep moving on.

It was as false to sentimentalise Africa as it was to despair over it. The agents of evil grabbed the attention but increasingly I saw a quieter landscape full of heroes. And I felt unworthy of them. I would have loved to have been able to help them in some practical way. Perhaps I could transport Santa and her son, or Nyibol and hers, to Australia and give them the life I enjoyed, in comfort and opportunity and peace. They were not, to be fair, asking that of me. And my impulse was no doubt wrong on all kinds of levels that my insensitive privileged soul couldn't measure. It was a fantasy.

So what could I do to make myself useful? It was slowly dawning on me that what people valued was their own story. It is one of the few things we own that we never grow out of, or lose, or set aside. The story of the poor woman is as powerful as that of the richest man. I have a story therefore I am.

I was aware of a Jewish proverb: 'God loves a good story.' It is really a statement of consolation. Most of the best stories are not of simple, easy, complacent lives. When your life is a tumult of pain and failure, of Job-like trials, that's when you want your Jewish mate to put an arm around your shoulder and remind you that you are pleasing God with the story you are living through.

For people who have been the victims of deep injustice, the need to tell the story becomes more urgent. I came to Santa and to Nyibol, and even to Riek Matar, the dying child in the hut, as a figure who would stay just briefly and then return to the outside world. Riek Matar was too far gone even to have seen me squatting beside him. Yet his story, the bare basics that I knew of it, became something important that had to be delivered to people living in safer places who could empathise in some small way. The pinpricks of acknowledgement of his life and death added up to something – but what? Did it make his death less lonely, his suffering less acute? No. But somehow, I was starting to believe, these stories made the world a little closer, our strangeness to each other a little less stark. They made our duties to each other a little clearer.

I was noticing something else as well. In my own tribe – unquestionably now Australia – to interview someone in their suffering seemed intrusive. As a reporter, sometimes I felt I was doing some good. Other times, it was as if I was taking something precious away from them, subtracting something further from people already crushed by their losses.

On foreign soil, I never felt the same way. Nor did I ever meet a hostile reaction. People wanted to talk. Twenty years into my reporting life, I was suddenly realising that stories matter. In fact, I started to realise that stories were the most important thing in the world. Nothing is truly understood unless it is bound in narrative. From the Old Testament to Shakespeare to national politics, anything of complex power requires a story.

It had taken a while, but telling people's stories became more than just a means to satisfy my own curiosity or to travel to places of interest. With those African journeys, it started to feel that honest stories, simply told, might even matter.

—

Steve and I flew into Sydney with a pile of stuff, including a feature on the extraordinary adventures of an Australian aid worker in the region, Bernard Vicary.

Channel Nine loved the slavery story. So did the Fairfax *Good Weekend* magazine, which ran my first long-form venture into print. I wrote it to honour the faith of Nyibol, the slave survivor. Hers was not a story that could have been told with a few grabs on TV.

But the LRA story was spiked. Nine hated it.

'Mate, kids raping, being raped . . . murdering, being murdered . . . we can't put that on at dinnertime,' grizzled the boss.

It never got a run. More than a decade later, a social media hashtag campaign – #Kony2012 – finally got the LRA's depredations discussed around the world. But its stated aim of seeing Kony brought to international justice by the end of 2012 failed. He is still running his army of stolen kids, still turning innocent victims into perpetrators, still as incoherent as ever about what his final strategic goal might be. In Western Africa, Boko Haram has copied his methods and attached them to the cause of radical Islam, ensuring even more children – and especially girls – live lives of terror and abuse.

The year after we left Gulu, the Australian foreign aid budget ceased funding the rehabilitation centre. Perhaps if our story had made it to air Canberra might have been motivated or pressured to sustain it. But commercial television has its rules. You can't really disturb the punters at dinnertime. My incapacity to work within those rules and still get the story out counts as one of my more painful failures.

32

JOHN MAC

THE STORIES I FILED FROM SOUTHERN SUDAN DID BRING AN UNEX-
pected and altogether delightful bonus.

As they went to air, I began getting calls from the very small
and somewhat bewildered community of South Sudanese expatriates living in Sydney. One of them, Mayom Tulba, invited me to a
meeting of Dinka elders at his home in Sydney's inner west.

It was a formal gathering that mirrored a village meeting back
in southern Sudan. The male elders sat around a coffee table laden
with plastic cups of Coca-Cola and took turns to expound on the
issues the community felt it was facing. They were trying to find a
useful place within Australian society but their political concerns
– and most of the conversation – dealt with issues back home.

After some time, the meeting broke up and we went into the backyard where the women folk had been preparing a feast. A tall, languid,
good-looking man strolled up and we began talking. His name was
John Mac Acuek and he was disdainful of the political minutiae that
preoccupied the others. He lionised neither the rebel army, the SPLA,
nor its political wing, the SPLM. His interest was Australia. I was
struck by his warmth, his intelligence, his easy humour.

A couple of days later he rang me. He was studying anthro-
pology and international development at the University of Western
Sydney (now WSU). He had written a paper on Dinka initiation

practices, which he had experienced first-hand. However, it had been delivered back to him with a complaint that he had failed to provide sources. The accepted source was a British anthropologist, E.E. Evans-Pritchard. I laughed that only an English don could tell a Dinka man what his initiation rites were all about but John confessed to a serious problem. He couldn't find the relevant book by Evans-Pritchard and even if he could he had no money to buy it.

By the weirdest chance, I found a second-hand copy at my local Berkelouw's bookshop and sent it on to him. Little by little, I was drawn into John's orbit. He was wildly funny, a clown and raconteur who always cracked me up – and delighted my then eight-year-old daughter, Cait. At his two-bedroom flat in Blacktown, provided by the Marist community in exchange for caretaker work, I met his younger brother. He was introduced to me as David, a ferociously fit teenager with a wild and wary eye. David kept his distance. Only later, when I came to know him a little better under his true name, Deng, did I realise that he spoke almost no English at that time.

Over time, I got to know John's story. He had been press-ganged as a thirteen-year-old to fight with the SPLA rebels against the Islamist government based in Khartoum. In his first battle, not far from his hometown in Bor, an artillery shell had sent shrapnel into the back of his head. He was carried to a crude field hospital, judged a hopeless case and left to die. The following day or so, he regained consciousness and the rough bush medics operated to remove metal fragments from his skull. There was no anaesthetic.

'I cried,' said John.

He became a skilled soldier, gaining officer rank and leading his own company. Once he was shot through the ribs and leg and was carried by his men across the nearby Ethiopian border. Again, he was left to recover without medical intervention.

On another occasion, he was again hit by artillery fire and transferred to a Red Cross hospital. That was the first time he received modern drugs to treat his wounds and to manage the pain.

In his long recovery, he heard of a beautiful woman, known to his family, who was in a displaced people's camp some fifty kilometres away. He walked there and they married.

John by now was sick of the war and the corruption he saw in the rebel movement. His wife, Elizabeth, had family contacts who managed to get her safely to Nairobi. John set off to pick up his mother-in-law to take her to join Elizabeth in Kenya. Along the way he discovered his kid brother Deng, then just twelve and a six-year war veteran, was in a child soldier camp. He busted Deng out and smuggled him across the border in a grain sack. Both would have been executed had they been caught.

In northern Kenya's huge Kakuma refugee camp, John plotted a way to get the family to safety. He met an Australian aid worker, Chris Harrison, who was having her own breakdown of sorts as she dealt with the sheer scale of the need. Chris had decided she would try to save 'just one' refugee.

She chose John, she told me later, because he was 'always charming, always cheerful, always optimistic'. She and her husband, Bob Campbell, fought the bureaucracy until John, Elizabeth, Deng, and John's infant son Joshua were put on a plane to Sydney carrying their special humanitarian visas, a bag of nappies, and nothing else.

Even that doesn't tell the whole story. On a trip from Kakuma to Nairobi to do some visa paperwork, John was spotted by some SPLA soldiers and seized as a deserter. He was tortured for several days. He was being taken out to be shot when a Kenyan police patrol spotted something amiss and came to his rescue.

At Sydney airport, John and his family were met by Bob Campbell who presented them with warm jumpers against the winter cold and announced he was taking them to Blacktown. John assumed it was a camp for black people, rather than a suburb in Sydney's west.

John had done the impossible. He, almost alone out of the millions of people suffering in southern Sudan, had found a way to bring his family to safety and a new kind of paradise. But they had never seen a fridge before, or an electric stove. Elizabeth destroyed their first oven when she lit a wood fire inside it. Deng blew up a microwave when he tried to take the chill off a can of Coke.

They discovered KFC and for months that was their diet staple.

John had one of the best brains I have ever encountered. Despite his education stopping at primary level, he was fluent in six or seven languages. He would become the first South Sudanese migrant to graduate from an Australian university.

He was a source of constant delight to me. The memory of him trying his hand at cricket and thundering in from a long run-up to deliver thunderbolts from his two-metre frame still terrifies me and cracks me up. I remember another day when I took John and a couple of his Dinka mates to Manly for the day. Walking through this white enclave in the company of some very tall black timber was an education. They had eyes only for the beauty of the beach and the long curling patterns of the surf.

One day John announced that he had been accepted for post-graduate study at the University of Geneva. All his tuition and board would be covered once he got to Switzerland but he had to find his own way there and provide his own out-of-pocket expenses. He asked me for the money. I didn't have it. I knew in Dinka terms, it was perfectly acceptable to ask someone else for something if you didn't have it yourself. But it is not really how it is done in Australia. So what is the Australian way? How do mates look out for each other?

I suggested we collaborate. I interviewed him. It turned out to be a wonderful opportunity to flesh out my understanding of his extraordinary life. I gave the article to the church press and the money donated by readers easily covered his needs.

John returned from Switzerland a highly educated, life-seasoned leader fully equipped to work in his selected field of international development. His ambition was to help the newborn nation of East Timor or do other work across the Asia–Pacific. Not a single job was offered to him. The only work he could find was in factories.

Meanwhile, contracts piled up for him from the world's leading aid bodies – the World Health Organization, the UN, major agencies like Oxfam – if only he would return to South Sudan. He wanted to leave that world behind. But his family was growing. He needed the money.

In South Sudan, while leading an aid team, he was captured by a rebel militia that wanted his fleet of four-wheel drives, his supply of diesel and his radio communications system. He refused. He was beaten unconscious and thrown into a deep pit. When he came around, he was lying in the faeces and blood of previous occupants. Our High Commission in Nairobi was eventually alerted that an Australian citizen was in peril and, to their credit, they worked tirelessly to negotiate John's release.

It was almost too late. John was in a critical condition and recovered only after an extended stay in intensive care in Nairobi. One consequence was a skin disorder that afflicted his arms and hands. He became super-sensitised to the cold. Even Sydney's mild winters were intolerable to him.

Over time, John accepted the inevitable and returned to South Sudan to live, hoping to find a useful place for himself as it moved towards independence. He established hotels, he built a school. He lived out his ethic of lifting those around him and eschewing all violence and corruption.

He returned to Sydney from time to time, establishing among other things a charity to fund vaccination programs for Dinka cattle herds which were being decimated by a virus. In this work, and in his businesses, he always invited me to join him. He was a man of many projects.

Nothing I could write about him could do him justice. In a fairer world, John would have become secretary-general of the United Nations. He had powerful skills with people, he built things up and he got things done. I have described him many times as my Mandela. He was elected administrator of his home county of Bor. By the end of 2013, his net assets were probably in the order of two to three million dollars, amassed entirely through his integrity, his intelligence and his knowledge of what needed to be done in a nation emerging from decades of war. He poured money into his school project. His heartbreak was that he was forced to live so far from his kids back in Sydney.

Throughout it all, he stayed in touch. At any hour, the clicks and whistles of a sat-phone call would break across whatever I was doing so that John, in his languid, easy way, could bring me up to date with his adventures. We would talk about our families and our hopes and frustrations more easily than I have ever spoken about such things with any man other than Steve Levitt and my brothers.

In the last days of 2013, the newly independent government of South Sudan split along its deepest ethnic lines. The vice-president Riek Machar pulled his Nuer tribe out of the government and the army. They went to war against the Dinka majority. The flashpoint was at Bor, where John had his home and his school.

As it happened, John was safely away further south at the time but he immediately set off to try to secure the school and its kids, and to find his mother who had been trapped in the fighting. Over a couple of nights, he helped smuggle Dinka refugees across the Nile from where they were trapped by Machar's so-called 'White Army'. Trying another approach, with a convoy of cars, John was ambushed, shot and killed.

That news, when it came, was utterly wrenching. I loved the man. He inspired me, and cheered me, and humbled me, and taught me so much. He was, in every sense that mattered, my brother. I feel his loss every day – not just for my sake, but for everyone he was helping and would have continued to help through what should have been a long and enormously productive life.

Life is not fair.

His brother Deng, whom he rescued from the child soldier camp, took John's advice and studied law. He now runs his own criminal law practice in Sydney. He gives tirelessly not just to the South Sudanese community but to anyone who seeks his help. He was named 2016 New South Wales Australian of the Year. His portrait, by Nick Stathopoulos, was voted People's Choice at the Archibald Prize. When Deng gave the 2016 New South Wales Australia Day address he said he was going to set up a foundation to honour the brother who saved his life and brought him to Australia. He has done so. Through public generosity and Deng's own, John Mac Foundation scholars are now being helped financially as they pursue their own degrees through Western Sydney University.

John and Deng are powerful examples of the great glory of Australia – this country's capacity to grant enormous opportunities to those who dream its dreams. Deng has told me solemnly that, with John's death, I have replaced him. I am now Deng's brother. It is typical of Deng's generosity. I accept that bond with the deepest seriousness and pride. I am one in a great group of people who work to make the John Mac Foundation a success in the name of a man we loved. But no one will ever replace John Mac.

I strongly recommend taking the time to read Deng's own account of his life as a child soldier and his escape and subsequent life in Australia. It is called *Songs of a War Boy*, written with Ben Mckelvey, and it will stay in your head forever.

33

ETHNIC CLEANSING

A MONTH AFTER I RETURNED FROM AFRICA, THE FORMER YUGOSLAVIA burst into flames again. It was 1999. For the best part of a decade, the Balkan stew held together for forty-five years by the Croatian Communist Tito had been falling bloodily apart.

The Serb centre couldn't hold, as first Slovenia and then Croatia and then Bosnia-Herzegovina broke off and fought for their independence. These wars had dominated Europe for years, spawning new place names to stand alongside the worst from World War II – Sarajevo, Gorazde, Srebrenica.

Once again, it was Steve Levitt who called in the middle of the night.

'Mate, Kosovo is going off.'

'Whassup . . . ?'

'Milosevic and the Serbs are stampeding through Kosovo, they're all ethnic Albanian Muslims down there . . . it's on again. Ethnic cleansing.'

The phrase had an electrifying power. Slobodan Milosevic, the Serbian ultra-nationalist who had waged the war against the former Yugoslavia's breakaway states, had spoken of 'ethnic cleansing' to explain both his vision and his methods. Where Serbs wanted control, other ethnicities would have to be purged.

'I'll make some calls,' I said.

It was true. A flood of people was fleeing Kosovo, a province of Serbia whose population was ninety-five percent non-Serb. They were pouring into little Montenegro and coming in even greater numbers over the mountain passes into Albania.

A few more calls and I discovered that Albania required no visas for entry. The ex-Maoist state was the poorest nation in Europe. It was hardly a mecca for tourists or business investment and had seen no need to put up any immigration barriers.

First thing in the morning, I was making my case to Peter Meakin.

'All right,' he grunted. Robbie Hopkins, the crack cameraman who had been with me in Tahiti and Port Arthur, was assigned to the case. Then David Hurley, the boss from *A Current Affair* was on the phone. He wanted me to do some reporting for his show, which ran right after the news at 6.30 pm. To make my current affairs stories look different from news he wanted to send a producer with me, but he had a problem. The obvious candidate was Tracey Hannaford. She was smart, keen and tough. But Hurley was leaning towards sending a bloke instead.

'Mate, I know all about that "rape-as-a-weapon-of-war" stuff they get up to over there,' he said. 'I could never live with myself if something happened to Trace.'

I felt a little of his concern. There was no question women had been singled out for appalling treatment by some of the paramilitaries operating in a very dirty war. I knew too much about men with guns to offer any glib undertakings – like 'Don't worry, boss, I'll look after her.'

I knew, if it came to it, I couldn't.

'Let me talk to her,' I replied.

I barely knew Tracey but I knew her reputation was first class. We discussed the issues and Hurley's concerns. My view was that if Tracey knew the particular risks facing women, and was willing to take them on, it was not the management's place to shut her down.

The conversation was brief and sensible. Tracey wanted in. I made my argument with Hurley and he relented. It is easy to see his approach as paternalistic. In the context of the times, I saw him as simply trying to manage risk. He was as big a fan of Tracey as anyone. He just needed an argument that would get him across the line.

By the late 1990s, the BBC's Kate Adie and CNN's Christiane Amanpour had forced a reimagining of women as reporters on the front line. Many of the best people I have worked with in the toughest of places have been women. CNN's Arwa Damon and Ingrid Formanek embodied courage and resilience on levels few men will ever match. But it was still a new and threatening idea to many male news bosses – and it must be said, some women in some war zones have suffered sexual attacks. Hurley's fear was not baseless.

But Tracey won, and joined our team as we scrambled for flights that would take us to a country I never imagined visiting, though it had always intrigued me during my boyhood examinations of the family atlas.

—

Even by the standards of busted old eastern bloc countries trying to find their way after the collapse of the Soviet Union, Albania was a sad old place. From the time of its liberation from the Nazis until 1985, it had been run by a paranoid Communist called Enver Hoxha. In the 1960s he had fallen out with the Soviets and thrown in his lot with Chairman Mao. Isolated politically, geographically and economically, he lived in perpetual fear of invasion from outside and dissent from within. Albania's Adriatic beaches were festooned with barbed wire. Its land borders were wired with electric fences. In every field were the little round concrete emplacements the locals called 'mushrooms'. These were machine-gun nests. Like little malevolent minions, they faced wherever the threat was seen as likely to come. In defensive terms, they were pointless. There was no system of trenches or bunkers to supply them. They were easy picking for any kind of air force and they used up so much of the national supply of cement that the cities and the roads had little improved since the age of the Ottomans.

At the time of Hoxha's fall, his secret police had 200,000 official informants. In a population of three million, from newborn infants to the few who might have made it to old age, that came to a ratio of one spy for every fifteen citizens. And that didn't include the regime's full-time agents.

Hoxha created a Mediterranean version of North Korea. His belief in Albanian self-sufficiency required bans on imports. We passed a vast, rusting factory that had once produced tractors – unsellable to anyone else and in numbers too great for the Albanian economy to need. Another factory had produced the tyres for those same unwanted tractors.

After Hoxha's death and the collapse of European communism, Albania's economy had relied on two things: pyramid schemes and crime. For a country so poor, the striking thing was how many of the cars on its roads were top-end Mercedes Benzes, Audis and BMWs. None had numberplates. All had been stolen from Germany, Switzerland and Austria and transported south by Albanian criminal gangs. The alternative forms of transport were donkey carts, tractors and scooters of dubious eastern bloc origins.

After clearing the crowded little immigration hut at the airfield, we did what any seasoned foreign reporting team did – we headed for the pub.

More accurately, we found our way to the hotel where the satellite dishes were clustered. There is some unwritten process by which one hotel gets selected as the hub for international media. In those days, the only way to file was through dishes established by the major networks and international agencies. If you wanted to get a story out, you had to go there.

Where the dishes were, production teams gathered. Among them would be official affiliates and lots of old friends from earlier adventures.

Sure enough, after a couple of coffees and a bit of industry gossip, we had acquired a local 'fixer' willing to work for fifty US dollars a day and a driver, Franko Marcou, with his own car more than happy with seventy-five US dollars.

Marcou was an ex-infantry lieutenant with a late model Mercedes sedan acquired through his brother's car-stealing gang. His English was rudimentary, his driving terrifying, his attitude sulky, but he was very good at 'reading the play'. He knew back ways around roadblocks and anticipated and fixed all kinds of problems.

The fixer, Arjan, was just twenty-one. He spoke pretty good English. He had won a Soros Foundation scholarship to study the language. But he already saw a future as a well-padded government official. He was lazy, arrogant and full of himself.

I spent much of my first couple of days assessing the strengths and personalities of this little team. When it works well, small-team reporting is one of the great pleasures of life. Great friendships are made, good work is done in which all can take pride, and humour and mutual affection can conquer most obstacles.

When small teams are toxic, a trip can be miserable. Getting it right early is a useful investment. The key is to identify and then encourage each person's strengths while sliding over their weaknesses. If people feel acknowledged for what they bring, they will seek to bring more of it. It is essential their more aggravating personality traits do not get rewarded.

There was never any doubt about Rob or Tracey. By the time I pulled out of the story weeks later, the little gang of five was operating as well as any I had worked with. If there are pleasures to be had in a place of widespread misery, this sense of teamwork is top of the list.

—

The Kosovo crisis saw the biggest and fastest refugee movements in Europe since the end of World War II. Franko's Mercedes took us over the rough mountain roads to a small town called Kukes nestled under snow-capped peaks on the border with Kosovo.

Across the border, came an endless stream of tractor-drawn carts laden with traumatised people. One woman on a packed wooden tray saw our camera and hoisted from her feet a boy of about eight. Shouting, she raised the boy's shirt to reveal a bullet wound, neat below his rib cage with a larger exit wound in his side. The boy, white with pain, resisted until he saw our camera too. Then he tried to stand manfully upright, until his knees buckled and the woman lowered him back to his place at her feet.

The Serbian style of ethnic cleansing relied heavily on lawless paramilitaries who acted with the approval of the Milosevic regime. Survivors spoke of a general technique where gunmen entered a village or suburb. A handful of people would be shot, the rest would flee. Sometimes, the paramilitaries would have a particular taste for murder, in which case the death rate would be higher and more arbitrary.

I heard one account of paramilitaries bursting into a home one evening when a family was eating. The gunmen taunted the parents. 'There is no meat in your soup.' They took a baby in the house, decapitated it and threw the head in the pot. The mother, days later in an Albanian refugee camp, was still incapable of speech. The story was told by neighbours who fled the same village and was confirmed by the nine-year-old daughter.

False atrocity stories are part of the grist of wartime. It is a natural human instinct to tell a more horrific tale than the last one. But the sourcing in this account was specific and close to the crime. A war crimes investigator I spoke with said he thought the description was credible.

Rape was another favoured practice. Refugees streaming into Albania frequently had heartbreaking tales of teenage girls and young women being selected out of the convoys and not being seen again. Among the crowds were many girls who had been dressed as boys or deliberately made to 'look ugly'.

The hospital in Kukes was a two-storey concrete building almost devoid of medical equipment. Its sagging iron cots were all filled. Two brothers sat side by side with faces shredded by shrapnel. Their mother lay alongside, shot through the abdomen. An old man nearby had had his nose cut off. Another woman had a bullet wound above her breast. Her baby, she told us, had been torn out of her arms.

And so it went on. There was little sign of medical intervention and what I saw of it was more terrifying than the injuries. I saw a tiny girl screaming her lungs out as a medic prodded the veins in her scalp with an oversized needle, trying to find one that would support an adult-sized drip.

At one point, someone started burning the little village of Morina, on the Kosovo side of the border. The refugee column continued without a break, the faces emerging out of the smoke. All, except the children who couldn't understand, wept when they crossed the border. Relief, grief at their losses, the final letting go of the tension of flight – whatever it was, women and men, young and old staggered into Albania and collapsed in tears.

—

For the Serbs, Kosovo was sacred ground. Even though they numbered only five percent of the provincial population, the Serbs' most precious national event had occurred on Kosovo land. In 1389, as the Ottoman Turks extended their domain westward into Europe, they fought a battle against a Serb army at Kosovo Polje, the Field of Blackbirds. It was a mutual slaughter, narrowly won by the Ottomans. At its end, a Serbian knight – or perhaps, according to some traditions, the Serbian Prince Lazar – was brought before the Ottoman ruler Sultan Murad. Pulling a hidden blade from his tunic, the Serb hacked the sultan to death before being killed himself. Six centuries later, this event still formed the rallying impetus for the Serbs to purge 'the Turks' – or more accurately the Muslim ethnic Albanians – from 'their' land.

The US and NATO had been stirred into action. Bill Clinton had pulled the US out of Somalia, he had done nothing during the Rwandan genocide, he intervened reluctantly and late in the Bosnian cataclysm – but suddenly he was in, boots and all, for Kosovo. NATO planes, flying above fifteen thousand feet to avoid anti-aircraft defences, targeted troops and militia movements on the ground. Sometimes, they got it wrong. They destroyed a train carrying refugees fleeing south. But even then, the Kosovo Muslims – known as Kosovars – cheered them on. It was as if a schoolchild made miserable by the school bully suddenly discovered he had a lion for a pet.

But the ending was still unclear. As NATO jets started hammering the Serbian capital Belgrade, the Serbs' traditional ally, Russia, was mobilising.

The Kosovars fleeing into Kukes found themselves in a small town groaning under the weight of the influx. A truck rolled up with bread. It was mobbed. But at least the people were temporarily safe.

Those who had fled on roads and rail lines further to the east found themselves blocked at the border to Macedonia. The Macedonian government was warned an influx of ethnic Albanians would disturb their own ethnic balance, with the Albanian population already over a quarter and growing. Some had spoken of a new nation called 'Greater Albania' in which present Albania would extend through Kosovo and Macedonia. Looking at the tragic dysfunction in Albania itself it seemed hard to imagine it could be great at anything, but Balkan ethnic jealousies are a powerful and eternal force.

The upshot was that thousands of refugees became trapped against the closed border fence at Macedonia with the Serbian killers at their heels. Exposed to the weather – it was snowing – people began dying in piteous scenes. There was no food, water or sanitation.

Suddenly a morning dawned, and all those people were gone.

What had happened? There were rumours of a massacre. The truth for once was thankfully more benign. The Macedonian authorities had brought in fleets of buses during the night. The refugees were crammed on board and driven through the night into southern Albania. The cloak-and-dagger approach was to get the job done before Albanian-hating Macedonians realised what was going on and attacked the buses.

We found some of these refugees in a series of cavernous wooden warehouses up a muddy track in the hills. The paranoid President Hoxha had created these places as food stores but never had the surplus to fill them. They were filled now. The weaker refugees lay on the hard dirt floors. The stronger ones stood guard at the entrance. Those from Kosovo may have fallen on hard times but they were used to far higher living standards than their Albanian hosts. Some Albanian toughs had already been around looking for things to steal.

The camp had a pipe that delivered water. A creaking truck turned up with a load of tomatoes. A woman of about sixty, elegant under the circumstances, walked up and addressed me in French.

'*C'est une catastrophe!*' she declared. A light snow began to fall.

Among the hundreds of people at the warehouse was a journalist, Flutura Bacaj, from the Kosovo capital Pristina.

'We have no food here,' Bacaj lamented. 'We cannot last.'

She presented her hands to me. All the little cuts and grazes of the past days and weeks on the road had begun to fester. People's immune systems were overloaded.

'We will survive . . . at the most . . .' Her head dropped. '. . . Maybe not even a month.'

Into this walked an Australian doctor. Rick Brennan was from the New York–based International Rescue Committee. He was assessing sanitation. A quick job. There was none.

'Could an epidemic go through here?' I asked, keeping my voice low in case I was overheard.

'Oh, certainly,' said Rick. 'I'd give it no more than a week.'

The nearest big town was Korce, a crossroads centre that had been controlled in the twentieth century by Turks, Macedonians, Bulgarians and even the French. In a modern basketball stadium we found more refugees from the border. The first man I met was an economics professor, his chin forested with white stubble over the still-immaculate knot of his tie.

His friend, a fellow academic from Pristina University, had died beside him in the mud along the border wire.

'Horrible,' he said. 'Horrible.'

Now he was looking for his daughter.

'When the buses came they pushed us on,' he explained. 'I was the last one onto one bus, my daughter was pushed onto the next. But who knows where that bus went?'

It was true. The bus could be in Macedonia. It could be in Greece, or Tirana, or in any one of the countless sports halls or warehouses or tented camps in between.

In the crowds on the floor, we also came upon a bright and pretty young woman of about eighteen. She was having a great refugee crisis. She had met a man. They were going to be married. Sure enough, a bloke turned up probably in his late twenties and clearly far more worldly than she.

He had the sly smarts of the black marketeer, a jaunty swagger and a knowing grin. She hugged him, her face beaming. He grinned his shark-fin grin. Still, who can resist love in the ruins? In fifteen minutes, we shot a quick story on them both. I got a bigger response to that yarn than to all the dozens of others I filed from Albania. I hope their lives have been rich and satisfying.

The plight of the Kosovars had struck a global chord. Every day the ferry from Italy arrived at the port of Durres filled with young men coming to sign up with the Kosovo Liberation Army – the KLA, or in Albanian script, the UCK. Many of the volunteers were ethnic Albanians from other parts of Europe or North America. Among their numbers, however, were some with no links to Albania at all. Some were idealistic. They likened the cause to the fight against

Spanish fascism in the 1930s, which had drawn in the muscular dreamers of that age – from Hemingway to Orwell to Laurie Lee. In Tirana, I met a senior Australian aid official who thundered that if she was thirty years younger she would be signing up herself.

I felt the romantic appeal of the Spanish analogy but I also had my doubts.

On the road south from Kukes, we had seen UCK roadblocks pulling teenage boys out of vehicles, insisting they 'volunteer' for the cause. I had also read enough about the Spanish cause to know how badly that had turned out. There are few innocents in dirty wars.

Among these recruits was a young rootless man from northern Adelaide, David Hicks. Whatever idealism drew him to the fight against Serbian nationalists, it led him also to Afghanistan and ultimately to Guantanamo Bay.

In a refugee camp in Tirana, I also met Senator Natasha Stott Despoja. The then deputy leader of the Australian Democrats was on a fact-finding mission accompanied by, of all people, my good mate Steve Levitt. She was low-key, serious and good company.

I spent weeks covering the Kosovo story, but had to bail out before the final capitulation by Belgrade. I was booked for a spell hosting the *Today* show. My replacement was the London correspondent, Lane Calcutt, a man impossible to dislike. He rolled into Tirana in a blue blazer and a Piccadilly shirt toting a pricey suitcase with tapestry embroidered on the sides. The ferry ride had been crowded and awful, he announced. We took him to our still only part-built townhouse on a hillside above Tirana. We loved the place. It had views. No matter that rain poured in through the unsealed windows and pooled on the tiled floor.

Lane looked horrified.

'A hotel, I think,' he said. And made for the door.

We had a laugh. The grown-ups had arrived.

In a gesture of gratitude to Franko Marcou, I gave him all my warm clothes and jackets. He had admired my American brands. I took the only flight available, an Albanian clunker to Bologna, and that evening found myself wandering the commercial cloisters of a beautiful Italian city. What a contrast. I spent an hour at the Museo Morandi, dedicated to the Bolognese artist who spent a long life painting bottles and jars in the colours of mud. Somehow, in his close, measured examination of the utterly ordinary, I found a calm to settle the jumbled impressions left by weeks of Kosovan chaos. I still keep a Morandi print on my wall, just for when the noises get jumpy.

34

A SCOOP

AS THE MILLENNIUM TURNED, I WAS ABOUT TO START A PHASE OF almost permanent travel.

In May 2000, yet another coup struck Fiji. This time it was launched not by the military but by a former Brisbane computer salesman called George Speight. With fewer than twenty mutinous soldiers on his side but darkly obscure support among Fiji's hard-line indigenous politicians, Speight seized thirty-six members of parliament, including the country's first Indo-Fijian Prime Minister Mahendra Chaudhry. Chaudhry had been a senior member of the Bavadra government overthrown in the first Fiji coup in 1987. He was marched out of parliament on the first anniversary of his election.

Once again, I was bound for Suva. We entered the capital late at night after driving across the island from the international airport at Nadi. The first thing we saw was looters cleaning out a shopping centre.

For weeks, ethnic Fijians had been stirred to anger by false claims the Chaudhry government planned to re-order the nation's land laws to favour Fijians of Indian descent. In fact, such a move was all but constitutionally impossible, but that had not stopped protests, some of them violent, in the lead-up to Speight's coup.

The captive politicians were being held behind the high fences of a government compound just outside the city centre. Supporters of the coup gathered in their hundreds. No one knew anything of the plotters' plan. What was their level of discipline? What was their capacity for violence? One evening, one of the coup foot-soldiers was expelled from the compound and left to stroll around outside, plainly very drunk and armed with an AK-47. He threatened passing traffic and made a dangerous goose of himself while we filmed him as surreptitiously as we could. The army did nothing.

The initial action was away from the compound. The old veteran Ratu Sir Kamisese Mara was now president. His daughter was among those being held hostage. He warned that another racist-inspired coup would consign the country to purgatory that had to be reversed immediately or the shift would be 'to hell'.

On the Saturday afternoon, the international media was camped outside the compound hoping for a glimpse of the hostages or some word from the still-mysterious coup leader. A thunderous tropical storm came in, bringing lashing rain. It was a signal for us and all the other media people to leave. We were all approaching deadline anyway and we had to get to the satellite dish stationed at a local airport.

Having filed our story, I realised we had left our camera tripod back outside the compound. For that reason, and no other, we returned. No other journalists were there. There was just a couple dozen coup supporters who had not been discouraged by the down-pour. The rain had stopped. Night had fallen.

As we spotted our tripod at the side of the driveway, Sam, our driver, said something.

'What's that, Sam?'

'George Speight.'

'What about him?'

'That's him. Just there.'

And sure enough it was. Walking down a path, almost unnoticed in the dark, was the diminutive figure of the most wanted man in

Fiji. He had come to say thanks to his supporters but had waited until the TV cameras had moved on.

He was surrounded by burly goons, a couple of them carrying assault rifles.

How to get to him? There could be nothing subtle about it. We needed to hit him with a light.

Anywhere you go, armed thugs are hostile to cameras. They can't help themselves. No amount of charm or wheedling will make any difference. The only thing that checks them is The Boss. Therefore, flatter the boss. If he values the attention, the goons keep their distance and you get your shot. If the boss reacts negatively, then you're in trouble.

Nothing to do but chance it.

We banged the light on Speight as he reached the line of supporters. The goons immediately reacted.

'Mr Speight, good to see you – how does it feel to know you have supporters willing to wait for you even in the rain, even at night-time?'

'Oh, hello Hugh,' he replied. I gave quiet thanks for Nine's strong ratings in Brisbane. 'Yes, I know I have support from the ordinary people of Fiji . . .' and on he went.

I could see he was distracted and our shot was not a good one. I invited him to go ahead and greet his supporters without my interruption while we got shots of that interaction. We then repositioned ourselves on the path back to the compound. As he returned, I walked with him, asking more pointedly political questions about his aims and whether he would abandon his cause if the primary body of indigenous power, the Great Council of Chiefs, ruled against him.

'Of course,' he said, but he didn't think they would. Speight was of mixed Fijian and European descent but his father was an MP under Rabuka, the leader of the 1987 coup. He expanded on his motives and his plans, as well as the condition of his hostages.

'This is a cause worth fighting for,' he said.

'Is it a cause worth dying for?' I asked.

'Absolutely.'

The interview was a dead-set scoop. All thanks to a forgotten tripod.

Further compounding our good luck, it was Saturday night. All we had to do was get back to the satellite dish and file it to Sydney and the *Sunday* program could run the whole thing to a national audience in the morning.

Once our story went to air, my competitors drove themselves nuts trying to get an interview of their own. My good friend Chris Reason was so desperate not to be beaten he provoked one of the coup gunmen into firing a shot into the air. Nice work. But Speight kept himself out of sight and the interview ran again that night on the peak audience Sunday evening bulletins.

I have lost stories because of plain bad luck. Awards, too. But for that one, my luck was in. After a few previous misses, that missing tripod brought me my first Walkley Award.

In the following days, as mobs roamed the capital and Fiji hung in the balance, Speight became such a fixture that journalists were soon declining his invitations for an interview. Turns out the bloke could hardly shut up.

Two months later, Speight released the last of his hostages under a peace deal that the military chief Frank Bainimarama immediately rescinded.

Speight was put on trial for treason. At his court hearing, he would wander over and chat like we were two mates remembering the good old days. I felt for him. He was a slick-talking salesman who was out of his depth and about to take a fall for other people he has never named.

George Speight was found guilty and sentenced to death. The sentence was commuted but, to this day, he remains a prisoner in the country he claimed he wanted to set free.

35

THE PLATES SHIFT

JOHN HOWARD WAS IN TROUBLE. HE HAD WON TWO ELECTIONS – THE first, against an exhausted Keating government, by a landslide; his follow-up in 1998 had been much closer. He had lost the popular vote while promoting a Great Big New tax, the GST. He had sneaked home in just enough of the marginal electorates to be returned to office.

It was now 2001 and a victory seemed unlikely. By March, the Coalition had been defeated in state elections in Queensland and Western Australia. All eyes turned to a federal by-election in the Brisbane seat of Ryan. It had never been anything other than Liberal.

But then, on a swing of nearly ten percent, it fell too.

The political obituaries were being written. Liberals were taking a closer look at the Treasurer Peter Costello. Could he save them?

Meanwhile, boatloads of refugees were arriving on our northern shores.

An old family friend of mine lived in a working-class suburb of Brisbane. He liked boats and fishing, his four-wheel drive and the traditions – if not the religious dogma – of the Catholic tribe. Over many decades he had been the surest one-person opinion poll I had ever encountered.

And he had a view on refugees.

'Why don't they send the navy out against those so-called refugees and bloody shoot them? Sink their boats! At the very least, send them back where they came from?'

The American newsman Ted Koppel had a simple theory when it came to interviews. Ask what people want answered.

So a couple of days later I was in Canberra interviewing the Immigration Minister Philip Ruddock. In the course of the interview, we had to stop the tape while he took a phone call from the Defence Minister Peter Reith. They discussed plans to build more asylum seeker accommodation on a defence site in Darwin. The other camps, mostly in remote parts of Australia, were filled to overflowing.

Quoting my Brisbane oracle, I asked him why Australia didn't simply force the boats to turn around.

'Australia is a humanitarian nation . . .' began Ruddock, and went on to explain why the current course of accepting refugees by sea, albeit after a long wait in desert detention centres, was the right policy.

The calls from the heartland, however, grew ever stronger. And John Howard's polling numbers grew ever weaker.

I was in the newsroom early on 26 August 2001. A Norwegian container ship, the MV *Tampa*, had picked up about 450 asylum seekers from a leaking boat seventy-five nautical miles north of Australian territory at Christmas Island.

I put in a call through ship-to-shore radio. The captain, Arne Rinnan, sounded reasonably relaxed. He said he was setting off to return his unexpected human cargo to Indonesia.

There was a flight to Jakarta at midday. I got the nod and headed for the airport.

By the time I landed, Rinnan had already turned his ship back towards Australia. The asylum seekers had realised the ship was heading north. Some stormed the bridge. Others threatened suicide by jumping overboard. Captain Rinnan noted that some of the refugees were sick. Christmas Island was much closer than

Indonesia. He took what he thought was the sensible action and set a course for Christmas Island, radioing ahead for medical help.

Four nautical miles short of the island, he was ordered to stop. And so began the stand-off that became known around the world as the *Tampa* crisis.

There is not much to Christmas Island. A dot of rock resembling a stretching cat, it was best known for its profusion of land crabs. Flying in on a light charter plane from Jakarta, the island seemed scarcely larger than the ship now stationary off its northern coastline.

Captain Rinnan wanted to offload the people he had been good enough to stop and rescue. Australia refused to let him do it. The asylum seekers refused to let him head to Indonesia.

It was then, and may still be the case, that Australians object to asylum seekers arriving by boat when they are perceived as mere statistics. When their faces are seen, when their individual identity becomes clearer, a different aspect of the Australian personality gets triggered – the friendly welcome that I received nearly two decades earlier.

John Howard had set a course of his own and could not bend from it. The asylum seekers must never be allowed to land on Australian soil. Their individual faces must never be seen.

The whole event became militarised in a way I have never seen and never imagined in Australia. Special forces troops were landed on the *Tampa*, essentially taking control of a ship carrying the flag of a friendly nation. At one stage, I drove to a viewpoint just to the west of the island's main settlement of Flying Fish Cove. After getting a few shots of a distant navy ship, HMAS *Manoora*, we were stopped by armed special forces soldiers.

'This road is closed,' they told me. 'You have to give us your tapes.'

I told them that unless martial law had been declared they could go and fuck themselves. An assistant commissioner of the federal police had been flown to Christmas Island and I knew him. While the soldiers stared through the windows I called the assistant commissioner on the mobile phone and he confirmed our right to use the queen's roads. The diggers seemed relaxed enough. They were just trying it on. But it is an indication of how quickly official respect for law dissolves once politicians give the military their head. It was unnerving to see behaviour I was familiar with from overseas military coups playing out in Australia.

The Foreign Minister Alexander Downer broke the deadlock by seizing on poor bankrupt Nauru as a dumping ground for the refugees. The almost 450 people who had hoped for a home in Australia were transferred at sea to the *Manoora*.

I got the order to head for Nauru.

Before I left, however, there was some housekeeping to attend to. There was no rental car service on Christmas Island. A Chinese gentleman let me use his beautifully maintained Honda Accord for sixty dollars a day. I paid three days in advance and promised to settle when I left.

Our satellite dish and live-point was at the airport. One evening, I was crossing live to Sydney when a roaring sound was followed by a terrible clash of metal and a car hurtled past me at full speed in reverse. It cannoned into the cyclone-wire fence immediately behind me.

I finished my cross and went to investigate. It was a Malaysian woman and her young adult son. The lad was driving. He had put the car in reverse when he had plainly intended to go forward. As the car sped up in an unexpected direction he had responded by pressing harder on the accelerator. What saved me from being hit was a car that had stood in the way.

My borrowed car.

The impact had smashed in the panels from nose to tail. The car was a write-off.

So, some time later, I fronted up at the Chinese gentleman's house with a sad tale to tell.

He listened to my story.

'When did this happen?' he asked. 'Which day?'

'It actually happened on the very first night,' I admitted.

The man's head drooped, his expression unreadable. Then he rose and went to the kitchen. I didn't know what to expect but if he had returned with a meat cleaver it would not have been unreasonable.

Instead he returned with $180 in cash.

'Refund for unused rental,' he said.

I felt shamed by his generosity. Naturally, I refused to take the money. I went with him to his insurance office and, between us, we were able to fix things up.

—

If Christmas Island was small, Nauru was even smaller – just one seventh of the size. It emerged from the wide blue Pacific as a tiny dot and seemed barely larger even once we had landed. A single road ringed the island. The centre was a wilderness of mined-out limestone. Less than ten thousand people lived there, clinging to the thin coastal fringe.

What had once been per capita the richest nation on earth, thanks to the phosphate mined from the interior, was now poor, exhausted and hopeless. Nauruans were among the least healthy people on earth. The country ranked 169th in the world for life expectancy, and number one for type 2 diabetes. Ninety-seven percent of Nauruan males were overweight or obese. Most middle-aged men had amputations they were willing to show you, or the proud scar of open heart surgery performed – if you were important enough – in New Zealand.

Years ago, a friend of mine had worked for the company that supplied Nauru with all its grocery items. Spam featured prominently. So, too, did Foster's beer. The primary system of transport were little motorbikes of the type Australian posties use. To cool off and see friends, Nauruans liked to pile their kids in their laps or on their shoulders and go for a ride around the island. After going around one way for a while, they would change direction and go the other way. This meant you could wave to all the people you might have missed on the first go-around. The Foster's would be drunk, the cans flicked to the roadside.

Over time, so many Foster's cans had piled up that the island appeared blue. The leaders gathered to discuss this issue. The resolution? The islanders would shift their allegiance to Victoria Bitter. Slowly over time, the landscape became green again.

Here we waited.

The president, René Harris, was an accommodating fellow. He invited the Australian crews to State House, the former official residence of the mining company boss. Here we were treated to a barbecue and a singalong, with President Harris leading the vocals. He did a nice job, too. It was then indicated that a song in reply was required. We journalists looked at each other in deep embarrassment. Eventually, a lame rendition of 'Waltzing Matilda' was offered up, becoming ragged as we realised no one knew past the chorus and the first verse.

Undeterred, President Harris offered to take a few of us out fishing in his boat the following morning before dawn. I turned in early. We were staying at the only hotel that had TV but the one set was down in the lobby. No distractions, then, to interrupt a good bit of kip.

Around 1 am, cameraman Paul Bousfield banged on my door.

'What time is it?' I groaned.

'I think you had better go down and watch the TV.'

'What's the time?'

'Just go down and watch the TV.'

Something in his tone suggested there was a purpose behind his strange behaviour.

I watched the scenes from New York City until the first images of people throwing themselves off the towers. That was enough for me. I went back to bed with the deep sick feeling shared by everyone that day – that the world had in a moment been utterly changed and the future would be worse than the past.

There was no way to get to New York. The airports were closed. And if you wanted to get there, Nauru would be about the worst place in the world to start the journey.

We kept covering the Nauru story.

HMAS *Manoora* arrived to offload its human cargo. For the first time we saw their faces. After all the fuss, they looked like . . . people. They were chiefly Iraqis fleeing Saddam Hussein and Afghans fleeing the Taliban. But the attacks in the United States, rather than stirring up sympathy, had just made Australians more suspicious and frightened of them.

In the early days, it was easy to walk up to the wire of the camp on the sun-blasted plateau in the centre of the island. Women told me of their husbands being shot on the orders of Saddam Hussein. Hazara Afghans, members of a Shia minority brutally persecuted by the Taliban, told me their tales of woe and of their hopes of freedom in Australia. In return, I told them of the terror attacks in the US and the early talk of retaliation against Afghanistan.

That was when Nauru still functioned as a sovereign nation and its relaxed Pacific attitude made free movement possible. The sight of articulate people telling sympathetic stories caused grief back in Canberra, however. Soon the Nauruans were bullied into shutting down access to the camp. Sixteen years on, Nauru and its current asylum seeker population remain largely closed to outside examination.

John Howard was in Washington when the United States came under attack on September 11. He invoked the ANZUS Alliance to throw Australia in unambiguously with our American friends. He won the election in November by a solid margin. President George W. Bush would soon be calling him the 'Man of Steel'. Some Australians would soon be calling him the 'Father of the Nation'.

'Offshore processing', the system of shipping asylum seekers who arrive by boat to Nauru or PNG remains the policy of both major Australian political parties. Towing or turning back asylum seeker boats is also a bipartisan position. The Coalition stopped the boats. Neither side wants to see them start again. My mate in Brisbane got his wish.

36

CASHED UP AND OFF TO WAR

I CAME HOME FROM THE *TAMPA* STORY TO FIND A WORLD CHANGED on every level. The terrorist attacks in the United States had changed global politics and ideas about security. And my job had changed, too.

The great Sydney newsreader Brian Henderson retired. *Nightline* host Jim Waley stepped up into his job and I stepped up into Jim's. It was a dream gig. I had a nightly national audience of 750,000 to one million viewers. There was a great little team on the show and we could take it wherever we wanted to.

I was also free to travel to the big stories and by January 2003 it was clear there would be none bigger than the coming invasion of Iraq.

I got the call-up one Sydney summer afternoon. The brief was to fly to London for some specialist training in surviving biological and chemical weapons attack. From there, it would be into Baghdad. Our goal was to stay there, survive the invasion phase, and still be reporting when the first US tanks came into the city.

There was no way I could say no. This would be the biggest US-led invasion since the D-Day landings at Normandy, quite simply the biggest story of my lifetime. And I would be reporting it from the receiving end.

Con Coughlin's biography of Saddam Hussein left no doubt about the appalling violence of the man. Murder, on large or small scale, was his answer to almost anything. From a dissenting minister whom he marched out of a cabinet meeting personally to shoot, to post-revolutionary Iran which he thought was ripe to invade, Saddam met any challenge with a doubling down of murder.

I had also come to know Richard Butler, the head of the United Nations Special Commission (UNSCOM), who was tasked with verifying the destruction of Saddam Hussein's chemical and biological weapons stocks. Butler owed his rise and his international career to contacts within the right wing of the New South Wales Labor party. He wasn't a John Howard man. Yet Butler's absolute conviction that Hussein was hiding illegal weapons stockpiles was one of the strongest arguments at Howard's disposal as he built the case for following the US into war.

Given all that, I didn't doubt at the time that Hussein had the weapons stockpiles. The best available experts were convinced of it.

My reservations were legal ones. There was no basis in international law for an invasion against a country that posed no immediate threat to the invaders. Iraq had not been involved in the September 11 attacks. Nor was it providing sanctuary to the attackers, as Afghanistan's Taliban had been. Hussein was a secularist. He was unquestionably a thug but his impulses were nationalistic and self-serving, rather than religious. He had organised the murder of prominent Middle Eastern jihadists who had sought sanctuary within his borders.

He remained a potential threat to others around him, including Israel, Kuwait, Iran, Saudi Arabia and others. But his main danger was to his own people. And a potential threat is not a justification for invasion under the law. All countries with military forces are a potential threat to others. Even if he did have stockpiles of banned weapons – as seemed likely – so too did the United States, Russia and other countries that were not under immediate threat of invasion.

All this disturbed me. International law is a grand but flimsy concept. It is largely unenforceable, particularly against great

powers. If attacking a nation that was offering no credible immediate threat to anyone else was okay, no nation on earth could be
safe from future unprovoked attack.

It was with these thoughts in my head that I packed a bag,
updated my vaccinations and prepared an extensive medical kit for
the trip. Times had changed since my first ventures overseas. Now TV
networks organised 'hostile environment courses'. Nine dispatched
a couple of us into the bush north of Sydney in the company of
some interesting characters. One was ex-Mossad, the Israeli secret
service. Another was a Swedish former special forces paramedic.
The rest were ex-commandos. They did what they could to terrify us
with explosives and mock hostage seizures. It was realistic enough
to get my heart rate up. Their scenarios were rarely what they said
they were. So, an exercise in stepping through the bush looking
for trip-wires would suddenly devolve into explosions and gunmen
running in to kidnap us. In one exercise, we were sent on a bush
track to 'look out for things'. Walking single file, eyes sharpened
for any hint of a mine or a trip-wire we reached the allotted end
point and proudly listed all the things we had spotted. The trainer
noted these solemnly down before asking if we had noticed any
enemy soldiers.

'Er, no.'

At that point, the Swedish paramedic stood up from where he
had been lying at our very feet. It was an astonishing example of the
powers of tactical concealment, at least to us. One lesson learnt was
that if we thought a path or trail carried the possibility of ambush
or bomb it was best avoided altogether. We had received a sobering
lesson on the limits of our ability to spot danger.

We were also given a sense of what it might be like to be seized
as hostages. It was my greatest fear, worse than bombs or bullets,
a feeling that only increased with time spent in the Middle East.

One thing I paid particular attention to was combat first aid.
I could imagine the helplessness of having a colleague shot or blown
up and being incapable of rendering any serious assistance. The

paramedics were tough and direct. Tourniquets, cannulas, airway and blood loss management, the search for things that are not obvious, how to triage multiple casualties . . . in a matter of days we were getting the kind of training that usually takes weeks or months. We had no illusions about our skill levels but they were better than nothing.

Before I left, I had a chat with the boss.

'If the intent is to keep us there through the invasion phase,' I said, 'we are going to need a plan if we have to carry out our own medical evacuation.'

'What do you have in mind?'

'If a cameraman gets his leg blown off, I will need the tools to save his life – tourniquets, dressings, morphine.'

'Okay.'

'And enough cash to be able to go to an Iraqi in the street, give him ten thousand US dollars, fifteen thousand, whatever it takes to get his car and head for the Syrian border.'

'Leave it with me.'

Nine was as good as its word. I left with an impressive medical kit and enough opioids to keep Kings Cross satisfied for a long weekend. Money, I was told, would be waiting for me in London.

The team was a crack one. I would be working with cameraman Richard Moran. He was a country boy from Shepparton, tirelessly good-natured and as cool-blooded as they came. A few weeks earlier he had shot vision of the Canberra bushfires that would win him the Gold Walkley – the first photojournalist to be awarded Australian journalism's highest honour. Nick Farrow, another future Gold Walkley–winning journalist, would be travelling as producer for the *Sunday* show. We had worked together on the Fiji coup. *A Current Affair* was sending Jane Hansen with a fine camera pairing, the veteran Drew Benjamin and a young bloke called Matty Brown (not the ABC's Matt Brown who would later acquit himself with such distinction as the ABC's Middle East correspondent). Matty was only twenty-two but was a calm and thoroughly professional operator.

—

From London, Richard Moran and I were transported to an army training facility in the depths of a very olde English wood. There was something medieval about the threats we were being trained to face. Crusaders laying a siege – or withstanding one – had boiling pitch and Greek fire to contend with. We were being trained in how to respond to anything from anthrax to sarin gas. Trying to get a gas mask on inside four seconds in total darkness while being shouted at by over-caffeinated British sergeants tipped us into laughter as much as terror. But the purpose was real enough. It was considered credible that if Saddam Hussein was going down, he would spray around a few of the illegal agents he was widely assumed to hold. A full jog through the woods in respirator and chemical weapons suit was enough to kill off any notion that escape would be easy if such a moment arrived.

We returned to our hotel in Piccadilly to be visited by a sober-looking gent who insisted on coming to my room.

'I have been instructed to give you something from your employer,' he said.

He handed over US$250,000 in cash in vacuum-sealed bricks, enough in those days to buy a family home in Sydney outright. I had hoped for ten grand. A sum this large had the fingerprints of the Big Man himself, Kerry Packer, Australia's richest tycoon and my ultimate boss.

The courier didn't even ask for a receipt. Job done, he was gone.

I immediately split the cash with Richard Moran and we set about trying to find places to conceal it in our personal baggage and gear.

The Nine team, representing news and two current affairs shows, set off from Heathrow airport with nearly half a tonne of gear. I had a satellite phone that I was required to declare to the

Iraqi authorities and another secret one, broken up into constituent parts and hidden in the luggage. We had been warned that paranoia about sat-phones trumped all other concerns for the Iraqis. Their fear was that spies were coming in amid the TV crews. With unregulated sat-phones spies could report back on defences and troop movements. If war was to come, they could call in air-strikes.

We had visas to work in Iraq. It was simply a matter of setting off, via Amman, Jordan, for Saddam Hussein International Airport.

We were on our way and stoked to be going.

—

My first act in Iraq was to corrupt a local official. A security agent at the airport had pulled out the cover to our undeclared satellite phone.

So there I was in the official's airport office knowing I was busted cold if he insisted on a piece-by-piece search of our entire load. Uniformed officers were coming and going. In a moment when the room was empty, I brought out my practised line, apologising for any confusion and offering to cover any administrative costs.

My reluctance to carry too much cash in any one place meant that I could only put my hand on one hundred-dollar note. I placed it quickly on the desk beside the official, hoping it would be enough. Benjamin Franklin, that iconic figure of liberty and the law, gazed serenely up from the greenback. The official looked startled, almost bouncing in his seat as he grabbed the note and with a single gesture slid it into his top drawer. He pulled out a rubber stamp and started furiously pounding a bunch of papers. He gave me one of them. I picked up the sat-phone part and headed for the exit.

First stop was the Ministry of Information where we were assigned our 'translator'. Nasir was his name, a former infantry officer who had fought in the hideous eight-year border war with Iran in the 1980s. His English was rudimentary at best but his real role was not to translate but to spy on us. We knew from old hands that Nasir would be required to file a daily report, not only on what we saw and reported but what we asked about, what our interests were and our political demeanour.

Our spy was a decent man. We became friends as much as our roles allowed. As the invasion day approached, he tried hard to improve our chances of survival. Which was just as well, because his translation skills were rubbish.

Many was the time we would throw a question to someone, who would answer at length in that harsh and guttural Iraqi Arabic.

'Nasir, what did he say?'

'He said same, like . . . I don't know,' Nasir would invariably reply. We had a laugh about it after a while. Luckily we had also hired Alaa, the son of the British ITN bureau producer, and his English more than covered our needs.

—

Baghdad in those last weeks under Saddam Hussein, blended a repressive state with a centre of ancient and subtle charms.

The great man's portrait dominated – by law – every public space. He gazed out from cement frames overlooking every intersection. His massive bust, styled with the headwear of that killer of crusaders, Salah ad-Din, stood atop the grandest of his Baghdad palaces. Iraqi television ran constant propaganda images of the president being greeted by adoring crowds. A little later, as anti-war protests gathered pace in the west, news agency vision would be spliced into the feed. It was a strange experience to be in a hotel room at the edge of the Tigris, picking out people I knew from demonstrations in Melbourne and Sydney.

At street level, the cafés were full. The men smoked their hookahs and drank their tea and argued at clattering volume as old Chevrolets and diesel trucks spouted fumes in the never-ending traffic. In the big hotels, lovers still trysted. In a remarkable display of defiance – or inertia – tradesmen continued to patch blemishes in the great walls around the official buildings until the very day before they were blown to pieces in Operation Shock and Awe.

In the thieves market, the influx of foreign journalists assured a roaring trade in watches carrying the face of Saddam Hussein. Key-rings, too. And dinner plates, carpets, framed mirrors . . . anything that could be made to carry the cheerful tyrant, the latest in a stream of despots who have ruled or attempted to rule this land of the two great rivers, going back beyond the days of Abraham.

Perhaps the most poignant item on sale was a one-dinar note from 1990. At the time of its issue, that Iraqi dinar was worth three American dollars. A dozen years later it was worth a twentieth of an American cent. The most common currency note in use was the 250 dinar. Eight of them equalled one American dollar. To buy anything of even modest value required great fistfuls of the shabby little purple notes. Government officials preferred the ten thousand dinar alternative – easier to slip into a coat pocket. US money was preferred above all.

In fact, the only thing in common between the 1990 dinar and its 2003 descendant was that both had Saddam Hussein's face on them. But for how much longer?

The United Nations still had weapons inspectors busily trying to find evidence of Saddam's arsenal of banned material. They couldn't find any but accused Hussein of being uncooperative. The dictator was playing his own game. He publicly stated that he had no such weapons – bizarrely he was telling the truth – but his only deterrent against invasion was the fear that he had them and might unleash them.

My own views were turned by a single incident at the daily news conference held at the Ministry of Information. These were frequently nonsensical events, the forerunners to the much-parodied 'everything is going fine' announcements that were made even as Baghdad was disappearing under a wall of flame. But the Iraqis had one senior figure who impressed me. Lieutenant General Amer al-Saadi spoke perfect English. He had a PhD in chemistry from the University of Surrey. He was the regime's chief scientific adviser and the main go-between with the UN weapons inspectors.

His news conference was bogged down in detailed questions about missile systems still held by Iraq and whether they technically breached the terms forced on Saddam by the first Gulf War defeat in 1991. At the end, though, he had a point he wanted to make. In the United States, the Defense Secretary Donald Rumsfeld had been asked about the dangers of unintended chemical or biological contamination once the messy business of war began.

Rumsfeld, according to al-Saadi, had soothed those concerns. 'Don't worry,' he quoted Rumsfeld as saying, 'the US has bunker-busting bombs that explode with such heat that any biological agents or nerve-killing chemicals will be neutralised.'

'Okay,' reasoned al-Saadi, 'if you are going to drop these high temperature bunker-busting bombs, you must know where you are going to land them. You must know where these agents are.'

Many of the journalists in the room were already shuffling towards the door. Their questions of the day had already been answered, or at the very least parried.

Al-Saadi pressed on: 'If you know where you are going to be dropping these bombs, upon these bunkers full of chemical and biological agents, you must have map co-ordinates.'

He leaned forward across the table. 'The UN inspectors are still here. Send those co-ordinates to the UN and they will go and discover these stockpiles and all of this will be over.'

He sat back. It was such a simple argument. Washington had been stressing for months the strength of its intelligence, its certitude that Saddam was lying and its faith in its own capacity to find and neutralise these weapons of mass destruction. Very quietly, using simple reasoning, al-Saadi had shown that the US was bluffing.

I was intrigued but still not completely convinced.

'Is there any chance that Iraq has stockpiles of chemical and biological agents that you simply don't know about?' I asked him.

'I can tell you that if we had them, I would know,' he replied. 'And we do not have them.'

This convinced me. In the Iraqi system, people taking personal responsibility for anything was very rare. Al-Saadi had taken the responsibility on himself. He had not fudged the answer. I realised at that moment with a clanging clarity that Iraq really did not have weapons of mass destruction. And I realised that the United States either knew it too, or couldn't care less one way or the other. The whole premise for the war was a smokescreen.

Now, I know many opponents of the invasion had been saying that from the start. But here, I felt, was the proof that satisfied me.

Lieutenant General al-Saadi surrendered himself to a German television crew in the days after the fall of Baghdad. As he was being handed over to the US authorities, he turned in his seat and addressed the camera.

'Everything I have said will turn out to be true,' he said. And with that he disappeared forever from public life.

—

Officially, as the month of March advanced, no final decision had been made in Washington about an invasion but the huge build-up of troops and materiel left no doubt where things were heading.

We took a short internal flight to the south, to Basra, a Shia city that had been violently repressed after some of its people had risen against Saddam during the war to liberate Kuwait. Air travel was such a novelty in Iraq that a photographer with an ancient but very sturdy Russian camera walked up the aisle and took photographs of every passenger. The prints would be available for purchase on the return trip. Nasir proudly got one of the two of us together in our seats. He had never been on a plane before.

Iraq claimed the west used depleted uranium munitions during the first Gulf War in 1991. In the desert south of Basra, the remains of Iraqi tanks lay blasted with what Nasir insisted were the telltale entry marks of the banned armaments. In a Basra hospital, a doctor who had trained in Birmingham told me the uranium had ended up in the water system and the soil. He showed me children with congenital defects he blamed on the effects of the radiation.

'They talk endlessly about weapons we don't have,' he said, 'but they are the war criminals.' Sanctions, he said, had limited the hospital's capacity to treat anyone.

'We had a middle class once, but now all of us are beggars.' Naturally, no part of the blame for this was laid at Saddam Hussein's feet. The doctor was no fool.

My overall impression was of the harshness of life. Baghdad was still in the last lick of the short Iraqi winter. We wore coats in the evening. But at the southern end of the country, the heat was already building. This was the landscape over which the invasion force would come. Basra looked already beaten and broken. Five thousand years ago, in the river flats just to the north of Basra, humankind first invented the wheel. Not much seemed to have happened since. Stagnant ponds stood in their stinking slime around rubble-strewn yards and compounds. Everything was the colour of the grey-white sand. Children looked hungry and filthy and the dogs and the donkeys looked exhausted. In the background, towers with crowning plumes of fire marched across the desert. This was oil country, the reason, many argued, the war was coming in the first place. But very little wealth seemed to reach down to the people on the ground.

—

We were locked into a daily round of reporting and filing. Every bulletin for weeks had led with the build-up to war or the reactions and counter-reactions to that plan. Sleep was short. Already much of the day was spent making calculations about where best we could bunker down for the invasion phase.

Our first hotel, the Al-Mansour seemed a good spot, with park-land on two sides and a good view of the river. But someone told us the building behind it was a target. We then secured rooms at the Al-Rashid hotel. Many of the big networks had rooms there.

It had been built to withstand attack. The double-glazed windows were said to be bulletproof and they sat behind concrete panels angled to deflect an incoming missile. The walls to the bathrooms were twenty centimetres thick and were said to provide a last refuge if the worst was to come. Saddam had even installed a portrait of President Bush Senior in the floor at the front entrance, so every guest and visitor would be compelled to stand on the face of the man Saddam claimed to have bested in the first Gulf War.

It was also said that the big heavy mirrors in each room concealed cameras to keep an eye on the guests. Who knows? They would have had a dull time with me.

Then the word went around that the regime was keen to have the foreign press at the Al-Rashid because directly underneath it was a command bunker linked to the Presidential Palace. Nothing safer than to have the world's press as unwitting human shields. And so we moved again.

By the eve of invasion day, we were at the Sheraton, directly across the river from the heartland of the Hussein administration. I had set up two safe houses with water and a generator, a sat-phone, essential food and medical supplies. It was impossible to conceal this process from Nasir the spy so I didn't try. He became an unexpectedly useful source of advice. When I had chosen one small family hotel, run by a Syrian Christian, as a potential bolthole if I needed one, Nasir gently pointed out a large but anonymous building next door.

'Barracks for Republican Guard,' he murmured. It was a very useful piece of intelligence and there were risks for Nasir in passing it on. After Iraqi forces were pasted by American air power in the Gulf War, Hussein had hidden his army in innocuous buildings in the suburbs. If the Americans identified this one for what it was, the air-strike would not have been so surgical as to leave our hotel next door still standing.

The mood on the ground was changing. Initially, we received nothing but warmth from people we encountered on the streets.

As war became more inevitable, however, tensions naturally rose. We went for Friday prayers at the Umm al-Ma'arik mosque on the outskirts of Baghdad. This was a place of worship like none other. Named after the 'Mother of All Battles' in which Saddam Hussein had vanquished the forces of America – or as the world saw it, the moment Iraqi forces were kicked out with extreme prejudice from their occupation of Kuwait – the minarets were designed in the shape of Scud missile launchers. The Friday sermon was as bellicose as the architecture. I asked Nasir to translate but he wouldn't. I turned instead to Alaa.

'The imam is saying "your duty to God is to kill the Americans when they come",' he recited. '"Shoot them with your gun. If you do not have a gun, stab them with your knife. If you do not have a knife, take a piece of metal – even a coathanger – and stab their throat."'

Occasionally, the worshippers would glance up in our direction, in the upper chamber of the mosque. We left before the end.

There was a pleasant social life in the middle of all of this. Where I could, I would grab a *shish tawook* with admired Australian colleagues like Paul McGeough from Fairfax and the brilliant photographer Jason South. The artist and film-maker George Gittoes, whom I had first met in Rwanda, was also great company in crazy times. And at the Al-Rashid hotel, from where he had reported the first Gulf War and made himself and CNN a global brand, I enjoyed a couple of lunches with the old lion Peter Arnett. He was a link to an earlier time, having won a Pulitzer Prize as a front-line correspondent in Vietnam. He was, by reputation, a terribly hard, irascible bastard but I broke down his defences by playing the New Zealand card. In fact, the South Island of New Zealand card. He came from Bluff, a town so far south the next stop was Antarctica.

By 2003, Arnett was nearly seventy. He had met Osama bin Laden and Saddam Hussein. There was nothing he hadn't done, including embroiling himself in a few scandals. He had made a lifetime calling it as he saw it. He viewed the coming invasion with absolute equanimity. I hoped to absorb a little of his sangfroid over our plates of bony Tigris River fish.

With Richard Moran and Nasir, I flew to Mosul for no reason other than a change of scenery. At the site of ancient Nineveh, Mosul was one of the oldest continually inhabited cities on earth. The Iraqi military authorities were busy preparing the defences of the city and weren't keen on us mooching around.

'Why don't you look at some of our historical sites,' said the local Baathist official. 'We have a very old Christian monastery near here, dating from the fourth century.'

I was about to dismiss that out of hand and press my case for free travel around the city, but Nasir interrupted. Holding my gaze, he said – yes, the monastery visit would be ideal.

The official stamped a piece of paper and was plainly glad to see the back of us.

'What are you doing, Nasir?' I complained.

'You will like the monastery,' he replied with a smile.

Indeed, I did. The church and monastery of St Matthews had clung to the steep slopes of Mount Alfaf since 363, when its founder fled persecution by the last pagan Roman Emperor Julian. To get there, we had to drive up a broad valley being made ready for the expected northern invasion through Turkey. Rocket launchers were stationed in fields, trenches had been dug and pits were filled with oil as tank traps. We were not so foolish as to film any of this – Nasir would have forbidden it anyway – but it was useful direct evidence for reporting back home. The monastery, with its elevated views, gave a perfect sense of how Iraq might face an attack from the NATO member on its northern border. As it happened, while we were there, Turkey announced they would not give approval for an attack to be launched from their territory.

The abbot of the monastery was a small man with a thoughtful face and the beard and vestments of the ancient Syriac Orthodox church. Services here were conducted in Aramaic, the language spoken by Jesus. Father Abdel Kheder showed me the tomb site of the original St Matthew. It was in a tiny soot-blackened room, the legacy of centuries of guttering candles. Attached to the stonework at the foot of the tomb was a manacle and chain. St Matthew had been called from his original cave in the mountainside by the Assyrian king with a promise that his people would convert to Christianity if the holy man could cure the king's son of madness. Tradition says he succeeded and the population converted. (It must be said there are other versions of this story but I am going with the one the monks told me.) The mad were still brought to that tiny black room to be chained to the tomb in the hope the spirit of the saint would miraculously cure their psychosis.

Most of the madness now, though, was taking place outside.

Father Abdel Kheder assured me of his loyalty to Saddam.

'We always pray to God to keep President Saddam Hussein,' he said. 'He is a good man, a brave man, a nice man and a leader of peace. All of us love him.'

As he intoned all this, his eyes never left Nasir, who gazed blandly back.

The old priest thought it best to keep going.

'We pray to give Saddam Hussein victory. You tell your government to open its eyes about Iraq and not stand with Bush and Blair because they are lying men and criminals.'

When you are the custodian of a place that has endured warring empires for more than 1600 years, it pays to take no chances.

I returned to the monastery four years later with a US patrol. The monks were too terrified to let me in. Saddam was gone. The al-Qaeda-linked Sunni insurgents who were the predecessors of Islamic State were now fully active. The last thing a Christian monk wanted was to be seen to be talking to American soldiers.

A decade later, and the monastery and the town at its feet came under attack from the heathens of Daesh. Before the recovery of Mosul, the monastery and its remaining holy men were being protected by a small force of Kurdish Peshmerga fighters, descendants of the Kurds who had ransacked the monastery centuries before. In Iraq, you take what friends you can get.

Driving back to Baghdad that night, we passed rows of massive tank-transporting trucks. Turkey's decision not to allow a northern invasion front meant Saddam could redeploy that section of his armour to the south.

'Not film this,' ordered Nasir. But he kept his eyes trained carefully forward while Richard surreptitiously filmed this scoop vision from the back seat.

—

As invasion day approached, the Australian TV journalists were one by one recalled by their head offices. Even the ABC left. The Nine team alone would tell the television story from the Iraqi side of the lines.

We prepared everything we could.

The UN inspection teams, the last symbol of the non-violent process for dealing with Saddam Hussein, announced they were pulling out. With just a few hours' notice, they headed to the airport, boarded a charter flight and were gone.

War was coming.

We raced across town to file from the remaining satellite dishes on the roof of the Ministry of Information. Everywhere, sites were being sandbagged, trenches dug, air-raid shelters with no chance of withstanding a full American aerial attack were being prepared.

Officials we had met suddenly turned up in my hotel room, as late as 2 am, wheedling for money. I gave some. It was sympathy now, not a bribe. There was no longer anything these apparatchiks could offer me.

'Don't forget us,' said one, as he gripped my hand.

And then a phone call from Sydney.

'You've got to get out,' said the boss.

I won't bore you with the arguments, but they were bitter. I won't recount the conversations exchanged with the rest of the team. Many wanted to defy the order. One wanted to get out. There is an old rule – one out, all out. We couldn't force a team member to stay in a war zone if they wanted to get out, especially if we were being ordered to leave.

There were other factors in play. Several of us had families and children. Life insurance policies were void in war zones. Channel Nine had taken out policies on our behalf but, if we defied an order to leave and then got killed, they could hardly be expected to look after us. That swayed some heads. So did another, more nebulous ethic. The good soldier follows legal orders even if he doesn't like them. If we were part of a journalistic chain of command, the generals had spoken.

We had no option.

We left.

It was the worst journalistic decision I ever saw at Nine. They were gutless. They lost their nerve.

As the US bombers were fuelling up, we were racing across the western Iraqi desert to Jordan. Richard and I grabbed a flight to Kuwait. We would have to go in from the south, across unknown countryside with far greater risks than staying in a place that we had come to know.

As we landed in Kuwait, the pilot came on the public address system. 'Welcome to Kuwait. It is twenty-two degrees and sunny. The war has started.'

We left the plane just as the air-raid sirens sounded. Hustled down steep, airless staircases, we entered a vast bomb shelter beneath the terminal. Most of our fellow inmates had been trying to flee Kuwait, not enter it. All had a very real fear that Hussein's vindictive nature would see poisonous chemicals or strains of disease fired at the Kuwaitis who were hosting the invasion force. Many in the air-raid shelter were in tears. None of them had gas masks. Some clutched hands or handkerchiefs to their faces in the hope that might save them.

In the shelter was a French couple, Nathalie and Atlantis Puisegur. They were on their way home to Paris after five months in India. They found themselves in Kuwait in transit. Their timing was poor. But they reacted to their circumstances and the shaking terror of their fellow travellers by moving into each other's arms and dancing, a brief but entirely elegant waltz. Little acts of grace and courage are all we ever have. So here's cheers, I thought, to the Puisegurs.

The rest of the Iraqi invasion phase felt dull to me. Hours passed in static live crosses from Kuwait City. Richard and I pushed up into southern Iraq as much as we could, stepping back onto the same dust where we had been just weeks before. But now the highways were nose to tail with convoys of American materiel. The story had moved on.

After Coalition forces met unexpectedly fierce resistance around Basra, US command said the advance on Baghdad would be halted to allow another full infantry division to get into place. That could take a month.

I took a break. I headed to Jordan. The weeks of sleeplessness and disruption in Iraq had seen my weight drop to fifty-nine kilos, about sixteen kilograms below normal. I went to Jerusalem. I visited Petra again, one of my favourite places on earth. On my way south to Aqaba at the head of the Red Sea, I picked up a Bedouin hitch-hiker. Ali took me back to his tented camp and I amused myself for a couple of days riding his camels and feasting on flat bread and labneh.

I went to Wadi Rum, Lawrence of Arabia's favourite place. I scrambled over its rocks and dunes. I had been there, years before after another Middle East reporting assignment. Now, I clambered up a cleft in the towering escarpment rising from the crimson sands. Descending in the very last of the light, I encountered a snake that rose to strike at me but slithered off its sloping rock shelf to fall into the inky darkness below me. That night, reflecting on my lucky escape, I sat in the sand and watched a vast moon rising above the mountains opposite.

This was a countryside that spoke to my soul. My bruised spirits restored themselves. I was ready to go back and finish the job.

I was in Petra when my mobile phone sang into life. It was my boss in Sydney. The Americans had chosen not to wait for the extra division. They had pushed on into Baghdad. The city had fallen.

Come home.

37

THE BOSS

'NO STORY IS WORTH DYING FOR,' INTONED MY BOSS, AS I CAME BACK and left him in little doubt about my views on his evacuation order.

'No story is worth the *certainty* of dying for,' I thundered back. 'We are not suicide bombers. But any story that big is worth taking a risk for.'

The Iraq experience was making me rethink the whole purpose of journalism.

I had always revered the Nine Network. It was by far the strongest commercial network in Australia and had built its success on news and current affairs. It hired the best people, backed them, and expected a lot of them. In the time I knew it, Nine was by far the best at talking to middle Australia about things that mattered while putting it in language that could be easily understood.

I was proud to be a part of it. But now I wondered if Nine was going soft. The world had changed since September 11, 2001. The long post-Vietnam peace was over. To report honestly on the conflicts that would define our times would require a new level of commitment. It would mean putting lives on the line, if need be. That was how it was in Vietnam, in Korea, in World War II.

I went back to work presenting *Nightline*. It was a good show. And the travel continued – to Israel and Gaza . . . to the Solomon Islands as Australia led a mission to stabilise a rapidly failing state.

And it turned out at least one person had enjoyed the work we had done in Iraq.

I was at home one morning when the phone rang.

'Hello, it's Pat from Mr Packer's office.'

'Hello, Pat.'

'Mr Packer was wondering if you might be free for lunch.'

My head was spinning a bit at this point. There was a very good chance this was a wind-up by my *Nightline* mates but something about the cool authority in the voice gave me pause.

'Well, I'd be honoured,' I said. 'When were you thinking?' With luck some distant date would be arranged, giving me time to find a pressing need to be in Jakarta or somewhere.

'Mr Packer was thinking twelve o'clock.'

'Today?' I choked. It was already past ten thirty.

Showered, combed, suited and only slightly out of breath, I presented myself at the great man's office in Park Street, Sydney. People used to imagine in those days that Kerry Packer was so hands-on he told us all what to say. In a dozen years working for him, I had seen him only once. I had no desire to change that. His temper was said to be nasty, his power so absolute that if he took a bad view of someone their careers were finished – at least at Nine. With Kerry Packer, there was no court of appeal.

I knew Packer had seen my work. Twice the radio man Alan Jones had complained directly to Kerry Packer when I reported on the 'cash for comment' scandal that had sparked a formal inquiry. Jones was a prime target of the inquiry. He demanded I be sacked. I was required to justify my reporting up the chain of command. I had no problem doing so. My work had been straight and square. On another occasion, just before the 2001 federal election, I got the message that Packer thought my *Nightline* interview with John Howard was too hard on the prime minister. Packer plainly wanted Howard to win. Again, it went nowhere because the interview had been standard fare, robust but – I blush to admit it – routine. Howard himself had no difficulties with it and had stuck around afterwards for a drink.

Other workmates had spoken of their sudden jolt of terror when they would bump into Kerry Packer in a stairwell or somewhere else around the Willoughby headquarters. But I spent so much of my time away, I had never exchanged a word with him.

And now, there I was, being directed into the darkly polished wooden interior of the Packer temple.

Sometimes explosively rude, famous for his powers of intimidation, Packer was also known for laying on great depths of charm. And this was the man I met.

'I didn't like you,' he began disarmingly. 'But I think I like you now.'

He was interested in Iraq. There was not a detail that didn't catch his eye. He was even intrigued by what we ate – towards the crazy end, as the restaurants closed, dates made up a large part of our diet. He loved the stories of how gangsters emerged as order began to fray. In the final thirty-six hours in Baghdad we had been unable to leave the hotel without men in suits demanding twenty US dollars a head for our 'security'. Given a high-school teacher in Iraq made eleven dollars a month, it was a good earner. At the Jordanian border, Iraqi guards threatened us with filthy hypodermic needles, warning us that an AIDS test was mandatory for foreigners leaving the country. However, for US$180 a head perhaps it could be overlooked.

Keeping Packer and I company was John Alexander, the supersharp print and magazine man whom Packer had put in charge of his television interests as well. Alexander was, and is, the ultimate sophisticate, an Italian speaker with the manners of a Florentine courtier.

'Would you like to join us for lunch?' asked Mr Packer.

Dark wooden doors slid back to reveal a dining table in the adjoining room, set out with a heavy tablecloth and silver.

A waiter approached. Would I like beef or fish? He did not ask the others.

A plate appeared before me with a piece of fish under a thick béarnaise sauce. The waiter went next to Kerry Packer and placed before him, on fine china, a meat pie. It was the bog standard, at-the-footy type. I had heard of the billionaire's preference for honest Aussie tucker. Apparently it was not a myth.

The waiter then went to John Alexander and placed before him . . . a meat pie.

I caught JA's twinkling eye. You bastard, I thought. You're no more a meat-pie muncher than Dame Barbara Cartland. But there I was picking my way through a pile of bony fish while the boss and his silky factotum chowed down on the chunky beef.

After lunch, John Alexander retired to catch a flight to Europe. For the next couple of hours, I enjoyed the company of one of the most extraordinary Australians of any age. His insights into political leaders were incredibly sharp. He expressed an admiration for Howard and a disdain for Fraser. He admired both Hawke and Keating, although Keating had fallen out with him spectacularly over the small matter of a piggery. Some of his comments about other personalities are unrepeatable, even if I was of a mind to repeat them.

It struck me that he was a man who was never interrupted. Where he wanted a conversation to go, he was used to being followed. I didn't mind at all. He gave me tips on horse-riding (I try to avoid the animals. I agree with the proposition that it is like riding a half-tonne two-year-old child.) He enjoyed my accounts of camel-riding. He discussed the rainfall patterns of southern Argentina. If his subject matter meandered a bit, he was always engaging and fun.

His health was plainly not great. He had had his kidney transplant three years earlier. His skin looked fragile. He didn't drink but I did because I had heard he didn't like men who didn't drink. He did smoke, however, an ordinary working-class brand.

I won't breach any confidences but I could see why he enjoyed huge loyalty from some of his people, despite his fearsome reputation. I also made my case about the need to accept more risk in reporting wars.

I am grateful for that day. Two years later, the old boy was gone.

38

TIME TO GET SERIOUS

BY 2004, HOPES FOR AN EASY VICTORY IN IRAQ, WITH DEMOCRACY flowing outward across the Middle East, were shown for what they always were – wishful thinking and spin.

A suicide truck bomber had blown up the UN headquarters in Baghdad, a building I knew well. Fatally wounded in the rubble was a man I had got to know a little in East Timor and Fiji and who seemed destined to be secretary-general of the United Nations, Sérgio Vieira de Mello. As so often, the optimists were learning hard lessons. Sunni bombers were killing Shias by the hundred. Ancient schisms were finding a new violent life in a nation fracturing in every direction.

From the *Nightline* desk, I watched and presented news and interviews on this new, darker world.

I would return home each day around midnight and read in silence until birdsong informed me of the coming dawn. I would then sleep until 11 am, jump on my bike and head to the beach. I was training for the new fad of ocean swims. I would swim across Bondi beach and back, or knock off a few kilometres in the famous Icebergs pool and be ready to front up at the studio at 5 pm.

It was the perfect life, interesting, well paid, selfish and comfortable.

It was time to move on.

In Iraq, I had spent a bit of time hanging out with the CNN correspondent Nic Robertson. For a man who had spent a lot of time at the pointy end of things, he was freakishly normal. He had been with Peter Arnett during the first Gulf War, not as a journalist but as the CNN satellite engineer. He had migrated into field producing work and was in Afghanistan when the September 11 attacks happened. He had been on the road almost non-stop ever since.

I rang him. He gave me a name at CNN to call.

I was owed a pile of holidays. I decided to take them, flying off to Paris and borrowing a friend's house for six weeks to think through my next move. I loved the Nine Network. It had given me the world. The people I worked with were my friends. We had a lot of fun. I also loved the great privilege of broadcasting to a nation I loved absolutely. The humour and character of Australians had created for me a tribe and a home.

But CNN was dead serious about reporting the shockwaves roiling around the world. They had lost staff in Iraq. A young Australian sound recordist, Jeremy Little, had been killed in Fallujah while working for the American network NBC. The cameraman with him, Marcus O'Brien, was a friend of mine. A school friend of mine from New Zealand, Alastair 'Sam' McLeod, had died in Afghanistan while working freelance. I felt others were taking the risks essential to reporting this new darker world and I was sitting in an air-conditioned studio taking it easy.

In Paris, it became clear. I had to at least try.

There was a direct flight from Paris to Atlanta. I rang Chris Cramer, the head of CNN International. I was travelling through Atlanta on my way home from Europe, I lied. Would it be okay if I dropped in?

'Sure,' he said.

There is a very useful quote in John Marsden's kids' adventure series *Tomorrow, When the War Began*. Apparently it was a favourite of the German general Erwin Rommel but I saw it first in Marsden's tale of Australian schoolkids resisting foreign invaders.

'Time spent in reconnaissance is seldom wasted.'

It was sound advice. I did not go to CNN cold. I had investigated the territory through my Australian mates who were already there: Stan Grant and Michael Holmes. I knew Stan was anchoring a show out of Hong Kong but was keen to move into a dedicated reporting position in Beijing. By going through Nic Robertson, rather than a member of that 'Australian mafia', I avoided the appearance that I was simply an Aussie trying to leverage his Aussie mates. The fact that I had met Nic in Iraq immediately signalled that I was a reporter used to that landscape. It also helped that I fronted – anchored in American parlance – a show called *Nightline*. The original American show carrying that name was an institution in the US and a by-word for serious, committed journalism. Had my Nine program been simply called *The Late News* it might have had less resonance.

I flew into Atlanta, taking care to book myself into the most expensive hotel. Derryn Hinch used to say, 'If you drive up in a Rolls-Royce they'll treat you like you drove up in a Rolls-Royce; if you drive up in a taxi, they'll treat you like you drove up in a taxi.' I was doing my best not to drive up in a taxi.

Chris Cramer took me on a tour of the building. The heart of the place was not the studio but a vast darkened room blinking with screens. This was 'the row', the editorial engine room of the whole global twenty-four-hour news network. It thrummed with a quiet seriousness of purpose. He was exposing me to the news version of crack cocaine. I immediately wanted to be a part of it.

'Do you see yourself as a reporter or an anchor?' asked Cramer.

'Both,' I said. 'The field work informs the studio work, and the studio profile gives authority to the field work.'

He excused himself and made a phone call.

'I want you to have a chat with Rena Golden,' said Cramer. 'She can see you in half an hour.'

Cramer had two deputies. Tony Maddox was responsible for all the reporting teams around the world. Rena Golden ran the studios and the presenters.

She was a huge character, an ebullient woman who had been born in a small Indian village near the Nepalese border and risen through talent and force of personality to one of the top journalism executive positions in the world. We hit it off immediately.

'Where would you want to go?' she asked.

I knew CNN had three global hubs from where the anchors presented as time zones shifted around the world. They were Atlanta, London and Hong Kong. I would have happily gone to any of them – but I knew Stan was moving on from Hong Kong. I started to bang on about the importance of the China story.

'When could you start?'

And with that, I was on my way.

39

THE GREAT WAVE

HONG KONG IN WINTER IS A GLOOMY PLACE. IN SUMMER THE WINDS push up from the Pacific, hot and muggy, rain-heavy but clean. In winter, the winds come from the north, foul with all the pollution generated by the world's manufacturing heartland in southern China.

I loved travel. I loved the creative disruption of shifting cities and countries. But I did wonder, as I gazed out on streetlights struggling with a grey sulphurous fog, if I would ever see Hong Kong as home.

I was due to start on 10 January 2005 but arrived a few days before Christmas to find an apartment and settle in. I spent Christmas Day with my new boss, Paul Cutler. A Kiwi who had been a senior player at TVNZ, Cutler had moved to Atlanta for a second career at CNN. He now managed the network's coverage of Asia and the Pacific. He had an apartment directly on the water at Shek O, the loveliest of Hong Kong's beaches, and here we passed a pleasant day discussing the ways of the world and the delights of West Texas country music, a Cutler obsession.

The next day, Boxing Day, passed in similar relaxed fashion until CNN's Indian correspondent, Satinder Bindra, rang through from Colombo, Sri Lanka, where he was on holiday. Waves had come ashore. CNN's veteran Sri Lanka producer, Iqbal Athas, was working the phone. Something huge and awful appeared to have engulfed the island's south and east.

In my hotel, I had CNN on in the background as I tried to immerse myself in its rhythms before I took over in a few days. As the news flashed I rang Paul Cutler and offered my services. Half an hour later he called back. A flight had been booked. Get to the airport.

Even as I raced for the flight, something troubled me. The epicentre to the quake was known within minutes to be off the west coast of Sumatra. Reports were coming in from Sri Lanka of thousands of people being washed away. The first fragments of amateur vision were emerging, showing people in the southern city of Galle being washed away at a bus depot, some of them scrambling to climb on top of buses as they were carried off by a filthy black tide. But there was no sound at all coming from Aceh, the Indonesian province closest to the centre of the earthquake. Journalism had taught me always to be alive to the sound that you are *not* hearing. I clambered on the plane wondering what on earth might have befallen those people much closer to the epicentre.

—

Sri Lanka was a homecoming of sorts. The airport we arrived at was where my mum had been posted as a Royal Air Force nurse forty-five years earlier. It was my first return to the land of my birth but it wasn't a happy one. Cameraman Mark Phillips and I went immediately from the arrivals hall to the departure area where we found tourists desperate to leave. One Englishwoman was in a wheelchair with deep bruising and grazes to her legs. The wave had come through her cabin on the beach, she said. She had somehow hung on but her clothes had been washed away. She had fled to higher ground stark naked. She was now wearing an arrangement of sarongs donated by concerned villagers.

Mark Phillips was an Australian from Wollongong who had built himself a stellar career as Christiane Amanpour's number one cameraman. He knew what CNN needed, quickly setting up a live spot at a temple at the southern edge of Colombo. Within minutes I was on air with Larry King. For the first eighteen hours I barely stopped broadcasting. I thought there was one CNN. It turns out CNN was a conglomeration of outlets – CNN USA, CNN International, CNN en Espanol, CNN Headline News, a broadband service called Pipeline and radio outlets. All wanted their man on the ground and I rotated constantly between them. Very soon, I had nothing fresh to say. I had to beg for a free hour to dart out to the local hospital to speak with injured survivors. I met an Australian man about sixty who didn't want to give his name. His leg had been opened up by something in the water. His wound was still packed with fine, silty mud. It was clearly an invitation for infection. The medical staff were flat out. The man seemed in some pain but remarkably unconcerned. But that would change once septicaemia set in. He persistently refused my offer to try to alert the doctors, or at least the nurses, to the danger. I offered to get a message back to his family. He declined. I couldn't shake a feeling that he had been in Sri Lanka doing something he didn't want people to know about. I left him to it.

An English tourist recounted how the wave had flooded over the resort swimming pool where he was having a morning dip with his wife. He had clung onto her hand but she had slipped away. He had not seen her since. It was a stark tale. I groped for something useful I could do for him.

'Is there anything I can get you?' I asked.

He held my eye.

'Hope?' he said.

As more CNN reporting reinforcements started to arrive, Mark and I pushed south. The main road around the island hugs the coast. Where the wave had crossed, the debris made progress impossible. CNN flew in a distinguished staffer, Phil Turner. He was a CNN original, one of those who had started with Ted Turner (no relation) back in the crazy beginning. Not only was he well experienced in making television in places where nothing worked, he also spoke

Tamil, a consequence of his childhood as the son of Christian missionaries in southern India.

We set up in the grounds of another Buddhist temple, where hundreds of traumatised people were sheltering, for the most part stunned and unmoving. Rena Golden got through to me on a phone from Atlanta.

'We're going to do two hours of special programming from there in one hour from now,' she said. 'You are going to be anchoring.'

The plan was to feed me information about what packages and live crosses and interviews were up next through an earpiece, while I ad-libbed and held together the broadcast. I was astonished. The risks of a stuff-up on air were high. Furthermore, CNN knew nothing about me. They were taking a total punt on an unknown quantity. I had to admire their chutzpah. The challenge for me was to live up to their faith.

So began days of a kind of free-form journalism. It was like jazz. You never knew the note you were going to play next. The producer in Atlanta was called Keith Wallace. I have never met him but in my mind's eye he looked like Barry White, with the deep *basso* voice of the disco king. Keith would growl out the next thing I had to link to, while the current packaged report was going to air. Fortunately I had a good basic grasp of Indian Ocean geography because CNN by now had reporters from Jakarta to the Maldives to Kenya, where a measurable wave had come ashore. Stan Grant had arrived in Sri Lanka and pushed on into the island's north-east, then still under the control of Tamil Tiger rebels.

The most extraordinary reports were coming out of Aceh, where CNN's veteran China bureau chief Mike Chinoy and correspondent Atika Shubert were giving the world the first real idea of one of the most deadly natural disasters in recorded history.

To hold all this together and make it coherent was the work of many amazing people. It felt like steering a rocket ship of news with just a busted oar. And this went on for day after day.

Phil Turner found us a hotel on a headland high enough to have escaped the waves. We produced our live shows from beach level in another hotel that had been completely shattered. The smell of dead bodies, buried somewhere in the debris and sand, became increasingly powerful over the days. There was no escaping that scent.

As we pushed south, we came to the site of the world's deadliest ever train disaster. At Hikkaduwa, a beach beauty spot where my parents had taken us as kids, the wave was somehow concentrated into a spectacular force that hit the Colombo to Galle train service. Over one thousand people died. I met a man who had just found the body of his one-year-old daughter. He had been travelling with seventeen other members of his extended family to visit temples on the holy Buddhist day of Poya. Of the eighteen of them, only his brother and he had survived unscathed. His wife had been washed a long way inland. They found her alive but she had to have her leg amputated.

This was just a man who stood there and told me these things, recounting losses as vast as galaxies.

Along the coast, an excavator had been brought in to dig a deep trench in the sand beneath the palm trees. Local men were carrying the bodies of the dead out of a shattered village and throwing them in the pit. Some of the dead were little children. It is hard to imagine a sadder sight. One man, stoically swinging a man's body into the open grave, over-balanced and fell in. He scrambled to get out, but the crumbling sand at the steep edges gave him nothing to grip. It was a moment of awfulness. I saw the hard mask he had maintained during this grim work dissolve into panic and horror. I managed to hoist him out by lying flat on the ground. He recovered his place in the land of the living and went back to carrying bodies.

Another village just south of there had been wiped clean. The only thing the waves had not taken were the gravestones.

Hambantota was a fishing town that faced directly into the oncoming wave. Seabed geology increased the power of the tsunami in some places, where others got away more lightly. Hambantota was one of the unlucky ones. A freighter lay stranded on a small rise overlooking the port, twenty metres above normal sea level, deposited there like Noah's Ark. Barely a building remained of the town itself. Cars and buses that hadn't sunk floated like the carcasses of whales in the lagoon that lay behind the town.

It is a sign of Beijing's strategic ambition that, within a few years of this devastation, China had rebuilt Hambantota to the point where it was bidding to host the 2018 Commonwealth Games. The Gold Coast won the event, but China had won a new ally and a friendly port from which to challenge Indian supremacy in the Indian Ocean.

But there was no sign of happy endings as 2004 ticked into the new year.

A few days after the disaster a local fortune-teller warned another wave was coming. Terrified people fled inland and for days refused to go back near the coast. At a Buddhist monastery in the green hills people crowded for shelter and the hope of food. The old head monk watched the influx with equanimity. He spoke excellent, careful English, constructing grammatically perfect sentences though I got the impression it had been a long time since he had been asked to try.

After recording an interview, I asked him where he had grown up. Galle, he told me, the southern city that had provided the world with the first images of the tsunami.

'Oh,' I said, 'do you still have family there? Are they okay?'

'Seven members of my family were taken by the waves,' he said.

'Oh, my Lord, I am sorry . . .'

'It was the matter of a second,' he said. 'There is no need for grief. It was all just a matter of a second.'

It was a lesson in Buddhist non-attachment. And in pragmatism. I felt the messy weight of my own emotions, let alone those of people struggling with the loss of more than thirty thousand lives in Sri Lanka and as many as 300,000 across the affected area.

I lost the services of Mark Phillips around this point. Christiane Amanpour turned up and requested – quite reasonably – her man. The new cameraman assigned to me was another legend of the game, Scott McWhinnie. A man of irrepressible good cheer, Scott had been shot in the head in Iraq just a few months before. He had been working with my old mate Michael Holmes on stories about preparations for Iraq's elections when a car drove up alongside them on the highway. A gunman suddenly stood up through the sunroof. His first spray of bullets killed two CNN producers in the second car. In the second burst, aimed at the lead car, bullets tore through the soft-skinned vehicle as Holmes and McWhinnie ducked for cover. Fortunately, CNN was a pioneer in the then controversial practice of having a highly trained personal security agent with them. The agent shot the gunman dead.

McWhinnie, falling sideways, had his head in Holmes's lap.

'Christ, Mike,' said McWhinnie, 'I think I've been shot.'

'Oh, Jesus!' lamented Holmes, feeling a warm rush of liquid in his groin. 'I think I've pissed my pants.'

They can laugh about it now. The bullet had passed through Scott's scalp, grazing his skull but not shattering it. He was quickly back at work, insisting on it. He and I would shoot a CNN documentary in Pakistan a few months later and I could attest to the full extent of his remarkable recovery, in spirit as much as body. It was a reminder of the dangers that went with the CNN world. Michael Holmes, for his part, keeps another reminder – a tattoo carrying the names of his two slain colleagues.

CNN's rising star Anderson Cooper also turned up at our little Sri Lankan camp. He was thoroughly impressive, a quiet man of great poise. I was in honoured company. I also got a sense of where CNN stood in the world when I came back one afternoon to find a US embassy official waiting. Would I mind meeting Senator Sam Brownback? The man who would run unsuccessfully for president in 2008 had come to Sri Lanka to see how the United States could help. He'd heard from the US ambassador and he had met Sri

Lankan government officials but he wanted to hear what 'the man from CNN' had to say.

And so I found myself briefing the US government at a senior level armed with nothing but a CNN business card. That was the power of the brand.

Gradually, as the heavy-hitters from CNN came in, I did less of the unscripted field anchoring. It seems I left some impression, however, on the great Amanpour. She was aghast at the live site to see no autocue. Where was it?

We don't have one, she was told. We don't even have a fax machine. It was just a camera and a new-fangled 'B-Gan' taking the place of a satellite dish.

But that Australian guy had an autocue, she grizzled.

No, he didn't, said the tech.

Boo-yah! I fooled even the best.

The warrior and the crook. Rebel army treasurer Arthur Akuen Chol was a good friend despite being later jailed for corruption. Between us, veteran SPLA commander Luol Ding Wol. Malual Kon, South Sudan, 1999. Photo: Steve Levitt

My great friend John Mac Acuek with my daughter Cait, around 2001.

Getting ready for whatever Saddam Hussein could throw at us. With the ever-smiling Richard Moran at a British chemical and biological warfare training ground, early 2003.

Riding with the Fifth Cavalry. Staff Sergeant Matt St Pierre is in the centre, without a helmet. David Allbritton is in the T-shirt and beard.

Helping lug possessions as people flee a rising 'quake lake' (behind) after the Sichuan earthquake, 2008. Photo: Scott Clotworthy

Barely a toddler and already a survivor, a boy from the village at the epicentre of the Sichuan quake, which killed some 100,000 people.

Photo: Xiaoni Chen

With the extraordinary Kristie Lu Stout, anchoring CNN's first ever live scheduled programming out of mainland China. Photo: Ben Adams

Inside the bunker at CNN House, Baghdad. Seated are Arwa Damon and Jomana Karadsheh with David Allbritton on the right, 2007.

Making camp, East Dorafshan, Afghanistan. Note the Red Crescent 'ambulance' on the left.

A deceptively peaceful moment in Uruzgan Province. Not long afterwards, the brave young sapper beside me, Jamie Larcombe, would become the 23rd Australian soldier killed in Afghanistan.

Photo: Lachlan Simond

Late at night in the Afghan mountains, reviewing the day's vision with Chris Campey.

Photo: Lachlan Simond

A moment's pause on patrol in the Baluchi Valley. This one ended with the capture of two Taliban bomb makers. A productive day.

Photo: Lachlan Simond

Returning home allowed me to indulge my passion for reporting politics. This was Tony Abbott before the hung Parliament election of 2010. His own prime ministership was brief but he has been, for better or worse, the dominant political personality of this decade.

Studio life, Channel Ten, Sydney.

Photo: Joel Pratley

With artist and provocateur George Gittoes at his Bundeena NSW studio, 2003. On the right is his mighty work, 'The Preacher', painted from a real event during the Kibeho massacre.

Journalism exposes its practitioners to an endless tide of giants and rogues, the truly great and the truly awful. Stephen Hawking was one profoundly memorable interview. The most expressive eyes I have ever seen.

With Brian Henderson and Ken Sutcliffe, who — with Brian Naylor in Melbourne — helped Channel Nine dominate Australian news ratings for decades.

Four and a half wits. Fill-in duties on *The Project* have sparked some great nights — for me at least. Here with Stephen Fry, Peter Helliar, Carrie Bickmore and Jennifer Byrne.

A chinwag of hacks. A dinner ahead of the official dedication of the Australian War Correspondents' Memorial in Canberra, 2015. Left to right: Mark Corcoran, Chris Reason, Peter Greste, the late Mark Colvin, Nick Greenaway, Shane Munro, Michael Brissenden, me, Neale Maude (back), Steve Levitt, Max Uechtritz, Chris Masters, Peter Cave and Mark Willacy. Absent: Many more friends, including all the women!

Jacob, Holly, Coco and Mary doing what we love: setting off into the Australian desert, finding a dune to camp by and knowing the meaning of peace.

40

CNN LIFE

THE TIME I SPENT AT CNN WAS THE PUREST PLEASURE. MY MAIN JOB was to present four hours a day from the Hong Kong studios. One-sixth of CNN's daily international programming was mine . . . all mine! Cue the mad cackle. Compared with Australian newsrooms, CNN's Hong Kong operation was magnificly multi-cultural and strikingly young. Most of the key players were under thirty-five.

At my first editorial meeting, I had the good sense to stay quiet. There had been new rumblings from North Korea. A brief debate broke out about how best to read the play and it became evident three of the people around the table had been reading the South Korean analysis that morning – in Korean. I was the only mono-lingual person in the room. One field producer, a north country Englishman called Tim Schwarz, spoke fourteen languages fluently, including Mongolian. The assignments editor, Andrew Henstock, spoke half-a-dozen languages, including Mandarin and Cantonese. He had also done a PhD on French literature in French. Most of the team were of Asian descent, chiefly Chinese, Korean and Indian, but many had educations and passports from Canada, the United States or the United Kingdom.

My co-presenter was the best example of the brilliance of the mix. Kristie Lu Stout was Californian, born to a Chinese mum and a German–American dad. Stanford educated, she had moved to Beijing to polish up her Mandarin with a master's degree at Tsinghua University. While there she became involved early on with Sohu.com, the first Chinese tech company to float on Wall Street. Aged thirty, she was wealthy, strikingly beautiful and a very generous co-host. We had a lot of fun.

My day began at 4 am. We were off air by 10.30 am and straight into editorial meetings to review the show and prepare for the following day. Very often, breaking news destroyed whatever fine plans we had and we would be ad-libbing and scrambling under the cold, ceaseless eye of the studio camera.

The CNN name carried incredible power. When Bolivia suffered a constitutional crisis, the country's chief justice found himself appointed president. He reached out to CNN and we put him to air. I conducted the interview with Eduardo Rodriguez Veltze, the man who never wanted to be president, with just a couple of minutes notice. Fortunately, being a foreign news nerd, I had been following Bolivia's difficulties at least enough to deliver a coherent interview.

Another time we went live to a man in a toilet. Joseph Estrada had been the thirteenth president of the Philippines. Alas, he was quite magnificently corrupt. In September 2007, he was found guilty of the splendid crime of 'plunder' – which under Filipino law carried the death penalty.

Moments after the verdict was announced, Estrada begged to be allowed to go to the toilet. Once there, he pulled a phone from his pocket and rang us. We put him to air as he proclaimed his innocence and his intention to fight on. It was my first and only interview with a condemned man and my first with a bloke in the shitter. He was eventually pardoned – and incredibly – lived to renew his political career as the mayor of Manila.

My day job was co-hosting the flagship show, CNN Today. On a quiet day, the global audience might not have been much larger than the one I had at Nine. But when something significant was happening globally, the world tuned in. CNN reckoned our tsunami coverage reached audiences of over 300 million people at a time. It made sense. With the wave crashing through tourist areas like Thailand, the victims came from every corner of the world. It was the world's worst natural disaster since the advent of television and CNN was the global broadcaster. Quite literally, no one had seen anything like it.

One result from the tsunami coverage was that CNN's bosses wanted to see me reporting as well as hosting the show. At any moment, I would be flying around Asia and the Pacific, in frigid wintry Japan one minute, the fetid backblocks of Indonesia the next. But there was a downside. The network never rested and its people weren't allowed to either. I could get back home to Hong Kong at midnight after a week of twenty-hour days at some Asian disaster and the program bosses – who were different from the news-gathering bosses – would still require me to turn up at 4 am for another four hours of rolling studio news.

I had travelled to Hong Kong with my second wife, Kumi Taguchi. When our daughter Coco came along I tried to help with night feeds. Before long I was constantly dizzy. The sensation, which I had to consciously combat, was that I was falling backwards and to my left. When I went to a landslide disaster in southern Leyte in the Philippines, the shifting ground became impossible to navigate with my uncertain footing. I had to retreat to solid ground, using a tripod for balance, the world whirling. Did I have multiple sclerosis . . . a brain tumour . . . ?

Finally, I did the un-male thing and went to a doctor. Scans were conducted. Nothing was found.

The doc ran through a checklist, finally asking, 'Are you getting enough sleep?'

'Not really,' I replied.

'How much?'

'Unbroken sleep? Maybe eight to ten hours.'

'Well, that should be enough.'

'That's per week.'

'That's your problem.'

I begged exemption from Coco's night feeds but the CNN work was as relentless as ever.

—

I didn't want to miss out on all the professional opportunities. I reported and fronted a CNN documentary on the toxic politics of Pakistan, working on long-form film-making with some of the best operators in the world. An absolute professional joy. During this time, I met a listed terrorist leader, a senior figure in one of the myriad Pakistani-based jihadist groups. It took weeks to set up, working with a courageous Pakistani journalist, Amir Mir, who had literally written the book on Pakistani terror groups. I was very conscious of the fate of Daniel Pearl, the *Wall Street Journal* reporter who had sought an interview with senior players in the jihadist movement in Pakistan. He allowed himself to be taken to meet them and was passed up the line to Khalid Sheikh Mohammed, the operational brains behind the 9/11 attacks. This appalling man had Pearl beheaded.

My experience could not have been more different. We were told to wait at the upmarket Pearl Oriental Hotel in Lahore. Someone would contact us. We took a room there. The hotel was subject to what we thought was fairly tight security, especially considering there was an American trade fair being staged in its convention rooms.

Finally, there was a knock at the door. It wasn't a go-between carrying a blindfold to take us to the wanted man. It was the wanted man himself. He breezed in with the full confidence of someone with no reason to fear the notoriously corrupt Pakistani security service. We did the interview in our hotel room, pausing only for him to perform his afternoon prayers. Most of what he had to say was soothing, reasonable nonsense but the mere fact of his being there, while American businesses were shopping their wares downstairs, revealed the layers of nods, winks and blind eyes that made up Pakistan's attitude to Islamist terrorism.

Soldiers talk in wartime of a 'target rich environment'. It simply means there are plenty of enemies to shoot at. For a journalist from CNN, Asia was a target rich environment. There were stories everywhere.

In the Philippines, I heard of a plan to regularise the growing trade in human organs. We went to one of the poorest parts of Manila, a slum known colloquially as 'Kidney Island'. So many men had sold a kidney that the scimitar scar of surgery was almost a rite of passage. The going rate was two thousand US dollars. Yet the windfall never seemed to make any lasting difference. In most cases, people stayed in the slum. Many of the men – and they always seemed to be men – expressed deep regret at their actions.

In his corrugated iron shanty, Ricky Villegas was concerned not so much about potential health challenges to himself as the insult he had committed to God. For his pieces of silver, he had sold something God had given him for free.

'I tell people it is a sin against God,' he said. And there was another downside the kidney agents hadn't warned him about.

'My scar still hurts.'

The buyers of these organs were chiefly from China or the Arab Gulf States, although they came from Europe, the United States and Australia too. And business for the middlemen was booming.

A move was underway among Filipino legislators to regulate the kidney trade, just like any other export business. Keen to push it along was a psychiatrist who worked with the transplant donors and patients, Dr Reynaldo Lesaca.

He saw himself as fixing a black market and bringing it into the light.

CNN was widely watched in the Philippines, especially among the elites. When our story went to air there was uproar. One Filipino politician, who had been backing Lesaca's plan, gave a furious speech to the senate, demanding I be found and thrown out of the country. I had already gone. But it was a reminder of the power latent in simple straight reporting. The Philippines government abandoned the official organ trade idea and instead announced tough new penalties – twenty-year jail terms – in a bid to stamp out the illegal trade.

The huge story, that trumped all others, was China. The Hong Kong posting came at the right time. My work up until then had been focused on Australasia, Europe, the Middle East and Africa. I had never sought a US posting. Indeed, I had turned one down at Nine. The United States seemed to me to be over-reported and the opportunities for adventurous travel comparatively limited.

Not a moment too soon, I was now immersed in 'The China Story'. Everything about China was important and newsworthy. Its economy, growing faster than any other nation's on earth, was the obvious and never-ending yarn. The impact of Chinese manufacturing on western economies was also enormous. As a friend of mine, the Mandarin-speaking economics writer Clay Chandler wrote, 'China has not been a threat to American capitalism – but it has been a disaster for American labour.' It is almost certain that rising robotics and automation would have wiped out lower skilled factory jobs anyway – in the US, Australia and everywhere else in the world – but the first step in the destruction of employment in the west came with the redeployment of factories to low-wage countries in Asia.

China wasn't just an economic story, however. It was wreaking changes across every aspect of human life. In simple environmental terms, it was the biggest story on earth. At one point, all ten of the most polluted cities on earth were in China. They have reined that in a little bit and now various Indian and Russian cities have overtaken them. China is still the biggest emitter of greenhouse gases in raw terms – though Australia outstrips it per head of population.

China represented a challenge to established thinking about political theory. Even when I arrived, in 2004, serious China watchers still argued that a growing middle class would inevitably demand democratic reforms. A liberalised economy would lead, as night follows day, to a liberalised polity. China is now, on some measures, the largest economy on earth. Hundreds of millions of people have been raised out of poverty. The big cities possess more people who might be counted as middle class than entire nations in the west. And yet, China remains a one-party state with no realistic prospect of change.

It was a style of government – sometimes called 'authoritarian capitalism' – that Beijing picked up from tiny Singapore. They now export the idea, most notably to Africa, where many despots are drawn to the notion of staying in power while reaping the benefits of economic growth.

When I helped CNN report a popular uprising in Tibet in 2008, our bureau in Beijing received thousands of death threats, ostensibly from Chinese citizens. Many came by fax, so that whole household removal boxes were filled with the outrage and invective, much of it in English. What was especially remarkable was that CNN wasn't broadcast inside China, except to international hotels, university faculties and the diplomatic quarter. Even then, Chinese censors blacked out anything they didn't like.

The full-time Beijing correspondent, John Vause – my colleague in covering the Port Arthur massacre a dozen years earlier – was personally named in repeated death threats. The entire bureau had to shut down for weeks and broadcast from a Japanese-owned hotel. When the Chinese authorities wanted to express displeasure, they left no one in any doubt.

And yet they wanted to be seen and understood by the world. In 2005, CNN staged its first week of live broadcasts from inside mainland China. Kristie and I hosted 'Eye on China' with a neat reversal of roles. I, the middle-aged bloke, was the wide-eyed innocent; Kristie was the seasoned interpreter of a land she knew so well. One highlight for me was giving a lecture to the elite Peking University master's degree course in journalism. I expected to be translated. In fact, the hundreds of terrifyingly bright students packing the lecture hall followed everything I said in English.

Of the many stories we covered in China, two stand out.

In January 2008, a huge snowstorm swept through China from the north. The timing was poor. About 180 million people, more than the total population of Russia, hits China's rail system during the lunar new year. It is more than just a break. It is often the only time China's army of migrant workers goes home to distant towns and villages to see family, settle business, and hand over some of their hard-won earnings from factories in the big cities.

That year, the trains stopped for days. In Guangzhou, the rail hub serviced a vast population of workers. And within thirty-six hours, 800,000 people were crowding the station waiting for their train.

For the Communist Party in Beijing, this was more than a logistical challenge. It was a potential flashpoint. For nine days, I stood among the crowds reporting. For nine days, apart from the fifty-metre struggle through the crowds to a local hotel for food and occasional rest, I didn't move.

So important is the workers' once-a-year opportunity to go home, the Communist Party feared an explosion of frustration and anger that could sweep across the country and threaten the central government itself. The most accessible member of the senior leadership, Premier Wen Jiabao, was dispatched to the station with a loudhailer to calm tempers and reassure a crowd that just kept growing.

In their puffy winter coats, through day and night, hundreds of thousands of people stood like penguins against the cold. No one wanted to leave and lose their place should the trains come back to life. They weren't happy. A crowd that big is unpredictable. In three days, the authorities deployed 140,000 fully armed paramilitary police to Guangzhou – the same number the United States deployed to Iraq at the height of 'the surge'. Had the crowd blown up and started rioting, a confrontation with a force highly trained in mob suppression would have been unavoidable. We would still be talking about the great crackdown in Guangzhou, just as we talk about Tiananmen Square thirty years after the armed forces moved in there.

Most of those workers never did make it home that year. But somehow, order held. The great Chinese government nightmare – the population angry and unleashed – was shelved for now.

To me, the experience revealed two things. One is the astonishing resilience of Chinese people. They expect life to be hard. They know there is nothing special about them as individuals, that their vast numbers mean their suffering is either a shared event or it is nothing in the scheme of things. They weather hardships communally but – and here was the second insight – if they react they do so *en masse*. For the first time, I saw the depth of Beijing's nervousness at what might happen if the people – with no access to democratic safety valves – decided to let loose a little rage.

—

Less than four months later, I would see that Chinese resilience on an even larger scale. On a fine spring afternoon in mid-May, a shattering earthquake struck Sichuan in central-western China. It was a magnitude eight quake, striking at the point where the lowland plains of the Sichuan basin rise in a series of precipitous folds to meet the eastern edge of the Tibetan plateau.

Some ninety thousand people died. Entire towns were levelled. It was a school day and the poorly reinforced multi-storey cement structures proudly raised for district schools collapsed on themselves. A disproportionate number of children died. In a nation still under the one-child policy, the death of a child is more than a tragic sadness – it is the end of the family line.

CNN's John Vause was quickly at the centre of the worst of it. I followed as soon as an emergency visa came through. The days had changed since my first experience of foreign reporting. There was no longer any need for big satellite dishes with supporting generators and transportation. I flew in to the provincial capital Chengdu with a fine New Zealand cameraman, Scott Clotworthy, and one of the wonderful producers from the Beijing bureau, Xiaoni Chen.

In the city of Jiangyou we found hundreds of high-school children playing soccer and strolling around rows of tents. They had been bused in from another town closer to the epicentre. Some seemed a little pensive, and here and there a child was sitting with an arm around a friend. Nothing else indicated that they had just lost a quarter of their schoolmates in collapsed buildings.

In the same town we found a very Chinese heroine. Thirty-year-old Jiang Xiaojuan was a police officer and a new mum. When the earthquake struck she left her baby with her mother and reported for duty. In the chaos of rescue and evacuation, tiny infants were being saved with no sign of their mothers. Jiang saw one was crying and breastfed her. She was given another baby and fed it, too.

'My milk kept coming so I kept feeding them,' she told me.

By the time we met her, sheltering in a multi-storey building with no external walls, she was feeding nine babies.

We pressed on into the mountain gorges, popping up our pup tents to catch a few hours' sleep. Powerful aftershocks were coming through. To travel the roads was to put yourself at risk of being swept away by rocks and mud falling from the raw hillsides. It was a landscape of scars: physical, human, emotional. Where the road had been buried, lines of Chinese soldiers worked at it with shovels, ants against rocks. It was an insanely risky use of human labour but there seemed no alternative.

We pressed on.

A story of that size didn't need to be found. We were in it. Every so often, in a shattered village or at the edge of a particularly forbidding landslide, we would stop, set up a link and file back to Atlanta and the world. With a twenty-four-hour news channel there was no deadline. There was freedom in our work. The people we met, their crises and griefs and dilemmas were the stories we told. And there were so many stories – they were just there to be picked up.

Between filing, we helped out. We shifted bricks, extracted pieces of furniture, rescued animals. Christopher Hitchens wrote of the importance of solidarity and while he was wrong about some things, he was dead right about that. It was an honour to help these tough and uncomplaining folk wherever we could.

The explosive power of the earthquake had blasted mountain-sides into the narrow gorges until the river lay beneath four hundred vertical metres of tortured and shifting rock. It was in western Sichuan that I realised the traditional Chinese ink painting on vertical scrolls showing a river rushing between craggy cliffs with a little house clinging to a ledge was simply an accurate reflection of landscape. We were there.

But with the rivers blocked by vast piles of rubble, the water was building up into so-called 'quake lakes'. The great fear was that the rubble dams would burst, sending tsunamis of water and mud into the cities on the plains below. Hundreds of thousands of people were evacuated.

We pressed on.

We decided to work our way up one long river gorge in search of the last village to get help. It took us days, filing stories along the way, waiting for roads to clear until finally the road stopped at a little place apparently famous for its peaches. It had a big school which had not fallen down. This was a signal the town was not corrupt because contractors and officials had not cut a deal to build the school from second-grade cement.

In China you could often sense quite quickly if the local communist party machine was corrupt or working in the interests of the community. Some places were unfriendly and fearful. If the local party heavy found a western TV crew they would fly into rages and there would be little option but to leave. In others, the spirit of the place would be open and welcoming, the party official would usually be smart, hard-working and humble in style. So it was in the village at the end of the line.

Due to the fears of a quake lake higher up the valley, the town had been substantially abandoned. People were sleeping under sheets and fluttering fabric in the terraced fields rising up from the river. After asking permission, we set up our little tents and stayed there. The spring weather was mild, the people were incredibly hardy and cheerful. Xiaoni, who knew so many Chinese dialects, admitted she was out of her range here. But a young woman from the village spoke standard Mandarin. She translated for Xiaoni who then translated for us.

In my fantasies sometimes, I dream of returning to this village at the head of the narrow gorge. Perhaps I could teach English at the school. I could live in a hut among the peach trees. I could learn to speak in a language incomprehensible even to other Chinese.

And there I could pass my days.

It is as good a fantasy as any other.

There on the hillside late one night, I had an extraordinary experience. A CNN colleague in Beijing, the Czech cameraman Tomas Etzler, mentioned once that the *sound* of an earthquake was awesome if you happened to have your ear to the ground.

One night, as I slept with just a millimetre of nylon between my ear and the earth, I woke to a howling scream that rose with astonishing speed. Even as adrenalin rushed my system, the ground suddenly thumped: three hard vertical shocks and then a rolling motion. In the darkness, I heard dense concussions as huge boulders bounded to the valley floor. I lay rigid and yet curiously relaxed. There was nowhere I could run in the darkness and it was too late anyway. The crashing sound resolved itself into a sizzling noise as smaller rocks slowed and settled. And then the deep mountain silence reasserted itself. It was broken only by shouts of query and reassurance across the hillside. The landslide had missed. The earth resumed its brooding sleep until the only thing still moving was my pounding heart.

Five million people were left homeless by the Sichuan earthquake. It was a human disaster on such huge scale words became feeble. It could only be comprehended at the personal, human level; the middle-aged parents clinging to each other in waves of grief; their one child gone, too old to hope for another. Everything ending. At a reporter's level, however, I think of it as among the most satisfying work. There was nothing we could do about a natural disaster. But as a small team of good people – Xiaoni with her empathy, Scott with his physical strength and Kiwi friendliness – we lived among people who lived up to the Chinese proverb and 'ate their bitterness'. They helped each other. They grieved. They bore their burdens. I came out of Sichuan with an even deeper respect for the ordinary folk of China.

—

CNN gave me so many experiences. Living in Hong Kong, having a daughter born there, the friends I made. I loved the sense of being immersed in Asia, working with people from all sorts of Asian backgrounds, travelling from Japan to Bali to the mountains of Pakistan. CNN extracted their fair price – until it became unendurable – but my overall emotion is of the deepest gratitude.

And there was one thing above all I was grateful for. They sent me back to Iraq. I believed journalists should risk their lives to report on people who were risking their lives. Call it solidarity. Now, in the worst of all times, in the worst of all post–9/11 wars, I was going to put my theory to the test.

41

BAGHDAD FOR BUSINESS

DAY ONE. WE JOINED A CONVOY OF FIVE US ARMY HUMVEES HEADING out from the Green Zone, the heavily fortified central government district. We were riding with the Fifth Cavalry. In the lead vehicle was the patrol leader, Staff Sergeant Matt St Pierre from Texas. He was twenty-four years old and on his third tour of Iraq. David Allbritton sat behind him, a much-scarred CNN camera veteran. His marriage was crumbling. His body was still a mess from a Sarajevo bomb and he carried and managed a more complex arrangement of stresses and anxieties than most of us could ever imagine.

The patrol was taking a newly arrived command sergeant major on a familiarisation tour of west Baghdad. That would work for us, too. But this was no bus tour. On the way to meet us, the lead vehicle was ambushed, a rocket-propelled grenade skimming over the top of the turret.

The first task was to take the airport road. The Americans named it Route Irish. It was the most bombed, most ambush-prone stretch of hardtop in all Iraq. Everyone working the Baghdad beat knew people who had been killed there.

Dave Allbritton kept his camera rolling. It would be too late to button on once a bomb went off. I kept a camera, a small handheld Sony. It was rolling, too.

Baghdad was unrecognisable from the city I left just four years before. It had never really been the 'Paris on the Tigris' that some had claimed for it. The baking heat, the flat-roofed sprawl, the desert dust and the garbage filth always worked against it. But with its bridges spanning the serpentine river, the grand displays of Saddam Hussein's ambition, and the hints of former Ottoman glory, Baghdad still held something of its ancient glamour.

Not anymore. The roads had become canyons. In a bid to stop hit-and-run ambushes, car bombs and sniper attacks, all traffic now ran between five-metre-high concrete blast walls. It was bewildering. A maze.

Everyone running on Route Irish looked upon every other traveller as a potential mortal threat. And they were. As well as US military vehicles, there were the Iraqi army and the poor, harried bastards of Baghdad who were just trying to get across town. Worst of all were the American security contractors. Hired on big money to protect technical advisers, aid agencies, the carpet-baggers and the money-men looking to make their fortunes, the cowboys drove fast, waved their weapons hard and looked for any opportunity to take a shot. It was called 'hi-pro' – or high-profile – security. Everyone knew when the contractors were on the move.

CNN took a different approach. When we moved in our private cars we went low profile. I had been picked up from the airport the night before in a factory armoured Mercedes Benz with two ex-special forces soldiers on board plus a trusted ex-Iraqi army infantryman.

On Route Irish, with the Hummers, we moved at a steady pace. Local traffic kept their distance. If any strayed close, they got a blast from the air horn and the attention of the top gunner in the turret. No car-bombers on this run, however.

Matt St Pierre led the convoy off the main highway into a suburban street. A little bit of the tension left me. Some old men were standing at a stall selling onions and tomatoes. A little girl ran across the road, hair streaming. Normal life. I buttoned off my camera to save the batteries.

BOOM! The explosion was a stunning blast. The road lifted in a monstrous flowering of earth. The shockwave hit instantly, a pulse through my organs. A reminder that we are mainly water.

Matt St Pierre was shouting. 'Go right! Go right!'

The driver responded. We plunged into a narrow lane.

A second blast, somewhere behind us. Not so strong. My body seemed to have disappeared, but my mind was incredibly clear. Questions and calculations.

Why had they blown the bomb in front of us?

The patrol commander sensed a trap.

'Dead end,' said St Pierre. 'Go back. Go back.'

The rest of the convoy had followed us into the tight lane. It was clear to me now what the tactic was – to direct us into a killing zone where we couldn't get out.

The turret gunner was wheeling his machine gun around, looking for targets. Not finding any. I tensed for incoming fire.

None came.

The Humvees, top heavy with all the extra armour the soldiers had been welding on to increase protection, rolled sickeningly as they tried to execute a rapid three-point-turn. We came out of the lane. There was a car blocking our way.

So that was it. We were being bottled in for a car bomb.

St Pierre got on the public address system – bellowing in Arabic for someone to move the car. To my surprise, someone did. An elderly man who had abandoned his car when the blast went off, emerged from a house and moved the vehicle. We moved on. But now the ambushers had regrouped. Small arms fire pinged off the Humvees. The engines roared. We burst back onto Route Irish. A hard dizzying left turn across the lanes. The clatter of the gun turret. And then nothing but the sounds of sustained acceleration, the hard-working diesel engine switching up the gears.

Welcome to Baghdad.

Safety. Movement. Escape.

The insurgents had set a bomb big enough to blow up the lead Humvee and everyone in it. That included David and me. They would have spent enough time watching American troops to know they never drove on through a bomb blast site. The practice was to find another route out. The second bomb we heard was on the only road out, a turn to the left.

Had the ambush worked, the first vehicle would have been destroyed with all dying or dead. The second vehicle would have followed procedure and gone left. It would have been hit by the second bomb. The insurgents would then have killed up to ten US troops, and they would have had small arms fire ready to pick off survivors or any other vehicles caught in the trap.

We lived, because they fired the first bomb two seconds early. That allowed Matt St Pierre to make an instinctive call to head down the lane, not realising it led nowhere. The insurgents had not been expecting that. But it meant we lived. It meant this time they missed out.

It was 2007. George W. Bush, in a belated recognition his Iraq adventure was failing, had ordered 'the surge' – boosting up troop numbers and taking the fight to the militias who were acting with increasing authority. By this time, April/May of 2007, US troops were being killed at the rate of four a week. That day we kept the averages down.

There was just one other thing.

'Did you get any of that?' I asked Dave Allbritton.

'Yeah,' the veteran cameraman said, 'I got it.'

—

The patrol headed north-west to the security of a burnt-out shopping mall overlooking the highway to Fallujah and Abu Ghraib. It was several storeys high. Inside, it was a sad and abandoned place, a monument to long-flown commercial dreams. With no electricity, the only light was a brilliant shaft of sunlight through the shattered ceiling, catching in its beam a thick suspension of concrete dust and God knows what sinister fibres. The place was a fortress. All sorts of weaponry was trained down on the highway and the suburbs where many of the senior Baath party operators still lived.

I followed Matt St Pierre up onto the roof. He agreed, without fuss, to an interview. An Australian sergeant would have run a mile. But the constitutional right to free speech is taken seriously in the United States and so he spoke free from fear. What strikes me, looking at that interview again a decade later, is the wisdom and clarity of his analysis.

'The surge' was the Bush administration's final play, to claw back success from the disastrous, arrogant, ill-considered invasion of four years earlier. Bush and his so-called 'neo-con' advisers, including Vice President Dick Cheney, Defense Secretary Donald Rumsfeld and Deputy Defense Secretary Paul Wolfowitz, had gone into Iraq with no strategy weightier than a press release. When Arab experts in the State Department had raised their concerns, they were sidelined. To run post-invasion Iraq, the US chose a mid-level diplomat whose most senior role had been as Ambassador to the Netherlands twenty years earlier. Paul Bremer had spent no time in the Arab world. But the ultimate blame for the miscalculations under his reign lie not with him but with those who put him there.

In 2016, Paul Bremer wrote that the United States had failed to prepare for the aftermath of the invasion phase. As the country fractured, and Sunni insurgents took on both the Coalition forces and their ancient Shia enemies, the US appeared bewildered.

By late 2006, when all else had failed, the administration finally took notice of some of the bright freethinkers in the military. Men like David Petraeus, Stanley McChrystal, HR McMaster, and Australian soldier and anthropologist David Kilcullen reasoned that stability could never come unless the Coalition understood Iraq from an Iraqi's perspective.

The surge was the result; a counter-insurgency plan backed up by extra troops and new intellectual rigour. It was the first smart thought of the war. But at the pointy end, a courageous, committed soldier like Matt St Pierre believed it doomed.

'This is our generation's Vietnam,' he told me. 'I don't think this can be won. We're caught in the middle of a civil war.'

He wasn't personally despondent. He believed morale among the US troops who went 'outside the wire' – into the badlands beyond the bases – was good. But he feared America would leave Iraq worse than it found it. And when they left, there would be a slaughter.

'We are the buffer right now. You pull us out and the people that support us are going to feel the wrath. The people who are against us – and I believe that's the majority – they're going to ultimately win.'

How many wars through history have been like that? Cynicism, political opportunism and miscalculation at the top end, sacrifice at the bottom. There has always been sacrifice at the bottom.

Matt St Pierre lives in Texas now with his wife and two daughters. Most of the team he led out of the ambush that day have got on with their lives, though one of them, Brian Bradley, had his right arm blown off in another ambush later in the tour. The Facebook page of one of them contains a seven-minute rant against counselling.

It is a tough adjustment from peace to war. It is just as tough going the other way. A National Mental Health Commission report in 2017 found suicide rates among those currently serving in the Australian Defence Force was half that of the general civilian population. Once people leave their service, however, the rate increases to double that of the civilian population. Unemployment post-service is also far worse than among the general population. Joblessness, depression, substance abuse, domestic stress and suicide seem a poor reward for very real courage and endurance.

One of the new counter-insurgency policies was to push US troops into small bases shared with the Iraqi troops they were supposed to be 'mentoring'. In fact, I never saw much contact between the US and the Iraqi soldiers. Language and trust were issues. The US troops' warmest exchanges were with Kurdish Peshmerga units, nominally Iraqi troops but with their own chain of command and their own interest in supporting the American effort.

The little suburban bases were prime targets for insurgent bombs. Al-Qaeda-linked websites loved nothing better than videos of trucks speeding towards the blast walls and exploding with shattering force. From one of these bases, on a foot patrol with US troops, I met 28-year-old Corporal Jack Androski. He had been a commodities trader at the World Trade Center in New York when the terrorists struck in 2001. Escaping from the towers, he found himself afterwards with no office to go to and an urge to get in the fight. He had never fired a gun.

'The US army is the greatest force in the world for good,' he enthused. Part of the counter-insurgency plan was to get the Iraqi economy moving again. As a grunt with an economics degree, Androski was entrusted with hundreds of thousands of dollars in cash. He often accompanied the unit captain to meet local leaders. Tea would be drunk. But these were watchful men. A suggestion might be made that the local economy would benefit if a small cluster of shuttered shops was to be re-opened. Perhaps money for new plate glass, for repairs to the electricity . . . ? The whiskery men would agree this would be useful. Androski would then peel off twenty thousand US dollars. He would solemnly enter the money and its purpose into his book and the Americans would leave. God knows where the money really went.

American patrols spent a lot of their time making connections, asking questions, showing the flag. On a typical patrol we dropped in on an Iraqi police base. Tea was drunk. Small talk exchanged. Outside the sun baked down. As the patrol leader and the Iraqi police boss chatted, flies rose and settled on a line of fresh corpses lying in the dust outside. In 2007 there were two wars in Iraq. One was by insurgents, mostly Sunni, against the US and Coalition troops. The other was between Sunnis and Shia. Saddam Hussein was a Sunni. Sunnis had run the country for decades. But they were a minority and now the hard-pressed Shia majority was asserting itself.

The killing followed patterns. Sunni insurgents had access to foreign fighters and bomb-making skills. The huge explosions that killed hundreds of people at a time were always the work of the Sunnis. But the Shia had their death squads. Every night, dozens of Sunnis would be shot and their bodies left as a warning to others. At some stage, someone would come along and collect the bodies and drop them outside a police station. The process was so unsentimental – and so common – the sight of the night's harvest attracted not even a glance from the Americans or the police, as the tea was drunk and the pleasantries exchanged.

But the sight of the flies blackening the latest silent victims of the madness is one of those images that stayed with me.

There was, however, some tenderness in this world of death.

On one patrol in west Baghdad, we stopped at the sight of a young woman's body at the roadside. Was there a sniper active? The soldiers dismounted – that is, got out of their Hummers – to investigate. Soldiers formed a defensive perimeter, watching for snipers, alert to ambush.

Her name was Sonia. She was twenty-three years old but looked half that age. She was unconscious. Her brother said she had cancer. The US patrol medic Giovanni Alvarez set up a drip while the interpreter waved off the flies gathering on her face. Soldiers investigating an abandoned house next door found a stash of rocket-propelled grenades. This was insurgent country.

Sonia started to regain consciousness.

'I am dying,' she moaned. 'I am dying.'

'This girl needs an ambulance,' said Alvarez, but there was the rub. The Americans were not allowed to take civilians back to the American casualty hospital with its first-world levels of care. The local Yarmouk hospital was not far off but it was in a Shia area. Shia thugs had been known to kill Sunnis who went there, even – it was said – walking in on doctors as they performed surgery.

Sonia's brothers and parents thought it better that she simply died where she was.

A small crowd gathered. Some brave soul volunteered to drive Sonia to hospital. Sonia pleaded to go. The car left with her while the rest of her family stayed behind. The patrol moved on having won Sonia, at best, a brief reprieve.

I would love to say there is an upside to war. I haven't found it. There are justifiable wars and there are times when people have to fight. Some people have a good time: the politicians, the strategists and the myth-makers. And some people have good wars. They emerge glorified by the fire, and good luck to them. For the most part, war is pain and suffering and waste.

In a Baghdad primary school, I watched the children play at lunchtime. Their games involved helicopter and shooting noises, bomb sounds and falling down. The boys seemed hyper-energetic, nervous and anxious. I was able to visit them only because CNN had given me personal armed security. They allowed me twenty minutes. Then we had to go.

My great fear was not guns or bombs but being kidnapped. Studies show ten percent of troops in combat will develop symptoms of post-traumatic stress disorder (PTSD) – I suspect the number is actually higher – but survivors of kidnap have a ninety-five percent PTSD rate. While I was there, a British engineer setting up IT systems at the Finance Ministry was kidnapped by a gang dressed as Iraqi police. It is likely they *were* Iraqi police, freelancing on the side. Four British security contractors with him were also taken. Years later, the IT man, Peter Moore, was finally freed in exchange for two Shia militia leaders. The security men were killed.

Russ Finn, the tough ex–British military man who looked after me, pledged to go down firing if we were targeted. I was oddly comforted by that thought. At a secret briefing in the Green Zone, US spooks told us what to expect if we were kidnapped. There were tricks to trying to survive longer. But it was made very clear that no US soldier would be put at risk coming for me. They would make every effort for US troops, some effort for Coalition troops, some effort for US citizens. The rest of us were on our own.

Baghdad smelled of dust, sewage and diesel fumes. One legacy of the invasion and its aftermath of violence was that the power grid no longer worked. At best, as the heat built towards the stunning furnace blast of summer, the electricity ran for four hours a day. The wealthy found other means. The convoys of trucks that every day made the risky run north from Kuwait carried an endless trail of diesel-powered generators. And in the refrigerated trucks came ice-cream for the US troops.

As one sergeant put it to me, 'My job is to fight the bad guys who attack the trucks that bring the ice-cream.'

Most US troops in Iraq never met an Iraqi. Forward Operating Base Speicher was a military town that had sprung up next to the old Iraqi Air Force Academy. Just down the road was Saddam Hussein's hometown of Tikrit. But few of Speicher's inhabitants ever saw it. The base displayed occupational health and safety warnings that would not have been out of place in a Californian warehouse complex. 'Watch your back: bend your knees when lifting.' Speed limits on the base were strictly enforced. Visitors passing through were put up in rows of semi-detached townhouses that might have sprung up in Texas or New Mexico. Food was handled by a US contractor who hired exclusively Filipino labour. No Iraqis got a job. They were not to be trusted. The food options were never-ending: Mexican tucker, roast of the day, salads, sodas and – yes, ice-cream. Many flavours. The big PX stores on site sold everything from souvenirs to personal military gear to supplement the official stuff. Demountables outside offered Ford pick-up trucks and Harley-Davidson motorcycles at tax-free prices. The troops could order them there in Iraq, lay a down-payment, and the shining prize would be waiting for them when they finally made it home. People bought Harleys out of boredom.

Iraq was the first war in which the invading force on average put on weight. It was also the first war where most of those killed died sitting down. I went on many foot patrols, from Baghdad to Mosul to the Syrian border. But most movement was in lightly armoured Humvees or other vehicles that were prey to buried bombs. Thousands died in their seats. It created a new kind of warrior. Some American troops were amazing physical specimens – big and strong and relentlessly disciplined in their fitness. Many were not. I spent a long afternoon with some Georgia National Guard troops waiting for a chopper to come. They were bored, insolent to their own officers, overweight and unimpressive. It made no difference. The fit and the lardy both met their ends in similar ways, blown up inside their vehicles.

It played in the heads of people. For some soldiers, sitting in a car waiting to be blown up didn't seem like a fair fight. It seemed almost unmanly.

I was up near Tal Afar close to the Syrian border when a bomb hidden in a culvert blew up beneath a Humvee. The turret gunner was blown clean out the top, breaking his back as he landed. For Lieutenant Colonel Malcolm Frost, this was personal. The crippled soldier had been a talented mountain biker. Colonel Frost had arranged for him to be assigned to an elite athlete stream back in the United States. There were hopes he would go to the Olympics – good PR for the army.

All that had gone in a microsecond of fire and wind.

Frost was furious. He knew someone in the little flat-roofed villages around the blown culvert must have sheltered the bomber. Frost got every military asset he could find and cordoned off the villages. Every building was searched. Every man was marched out to sit beneath the oven of the sun. I could feel my helmet heating up until the centre of my brain felt like it was in a microwave. I was lucky. As a civilian I could take off my helmet, and did. The US troops sweated it out.

Frost gathered the 'sheikhs', the village leaders. They were a grubby, ill-dressed lot. This part of Iraq was strategically significant but impoverished. Survival for these men depended on shifting loyalties as the winds required. Frost, lean and intense, the son of a general, warned the men of what would happen if any more attacks were made on US forces from their area. He didn't care who did it.

'I'm coming after you . . . and you . . . and you!'

He was enraged, working himself up, spit flicking from his mouth, thrusting his finger into the chest of each of the men, bringing his face up into their space. The subtext seemed to be: give us a fair fight and see how you like it. (Malcolm B. Frost went on to make Major General, as head of US Army Public Relations.)

But nothing about Iraq was fair.

In Mosul I joined a raid on a bomb-making factory. The biggest bombs of the war always came from the Mosul district. It seemed to be a regional specialty. A well-packed truck could carry two tonnes of fertiliser bomb, enough to flatten almost everything within four hundred metres. I had walked through the kill zones after these things had gone off. In Mosul, you would hear one every night, the shattering concussion across the ancient city. Now, in an industrial area, we came across a shining oil tank ready to be fitted to the back of a truck. But there were no pipes or arrangements for pouring off the oil. The truck's sole purpose was to carry explosives ready to blow.

While troops swarmed the building, a departing insurgent let loose a spray of bullets. I didn't see where they came from. The only person hit was a simple, poor Iraqi manning a little stall selling cigarettes and snacks. As I clambered back into the Humvee, I saw his legs stretched out unmoving beneath the wheels of his stand.

At that stage, even with the surge, the US had just one combat battalion in Mosul – three hundred outside-the-wire troops in a city of nearly two million people. The insurgents there were constantly being resupplied with foreign fighters from across the nearby Syrian border.

In the American military, the rank of command sergeant major (CSM) carries huge respect. On even the biggest bases, the entrance features a photograph of the commanding officer, often a general, and the CSM. In Mosul at that time, the CSM was James D. Pippin. He had survived more combat parachute jumps than any still-serving US soldier and had been among the first to parachute into Afghanistan after 9/11.

Pippin was a slow-drawling, tobacco-spitting Texan, as tough as rock. He had no love for reporters. The first thing he did was sit me down and give me a lecture about respect.

He came out with me on a patrol, though. We passed by the Mosul jail. Two suicide bombers, including one in a truck, had recently attempted to blast into the jail to release the many insurgents and terrorist leaders incarcerated there.

'We get fifteen to twenty combat incidents on this patch every day,' said Pippin. 'That was just one of them.'

The next day there was another combat incident. Pippin was shot. A sniper got him through the legs.

He had served two long tours in Afghanistan and three in Iraq. The combat medics saved his life but the day I saw him was the old warrior's last full day in war.

Deeply written into the United States' sense of itself is the story of sacrifice in foreign fields. The perfect rows of white crosses at Arlington cemetery in Washington attest to the costs of America's self-appointed role as guardian of the free world. Cynicism is easy. The US has got the world into wholly unnecessary wars in Vietnam and Iraq. But the legacy of freedoms from American sacrifice in World War I and, particularly, World War II are immeasurable.

President Eisenhower, the warrior statesmen, warned on his departure from office of the 'military–industrial complex' that makes new wars inevitable as the machine keeps needing to feed itself. No one should dismiss those insights lightly. They have proven themselves a predictor of much of what followed the Eisenhower presidency.

At his temporary home in a former Saddam Hussein bungalow in the Green Zone, Major General Rick Lynch knew a thing or two about what Eisenhower called 'the certain agonies of the battlefield'.

General Lynch had invited me to lunch. The *New York Times*' great sage John Burns was there as well. Lynch wanted to explain his tactics and methods as he took over responsibility for the insurgent-rich territory to the immediate south of Baghdad. The area of operations for his division included the Shia shrine towns of Karbala and Najaf, scenes of repeated large-scale bombings by their Sunni rivals.

'I am doing this,' said Rick Lynch, 'so my wife and kids can get on a bus back in the US and not get blown up by terrorists there.'

It was a line you heard a lot. It made Iraq's tortures a domestic American issue. It justified the sacrifice.

'I am fighting the terrorists here, so I don't have to fight them at home.'

We had finished lunch and were sitting on floral, chintzy armchairs that I suspect were the taste of the previous owner.

Suddenly, Lynch pitched forward onto one knee. Reaching into a shoulder pocket on his army fatigues, he pulled out a thick fistful of laminated cards, each one with the face of a soldier. These were the men who had died under his command. He lay them down one after the other. As he did, he recited the names of each man, their rank and something about them. This one had just become a father. This one was just nineteen. This one had been decorated for valour the previous year. This one . . .

His voice thickened and became hoarse. He kept looking down at the cards, shaking with sobs. After a while, he controlled himself, wiped his eyes and sat back up again to continue his briefing.

During the US invasion and occupation of Iraq, 4500 US troops died and 32,000 were wounded. The wide use of roadside bombs combined with the increasingly sophisticated body armour meant many Coalition troops survived with limbs blown off. Blast shockwaves have left many veterans with brain injuries whose long-term impact is still being measured.

The real story, of course, is the number of Iraqi deaths. These are contested and impossible to verify. The lowest count is over

100,000, based on official reports. Estimates using other methodologies run to well over one million. Whatever the number, they were all real people.

Many died without a bullet or a bomb in sight.

The shortage of power meant Baghdad's water-pumping machinery didn't work properly. In a city of seven million people, much of the drinking water was simply pumped out of the vile and fetid Tigris and delivered to the slums by local entrepreneurs with water tankers.

The hospitals were overflowing with children dying from gastro. We took a bit of a risk and drove two of the armoured CNN sedans down to the edge of the Tigris, so we could film pipes pouring filthy effluent into the river. Tractor tyres had cut a little channel in the mud at the edge of the water. The ridges had dried solid in the sun. While we were filming, a sniper took a shot at us. Russ Finn, our doughty British security man, threw me face first into the only cover available, the tyre track. Hassan Aljaber, our wonderful Iraqi cameraman, hesitated a moment too long, trying to get his camera off the tripod. Russ virtually crash-tackled him. From the embankment, our back-up security, Hamdi Alkhshali, scoped the opposite shore with his M4. We saw nothing more. I lay in the stinking dirt and enjoyed the strange serenity that comes with knowing they had missed. After a while we bolted up to the armoured Mercedes and drove back to the office.

I remember this incident because when I was back at CNN House writing up the water story someone came in and asked how my day was and I said 'good'. I kept typing. Then, I recalled I had been crawling around in dried mud just two hours before, trying to avoid getting hit by a sniper. An Iraqi reporting life was so full of incident nothing stuck in the mind. So I made a point of remembering that day so I would know what a normal, 'good' day was.

I was a visitor to the CNN operation in Baghdad. A tourist. The place had its residents. First among them was fellow Australian Michael Ware, probably the gutsiest foreign correspondent in the entire theatre. When I was there he had been working non-stop in war zones for six years. He was half mad with daring. One of our Iraqi security guys, Walid, had knocked off work when a Sunni road-block mistook him for a Shia assassin. In fact, he was a Sunni, trying to get home. No matter, the self-appointed guardians of the Sunni neighbourhood shot him. In a reflex, Walid flung up his hand. The bullet aimed at his head ricocheted off a bone in his wrist and settled in his thigh. He somehow managed to sprint towards some Iraqi soldiers, as his would-be killers made a run for it themselves.

With Walid losing blood fast from his leg wound, a resourceful Iraqi soldier grabbed his mobile phone and hit 'last number redial'. It came through to our office. The soldier said Walid was being taken to Yarmouk hospital, in the Shia district.

So the Sunni man who had been shot by Sunnis who mistook him for a Shia was now going to a Shia hospital where he would be killed if they knew he was a Sunni. Such were the complexities. And if they knew he worked for an American outfit, death would be certain.

Michael Ware organised a mission to bust Walid out. Leading from the front, he and a team of our security 'assets' took off to Yarmouk in armoured sedans. They held off the Shia thugs guarding the place while Mike went into the hospital, found Walid and got him out. CNN then pulled favours to ensure he got treatment at the US military hospital.

Such things made Mike an absolute hero to the Iraqis on the CNN staff, especially the tough nuts on the security desk. All of them would follow him anywhere.

CNN's compound was made up of three large terraced houses in a row with inter-connecting walkways and an armoured 'panic room' in the basement. It was not in the protected Green Zone. It was out in the badlands. CNN had paid for blast walls in the little street, and maintained checkpoints on the approaches. It cost a fortune. Other international outfits saw what CNN was doing and got hold of other houses in the street so the protection – and the costs – could be shared. ABC America was just across the road. Fox News, our main US cable rivals, were around the corner.

Inside CNN House, you could not imagine a better team. Running the joint when I was there was the formidable Ingrid Formanek, a gravel-voiced veteran who had been Peter Arnett's producer during the first Gulf War. Nic Robertson, CNN's senior international correspondent who had helped engineer my arrival at CNN, came and went. If Michael Ware knew everything happening at street level in the fight, Nic knew every shift in the strategic battle, the slippery alliances between US counter-insurgency experts and all the various power players inside Iraq. Arwa Damon, fluent Arabic speaker and woman of insane physical courage, was also in the house – when she wasn't out on some new front line. She's still doing it. As I was writing this book, she was on the front line in the liberation of Mosul.

The cameramen, Gabe Ramirez, Hassan Aljaber and the scarred veteran David Allbritton . . . they were all a joy. And the security men who went out with us and kept us alive when we weren't embedded with a US unit were the best of men.

To have been a part of the CNN Baghdad operation, however briefly, was the greatest privilege of my reporting life.

One of the best parts was that the US military didn't care if the reporters travelling with them lived or died. They expected casualties in their uniformed ranks; they were agnostic about casualties among the press corps. They treated reporters like grown-ups. They were not always ecstatic about what was written but they knew that if enough reporters were on the ground, the population back home would have some idea of what was going on. No colonel was going to lose promotion if a reporter died on their watch in the normal business of covering a war.

There were no public affairs officers hopping from foot to foot whenever a camera team wanted to interview a front-line soldier, no implied threat to the soldier himself. We interviewed the generals, but rode with the sergeants and the privates. The war the soldiers knew was the war we reported.

Importantly, the generals and the colonels were keen for our attention. They knew their bosses were watching CNN. It was a way to communicate directly to the top if the official chain was getting a little blocked.

Late in my posting, I injured myself. At a base called FOB Sykes outside Tal Afar – one of the most intriguing battle spaces of the war – our three-man team was looking for a flight out. We were at the end of the line. Choppers might come, they might not. And we were low on the priority list. While we were waiting at the hangar, a huge dust storm welled up out of the desert.

The first hint of it was a door suddenly blowing open, with a cloud of grit billowing into the air. A sergeant in full body armour jogged over to shut the door and I went with him. Within seconds the wind was bashing the building with an awesome howl outside. The sergeant and I reached the door, but it took all our weight to shut it. It was like trying to keep poltergeists in a bottle. We put our backs against the door and tried to keep it shut but the hangar roof was bowing under the force of the wind. The wall behind us started to tilt inwards.

'It's going!' said the sergeant. He dived for the floor. For a fraction of a second I stood with my back against the door, watching the entire hangar leaning and falling. The pressure against my back was astonishing. I had a fleeting awareness that my spine was about to break. The door and wall were falling in, driven by a force beyond all imagining. A searing pain went through my knee and I was crushed flat to the ground.

By chance, I had a tiny gap around me, thanks to a heavy metal sandbox the army kept so soldiers could clear their weapons of rounds. It had held up and it was close enough to leave me a little triangle of space no larger than I was. My big fear was that the steel girders of the roof had come down on my colleagues, Gabe Ramirez and Ben Blake. Extracting myself from the ruins of the hangar I hobbled around to find them in a red whirl of choking, blinding dust.

They were uninjured. I couldn't say the same about myself. My knee wasn't working. I hobbled to the CO's hut where we had been working out of an office. With some military-strength anti-inflammatories, some painkillers and a bit of my own handiwork on the compression bandages, I was able to hobble off to a donga and hope for a flight the following day.

I thought it likely I had sprung my AC ligament. When I finally got back to Hong Kong an orthopaedic surgeon discovered I had, in fact, fractured my leg in about twenty places across the head of the tibia. A classic pile-driving crush injury. That was weeks later. In the meantime, I had my northern Iraq stories to write, cut and file and then I was getting out of there. I hoped to return. But I also knew my leg was stuffed.

I took Route Irish back to the airport. There is no serenity like that which comes when you leave a war zone in one piece, with your work done and your conscience clear. I had a wonderful ten-day break in Jordan, my favourite country in the Middle East, and in Turkey. I was in tolerable levels of physical pain and my soul was at peace. I had put my Iraq bogie to rest. I had put into practice my desire to share the risks of the people I was reporting on. And I had worked with and among the very best in the business on a story of genuine complexity and importance. It was as good as it gets.

42

THE LITTLE BUDDHA BAR

IN HONG KONG, THINGS WERE CHANGING. AND MUCH OF IT WAS personal.

Helen Garner reckoned every time she wrote a book she lost a husband. It seemed every time I got a foreign posting I lost a wife. My second marriage ended in 2006. Our daughter, Coco, was not yet one. She now became my focus. I had the great good fortune of having a steadfast Filipino nanny who looked after Coco when I was at work. My normal workday involved a very early start. Most days I was home by two thirty as Coco woke from her afternoon nap and I'd spend the rest of the day with her.

When I returned from Iraq in mid 2007, a new producer had taken up the desk opposite mine. She was a Cape Town South African, though she had lived in Hong Kong for many years and spoke the earthy music of street level Cantonese. Her name was Mary Lloyd.

Mary was the no-nonsense type. She was strong on economics and global business. She produced shows and framed up ideas with a ringing clarity. We got a professional thing going where I knew where I stood. I also noticed that I tended to agree with her a lot, her ideas, her world view, her sense of things. She had a crystalline intelligence, hard and sharp, yet her lifestyle was laidback to the point of hippiedom. She lived in a little village house at the top of a hill on Lamma Island, a twenty-minute ferry ride out of Hong Kong. There were no cars there. Mary lived with two cats, hundreds of orchids and a view over rainforest jungle and the sea. Her neighbour, somewhere through the trees, was Han Dongfang, a labour rights activist who had been one of the leaders of the Tiananmen Square protests in 1989 that ended in the famous massacre. Han had been jailed, then exiled.

Mary's world combined the louche Byron Bay–style life of the island, with the Manhattan-like gleam of downtown Hong Kong. Before doing her Master's in Journalism at Hong Kong University, she had done English Literature honours at the University of Cape Town where her tutor had been the Nobel Prize winning J.M. Coetzee. Everything that interested me, she had done better and smarter.

I fell hopelessly in love with her.

Not that I could let on.

We were work colleagues, I was older, twice divorced, a solo dad. I was not about to risk being the creepy guy in the office. I kept my silence.

Months passed.

The Friday shift ended effectively around midday and Mary instituted the FBL (the Friday Boozy Lunch). Some of the CNN crew joined in. Mary, with her extensive Hong Kong contacts, drew in all manner of other interesting people. Needless to say, I found myself available to attend.

After weeks of this, I shared a cab with her from the office to an FBL. We had parted company with another couple of CNN friends who weren't joining us. I thought I might try an oblique approach.

'I suspect some of the people at work think we're dating,' I said breezily.

Perhaps she might say, 'Yes, why don't we go dating?' Perhaps she might say, 'I do consider these dates and I think it's time we started doing this properly.'

And what did she say?

'I don't date.'

Right-oh.

And with that her interest was taken by some shipping out on the harbour.

About this time, I spent a few days off the west coast of Sumatra with American earthquake experts trying to measure the growing load in the underground plates. They suspected a five hundred–kilometre length of the same fault line that had triggered the 2004 tsunami was still 'due to go'. (It did go, in two big shifts. In 2009, a 7.6 magnitude quake killed over a thousand people in Padang. In 2016, a 7.8 quake killed over five hundred.)

After romping around on the equator watching these guys securing high-tech measuring equipment on tiny outlying islands, I returned to Jakarta. My flight to Hong Kong was not until the afternoon. I took to the pool at the Mandarin Oriental. Mary dominated my thoughts. What to do about Mary.

On one lap, I would convince myself to declare my feelings to her whatever the consequences. On the return lap, I would be sternly rebuking myself for putting a colleague in such an unpleasant position. Her friendliness had not implied romantic encouragement. Behave, you bastard, behave. I had a good life without Mary and it was best I pursue it.

And so it went.

The year was getting old. Mary had been moved to the late shift. I had taken some time off to act in a play – a friend of mine had a part that he couldn't see through. Mary and I arranged to meet up for an after-work, after-show beer at Hong Kong's Little Buddha Bar.

We bantered on as normal.

In a momentary pause, I looked at her and said: 'What am I to you?'

She looked at me, mildly alarmed.

A line had been crossed.

'I'm going to miss my ferry,' she said and she left.

I felt the clarity of a soldier in wartime. I was floating. Alive with joy. For in that gap of silence, which for once I had not attempted to fill, I knew that she was not utterly indifferent to me.

A few minutes later I got a text message.

It said: '?'

I rang her and pronounced a torrent of love. She was entirely free to tell me to bugger off but if she didn't I promised to love her every day for the rest of her life. It was, effectively, a proposal of marriage.

We had not so much as kissed.

The next day came her reply, by text.

'Give me five days.'

Mary was the greatest thing that came out of my time at CNN and the greatest good luck of my life. We can talk about wars and expeditions, jobs and fame. Love is the human adventure that trumps all others. All of us get to write our story – our love stories. They are as rich in frustration and loss as any epic of empire. Sometimes they have happy endings or at the very least long periods of grace. Like all empires, even the best must ultimately fall. That is life. But like Dylan Thomas in his loveliest poem, love lets us 'sing in our chains' and I will go to my grave grateful for Mary Lloyd.

43

THE RUBBER BAND

ON 15 SEPTEMBER 2008, THE NEW YORK–BASED INVESTMENT BANK Lehman Brothers collapsed in the biggest bankruptcy filing in US history. The Global Financial Crisis had begun.

Mary was working with me on the morning shift, driving the business and economic data as Kristie and I went to air with the collapse of the western economy. It was ridiculous. The Nikkei opened in Tokyo and dropped almost ten percent within minutes. In a week it lost a quarter of its value. The contagion spread with such speed that the Reuters data on which much of the market relied went into meltdown. At one point, it appeared there had been a sudden buying splurge as the Asian indices rocketed back up again. In fact, the data feed had a long-forgotten safety program where, if the numbers were just too insane to be true, the computer would reset to the previous night's close.

There was no buying. There was no bounce. The markets had fallen off a cliff.

I remembered covering the 1987 stock market crash from the trading floor in Melbourne, when the prices were still written up on a vast wall by the 'chalkies'. Then, as now, the days were full of mixed feelings. Economic certainties had turned to illusions. The insane greed and dishonesty of Wall Street was taking down the world. Banks were shutting. Insurance giants were begging for bailouts. Vast global finance houses were refusing to lend to each other. The oil in the global economy had turned to sand. Yet to report it, live on air to a global audience, from one of the great finance hubs, was a rush of pure adrenalin. It was like tobogganing on an avalanche.

In Hong Kong, a bloke who had a business buying and selling second-hand luxury cars had so many people trying to dump their vehicles with him, he rented the top five floors of a huge car park building. There it was, a graveyard of Rolls-Royces and Maseratis, the wily Chinese hustler confident that Hong Kong would turn as it always had in the past and he would multiply his fortune.

Being a finance town, Hong Kong was hugely exposed. Properties were suddenly worth half of what they were yesterday as the lords of the investment game found themselves jobless or their firms dissolved. I could have bought a late-model Turbo Bentley for the price of a Camry.

Mary was pregnant.

We had been looking to buy a larger apartment to accommodate what would be a family of four. The prices were falling fast but no banks were lending.

CNN was also starting to be a problem.

The culture at CNN was relentless work, especially for those who bridged presenting and reporting roles. It was an article of faith that no matter how many days you had worked on end, under whatever conditions, there was no such concept as a catch-up day. The one exception was Iraq war duty, where after six straight weeks of intense danger and minimum sixteen-hour days, CNN graciously granted ten days in order for you to get back home. Those days were nice but even if you were only getting your weekends back, you would have been entitled to twelve days.

My friend and colleague Stan Grant, in his bestseller *Talking to my Country*, writes about his mental breakdown while on a CNN assignment in Mongolia. He ascribes his dangerous state of collapse to the final deep realisation of the accumulated losses suffered by his Wiradjuri people. It was the moment, he wrote, 'I fell under the weight of my history.'

I wouldn't gainsay him.

But he had also been working insane hours at the CNN Beijing bureau. 'My crazy work ethic had hollowed me out,' he wrote. 'My body was beyond exhaustion, I had a head full of death and misery.'

These words speak to me.

Sometime before, after a small Indonesian earthquake – just seven thousand dead – I found myself in the matchstick ruins of a little village of wooden houses. At first the whole place seemed abandoned, but in the middle of the devastation was a man trying to extract a cooking pot. I went to help him.

Was his family all right?

No, his wife and two children were dead.

He stopped working on the pot and sat down where he was. I sat down near him. I put my arms around him and we wept.

I had set out as a young man wanting to know about life on earth. I wanted to understand people and events and how things were. After that moment, with that young man, I knew there was nothing more I wanted to know about human suffering or loss. I had chipped away at understanding for so long and now I had broken through and there was no Golden Buddha, there was no enlightenment. There was just a void, bottomless and black. And that was the knowledge I now carried.

I noticed no one at CNN, none of my bosses, had children. Few were married. CNN consumed them and their passion for it was part of what made it great. I also knew that bonuses were paid to managers who left bureaus unfilled. The reporter's pay would be in the budget. By not filling the jobs, the managers would come in under budget and be rewarded for it. But someone had to 'backfill', to deliver the stories from those locations, and that was often me.

A friendly assignments editor tried to organise flights for me that would arrive back around midday, so that at least I would have an afternoon to get home, see Mary and Coco, and get some rest before being up at 4 am to start again.

Stan Grant writes, 'CNN took the welfare of its staff very seriously.' I don't think they did. They ran their star Iraq reporter, Michael Ware, until his mental health utterly collapsed. Perhaps, if I had done as Stan was wise enough to do, and rung the network's consulting psychiatrist, I might still be there. But I didn't.

The last straw came when I called in sick. My vertigo was back and I had the flu or something.

My boss called to say he expected me back on air in the morning. I told him I thought it unlikely.

He implied I was 'pulling a sickie'.

I told him I had never pulled a sickie in my life. Even when I fractured my leg in Iraq I worked through it. I had not taken a single day off the roster.

'So you're telling me you are not coming in to work tomorrow?'

'No.'

'Well, I want to see a doctor's certificate.'

'You're serious?'

'Yes, I am.'

And for me, that was the moment it ended with CNN.

I waited for Mary to get home so she could help me get to the doctor's. I was too dizzy and feverish to manage it alone. We got the certificate. But it was time to go. Working at CNN was not going to be possible if family life was to mean anything at all. But what next?

More than a year earlier, I had received a call from my old *Nightline* boss Jim Carroll. He was now head of news and current affairs at the Ten Network and he wanted a transition plan for the retirement of the long-serving multiple Walkley award–winning political editor Paul Bongiorno.

'Canberra,' I said to Mary. 'A house, a garden, clean air for the kids to breathe and one of the few areas in journalism where your value increases the longer you stay.'

'Canberra it is,' she said.

Stan says nothing comes close to CNN. In many ways, I agree. It was a ticket to the world like no other but it came with a price that at a certain point I was no longer willing to pay.

All in all, CNN were wonderful people to work *with*, terrible people to work *for*.

My parting gift was to arrange my own replacement, the wonderful Anna Coren whom I had watched from her early days as a morning news producer in Sydney. She became a true star of the network and was perfect for the job.

And CNN gave me a parting gift.

Throughout 2008, the lead-up to the US election dominated CNN's airtime. As Barack Obama swept up from nowhere towards victory, I wondered how another man once touted as the potential first black American president might be feeling. As it happened, Colin Powell was in Hong Kong on election night. He agreed to do just one interview and it was with CNN.

Here was the man who had been Ronald Reagan's national security adviser, who had risen to the most senior rank in the US military as chairman of the Joint Chiefs of Staff, who had become secretary of state under President George W. Bush. A man for whom the presidency seemed at times to be the next logical step.

He was a Republican. Obama was a Democrat. But as I spoke to him, he wept. Much as he admired his own party candidate, John McCain, the significance of a black man making it to the White House was too powerful for emotions to be held in check.

We spoke on for a while, the easiest major interview I have ever done. The questions were heartfelt and natural, his answers were honest and true. Great chunks of the interview appeared quoted the following day in the *New York Times*. And at the end, he stood up and gave me a hug.

So thank you, CNN, for that and many things.

But Australia, my other great love, was calling. And I was happy to be heading home.

44

DIGGERS IN THE DUST

THE QUIET SUBURBAN POND OF CANBERRA MIGHT HAVE SEEMED DULL after my years reporting with CNN but once again my timing was good.

We arrived just in time for the 2009 Press Gallery Mid-Winter Ball where Opposition leader Malcolm Turnbull confronted Kevin Rudd's economics adviser Andrew Charlton with an apparent scandal over favours being sought for a Labor Party donor. The apparent scandal was quickly dubbed 'ute-gate'.

But Turnbull's smoking-gun evidence turned out to be a fake email created by a treasury official, Godwin Grech. Turnbull had gone in hard, believing he had the prime minister cold. When it was revealed it was all just the work of an eccentric public servant's imagination, Rudd was exonerated and Turnbull's prestige was severely dented. His leadership – at least in that phase – never fully recovered.

By year's end, Turnbull was sacked by his own party. Tony Abbott surfed in by a single vote as he rallied the conservatives and the climate-change sceptics to his banner.

And so the blood-letting progressed. Barely six months later, Kevin Rudd had been chopped – a sitting prime minister in his first term. Soon after Julia Gillard went to the polls and hung onto power only thanks to the help of three independents. Then Rudd briefly clawed back and soon after Tony Abbott gained power in a landslide. And then he fell . . . and Turnbull was back.

My ringside seat to all this national self-destruction deserves a book of its own. It was the kind of rolling tragedy that can only be written as comedy; the high hopes, the venality, the sheer savagery of the process.

When we arrived, Mary was thirty-six weeks' pregnant. Our son Jacob would soon be born – the first native-born Australian in our tribe. The winds off the Snowy Mountains were raw and cold. After Hong Kong, Canberra's streets seemed bleak and deserted. I wondered if I had made a terrible error.

After a few days, I took Coco aside. She was three and a half. All she had known was Hong Kong. How was she feeling?

'Great!'

'Really?'

'I love Australia.'

'Do you?' I was genuinely puzzled. 'Why?'

'All the leaves . . . and the birds.'

I realised she had never seen autumn before. The bright wind-drifts of leaf-fall were an adventure to her. And she was delighted by the raucous screeching of the cockatoos and the little pink and grey nodding galahs.

I stopped worrying after that. Canberra was going to be okay.

One night, walking back from parliament to our rented house in Forrest, I gazed up at the cracking cold night sky, the spray of stars, the utter silence of the winter streets and a thought struck me like a shooting star.

'I could get old.'

For years, I had quietly assumed I would meet my end in some shithole somewhere. Not a glorious reporter's death, caught in the crossfire while reporting a mighty battle, instead experience suggested it would be from the fumblings of a drunken militiaman at a roadblock, a vehicle sliding off a cliff, a plane making one journey too many with an engine too far gone from its last maintenance check, a blind bit of ordnance fired off by someone taking a chance, or some hideous, untreatable virus. These were the deaths of foreign correspondents. I had known enough friends who had met them.

The idea that I might live to an old age had never occurred to me. If I was to live, I might have to grow up. I might have to save money for retirement. I might need to consider how to educate my kids. I was closing in on fifty. I certainly shouldn't take a long life for granted. Plenty of noble people were taken while still vigorous to the routine ends of cancer and stroke and a careless lane change on a highway. But I knew my long adventure holiday would have to end.

But not quite yet.

One of the first things I did in Canberra was to take some of my CNN stories to the Australian Defence Force Joint Public Affairs Unit. I wanted to make a polite point about the kinds of stories that came when the military relaxed a little and let reporters do their job.

The Australian Defence Force (ADF) was still shaped by the Vietnam War. It was holy writ that the media – and especially television – had 'lost the war' by removing support for the ADF back home. Their answer was to control the media and to distrust it utterly.

The military has an excuse. It is called 'Op-Sec', operational security. You don't tell your enemy what you are doing, where you are going, the numbers or types of your troops or military assets. Some generals and planners use operational security as an excuse to shut down anything. Ultimately, almost any detail – from the morale of the troops, to the internal layout of a base as revealed in the backdrop to a TV interview – can be of value to the enemy.

But when troops work in a vacuum, where there is no public insight into what they do, the strategic dangers are just as real. Practical experience shows that when the military provides only their pre-vetted vision of an engagement or operation, it gains very little traction with the public. Everyone knows they are watching censored vision and an official line. It lacks credibility and therefore interest.

What is left, then, in the coverage of a war?

Well, there is always the death of our troops.

These losses were announced with all possible solemnity and tact. But in the Afghanistan campaign, the drumbeat of our losses was about all people knew or saw. If people couldn't understand what an operation was about, but could only see the cost in young Australian lives, who could blame them for calling for Australia to get out of there. *Not* having the media can also lose you a war.

A little while after my presentation to the defence force media team, the Chief of the Defence Force Angus Houston pulled me aside after one of his semi-regular Canberra briefings.

'If you put in for a trip to Afghanistan, I am sure we can get you there.'

I pointed out that other journalists embedded with Australian troops in Afghanistan, some of them very seasoned hands, had been frustrated to the point of exasperation at the controls they were under.

'I understand,' he said. 'We are working on it.'

I put the proposition to Mary. I was going to be in India for a month with the Commonwealth Games in October. We were going to get married in Cambodia in December. That left a window for Afghanistan in November.

'And I promise that will be it,' I said glibly. 'Once we are married, no more war zones.'

—

I couldn't really fault the ADF's approach to transparency on that Afghanistan mission. In the UAE, I underwent the training course given to all personnel heading in-country. Much of it was mine and bomb recognition work, including a field examination in a mocked-up Afghanistan landscape. It was a lesson in how well a good bombmaker could hide his craft. There was more medical trauma training, including under mock fire and explosions, and some time on the range.

The commanding officer, Major General John Cantwell, was on leave. So cameraman Chris Campey and I were briefed by his deputy, Commodore (now Vice Admiral) David Johnston and the Regimental Sergeant Major Don Spinks. They were fantastic. Over more than an hour, I got a good sense of what the Australians were trying to do, how they were doing it, and the tactics being used by insurgents across Uruzgan and southern Afghanistan.

At one point a photograph appeared on the large briefing screen, a tiny base deep in a valley.

'What's that?' I asked.

'That's Combat Outpost [COP] Mashal,' said Johnston.

'It looks pretty lonely.'

'That's the hottest COP we've got at the moment,' he said. 'They are getting into contacts four out of five times they leave the base.'

'Can we go there?'

Spinks and Johnston exchanged glances.

'We'll get you there.'

—

The road from the main Australian base at Tarin Kowt to COP Mashal was only sixty kilometres. But it took us ten hours to get there. It was a bold move to attempt it at all. For months, the tiny outpost had been resupplied by helicopter drops. For the most part, the road was a gravel and dust track. Anything driving on it was easy picking for Taliban bombmakers and other local insurgents out to settle a score.

Our little convoy of armoured Bushmaster trucks and eight-wheeled Australian light armoured vehicles (ASLAVs) stopped frequently so combat engineers – the famous 'sappers' – could get out and search the ground for buried bombs. A favourite local technique was to load up explosives in yellow plastic containers designed for palm oil. The containers were everywhere, a person seen carrying one did not necessarily raise suspicions. But packed with ammonium nitrate and aluminium explosives they could blow a vehicle into the air. And, being chiefly plastic, they were hard to find with metal detectors once they were buried in the dust.

They were known to Aussie diggers by the acronym Y-POC (Yellow palm oil containers) and they killed more Australians in Afghanistan than any other weapon.

So progress was slow. Slow enough for insurgent spotters to send word ahead that a juicy target was on its way. Deep evening shadows were lengthening across the Baluchi Valley when our convoy caught sight of COP Mashal. We were just pulling up when the ambush was sprung.

The first blow was a rocket-propelled grenade fired at an ASLAV standing on a small rise to guard our arrival. The anti-tank warhead crossed the three hundred metres of open ground in barely a second. But it was shot too high, skimming over the ASLAV's turret.

Then it was on for young and old. The tree line and the mud-walled compounds at the bottom of the valley were suddenly alive with muzzle flashes. In an instant there was the far louder noise of the diggers returning fire.

Without a word between us, Chris Campey and I put our combat plan into action. His job, with the heavy, high-tech camera, was to get the overall view of any firefight. He immediately took a position in the rear of the Bushmaster where a gunman normally stands. A soldier took up a position on the other fire-step and began blazing away at the muzzle flashes.

With a smaller handheld camera, my job was to get close-up shots of our troops, capturing their facial expressions and shouts as they returned fire.

It worked a treat. I bolted from the Bushmaster and made for where the diggers were most concentrated as they tried to pick out targets. A curious effect of being under fire is the confusion about where the bullets are coming from. This time it wasn't such a problem. In the evening light, the Taliban muzzle flashes were all too visible. The Australian infantrymen, overwhelmingly men in their twenties, blazed away for all they were worth.

Above them, from a guard tower, two diggers were manning a heavy fifty-calibre machine gun. The shooting platform was largely protected by sandbags but the steps leading to it were exposed. With adrenalin fuelling my efforts, I bounded up the steps to get in behind the machine gun for a better look at the Taliban line. Private Ben Clifford was sighting up the gun on a mud wall 350 metres away. The air was thick with the clamouring noise of the fifty-cal and the smoke pouring from the barrel.

'Is this unusual?' I shouted to Clifford during a break in the firing.

'Not round here, it's not.'

Slowly the fire from the tree line became more ragged. And then it stopped. The artillery team pumped up some flares that lit the green base of the valley as if it was an outdoor theatre. It was partly intimidation, partly an attempt to see where the insurgents were moving.

Then it was time to assess casualties. There was only one on the Australian side. Private Brady Morrissey had turned his ankle when running for more ammunition. He was already being bandaged up under the merciless ribbing of his mates.

A gangly young man strode up and thrust out his hand. He was the officer commanding the base, Captain Nick Perriman, all of twenty-six years old.

'Welcome to COP Mashal,' he said, with a friendly grin.

—

Commodore Johnston had been as good as his word. Other than the special operations group teams – the SAS and commando units – we had a pretty free run across the Australian area of operations. It helped that in Lachie Simond we had a public affairs escort officer whose happiness seemed to increase the further he was from the main base. He was up for anything, as keen to get us to places as we were keen to get there ourselves. Chris Campey was also an ideal companion, laconic, tireless, a perfectionist with shooting and editing and an easy mixer with the troops.

By late 2010, the Australian effort was focused on clearing insurgents out of East Dorafshan, the wide plain that ran north of the provincial capital of Tarin Kowt. To go on foot patrol with the diggers by day and camp under the stars with them at night was deeply satisfying even if the ground – as the sappers constantly discovered – was alive with buried threats. If soldiers were taking risks in my name, it was a privilege to walk with them for at least a little part of their journey.

When patrolling, or sleeping 'in the weeds' in a swag, I had that old familiar sense of fatalism. What might come in the next step would come. For the moment, the sun was mild and the company strong. It helped that Uruzgan was strikingly beautiful. In the full blaze of day, the ragged peaks lost all colour. The fine dust of Uruzgan blurred the distance. Only the deep green of the irrigated valley floor seemed to hold any substance. In early morning, however, or towards evening, the angling sun would pick out the dramatic crags in sharp relief. Moonrise brought drama to the sky in this land without electricity. I could see why people across the broader Middle East held the moon, sailing cool and serene above the agonies of earthly concerns, as their consistent motif.

And there was no escaping the agonies. On our first day out, a suicide bomber took out a tribal leader who had been helpful to the Australians. That same day a young sapper from Kangaroo Island, Jamie Larcombe, proudly laid out a cache of weapons for us that he and his team had seized from the Taliban. Within weeks, proud, fit Jamie Larcombe was dead. His patrol had run into insurgents in the neighbouring valley. The lad who had signed up at eighteen, was dead at twenty-one.

—

It was in the Baluchi Valley that Private Paul Warren, a former Australian kickboxing champion, touched a pressure plate that

detonated a buried bomb. It blew his leg off and killed his mate
Ben Ranaudo. I got to know Paul and his extraordinary wife Dee
over the subsequent years: brave, resourceful people who have made
an inspiring life for themselves. But the wounds that rob a young
athlete of a leg run deep. And the wounds of losing a mate and
feeling – unfairly – to blame for it run even deeper.

It was at COP Mashal that Lance Corporal Andrew Jones, the
base cook, was gunned down from the guard tower by a rogue
Afghan soldier. Captain Perriman still calls it the worst day of his life.

Only fools and people who have never seen one glorify war.

An interpreter who patrolled with us in the Baluchi Valley
stepped on a buried bomb a few weeks later. He bled out. The
same blast blew shrapnel through the arm and shoulder of
Corporal Brodie Naunton, leaving him also with a traumatic brain
injury. Brodie and Chris Campey had particularly hit it off. It was
a shock to see him again some months later still working on his
recovery, though he seems to be doing well and is still serving
in uniform.

I won't attempt to hide my admiration for Australian troops.
Preparing to set off before dawn one morning on a patrol that the
intelligence team fully expected would put us into a Taliban ambush,
I had some tiny taste of the ancient human feeling: the mixture
of anxiety and strange arousal before battle. A sharpening of the
senses. A gut-scouring sense of dread. A feeling that can only be
allayed by movement, an urge to get on with it even though that
was where the danger lies.

So much literature has been dedicated to that feeling. The scenes
before Agincourt in *Henry V*, the agonies of Gethsemane. But I
was just a dilettante. If all went well, I would be gone again in a
few days or weeks. These men and women would stay for months.
Every day the same risk. And over time, the inevitable loss of mates.

So much about the Australians was impressive. The leadership
of a young man like Captain 'Pez' Perriman, the daily courage of
the sappers who went out looking for the bombs, or the 'point-men',

riflemen scouts like Todd Small who led the patrols I went on at COP Mashal. The lives of everyone depended on the quicksilver instincts of the man stepping out in front.

They weren't all army, either. The shortage of army explosives specialists in a war where the homemade bomb trumped more-conventional arms meant the call went out to other services. I patrolled several times with a navy explosives specialist, a sailor a thousand kilometres from the sea. Other than his resplendent naval beard, he was indistinguishable from his army mates.

And nor were they all men. Riding on the Bushmaster on my way into COP Mashal was a female army medic. And every foot patrol was made safer by a female electronics warfare officer working her spyware magic from a bunker within the base. With a security-cleared Afghan interpreter, she monitored radio chatter among the insurgents in the mountains and the valley.

And nor were they all military. The mission of rebuilding a functioning state so that the Taliban had less to offer the people fell to a dedicated bunch of pretty tough public servants. Bernard Philip seemed to run the show, his fair skin fairly cooked from all his time in the Afghan sun. He was low-key, approachable and tough. Another man doing good work was David Savage, a former Australian Federal Police officer who had seen horrendous things as an unarmed observer in East Timor before the independence vote. In the Chora Valley north of Tarin Kowt, a suicide bomber – just a boy – blew himself up causing David horrendous wounds. He and I work together now with the veterans' support charity Soldier On, which aims to help veterans of post-1990 conflicts, many of whom suffer physical and psychological wounds. Despite everything that has happened to him, he is still out there helping others.

Another great discovery was Fred Smith, Uruzgan's first and last Australian-appointed diplomat. An American sergeant first alerted me to him, enthusing about this Australian guy who wrote songs that explained everything. He burned off a CD of Fred's music while I waited to interview a general.

'Who's this Fred Smith guy?' I asked back at the Aussie base.

'You'll probably meet him,' I was told. 'Whatever you do, don't ask him to play guitar.'

I imagined that daggiest of things – an amateur musician with a painful blindness to his own incompetence.

Well, I met Fred Smith and we went out with a military escort to look at some of the work Australia was doing. Aussie taxpayers were paying for schools to be built – including, significantly, one for girls. Australia built a new medical clinic halfway to Chora, and a marketplace to attract commerce and kickstart the economy. We even visited a mosque being built on the Australian taxpayers' dime to win the favour of a powerful local Ghilzai chief. Fred was low-key, dryly funny and plainly very well informed about the complex local power structures.

Near our last day, I thought we had better get Fred on his guitar. If nothing else, it might provide a brief burst of aural variety in a feature story on the Australian effort. Shots of a homesick Aussie amusing himself by picking out a few tunes – that sort of thing.

The brief twilight was already on us when Fred sat behind a concrete blast barrier and went to work. The first song was 'Dust of Uruzgan' – a chilling epic written from the perspective of Private Paul Warren who had lost his leg – and his mate – in that Baluchi blast. I was stunned. Chris Campey looked at me with cameraman eye-language for 'we're on a winner'. We got Fred to play it again, as Chris picked up extra camera angles. The last notes rang off as a Black Hawk helicopter came in to land on a nearby field, adding a little authentic percussion to the mix.

After that, we raced against the dying light to record as many extra songs as we could. The next one was 'Sapper's Lullaby' about the death of Jake Moerland and Darren Smith to a single bomb in the Mirabad Valley a few months before.

Those two songs especially are the soundtrack to the Afghanistan war. 'Sapper's Lullaby' will be sung as long as there are Australian combat engineers.

My job was simply to report it straight, to give a sense back home of the daily realities of the diggers' lives, of the work they were doing, and the lives of the people they were trying to help. There were serious questions about a mission costing so much money and so many lives: was any of this going to make any difference? Would any advances last once Coalition troops withdrew? The supposed comment of a Taliban leader was constantly requoted: 'The foreigners have watches, but we have the time.'

—

An implicit part of my job was to watch for anything scandalous. I was not, to use an old legal phrase, 'avid for scandal'. But the armed forces are an institution and it is the permanent temptation of institutions to let things slide, to cover them up, to rationalise things away. Exposure by an outside eye can be therapeutic. The alternative is to drift into the darkness, like the churches that covered up sex crimes to protect their reputations. Would I find anything? The answer was yes and no.

When, at the end of an eight-hour patrol in the Baluchi Valley, Nick Perriman and his team nabbed two senior Taliban bomb-makers, I kept a close eye on how they were handled. They were cuffed and blindfolded and marched through a moonless night to the base at Mashal. They were kept in a demountable shower block where there was a heater against the sub-zero Afghan night. I checked in on them several times. They weren't particularly comfortable but neither were the soldiers guarding them. They certainly weren't manhandled at any time that I observed them. Considering the bombmakers had almost certainly been involved in devices that targeted Australian troops, including twenty-three-year-old Private Nathan Bewes who had been killed not long before, the diggers showed significant and proper restraint. The bombmakers were considered such valuable assets that the Americans sent a helicopter in at dawn the following morning and flew them off to whatever fate they had in mind for them. I was satisfied the

Australians had handled themselves well. And they had done well to catch them. Their location had been revealed by a blood trail left by one of the Afghan casualties in the attempted ambush a couple of days before.

The biggest impropriety I witnessed involved the Afghan National Army, who we were there to mentor and train. I felt sorry for the Afghan soldiers. With a rudimentary national banking system, many of them weren't even getting paid. Their boots were often worn out or the wrong size and their clothes, heading into that harsh mountain winter, were thin and second-rate. At all times, the Afghan security forces were dying at a much faster rate than the Australians. On one foot patrol, we heard a terrible concussion just on the other side of the nearby Kmaisan River. That one bomb killed five members of the Afghan police.

One evening, after they had wrapped up prayers, an Afghan contingent challenged us to a game of cricket. A fuel drum did for a wicket, someone had the rough shape of a bat and it was on. They could do a pretty good slog sweep off a rough track. But the teamwork only went so far.

The Australians got around in Bushmaster vehicles that were rated among the best in the world for surviving buried bombs. But the local forces travelled in soft-skinned Ford Rangers offering effectively no protection at all. The Afghans were also denied the electronic jamming packs that were carried on every Australian patrol. These interrupted radio signals designed to set off bombs from a distance, rendering that bombing technique ineffective. For all the talk of partnership, we didn't trust the Afghans with this technology. The Australians reasoned the high-tech gear would quickly be stolen and smuggled over the border to Pakistan. There, some very smart Pashtun engineers would quickly figure out a way to defeat it.

The Afghan major who managed the theatre just north of Tarin Kowt was a lifelong soldier, a veteran of bitter fighting and shifting allegiances since the Soviet occupation. He had seen a lot of death.

Over flat bread, chicken and pomegranate seeds on a carpet rolled out beneath the cold mountain skies, he was a good companion. But he had one problem. His staff car was an ambulance. There it was, clearly marked with the Red Crescent that should, under the rules of war, guarantee its safe passage because of its purely humanitarian purpose.

What to do about it?

For me, it would have been an easy splash exclusive: Australia's military partner caught in breach of the Geneva Conventions. We had photographic evidence. International law quite clearly forbids the military use of protected vehicles. It was not only a potential international incident for the Afghan Army, it was also hugely damaging to Australia. After all, we were turning a blind eye.

And if the Australian command tried to suppress the story – even better! Censorship. The heavy hand of military chiefs trying to cover up a scandal. God, it would run for weeks. Walkley Awards and who knows what?

So then, what should I do?

I didn't run it. My main hesitation was not because I wanted to protect Australian or Afghan army reputations. Rather, I knew there was a pretty good chance that kind of story would filter back to Afghanistan. The Taliban could use it as an excuse to start blowing up ambulances. Innocent people would die.

I took a different approach. I went to the most senior Australian officer in the province – a decent and straight-up officer. I told him what was going on and I told him we had enough pictures to go hard.

'Leave it with me,' he said.

Two days later, we bumped into the Afghan major again. He was getting around in a Ford Ranger.

45

SCANDAL AND REFORM

AFGHANISTAN WAS MY LAST WAR. WHEN A SENIOR AUSTRALIAN OFFICER invited me to go back, Mary gently reminded me of my promise.

I couldn't argue. She had given me everything.

In February 2011, I asked her what she wanted for her birthday. 'Another child,' she said.

I was already fifty. Coco had just started school. Jacob was eighteen months old. Another child meant I would be seventy with a teenager. On the other hand, Mary had given up her CNN job, followed me to a country she had never seen, become a mother to Coco, raised Jacob through the hardest days, all while knocking off a Master's of International Relations at ANU – her third higher degree. All this time, I had the easy shift. I worked six to seven days a week as a political reporter and editor, with the weekends often taken up with writing and presenting the Sunday morning political interview program, *Meet the Press*. I was forming up a great new political bureau, putting into practice the ideas about people management that had increasingly started to intrigue me. Every single person whom it was my privilege to hire turned out to be a winner. On top of that, I was still gadding off when the mood or the story took me.

I owed Mary, big time.

In any case, all the war and death had given me a fondness for life and for love. When Mary told me she was pregnant we were on our deck looking westward to the Brindabellas. The golden light was picking out the tree-dense slope of Red Hill a short walk to the south. A few thin clouds sailed in the deepening blue of the sky. We were contemplating the arrival of a new life. I felt nothing but gratitude and peace.

Holly arrived in December.

Unexpectedly, in the middle of all of this, came a story that compelled me to take on the defence establishment. It would test loyalties and fundamental principles. It pitched me into ethical minefields on a level I had never known.

—

On an autumn Canberra evening, Kate was excited. She was planning a hook-up with a young man who had caught her eye. She had just turned eighteen but it was not her age that made what she was contemplating dangerous. She was an officer cadet living on the Australian Defence Force Academy campus. Like the rest of her intake, she had just begun the training required to make her a military officer. Sexual contact between cadets was forbidden.

Still, it was surely a victimless crime. Kate was a country girl, feisty and forceful but a little naïve. Her ambition was to be an air force logistics officer, the person who arranged the movement of equipment and personnel. The object of her interest was one of the alpha males of the intake, the product of a top-end private school in Perth, a state age-level representative at AFL, a lad from a military family. His name was Daniel McDonald and there was no reason to suppose he wouldn't go on to become a general. Kate was flattered by his attention. He already had a large following among the cadets. He seemed 'a nice guy'. If she was in his group, she thought, she would be socially safe. It would help her fit in.

The cadets had individual rooms in multi-storey buildings on campus. She went to his room.

But Daniel McDonald was not quite the nice guy she imagined.

McDonald had wired up a camera to his computer. He had arranged to livestream their sexual encounter to a mate's room. Six male cadets were in there, watching. McDonald had already boasted of his plan to another friend on Facebook. His friend's name was Tim Hazlett. The exchange was later presented in court.

McDonald: I'm about to root a girl n have webcam set up to the boys in another room

Hazlett: win, hahahahaha, oh friggen hell is she aware of this or not

McDonald: Nope

Hazlett: Oh good it just gets better and better. Haha you sure you are about to bang her?

McDonald: Yer 15 min she will be here.

—

Kate returned to her room, unsuspecting. But what had just happened would trigger events that would spark six government inquiries, a renewed police investigation, charges and convictions, and – ultimately – fundamental change in Australian Defence Force culture.

And it all came down to what Kate did next.

Daniel McDonald and the other male cadets – the voyeurs in the other room – would almost certainly have got away with it had they simply watched the Skype feed. There was no recording of it, therefore no proof. But at least one of the young men used a smartphone to grab screenshots of the action.

In the following days, he couldn't resist showing this to other cadets around campus. One cadet, a naval midshipman, didn't see it as a harmless lark. He reported it.

The first Kate knew of her privacy being invaded was when she was confronted by a sergeant from the Australian Defence Force Investigative Service (ADFIS). Kate later said the tone of that meeting was that she had been caught out and was going to cop a punishment. The police account was simply that she had been informed that she had been filmed.

While Kate felt her world crashing in, things were about to get worse. ADFIS sought the advice of the civilian police, in Canberra the Australian Federal Police. Whether the briefing was inadequate or the police slack, the word came back to ADFIS that there had been no crime committed.

Kate was told the matter would be dealt with 'administratively'. The male cadets might lose a couple of weekends' leave. Meanwhile, she was separately in trouble for coming back from a night out in town after the curfew. None of it made sense.

'There's really no words to describe the hollow feeling that I felt when I found out,' she told me later. 'I felt sick to the stomach.'

Kate was getting leered at as she walked around the campus. Nothing was going to happen to the young men, no one was leering at them. She felt embarrassed, ashamed, furious. On a sleepless night she thought about her fifteen-year-old cousin, to whom she was close. If it could happen to Kate it could happen to her.

She decided, whatever the cost, she was going to make a stand.

The following morning she called Channel Seven in Sydney. The woman brushed her off.

'I don't think we'd be interested in something like that,' Kate says she was told.

She tried Channel Nine. It went to voicemail. No one called back.

She rang Channel Ten. The details were sent through to the Canberra bureau. The reporter on duty, Matt Moran, had been in Canberra only six weeks but he was uniquely qualified to understand the implications of the call. At thirty, Moran had been a full-time army officer and was still a reservist. He was an Afghan veteran. To Moran, Kate didn't sound like a crank. He called her up and agreed to meet her after her English lecture.

To his credit, when we called defence for comment, the ADFA Commandant, Commodore Bruce Kafer, made himself available immediately for an interview. He confirmed the broad details of

Kate's story and said it was under investigation. He wanted to stress that it was being taken seriously.

He then made a telling statement.

'If the perpetrators who were alleged to have been involved were found guilty of a crime, this could result in the termination of their military careers.'

It seems bizarre to consider it now, but the whole blow-up about the Skype scandal rested on that innocuous little word: 'could'.

Matt Moran brought his interview back into the bureau. Kate struck me as young, brave and credible. The betrayal she had suffered was certainly not unique to the world of defence. In 2011, there were still just the beginnings of the queasy understanding that every private sexual activity could potentially be part of a public show if one of the parties set it up that way. The law seemed ill prepared to deal with it. Was it a crime on the level of rape as some people argued? Or just part of the new rites of passage in the digital world?

I had no doubt where I stood. It was to me an appalling abuse, a breach of trust, an invasion of privacy of the most egregious kind and one aggravated by the age of the victim.

I looked at the Kafer interview again. If found guilty of a crime . . . 'could' . . . 'result in the termination of their military careers'.

Like every self-respecting newsroom, the bureau was open plan. Even my office had glass walls. I briefly caught the eye of one of the young women working there. How, I thought, should I react if I had learned that two young colleagues in that office had had a perfectly consensual sexual encounter but the male had streamed it without her knowledge to the other young men in the office, and even now screen grabs were being distributed among other young men up and down the press gallery where the woman would still be expected and required to work.

Would I be waiting for a court process to return a guilty verdict before acting?

Would it even then only be an option – a matter of 'could' – to fire the perpetrator?

How could the woman involved survive that combination of shock, humiliation and betrayal – while still being expected to front up every day to work with the same people who had abused her so appallingly.

They had to be joking.

'Fuck it,' I told my troops. 'We're going nuclear.'

I had contacts in the defence minister's office. I started working them. I took Matt Moran's perfectly straight script and added a little anger to it. I had no beef with Commodore Kafer. Many people have told me subsequently on and off the record that he is a decent man. One of the good ones.

But an institution that would consider protecting the careers of men who had behaved so revoltingly to a female colleague deserved the biggest whipping and scourging I had in my power to deliver. It went beyond their crimes. It went to the utter lack of self-awareness in the military institution itself.

On that first day, I had no idea where this might go. I wanted Kate's story noticed and I wanted her not to feel so alone.

At that stage Ten had not just its main news bulletin at five o'clock, it also had a half-hour prime-time current affairs show fronted by George Negus, followed by *The Project*. Matt's story went to air at 5 pm. I had a longer version delving more deeply into defence sex scandals and the law for the Negus show, and we hit *The Project* too. I alerted some newspaper mates that the story was coming and it made some front pages the following morning.

For me, it was never primarily a defence story. It was about where a society should stand on a new, growing and particular crime. I would have gone just as hard had it been at a big bank or a mining giant or – heaven forbid – a church or major charity.

My first aim was just to get the story noticed. What took me by surprise was the tidal wave of emotion Kate's story triggered. By noon the next day, Prime Minister Julia Gillard had weighed in on Kate's behalf. Defence Minister Stephen Smith was strong and would get stronger.

And others, who saw it all as an unfair attack on defence, were climbing in as well. The Leader of the Opposition in the Senate, Nick Minchin, spoke of Commodore Kafer's kindness when Minchin's son had been seriously injured in a cadet training accident. Old-school military boosters were rushing to defend the institution. One busily briefed Canberra journalists that Kate, after just six weeks at ADFA, was known as 'the town bike'. It was scandalous and utterly false. Kate's problems stemmed from naïvete and inexperience. She was the least likely candidate to be cast as a femme fatale. But even if the claim was true, it was an appalling example of victim blaming.

On social media, some with defence backgrounds pointed out that Kate had also broken the rules by engaging in sexual activity, so why was it only the males who were in trouble? There seemed an inability to acknowledge what the young men had actually done.

Far more powerful, however, was the huge uprush of support. Kate's plight sparked a national conversation about the vulnerabilities of young women, in particular, in the social media and digital age. And it had tapped into something else specific to defence. The rage being directed at the defence establishment was coming most strongly from veterans of that system, people who had suffered sexual and other abuse and had never been supported or heard.

It was plain Kate had started something.

But her life was spiralling out of control. Still at the academy, she was copping abuse from both male and female cadets, who called her variously a 'skank', a 'slut' and a 'dirty whore'. And worse. A sergeant walking past her sneered 'You've gotta be kidding, don't you?'

Many others, including particularly the officers, were very supportive of her.

But defence officials stressed to her – and to the wider public – that the welfare of all cadets, including the perpetrators, was of 'utmost concern' and all were being provided with 'full support'.

Once again, there was no distinction between those allegedly responsible for a criminal act and the victim of that act.

Bizarrely, a later secret official report said Kate was never subject to vilification. It painted her as a liar. But how could it know? Did her word count for nothing? Were those who denied vilifying her to be believed, when she was not?

Stephen Smith also said at a news conference that shaving foam had been plastered on her door. This was later officially denied but even that denial involved a cover-up: the secret report, later leaked to me, revealed that a substance *had* been sprayed on her door – but it was Jif cleaning liquid, not shaving foam.

It was a stitch-up.

A couple of days in, Defence Minister Smith had doubled down. Kate had a pre-existing minor breach against her. Commodore Kafer had pressed on with it. Stephen Smith went ballistic, calling it an act of stupidity. Kafer was later stood aside, in part – said Defence Force Chief Angus Houston – to protect him from abuse that had been directed at him by members of the public.

This itself was problematic. It was quite possible that Commodore Kafer was subjected to abuse. Emotions were running high. But defence was still claiming Kate was lying about the abuse she was suffering at the academy. So a senior officer was being abused but a vulnerable teenager was not? The defence position, including that of its highly respected chief, Angus Houston, was simply not credible.

Kate had been told the offending male cadets would be dealt with at a misdemeanour level, under the catch-all low-grade charge of 'prejudicial conduct'. At most they could expect to be docked a few days' leave.

The official line was that the Australian Federal Police were called back to reassess the case *before* our first story went to air. This was technically true but also misleading. The call to get the police involved again came before we went to air, but after we had contacted defence to tell them Kate had given us an interview. Perhaps the police might have been called back anyway. We don't know. What was clear was that Kate's decision to go public galvanised the defence hierarchy into action

Two of the young men were charged. One was Daniel McDonald. The other was Dylan De Blaquiere, the cadet who had worked with McDonald to set up the Skype connection. The other voyeurs were not charged. McDonald was charged with committing an act of indecency without consent. Both men were also charged with using a carriage service to menace, harass or offend.

McDonald and De Blaquiere pleaded not guilty. Their bail conditions effectively banned them from ADFA because they were not allowed to approach within one hundred metres of Kate. Their lawyers, paid for by defence, appealed and the distance element disappeared. This meant if Kate remained at ADFA, she would have to accept close proximity with the men who had abused her. It was an impossible position. She left ADFA and never returned. For a while she remained in defence, posted to an RAAF airfield. Her studies stopped. The accused men returned to the ADFA campus and continued on towards their degrees.

Plenty of people in defence were happy to see Kate go. For many, the primary crime committed that autumn was Kate's decision to go to the media. Whatever the young men had done, it was she who had exposed the defence family to contempt and shame. Institutions protect their own. Many believed the one blameless victim was Commodore Kafer.

But Kate had opened a door and light was shining through. Hundreds of people started telling their own story of abuses, dating back decades. Deep in these expressions of pain was the anger of being brushed aside, told to deal with it, told not to damage their careers with complaints. Stories emerged of rapes and suicides. It became clear some people accused of sexual assault and other abuses were still in the military, some in senior ranks. But they were never named.

Defence Minister Smith ordered half-a-dozen inquiries, including two reports from the Sex Discrimination Commissioner Elizabeth Broderick. She found a little over one in fifty of the female cadets reported 'being forced into sex without their consent or against their will'. Nearly one in twenty said they had been 'treated badly for refusing to have sex'.

It wasn't clear, she wrote, how that compared with sexual assault rates at other universities. It might have been lower.

Many cadets and staff at ADFA, however, 'expressed frustration about the negative publicity' caused by the Skype scandal.

Among the consequences of Kate's case was a decision to bring forward an order to open all military positions – including those of elite units like the commandos and the SAS – to women. They would have to meet the same training and fitness standards as men but gender alone would no longer eliminate them. Some old soldiers reckoned the place was going to the dogs.

One of the most significant initiatives Stephen Smith put in place was the Defence Abuse Response Taskforce (DART). This allowed people who had been sexually abused within defence in the past to tell their stories to an independent body. An incredible 2400 claims of abuse emerged. The taskforce's report recommended a Royal Commission, finding some eight hundred alleged abusers were still serving in the military.

The Royal Commission recommendation was later withdrawn and the alternative plan for the Australian Crime Commission to join the investigation also lapsed.

Many previous victims did have their accounts treated with respect and some gained financial settlements.

Years later, I was at the headquarters of Soldier On in Canberra. There had been a large event at the site, timed to coincide with the board meeting I was attending. At the end of it, a woman offered to give me a lift to the airport.

'I know you were involved in reporting the Skype scandal,' she said, once the doors were closed. 'Please tell Kate that she saved my life.'

The woman said she had been raped while in defence. She had complained but the man, of more senior rank, said it was consensual. It went nowhere. She had had to continue working with her rapist. It had almost destroyed her. She had not wanted to leave her defence career because that meant her attacker would have won. But she was struggling. She was depressed and anxious.

The DART process meant she could talk again to someone in a position of importance about what had happened to her.

Oddly, the DART process enabled her to leave defence. She received some money, enough to start her own business, which was going well.

'They said to me "we believe you". When it happened, no one said that. I can't tell you what that meant to me.'

For no other reason but that, the whole Skype business was worth it.

Over time, every one of the cadets involved in the events of that night left the defence force. McDonald and De Blaquiere were found guilty. De Blaquiere quit ADFA soon after the scandal was exposed. McDonald was punted after his conviction. The five others who watched on were also shown the door.

Commodore Kafer was formally exonerated by an inquiry process. He was restored to leadership at ADFA and retired as a rear admiral.

Kate's dreams of a defence career – and a degree through ADFA – were crushed. It has been a tough few years. She has lived for some time now in remote parts of Australia but has always been employed and clear-sighted about where her choices have taken her.

Had she stayed silent at ADFA, copped her punishments, borne the weight of it all within the defence system, might she have survived, graduated, gained the career she went in for?

Possibly. But defence would have been far worse for her having done so.

In recent times, a lightness has come to my conversations with Kate. She is happy and fulfilled with a purpose in her life. She remains, as she always was, proud of the stand she took. The defence hierarchy will never see it that way but her defiant courage did them all a favour. It blew into the open with such power the issues had to be dealt with. Defence is a better place for all its honest and decent members because of what she did.

As so, to my mind, is Australia. The conversation around secretly filming or streaming sexual encounters ran for days and weeks. It was entirely correct to say that the impulses that drove McDonald and his mates were not part of defence culture. They were part of Australian culture. That McDonald's Facebook mate, who stood outside the defence world, was so enthusiastic in egging him on proved that. Everyone should now know that such behaviour is no victimless joke, an excusable piece of laddish fun. It is a crime with consequences.

Kate never asked for money. We never gave her any. She was never interviewed by anyone but Ten. She remains, to me, a proud and heroic figure. I hope if anyone in defence now – and this includes men – feels the need to go outside to the police or the media they will not be crushed for doing so. If defence has its act together, no one would ever need to.

Two final notes on the Skype scandal. The lead actor in reporting the story was Matt Moran. He deserved all the accolades that came his way. If I was the campaigner, Matt was the cooler head. He was the primary contact with Kate. He brought to the task the dispassionate focus of a good army officer.

A high-profile general rang me at home one day when the Skype scandal was at full boil. He was calling to tear strips off me, expressing his disappointment at my involvement. To his credit, he stayed on the line for forty-five minutes while we talked it through. He was a much calmer man by the end of it.

As he rang off he said, 'Thanks for caring about that girl.'

I have remained on good terms with that general – and several others – ever since.

As controversial as it remains, I count my involvement in reporting the Skype scandal as one of the few genuinely important pieces of work I have done.

46

GRATITUDE

WHATEVER I MIGHT HAVE HOPED FOR IN THAT INSTANT AS A seventeen-year-old when I agreed to a job I wasn't even seeking, my dreams have been rewarded beyond all imaginings.

As a journalist, I have had access to the most powerful people on earth. I have stood in the Oval Office of the White House exchanging banter with Barack Obama, the President of the United States.

But I have also seen the least powerful. And they have made me who I am. Those children dying in the dust in southern Sudan are never far from my mind.

Few callings expose their practitioners to a wider range of human experiences.

I have seen the world. I have lived in it. I have seen its music and have seen its art.

In early 2014, I finally bowed to pressure from Ten to leave the Canberra round to take a newsreading job in Sydney. The big draw was presenting the *Late News*, which my talented young colleague Hamish Macdonald had turned into a distinctive, smart product. It was an ideal show. I could shape it, it had a national audience, and we could focus on one or two main stories, with time for some interviews. I would also read the Sydney 5 pm bulletin with Sandra Sully.

A couple of months after I started, Ten went through one of its periodic financial crises and the *Late News* was axed. I suggested the network fling me some money to cover my blushes and let me go. But, bless them, they insisted on keeping me on.

For the first time in my life I wasn't working flat out. I was around to play with Holly during the day before heading in to read the news. I was able to support Mary's career for once, as she juggled work as a criminology lecturer at Macquarie University with journalism at the ABC. I became, at last, a proper family man.

But I still kept some skin in the game.

In November 2016, I found myself in the United States again reporting on the presidential election between Clinton and Trump.

I had my doubts about Hillary Clinton's prospects. In Virginia, a swing state that should have been safe given her vice-presidential running mate was a state senator, all the front lawns seemed to be sprouting Trump/Pence signage. She might have had the establishment, but Trump had the enthusiasm.

The gun show I visited in semi-rural Virginia was predictably hostile to Clinton. No surprises there. But I realised she was in real danger when I interviewed an African-American family checking out the Washington monument. The mum was a classic smart, middle-class, educated black woman. Yes, she thought she would vote for Clinton because she was the 'lesser of two evils'.

'But, you know . . .' and she shrugged.

Wow! I thought. If a voter from that demographic can't get enthused about Hillary Clinton, there is not a lot of love in the room.

Everyone, of course, is wise after the event but my reports predicting a possible Trump boilover are there to be seen.

On election night in New York City, I wanted to be with the Trump campaign but he was letting no one in. The Clinton campaign, however, was open to all comers at a giant convention centre on the banks of the Hudson River. Thousands of journalists were there. It was like an old school reunion – friends from CNN, from Britain, from other networks in Australia, colleagues and rivals I had met in countless messes across the world over decades of time.

And then the results started coming in . . . the slow confirmation that Donald Trump, the outsider, the oaf, the braggart and the misogynist, had outsmarted them all. The podium set up for Hillary Clinton's victory speech – beneath, yes, a high glass ceiling – remained empty. No concession of defeat. No show at all. A message was read out. She wasn't coming. She was tired. She had gone to bed.

—

History still rolls and will ever roll.

But the job of reporting the events that will become history has also rolled on. Journalism is in a state of financial collapse. The advertising money that has sustained it for two hundred years now floods to other platforms. At the time of writing, the Ten network, which just five years ago carried a full suite of news programming and which garnered its share of major awards, is in receivership. At the 2017 Press Freedom dinner in Sydney (an annual fundraiser to support the families of journalists killed in the line of work) people from every major strand of Australian journalism – News Corp, Fairfax, commercial TV and the ABC – were discussing active rounds of redundancies.

Sound information will always be in demand. It seems shonky information will be in even greater demand. But whatever shape the future takes, the old model of the journalist as the well-paid reporter and interpreter of the times is gone. For better or worse.

I hope I have done my bit to do my calling justice. It has been a wonderful ride.

ACKNOWLEDGEMENTS

THIS BOOK IS THE PRODUCT OF THE ENTHUSIASM AND TALENT OF Vanessa Radnidge and the team at Hachette. It was said of Ronald Reagan that if he had met Nancy earlier, he would have won an Oscar. If I had met Vanessa earlier, I would now be WH Auden. I am indebted also to my editor, Deonie Fiford, for her meticulous care and her tact.

We learn from each other in life so it is important to get good teachers. Particular credit must go to the cameramen and women who have been my companions and collaborators in all sorts of conditions all over the world. I have named some in the text but I have learned from all of them about how to make television and how to get along in the world. My thanks and respect to you all. The same goes for those brilliant vision editors I have had the privilege of working with over the years and whose work is so often overlooked. Whenever a story has truly sung, it is because of the way the pictures, the sound and the text have been sculpted together. Editing is another craft under siege in these more straitened times.

No foreign correspondent's work is possible without the patient and courageous work of local producers and fixers on the ground. The best are translators, arrangers, cultural interpreters, dietary advisers, journalists and humorists all rolled into one. Very often we have met under times of great stress but in every case I can think of we have parted as friends. I have always been the richer for the encounter.

I have been fortunate to have had incredibly generous mentors and backers: Tom Clarke, Nigel Horrocks, Terry Spence, Michael Frazer, Colin Tyrus, John Sorell, Robert Penfold, Peter Meakin, Jim Carroll, the late Rena Golden, Paul Cutler, Paul Bongiorno, Anthony Flannery, Hamish McLennan, Anthony 'Bug' Murdoch and John Choueifate, to name just a few. If I have ever encouraged or guided younger journalists, I have simply been passing on the favours I myself received in such abundance.

Of my peers, there are too many to thank. It has been my fortune to work with or against the very finest television journalists of my generation, both in Australia and overseas. For all the disdain handed out to journalists and journalism, every one of those I admire has added powerfully to the good of the world.

Speaking of good, I acknowledge the great satisfactions I have received in working on two causes close to my heart. Through Soldier On, founded by John Bale and chaired by former Chief of Army Peter Leahy, it has been my privilege to give something back to those Australian soldiers, sailors and airmen and women, whom I have seen at work in so many theatres. Soldier On is committed to supporting those wounded or affected by their service and I commend it to anyone reading this book. You can find us at www.soldieron.org.au.

The tragic murder of my beloved friend John Mac Acuek, in South Sudan in 2014, was a loss without measure. However, his equally remarkable brother Deng Adut has founded a charity in his name – the John Mac Foundation (www.johnmacfoundation.org). It is my privilege to chair this organisation which, among other things, provides university scholarships and support for people who have survived the worst of backgrounds and who come to Australia – as so many have over the generations – in pursuit of peace and hope and a chance to contribute their own genius to this great country. Please join us.

Some particular extra thanks: to Deng Adut and Ben Mckelvey for showing the way; and to Stan Grant for leading me always deeper into the profound questions of our times. It has been a privilege to know you.

My debt to my parents and to my brothers, Paul, Sean and Adrian, is only hinted at in these pages. It is measureless not least because you require such light repayments.

My deepest thanks go to Mary, the most powerful force I have ever known, and my sparkling and wonderful children, Cait, Coco, Jacob and Holly. Nothing I can ever write will do you justice. You are my world entire.

INDEX

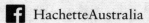